THE LAW OF PROPERTY

Other Books in the *Essentials of Canadian Law* Series

International Trade Law

Family Law

Copyright Law

The Law of Sentencing

Administrative Law

Computer Law 2/e

International Human Rights Law

Franchise Law

Legal Ethics and Professional Responsibility 2/e

Public International Law 2/e

Individual Employment Law 2/e

Civil Litigation

Canadian Telecommunications Law

Intellectual Property Law 2/e

Animals and the Law

Income Tax Law 2/e

Personal Property Security Law 2/e

Youth Criminal Justice Law 3/e

Bank and Customer Law in Canada 2/e

The Law of Equitable Remedies 2/e

Pension Law 2/e

Remedies: The Law of Damages 3/e

Freedom of Conscience and Religion

The Law of Trusts 3/e

Ethics and Criminal Law 2/e

Insurance Law 2/e

Immigration Law 2/e

Bankruptcy and Insolvency Law 2/e

Legal Research and Writing 4/e

Canadian Maritime Law 2/e

Public Lands and Resources in Canada

Conflict of Laws 2/e

Statutory Interpretation 3/e

The Charter of Rights and Freedoms 6/e

Constitutional Law 5/e

Land-Use Planning

Detention and Arrest 2/e

Refugee Law 2/e

Religious Institutions and the Law 4/e

Securities Law 2/e

Criminal Law 7/e

The Law of Partnerships and Corporations 4/e

Environmental Law 5/e

Fundamental Justice 2/e

International and Transnational Criminal Law 3/e

The Law of Torts 6/e

Mergers, Acquisitions, and Other Changes of Corporate Control 3/e

Criminal Procedure 4/e

Information and Privacy Law in Canada

The Law of Evidence 8/e

The Law of Contracts 3/e

National Security Law 2/e

Canadian Competition Law and Policy

ESSENTIALS OF
CANADIAN LAW

THE LAW OF PROPERTY

ROBERT CHAMBERS

Professor, Faculty of Law
Thompson Rivers University

The Law of Property
© Irwin Law Inc., 2021

Published in 2021 by

Irwin Law Inc.
14 Duncan Street
Suite 206
Toronto, ON
M5H 3G8

irwinlaw.com

ISBN: 978-1-55221-563-0 | e-book ISBN: 978-1-55221-564-7

Library and Archives Canada Cataloguing in Publication

Title: The law of property / Robert Chambers (Professor, Faculty of Law, Thompson Rivers University).
Names: Chambers, Robert, 1957– author.
Series: Essentials of Canadian law.
Description: Series statement: Essentials of Canadian law | Includes bibliographical references and index.
Identifiers: Canadiana (print) 20210126310 | Canadiana (ebook) 20210126612 | ISBN 9781552215630 (softcover) | ISBN 9781552215647 (PDF)
Subjects: LCSH: Real property—Canada. | LCSH: Right of property—Canada.
Classification: LCC KE625 .C53 2021 | LCC KF561 .C53 2021 kfmod | DDC 346.7104—dc23

Canada｜ Ontario
Ontario Media Development
Corporation
Société de développement
de l'industrie des médias
de l'Ontario

Printed and bound in Canada.

1 2 3 4 5   25 24 23 22 21

SUMMARY
TABLE OF CONTENTS

FOREWORD   xv

PREFACE   xvii

CHAPTER 1:   What Is Property?   1

CHAPTER 2:   Ownership and Possession   14

CHAPTER 3:   Title to Land   31

CHAPTER 4:   Equity and Trusts   66

CHAPTER 5:   Co-ownership   82

CHAPTER 6:   Security Interests   102

CHAPTER 7:   Other Interests in Land   128

CHAPTER 8:   Sources of Rights   166

CHAPTER 9:   Competing Rights   235

TABLE OF CASES   295

TABLE OF LEGISLATION   315

INDEX   323

ABOUT THE AUTHOR   337

DETAILED
TABLE OF CONTENTS

FOREWORD   *xv*

PREFACE   *xvii*

CHAPTER 1:
WHAT IS PROPERTY?   *1*

A. The Law of Property   *1*

B. The Meaning of Property   *2*

C. Rights   *2*

    1) Rights *In Personam* and Rights *In Rem*   *2*
    2) Assignable Rights   *3*

D. Things   *6*

    1) Land   *6*
    2) Goods   *6*
    3) Money   *7*
    4) Documents   *7*
    5) Intellectual Property   *7*
    6) Confidential Information   *8*
    7) Living Things   *9*
    8) Human Tissue   *11*

CHAPTER 2:
OWNERSHIP AND POSSESSION   *14*

A. Introduction   *14*

B. **Ownership**   *14*

1) Professor Honoré   *15*
2) Crown Ownership   *17*

C. **Possession**   *20*

1) Control   *20*
2) Intention to Possess   *22*
3) Possession of Things in Public Places   *23*
4) Wrongdoing   *24*
5) Rights to Possession   *26*
6) Relativity of Title   *28*
7) Adverse Possession   *29*

CHAPTER 3:
TITLE TO LAND   *31*

A. **Introduction**   *31*

B. **Tenure**   *31*

1) Subinfeudation   *32*
2) Feudal Services   *33*
3) Radical Title   *34*

C. **Estates**   *35*

1) Air Space   *36*
2) Underground   *37*

D. **Freehold Estates**   *39*

1) Fee Simple   *39*
2) Fee Tail   *41*
3) Life Estate   *42*

E. **Leasehold Estates**   *42*

1) Possession   *43*
2) Certainty of Term   *44*
3) Leasehold Covenants   *46*
4) Residential Tenancies   *49*
5) Privity of Estate   *50*

F. **Future Interests**   *51*

1) Remainders   *52*
2) Reversions   *52*
3) Defeasible and Determinable Estates   *53*
4) Rule Against Perpetuities   *55*

G. Aboriginal Title   *58*

    1) Aboriginal Title in Canadian Law   *58*
    2) Content of Aboriginal Title   *59*
    3) Proof of Aboriginal Title   *62*
    4) Constitutional Protection of Aboriginal Title   *63*

CHAPTER 4:
EQUITY AND TRUSTS   *66*

A. Equity   *66*

B. Equitable Remedies   *68*

C. Trusts   *70*

    1) The Settlor   *70*
    2) Subject of the Trust   *70*
    3) The Beneficiaries   *71*
    4) Charitable Purposes   *73*
    5) Duties of Trustees   *75*
    6) Modern Discretionary Trusts   *77*
    7) Rights of Beneficiaries   *78*
    8) Beneficial Ownership   *79*

CHAPTER 5:
CO-OWNERSHIP   *82*

A. Introduction   *82*

B. Joint and Common Ownership   *83*

    1) Four Unities   *83*
    2) Joint or Common?   *85*
    3) Survivorship   *89*

C. Severance   *91*

    1) Unilateral Act   *92*
    2) Mutual Agreement and Course of Dealing   *95*
    3) Operation of Law   *96*
    4) Effect of Severance   *97*

D. Partition   *98*

E. Condominiums   *100*

CHAPTER 6:
SECURITY INTERESTS   *102*

A. Introduction   *102*

B. **Possession**   *103*

　　1) Pawn or Pledge   *103*
　　2) Common Law Lien   *104*

C. **Title**   *108*

　　1) Creditor Selling to the Debtor   *108*
　　2) Debtor Transfers Title to the Creditor   *110*

D. **Encumbrance**   *111*

　　1) Equitable Charge   *111*
　　2) Equitable Lien   *112*

E. **Mortgages**   *114*

　　1) Common Law Mortgage   *114*
　　2) Equity of Redemption   *115*
　　3) Land Title Mortgage   *117*
　　4) Enforcement   *119*

F. **Personal Property Security**   *122*

　　1) Security Interests   *123*
　　2) Registration   *124*
　　3) Collateral and Proceeds   *125*
　　4) Attachment and Enforceability   *126*
　　5) Perfection   *126*
　　6) After-Acquired Property   *127*

CHAPTER 7:
OTHER INTERESTS IN LAND   *128*

A. **Introduction**   *128*

　　1) Incorporeal Hereditaments   *128*
　　2) Limits on Property Rights to Use Land   *130*

B. **Rentcharges**   *134*

C. **Profits**   *135*

　　1) Profits in Gross and Profits Appurtenant   *136*
　　2) Exclusive and Non-exclusive Profits   *136*
　　3) Duration of the Profit   *137*
　　4) Profit or Sale of Goods?   *137*

D. **Easements**   *138*

　　1) Positive and Negative Easements   *139*
　　2) Four Requirements for a Valid Easement   *143*
　　3) Accommodate the Dominant Tenement   *143*
　　4) Subject Matter of a Grant   *145*

5) Dominant and Servient Tenements *147*
6) Creation of Easements *149*

E. **Covenants** *155*

1) Positive and Negative Covenants *157*
2) Use of the Servient Tenement *161*
3) Benefit to the Dominant Tenement *163*

CHAPTER 8:
SOURCES OF RIGHTS *166*

A. **Introduction** *166*

1) Intention or Operation of Law *166*
2) Creation or Transfer *167*
3) *Inter Vivos* or Testamentary *167*
4) Gift or Contract *167*
5) Law or Equity *168*

B. **Gifts** *168*

1) Delivery of Goods *168*
2) Transfer of Land *174*

C. **Trusts** *179*

1) Express, Resulting, and Constructive Trusts *179*
2) The Settlor *180*
3) Three Certainties *181*
   a) Certainty of Intention *181*
   b) Certainty of Subject Matter *183*
   c) Certainty of Objects *185*
4) Constitution *186*
5) Formality *187*
6) Incomplete Gifts *190*

D. **Wills and Estates** *192*

1) Wills *193*
2) Intestate Succession *194*
3) Adequate Provision for Families *195*
4) *Donatio Mortis Causa* *198*
   a) Conditional Gift *198*
   b) Delivery *200*
   c) Land *201*
   d) *Inter Vivos* or Testamentary? *203*
5) Incomplete Gifts to Executors *204*
6) Secret Trusts *206*
7) Mutual Wills *211*

E. **Land Contracts**   *214*

1) Formalities   *214*
2) Specific Performance   *218*
3) Options to Purchase and Rights of First Refusal   *223*

F. **Proprietary Estoppel**   *225*

G. **Sale of Goods**   *229*

1) What Is a Sale of Goods?   *230*
2) Transfer of Property   *231*

CHAPTER 9:

COMPETING RIGHTS   *235*

A. **Introduction**   *235*

B. **Common Law**   *237*

1) *Nemo Dat*   *237*
2) Money   *238*
3) Agents   *239*
4) Estoppel   *240*
5) Buyer or Seller in Possession   *243*
6) Voidable Title   *244*
7) Market Overt   *247*

C. **Equity**   *249*

1) Bona Fide Purchase   *250*
2) First in Time   *254*
3) Mere Equities   *256*

D. **Land Registration**   *257*

1) Deed Registration   *258*
   a) Notice   *259*
   b) *Nemo Dat*   *261*
   c) Short Leases   *262*
2) Land Title Registration   *262*
   a) Fraud   *264*
   b) Forgery   *269*

E. **Personal Property Security**   *272*

1) Priority Between Security Interests   *273*
2) Priority over Other Interests   *274*

F. **Fixtures**   *276*

1) Goods or Fixtures?   *277*
2) Tenant's Fixtures   *280*
3) Personal Property Security   *282*

G. Specification, Accession, and Mixtures   *283*

   1) Specification   *284*
   2) Accession   *286*
   3) Mixtures   *288*
   4) Personal Property Security   *291*
      a) Accessions   *291*
      b) Specification and Mixtures   *292*

TABLE OF CASES   *295*

TABLE OF LEGISLATION   *315*

INDEX   *323*

ABOUT THE AUTHOR   *337*

FOREWORD

I am honoured to provide this brief foreword to Professor Robert Chambers's important introductory text, *The Law of Property*.

As Professor Chambers observes, almost certainly correctly, many first-year law students find property law to be their most difficult course of study. The terminology is sometimes archaic, the ideas being taught are often abstract and abstruse, and it is almost always highly technical. Taught well and with the aid of a good textbook, however, property law is one of those courses—along with, I think, the law of trusts and the law of wills—that tends to inspire trepidation at first approach, but that students become more interested in as they gradually immerse themselves, step by step, further into the subject matter.

The structure of Professor Chambers's pithy but comprehensive book is sure to create just that kind of gradual appreciation in its readers. Starting with first principles (rights in property), it pulls us further (for example, into what sorts of things can be subject to rights in property, how they can be held, with whom they can be held), and then even further into security interests, other interests in land, and then into an elegant and persuasive discussion on the sources of rights and competing rights.

There are, of course, different ways to learn and to teach property law. As a student I learned it by following a very different syllabus than what Professor Chambers sets out in this book, and as a professor I taught it with a different syllabus yet, although with an early focus on the first principles—rights in property—that Professor Chambers imparts. While I hope that doing so helped my students learn, I also found that it helped *me* in my own thinking *not just* about property law, but about its relationship to contract law and to my main research area of tort law—which is, after all, simply the vehicle by which wrongful interference with those rights are corrected. By setting and building on that foundation, *The Law of Property* does a service to law students by helping them understand the fundamental concern of their entire first-year private law course load.

Years ago, for my sins I was assigned by my associate dean to teach property law. Panic gripped me. Fortunately, just down the hall was a collection of first-rate teachers, esteemed scholars, and (above all) generous property law colleagues whose doors were open to me, and from whom I grabbed knowledge in handfuls. Professor Chambers was one among them. When I read this book, I am constantly reminded of the clarity of his patient explanations, and I am delighted that the benefit of his gifts as a teacher and a scholar can now be widely shared.

Russell Brown
Supreme Court of Canada
November, 2020

PREFACE

Property law has a fearsome reputation, which is only partly deserved. Every subject has its own specialist vocabulary, but property has more than its fair share. It is filled with terms like fee simple estate, mortgage, and incorporeal hereditament, which are still in use today but derive their meaning from laws and conditions that existed in England in centuries past. It can be difficult to see beyond the complexity to grasp the coherent structure of the subject. This book is intended to provide an accessible and enjoyable introduction to the law of property that will help the reader understand both the subject as a whole and its finer details.

I first studied property law as an LLB student in the 1980s before the internet age. We spent long hours reading badly photocopied cases, trying to decipher not just the meaning of strange words but the actual words themselves. I struggled to make sense of it. For much of that year, property law seemed an overwhelming jumble of antiques and I could see no pattern or structure to them. Fortunately, it began to make sense shortly before the final exam or I would have had a different career.

It has been my great privilege to teach property for the past twenty-five years in Melbourne, Edmonton, London, and now in Kamloops. It is so rewarding to see students unravel its mysteries and come to enjoy—and perhaps even love—a subject they once feared. This book has been shaped by those experiences.

There are many different ways to approach property law and there is a wide variety of syllabuses used in property law courses across Canada and throughout the Commonwealth. This book begins by answering the basic question, "What is property?" It then explores and explains the variety of different property rights that exist in Canadian law. Chapter 8 deals with the ways in which property rights can be created or transferred to others. The final chapter concerns the resolution of disputes between people who claim competing property rights to the same thing. You may find it most helpful to read the chapters in order since they build in complexity (and length). If you would rather dip in and out, the index can help you find explanations of terms and concepts. Some parts may be beyond the scope of your study of property law; they can be saved for later or skipped altogether.

This book deals with the law in every common law province and territory. The footnotes refer to statutes in order from west to east with provinces first and territories second. I owe two apologies to fellow Canadians who may feel ignored. First, references to statutes in Nunavut are included only where they are different from those in the Northwest Territories. Secondly, the civil law of property in Quebec is absent apart from a few references. I do hope that you do not feel alienated by these choices.

There are many people who deserve thanks for helping to make this book possible, including my students and colleagues. But this preface cannot go on and on like the credits to a modern movie, so I will limit my thanks first to my former colleagues who inspired me as a fellow property lawyer: Paul Matthews, Sonny Mirth, Charles Mitchell, James Penner, Sir Francis Price, Murray Raff, and Rod Wood. There are two people not on that list to whom I owe my greatest debts for helping me to become the academic lawyer that I am today: my DPhil supervisor Peter Birks, and my wife Carol.

Over the past forty years, Carol has lived with me in a dozen different homes in three countries. Year after year, I have been promising to work less, and that it will be better next year. Hopefully next year.

Finally, I thank Jeff Miller and Lesley Steeve at Irwin Law for adding this to their wonderful Essentials of Canadian Law series. Like Carol, Jeff has been patiently waiting on "next year" for more years than I care to mention.

Robert Chambers
2 November 2020
Kamloops BC

CHAPTER 1

WHAT IS PROPERTY?

A. THE LAW OF PROPERTY

The law of property is the most commonly encountered area of law but perhaps the least understood. It can be complicated and counterintuitive, yet we rely on it every day. The simple act of getting dressed in the morning involves having the right to some clothes to wear and the right to be in some private space in which to put them on. Children can own things long before they are able to make contracts. Property law is important to us because it defines and protects our rights to things and provides a framework for sharing them with others.

Most law students begin their study of property law in their first year, and many find it to be the most challenging part of the first-year program. Property law is an old subject in which ancient concepts and terms are still in use. It is also a broad subject, intruding on other areas of law. It intersects with the law of contracts whenever people buy and sell things. The wrongful interference with property may be a tort or a crime. The power to make laws concerning property involves constitutional law, as does the protection of Aboriginal title.

This book provides an introduction to the law of property that is meant to be accessible to law students and lay people. The key to understanding property law is to acquire a solid grasp of its fundamental concepts and to keep them in mind when exploring the topic in detail. And there is a lot of detail. This is one area of law in which it is very easy to lose sight of the forest for the trees.

This chapter explains the meaning of property and the two definitions of property that are used in the law. It then describes various things that can be the subject of property rights.

B. THE MEANING OF PROPERTY

We use the word *property* to mean different things in different contexts. It is often used to denote the things we own. When we see a box marked "Lost Property," we understand property to be the things inside the box. If asked if we own any property, we might understand property to mean land in that context. It is perfectly acceptable to use the word *property* in those ways. However, in the law of property, the word *property* is used to refer to the rights that people have to their things and not to the things themselves. Property is a kind of legal right. The first step in understanding property law is understanding the nature of property rights and what makes them different from other rights.

C. RIGHTS

All rights have corresponding duties. If you have a right to be paid a sum of money, it is only because someone else is under a corresponding duty to pay it to you. If there is no duty, there is no right. You might hope to be paid or even deserve to be paid, but you can have no legal right to be paid unless someone else is under a legal duty to pay you.

1) Rights *In Personam* and Rights *In Rem*

Rights can be divided into two broad categories: rights *in personam* and rights *in rem*. A right *in personam* is enforceable only against a specific person or persons. A right to a payment is just such a right. The creditor has the right to be paid, and the debtor is under the corresponding duty to pay. They have a relationship called debt. Whereas the creditor is normally free to assign that right (i.e., transfer it) to someone else, the debtor cannot assign the duty. The debtor is the specific person against whom the creditor's right can be enforced.

Rights *in rem* are different from rights *in personam* in two ways. First, a right *in rem* always relates to a specific thing, such as an animal, a car, or a piece of land. Rights *in personam* need not relate to anything in particular. A debt, for example, is a right to be paid a specific sum of money but not to any specific coins or bills. If I owe $100 to you, that does not give you a right to any cash in my wallet or funds in my bank account. I can pay that debt from any source I choose.

Second, rights *in rem* are enforceable generally against others and not just against specific persons. You have rights to possess and use the things you own, and other members of society are under the corresponding duty not to interfere with your rights to those things. This general duty of non-interference makes it possible for rights *in rem* to exist.

Although, generally, a right *in rem* is enforceable against others, no steps are taken to enforce that right unless someone wrongly interferes with it. The breach of the general duty of non-interference by a specific person gives rise to a claim against that person to stop that interference and possibly to pay damages. In the same way, it is necessary to take steps to enforce a right *in personam* only when the person who owes the corresponding duty is in breach of that duty.

The law of property is primarily concerned with rights *in rem*. We usually refer to rights *in rem* as property rights, which we contrast with personal rights, meaning rights *in personam*. However, a study of the law of property is not restricted to a study of rights *in rem*. There are two main reasons for this. First, many relationships involve a combination of personal and property rights. For example, if the owners of a house mortgage it to the bank as security for the payment of a loan, the bank will have both a property right to the house and a personal right to be paid that debt by the owners. Second, people often have rights *in personam* to use things. For example, a guest in a hotel has a personal right (called a licence) to be there but no property right to their room. Licences are commonly studied in courses on property law because they often relate to land and because it is important to know the difference between a licence and a property right, such as a lease.

2) Assignable Rights

We usually think of property rights as rights *in rem*, and courses on property law are based on that understanding. But it is important to note that a completely different concept of property is used in some legal contexts. Sometimes the issue is not whether the right in question is a right to a thing enforceable generally against others but whether that right can be assigned, that is, transferred to someone else. In some contexts, the term *property* is used to mean assignable rights and includes both rights *in rem* and rights *in personam*. Although this can be confusing, it is important to be able to distinguish between these two different meanings.

There are two areas of law in which the term *property* is most commonly used to mean assignable rights: the administration of a deceased person's estate and bankruptcy. When someone dies, all of their assignable rights form their *estate*, which is transferred to their personal representative (who is either an executor appointed by the will or an administrator appointed by the court). The personal representative has the duty to gather in the estate, pay the debts and taxes, and distribute what remains according to law. In British Columbia, the *Wills, Estates and Succession Act* defines "estate" as "the property of a deceased person."[1] It is clear that "property" is being used to mean all assignable rights, including rights *in personam*, such as bank accounts, insurance benefits, and other debts due to the deceased.

When a person becomes bankrupt, most of their assignable rights are transferred to their trustee in bankruptcy,[2] who will sell them and use the proceeds to pay the bankrupt's creditors. Those assignable rights are known as the property of the bankrupt, and the term property is defined in the *Bankruptcy and Insolvency Act* as follows:

> In this Act, ... property means any type of property, whether situated in Canada or elsewhere, and includes money, goods, things in action, land and every description of property, whether real or personal, legal or equitable, as well as obligations, easements and every description of estate, interest and profit, present or future, vested or contingent, in, arising out of or incident to property.[3]

It is an oddly circular definition that begins with "property means any type of property," but a key feature is the inclusion of "things in action." A thing in action (also known as a *chose in action*)[4] is a right *in personam* that is enforceable in a court of law, and the most common thing in action is a debt. The *Bankruptcy and Insolvency Act* uses this definition of property because the issue at stake is not whether the rights of the bankrupt can be enforced generally against others but whether they can be assigned to the trustee in bankruptcy and used to pay the creditors. For example, a bankrupt's right to appeal from a court judgment against them for the payment of money is considered to be the property of the bankrupt that is transferred to their trustee in

---

1   SBC 2009, c 13, s 1. See also *Wills and Succession Act*, SA 2010, c W-12.2, s 1(1)(i); *Estate Administration Act*, SA 2014, c E-12.5, s 1(h); *Probate Act*, SNS 2000, c 31, s 2(k); *Probate Act*, RSPEI 1988, c P-21, s 1(l).
2   *Bankruptcy and Insolvency Act*, RSC 1985, c B-3, s 71.
3   *Ibid*, s 2.
4   See *Torkington v Magee*, [1902] 2 KB 427 at 430.

bankruptcy,[5] yet it is a right *in personam* that would not be regarded as property in other contexts.

When property is used to mean assignable rights, it is a very broad concept since most rights are assignable. Some rights are not, such as the right to vote in a parliamentary election or the rights represented by a university degree or professional qualification.[6] Those rights are truly personal in the sense that they can only be exercised by the specific person to whom they were granted. Unlike rights *in personam*, which can only be enforced *against* specific persons, these non-assignable rights can only by enforced *by* specific persons.

As mentioned above, the law's use of two completely different definitions of property can be confusing, especially to those who are new to the subject. It can even cause confusion among lawyers and judges. A surprising example is the case of *Saulnier v Royal Bank of Canada*,[7] in which the Supreme Court of Canada was asked to decide whether a commercial fishing licence was property that fell within the definition in the *Bankruptcy and Insolvency Act*, quoted above. The Court reached the right answer but struggled to get there because it asked the wrong question. Instead of asking whether the licence was assignable, it asked whether it was sufficiently similar to a right *in rem* known as a *profit à prendre*.

A *profit à prendre* (discussed in Chapter 7) is a right to enter someone else's land and take away minerals, soil, wild animals, fish, or natural vegetation. It is not a right to things that may be taken away in the future but a right to the land itself. It is a right *in rem* because it relates to a specific thing (the land) and is enforceable generally against others. A commercial fishing licence is not a right *in rem* because it does not confer rights to any land, water, or fish (before they are caught) and is not enforceable generally against others. Its similarity to a *profit à prendre* should have been irrelevant in *Saulnier v Royal Bank of Canada* and would have been if the Court had asked the right question.

On reading this, a new student of property law might despair: "What hope do I have if the Supreme Court of Canada does not understand it?" A good lesson to be learned is that we all make mistakes, even senior lawyers, judges, and law professors. The authorities on which the law is based are not beyond question.

There is another form of despair that should also be avoided, which is the idea that property is a vague concept that can mean whatever we want it to mean. Each of our two definitions of property is clear and

---

5   *Heath v Tang*, [1993] 1 WLR 1421 (CA); *Cummings v Claremont Petroleum NL*, [1996] HCA 19, 185 CLR 124.

6   See *Caratun v Caratun* (1992), 96 DLR (4th) 404 (Ont CA).

7   2008 SCC 58.

stable. The problem arises when the wrong definition is chosen. When asking whether a particular right is property, we are asking one of two questions depending on the context: *against* whom can it be enforced, or *by* whom can it be enforced? Rights *in rem* can be enforced generally against others, whereas rights *in personam* can be enforced only against specific persons. Most rights *in rem* and rights *in personam* can be assigned by others and enforced by whoever holds them, but some rights are non-assignable and can be enforced only by the specific persons to whom they were granted.

D. THINGS

As discussed above, all rights *in rem* relate to things. This raises a key question: What things can be the subject of property rights?

1) Land

Land is central to the law of property. It is a finite resource (although that is not always apparent in many parts of Canada) and will continue to exist long after we are gone. Everyone needs some place to be. For many people, their home is the most valuable asset they will ever own. Land is often treated differently from other things, which is why two chapters of this book are devoted to that subject.

2) Goods

Goods are tangible things other than land and money. They may be manufactured (such as phones and furniture) or grow naturally (such as plants or animals). Plants attached to the land are normally regarded as part of the land and not as goods before they are severed from it, but the law will treat growing crops as goods for some purposes.[8] Rocks, minerals, and soil become goods when they are removed from the land. Manufactured goods may cease to be goods if they are attached to the land, such as wood used to build a fence or windows installed in a house. They become *fixtures* that are part of the land.

---

8   See, for example, the definition of goods in the *Sale of Goods Act* in each province and territory: RSBC 1996, c 410; RSA 2000, c S-2; RSS 1978, c S-1; CCSM, c S10; RSO 1990, c S.1; RSNB 2016, c 110; RSNS 1989, c 408; RSPEI 1988, c S-1; RSNL 1990, c S-6; RSY 2002, c 198; RSNWT 1988, c S-2.

3) Money

We think of money as either cash in hand or money in the bank. We have rights *in rem* to our cash. The bills and coins that we possess are tangible things, like goods, but they are not normally regarded as goods when they are used as currency to pay for things. A set of rare or commemorative coins could be treated as goods if it is sold as a set and not used as currency to pay for something.

Money in a bank account is a valuable asset, but we do not have a right *in rem* to that money. The bank account is a debt due to the customer by the bank.[9] There is no cash set aside for the customer. The account is simply the bank's statement of what it owes the customer, who has a right *in personam* to be paid that amount by a specific person: the bank. If the account is overdrawn, then it becomes a debt due from the customer to the bank.

4) Documents

Documents, such as books and manuscripts, can be goods, but they can have value not as goods but for the rights they confer. For example, a cheque for $1,000 is not just an ordinary piece of paper but can give its holder the right to be paid $1,000. Of course, one can have a property right to any piece of paper, but the real value of the cheque is the right to payment. There are many other types of documents that can have value far beyond the paper on which they are written. These include bearer bonds, bills of lading, and company share certificates. Deeds and wills also have significance, not as goods but as documents that can create and transfer legal rights.

5) Intellectual Property

We can have property rights to intangible things. Intellectual property is a generic term for a variety of different rights to exploit the value of ideas. Copyrights and patents are the best-known forms of intellectual property, but there are others, including industrial designs,[10] trademarks,[11] and plant breeders' rights.[12] Copyright protects original forms of expression, including artistic, dramatic, literary, and musical works, and gives the holder the exclusive right to perform or reproduce those

---

9   See *Foley v Hill* (1848), 2 HLC 28, 9 ER 1002.
10   *Industrial Design Act*, RSC 1985, c I-9.
11   *Trademarks Act*, RSC 1985, c T-13.
12   *Plant Breeders' Rights Act*, SC 1990, c 20.

works.[13] It is the form of expression, not the ideas expressed, that is protected. A patent provides an exclusive right to exploit an invention, which is a new, inventive, and useful way to manufacture something.[14] A scientific discovery (e.g., gravity or a new form of undersea life) is not an invention.

A feature of all forms of intellectual property is that they provide monopolies that are limited in time (e.g., fifty years after the author's death) and relate to specific types of ideas and information. The monopolies are justified because they provide financial incentives for creating intellectual property. They are specific, limited exceptions to freedom of information, which is essential in a free and democratic society.[15]

6) Confidential Information

Confidential information is often regarded as a type of intellectual property.[16] A secret recipe or idea for a new television series can be a valuable asset that can be sold or licensed to others.[17] Although other forms of intellectual property are undoubtedly property rights that can be enforced generally against others, the status of confidential information is subject to debate.

Every right to confidential information corresponds to a duty of confidence, which is the duty not to misuse that information. That duty may be created by contract, such as a contract of employment or confidentiality agreement, but a contract is not required. The duty of confidence can also be created by a non-contractual undertaking, for example, when secrets are shared between lovers.[18] The undertaking may be expressed but is often implied from the circumstances.

If duties of confidence were imposed only on those who undertook them, then the corresponding rights would be rights *in personam* since they would be enforceable only against specific persons. However, an undertaking is not required. If someone receives information and knows or ought to know that it is confidential, then a duty of confidence will be imposed on them. In *Attorney General v Guardian (No 2)*, Lord Goff said that the duty would even arise "where an obviously

---

13   *Copyright Act*, RSC 1985, c C-42, s 3.

14   *Patent Act*, RSC 1985, c P-4.

15   *Constitution Act, 1982*, s 2(b), being Schedule B to the *Canada Act 1982* (UK), 1982, c 11.

16   See, for example, *Coogan v News Group Newspapers Ltd*, [2012] EWCA Civ 48 at para 39, [2012] 2 WLR 848.

17   See *Cadbury Schweppes Inc v FBI Foods Ltd*, [1999] 1 SCR 142, 167 DLR (4th) 577; *Fraser v Thames Television Ltd*, [1984] QB 44.

18   *Duchess of Argyll v Duke of Argyll*, [1967] 1 Ch 302.

confidential document is wafted by an electric fan out of a window into a crowded street, or where an obviously confidential document, such as a private diary, is dropped in a public place, and is then picked up by a passer-by."[19] Since the right to confidential information can be enforced against people who do nothing more than receive that information, it appears to be a right *in rem* enforceable generally against others.

If confidential information ceases to be confidential (e.g., when it is published in a newspaper), there can be no further duties of confidence with respect to it. However, the people who disclosed that information in breach of confidence may still be personally liable for the breach.

7) Living Things

As mentioned above, plants and animals are goods. When animals are referred to as "livestock," their status as goods is made clear. However, it does seem odd to think of family pets as goods in the same legal category as clothes and groceries. A pet may be a loyal, loving, and much-loved member of the family. A divorcing couple may see their competing claims to it as something akin to a dispute over child custody. However, it is an aspect of their division of the family property, as Danyliuk J made clear in *Henderson v Henderson*:

> Granted, dogs and other pets are treated somewhat differently than other personal property. Statutory protection for pets exists to prevent them from being treated with cruelty or neglect. On a practical level, most people do not see their pet as something to be discarded or sold on Kijiji when they are done with it. While that is true, and while there is a distinction between animals and inanimate objects, it is also true that both are property and are not dealt with under child custody principles.[20]

Animals are significantly different from other goods because we owe duties to care for them and treat them humanely. We do not owe duties to them because animals are not legal persons who are capable of holding the corresponding rights (as discussed below). Our duties to care for animals can be enforced by the state.

A striking example of this is provided by the old Australian case of *Backhouse v Judd*.[21] The owner of horses allowed them to starve to death. He was charged under the South Australian *Prevention of Cruelty to Animals Act 1908*, which imposed a penalty of up to 10 pounds on

---

19   [1990] 1 AC 109 at 281.
20   2016 SKQB 282 at para 24.
21   [1925] SASR 16 [*Backhouse*].

anyone who "wantonly or negligently fails to supply any animal with proper and sufficient food, or water."[22]

Unfortunately, the statute was not well drafted and did not expressly impose the duty to supply food and water on anyone. The owner argued that he could not be convicted of a failure to supply food and water in the absence of a duty to do so. Justice Napier rejected that argument and convicted the owner. He said,

> The only possible meaning is that here, as in other respects, the Statute is intended to give legal force and efficacy to obligations which are already accepted as social duties, and as binding, in conscience, upon civilized people. The Statute presupposes the existence of some such moral duty, and provides for its enforcement. . . . [I]t seems to me that the only satisfactory basis for the duty is that of ownership. There is nothing novel in the idea that property is a responsibility as well as a privilege. The law which confers and protects the right of property in any animal may well throw the burden of the responsibility for its care upon the owner as a public duty incidental to the ownership.[23]

We treat animals differently from other goods, but why do we treat them differently from human beings? Humans are legal persons, but animals are not. That distinction does not depend on intelligence, empathy, or the ability to feel pain. A human infant in a coma is a person, but healthy adult chimpanzees, dogs, dolphins, and whales are not. The line between persons and things is artificial. Persons hold rights, whereas things are the subject of rights.

All living human beings are persons, regardless of their capacity, but they are not the only persons. Corporations are also persons. They are artificial persons. They can hold rights and be subject to duties just like human beings, who are called natural persons or individuals when it is necessary to distinguish them from corporations.

The distinction between persons and things is demonstrated by the whimsical case of *Joly v Pelletier*.[24] The plaintiff claimed that he was a Martian and that the president of the United States (Bill Clinton) and deputy prime minister of Canada (Anne McLellan) had conspired with the FBI to conceal his Martian origins. The defendants applied to strike out the claim before trial. This required the judge to assume that the facts claimed by the plaintiff were true and then decide whether the plaintiff had any hope of success based on those facts. Justice Epstein struck out the claim: "The entire basis of Mr Joly's actions is that he is

---

22   *Prevention of Cruelty to Animals Act 1908* (No 995), s 4(1)(b).

23   *Backhouse*, above note 21 at 20–21.

24   [1999] OJ No 1728 (Ont HC).

a Martian, not a human being. There is certainly no suggestion that he is a corporation. I conclude therefore, that Mr Joly, on his pleading as drafted, has no status before the Court."

Corporations are both persons and things. They hold rights and owe duties like human persons, but they are also owned by other persons. Most corporations are owned by their shareholders, who can be humans and other corporations. As owners, the shareholders can decide to wind up the corporation and terminate its existence.

At one time, human beings could be persons, things, or both. Slavery was allowed under Roman law (which provided the basis for most legal systems in the modern world) and existed lawfully in the United States of America until 1865. In 1953, Canada signed the United Nations' *Slavery Convention*, which defines slavery as "the status or condition of a person over whom any or all of the powers attaching to the right of ownership are exercised" and requires contracting parties to "bring about, progressively and as soon as possible, the complete abolition of slavery in all its forms."[25]

Human beings can no longer be things subject to property rights. However, many people are still being treated as slaves even though their captors have no legal right to do so. The fight continues against human trafficking and what is known as *modern slavery*.[26]

8) Human Tissue

Living human beings cannot be the subject of property rights, but it is possible to have property rights to human tissue once it is no longer part of a living human being. It has taken a long time for the law to work this out, starting with the traditional rule that there was no property in a human corpse.[27]

When someone dies, they cease to be a legal person. They can no longer hold rights, nor can they be subject to duties. Some of those rights will cease to exist (e.g., the right to practise a profession), but most will be transferred to their personal representative and distributed according to law. The personal representative also has custody of the body of the deceased and the duty to dispose of it properly. This right to custody of the body is remarkably similar to a right *in rem* since it relates to something tangible and is enforceable generally against

---

25 *Slavery Convention*, 15 September 1926 and amended 7 December 1953, 212 UNTS 2861, arts 1 & 2 (entered into force 7 July 1955).

26 See *R v Tang*, [2008] HCA 39, 237 CLR 1; *Modern Slavery Act 2015* (UK); *Nevsun Resources Ltd v Araya*, 2020 SCC 5.

27 See *Doodeward v Spence*, [1908] HCA 45, 6 CLR 406 [*Doodeward*].

others.[28] However, we are reluctant to say that the body of someone we have known and loved is now a "thing" subject to property rights. In the United States, this right to custody of the body is referred to as "quasi-property."[29]

In *Doodeward v Spence*,[30] the High Court of Australia recognized that possession of human remains is lawful for some purposes, such as a mummy for display in a museum or specimens for medical research and teaching. Since it is lawful to possess human remains for purposes other than burial, the law will protect the right to possess those remains. Chief Justice Griffith said that "when a person has by the lawful exercise of work or skill so dealt with a human body or part of a human body in his lawful possession that it has acquired some attributes differentiating it from a mere corpse awaiting burial, he acquires a right to retain possession of it."[31]

It is possible to have property rights to human tissue that has been removed from a living human being. Hair, urine, blood, and semen are all things that can be subject to property rights.[32] Doubt about the status of other types of tissue was created by *Moore v Regents of the University of California*,[33] in which the Supreme Court of California held that a patient did not own the tissue that had been surgically removed from his body. However, it is clear from other American cases that laboratories and universities do have property rights to human tissue that has been collected for research.[34] The Supreme Court of Western Australia held in *Roche v Douglas* that tissue that had been removed during surgery was subject to property rights:

> [I]t defies reason to not regard tissue samples as property. Such samples have a real physical presence. They exist and will continue to exist until some step is taken to effect destruction. There is no purpose to be served in ignoring physical reality. To deny that the tissue samples are property, in contrast to the paraffin in which the samples are kept or the jar in which both the paraffin and the samples

---

28   See *Edmonds v Armstrong Funeral Home Ltd*, [1931] 1 DLR 676 (Alta CA).

29   *Pierce v Proprietors of Swan Point Cemetery*, 14 Am Rep 667 at 681 (1872); *Janicki v Hospital of St Raphael*, 744 A (2d) 963 (Superior Ct Connecticut 1999).

30   *Doodeward*, above note 27.

31   *Ibid* at 414; see also *R v Kelly*, [1998] EWCA Crim 1578, [1999] QB 621 at 631.

32   See *Yearworth v North Bristol NHS Trust*, [2009] EWCA Civ 37, [2010] QB 1; *JCM v ANA*, 2012 BCSC 584.

33   793 P (2d) 479 (1990).

34   *United States v Arora*, 860 F Supp 1091 (US DC Maryland 1994); *Washington University v Catalona*, 490 F (3d) 667 (USCA 8th 2007).

are stored, would be in my view to create a legal fiction. There is no rational or logical justification for such a result.[35]

Human tissue can be subject to property rights after its removal from a living human being but cannot be property while it is still attached. It is part of the person and does not exist as a separate thing. This was demonstrated in the English case of *R v Bentham*.[36] The defendant had pretended that his hand in his pocket was a gun when he robbed his former employer. He was convicted of having possession of an imitation firearm but was acquitted on appeal. Lord Bingham said, "One cannot possess something which is not separate and distinct from oneself. An unsevered hand or finger is part of oneself. . . . A person's hand or fingers are not a thing."[37]

We do not own our bodies. They are part of who we are. The law protects our bodies in much the same way that it protects our things. Everyone else in society is under a general duty not to interfere with the persons or property of others. Anyone who breaches that duty commits a tort, but wrongful interference with the body of a living human being is trespass to the person, not trespass to goods.

35   [2000] WASC 146, 22 WAR 331, Master Sanderson.
36   [2005] UKHL 18, [2005] WLR 1057.
37   *Ibid* at para 8.

CHAPTER 2

OWNERSHIP AND POSSESSION

A. INTRODUCTION

Most people have an intuitive understanding of ownership and possession. We know that we can possess things without owning them (e.g., when we borrow a book from the library or rent an apartment), just as we can own things that are currently possessed by others. We usually think of ownership as being superior to possession, but possession has a more important role (as many students of property law are surprised to discover). When resolving disputes over property, the common law does not much care about who owns the things but merely which of the rival claimants has the better right to possess them.

B. OWNERSHIP

There is a wide variety of different property rights discussed in the chapters that follow, including easements, estates, mortgages, and trusts. For the most part, they are clearly defined. Although there is uncertainty on the boundaries between legal categories, the precise nature of each of these property rights has been worked out over time. Curiously, ownership is not among them. It is a concept, not a specific right. For example, the owner of land in a common law system is usually the person who holds the fee simple estate (which, as explained in the next chapter, is the right to possess land indefinitely). The owner of goods is simply the person with the best right to possess them. Estates and possession are property rights. People with those rights are often the owners, but they might not be.

Our statutes are filled with references to the "owner." In each case, it is necessary to see how that term is defined for the purpose of that particular statute. For example, the *Home Owner Grant Act* in British Columbia defines "owner" to include a tenant under a lease for ninety-nine years or longer.[1] We do not usually think of the tenant as being the owner of the land, but they do start to look the owner when land is leased for a very long time. If I leased my land to you for 250 years, your rights to possess, use, and enjoy the land would last for generations. In what sense am I still the owner?

1) Professor Honoré

In 1961, Tony Honoré published an important essay on the nature of ownership.[2] He was a brilliant comparative lawyer and began by noting that ownership is surprisingly similar in different countries despite major differences in their legal systems:

> There is indeed, a substantial similarity in the position of one who "owns" an umbrella in England, France, Russia, China, and any other modern country one may care to mention. Everywhere the "owner" can, in the simple uncomplicated case, in which no other person has an interest in the thing, use it, stop others using it, lend it, sell it, or leave it by will. Nowhere may he use it to poke his neighbour in the ribs or to knock over his vase. Ownership, *dominium*, *propriété*, *Eigentum* and similar words stand not merely for the greatest interest in things in particular systems but for a type of interest with common features transcending particular systems.[3]

Honoré then described what he called the "standard incidents" of ownership that are common to most legal systems:

> Ownership comprises the right to possess, the right to use, the right to manage, the right to the income of the thing, the right to the capital, the right to security, the rights or incidents of transmissibility and absence of term, the prohibition of harmful use, liability to execution, and the incident of residuarity: this makes eleven leading incidents.[4]

---

1   RSBC 1996, c 194, s 1.
2   AM Honoré, "Ownership" in AG Guest, ed, *Oxford Essays in Jurisprudence* (Oxford: Oxford University Press, 1961) 107.
3   *Ibid* at 108.
4   *Ibid* at 113.

Before looking more closely at these standard incidents, there are two things to note. First, this is a *description* of ownership, not a *definition*. Something can be owned even if some of those incidents are missing. Second, this is a description of *ownership*, not *property*. There is a wide variety of different property rights less than ownership. A right of way, for example, is a limited right to make use of someone else's land. It is a property right in the sense that it is a right to the land that is enforceable generally against others, but it is a far cry from ownership.

Most of Honoré's standard incidents apply to possession as well as ownership. Take the example of a ten-year lease of farmland. The tenant has the right to possess the farm, the right to use it, the right to manage how it is used, the right to the income from it, and the right to be secure from interference with their tenancy. The incident of transmissibility would also apply: if the tenant died, the lease would form one of the assets in their estate, to be distributed according to law. The lease would also be liable to execution. It is a valuable asset that could be sold to pay the tenant's creditors (although it is more likely that the lease would be forfeited because of the tenant's failure to pay rent). If the government needed the land for public purposes, it could expropriate the tenant's and landlord's rights and pay suitable compensation to both.[5]

The tenant would have a duty to avoid harmful use. They could not use the farm in a way that caused a nuisance to their neighbours, and they would have the occupier's duty of care to keep the farm in a condition that does not endanger those who enter it.[6]

There are three incidents that apply to the landlord and not the tenant: the right to the capital, absence of term, and incident of residuarity. These are what separate ownership from possession. A right to capital is the right to dispose of an asset by selling or giving it to someone else or by consuming or destroying it. Although the tenant would normally be entitled to assign the lease, that would not affect the landlord's right to the farm. In other words, the tenant has the power to transfer the

---

5   *Expropriation Act*, RSBC 1996, c 125; *Expropriation Act*, RSA 2000, c E-13; *Expropriation Act*, RSS 1978, c E-15; *Expropriation Act*, CCSM, c E190; *Expropriations Act*, RSO 1990, c E.26; *Expropriation Act*, RSNB 1973, c E-14; *Expropriation Act*, RSNS 1989, c 156; *Expropriation Act*, RSPEI 1988, c E-13; *Expropriation Act*, RSNL 1990, c E-19; *Expropriation Act*, RSY 2002, c 81; *Expropriation Act*, RSNWT 1988, c E-11.

6   See *Occupiers Liability Act*, RSBC 1996, c 337; *Occupiers' Liability Act*, RSA 2000, c O-4; *Occupiers' Liability Act*, CCSM, c O8; *Occupiers' Liability Act*, RSO 1990, c O.2; *Law Reform Act*, RSNB 2011, c 184; *Occupiers' Liability Act*, SNS 1996, c 27; *Occupiers' Liability Act*, RSPEI 1988, c O-2; *Hale v Westfair Foods Ltd*, [1995] 3 WWR 293, 127 Sask R 223 (QB); *Stacey v Anglican Churches of Canada* (1999), 182 Nfld & PEIR 1, 554 APR 1 (NL CA).

use of the farm for the remainder of the lease, whereas the landlord has the power to transfer the right to the farm indefinitely (subject to the tenant's lease). From the landlord's perspective, the rent received from the tenant is income, whereas the market value of the landlord's interest is the capital.

We do not normally think of land as something that can be consumed or destroyed. However, the tenant owes a duty to the landlord to return the farm in a satisfactory condition when the lease comes to an end. In contrast, the landlord would then be free (subject to local land use regulations) to do whatever they wish with the farm. They could tear down the buildings and fences, uproot the trees, dig up the soil, and so on.

Absence of term means that ownership has the potential to go on indefinitely. The tenant's right to the farm (like all leases) has a defined limit, whereas the landlord's ownership does not. The landlord will die someday, but their right to the farm will continue and be transferred to others. The incident of residuarity means that, regardless of how many lesser rights are granted by the owner, ultimately, the asset will come back to its owner. In our example, the landlord will once again have a right to possess the farm when the lease comes to an end.

2) Crown Ownership

Many things are owned by the Crown (i.e., Her Majesty the Queen in right of Canada or a province or, as most people think of Her Majesty, the government). Crown ownership is often just like private ownership. Honoré's standard incidents apply to government office buildings, furniture, vehicles, and so on. However, there are important ways in which public property is different from private property.

Crown land is held on behalf of the people of Canada or a particular province, but much of it is off-limits to members of the public. Access to a military base is a prime example. However, Crown land is often held for the purpose of being used by the public to a greater or lesser extent. We have public roads, sidewalks, trails, parks, and beaches, as well as public buildings, such as museums and libraries, to which members of the public routinely have access. Although the government can restrict access to public places and regulate their use,[7] it does not have the same degree of control as a private person would have over their own private spaces.

A good example is provided by *Committee for the Commonwealth of Canada v Canada*.[8] Although that case took place in Quebec, where property rights are governed by a civil code instead of the common

---

7   See, for example, *Batty v Toronto*, 2011 ONSC 6862.

8   [1991] 1 SCR 139, 77 DLR (4th) 385 [*Committee for the Commonwealth of Canada*].

law, the fundamental principle is the same. The plaintiffs claimed that their *Charter*[9] right to freedom of expression was violated when they were prevented from distributing political materials at Dorval Airport (now Montréal-Trudeau International Airport). The Supreme Court of Canada decided that their right to freedom of expression trumped the government's property rights.

Article 399 of the *Civil Code of Lower Canada* states: "Property belongs either to the Crown, or to municipalities or other corporations, or to individuals." As L'Heureux-Dubé J noted, this means that "all lands belong to someone."[10] She went on to say that

> [i]f members of the public had no right whatsoever to distribute leaflets or engage in other expressive activity on government-owned property (except with permission), then there would be little if any opportunity to exercise their rights of freedom of expression. Only those with enough wealth to own land, or mass media facilities (whose ownership is largely concentrated), would be able to engage in free expression.[11]

The right to freedom of expression applies in places to which the public are routinely granted access. It does not require the government to open up all of its land for that purpose. As L'Heureux-Dubé J said, "the *Charter's* framers did not intend internal government offices, air traffic control towers, prison cells and Judges' Chambers to be made available for leafletting or demonstrations."[12]

In *PruneYard Shopping Center v Robins*,[13] the US Supreme Court held that the right to freedom of expression applied to the distribution of political materials in a privately owned shopping mall. The court applied a principle it had established in *Marsh v Alabama*: "Ownership does not always mean absolute dominion. The more an owner, for his advantage, opens up his property for use by the public in general, the more do his rights become circumscribed by the statutory and constitutional rights of those who use it."[14]

This was quoted with approval by L'Heureux-Dubé J in *Committee for the Commonwealth of Canada v Canada*, but she stated that her decision related only to government property.[15] The distinction between Crown

---

9   *Canadian Charter of Rights and Freedoms*, Part I of the *Constitution Act, 1982*, being Schedule B to the Canada Act 1982 (UK), 1982, c 11.

10   *Committee for Commonwealth of Canada*, above note 8 at 195.

11   *Ibid* at 198.

12   *Ibid*.

13   447 US 74 (1980).

14   326 US 501 at 506 (1946).

15   *Committee for the Commonwealth of Canada*, above note 8 at 197.

land and privately owned land may be less important than the extent to which the land is open to public access. However, in *Harrison v Carswell*,[16] a majority of the Supreme Court of Canada held that employees on strike did not have a right to picket in a privately owned shopping mall. Although that case was decided before the *Charter* came into force, it continues to be followed by lower courts.[17]

The Crown often claims ownership of natural resources other than land. For example, the Crown is the owner of much of the wildlife in most Canadian jurisdictions.[18] In Alberta, the Crown owns "all water on or under the surface of the ground, whether in liquid or solid state."[19] This suggests that every snowman in the province is government property. However, the Crown's ownership of natural resources is really a device for the regulation of those resources and is not the same as private ownership. This was demonstrated in *Yanner v Eaton*,[20] in which an Aboriginal Australian was charged with hunting crocodiles without a licence. It was argued that the Crown's ownership of the crocodiles had extinguished his native title right to hunt them. This was rejected by the High Court of Australia, which held that the Crown's ownership was "nothing more than 'a fiction expressive in legal shorthand of the importance to its people that a State have power to preserve and regulate the exploitation of an important resource.'"[21] The court went on to quote Roscoe Pound:

> The state as a corporation does not own a river as it owns the furniture in the state house. It does not own wild game as it owns the cash in the vaults of the treasury. What is meant is that conservation of important social resources requires regulation of the use of *res communes* to eliminate friction and prevent waste, and requires limitation of the times when, places where, and persons by whom *res nullius* may be acquired in order to prevent their extermination. Our modern way of putting it is only an incident of the nineteenth-century dogma that everything must be owned.[22]

---

16 [1976] 2 SCR 200.

17 See, for example, *RMH Teleservices v BCGEU*, 2003 BCSC 278.

18 *Wildlife Act*, RSBC 1996, c 488, s 2; *Wildlife Act*, RSA 2000, c W-10, s 7; *Wildlife Act, 1998*, SS 1998, c W-13.12, s 23; *Wildlife Act*, CCSM, c W130, s 85; *Fish and Wildlife Act*, SNB 1980, c F-14.1, s 3; *Wildlife Act*, RSNS 1989, c 504, s 4; *Wildlife Conservation Act*, RSPEI 1988, c W-4.1, s 2; *Wildlife Act*, RSY 2002, c 229, s 101.

19 *Water Act*, RSA 2000, c W-3, ss 1(1)(fff) and 3(2).

20 [1999] HCA 53, 201 CLR 351.

21 *Ibid* at para 28, quoting *Toomer v Witsell*, 334 US 385 at 402 (1948).

22 Roscoe Pound, *An Introduction to the Philosophy of Law*, rev ed (New Haven: Yale University Press, 1954) at 111.

C. POSSESSION

Possession is different from ownership in the ways discussed above. It is more than just a concept. It is a specific legal right that exists when someone has control of a tangible thing with the intention to possess it. As Lord Browne-Wilkinson said in *JA Pye (Oxford) Ltd v Graham*, "there are two elements necessary for legal possession: (1) a sufficient degree of physical custody and control ('factual possession'); (2) an intention to exercise such custody and control on one's own behalf and for one's own benefit ('intention to possess')."[23]

1) Control

Control of a tangible thing is often called *factual possession*, but that can be confusing since it sounds a lot like *actual possession* and is just one of the two elements required to have possession at law. Control usually means limiting or regulating access to land or goods by other people, but sometimes it depends on keeping wild animals or other goods (such as fluids or floating logs) from getting away.

The best way to control land is with a fence, but a fence is not required. Unfenced land can be controlled by using it in a way that is inconsistent with its use by others, for example, by cultivating it or building something on it.[24] Just as a fence is not necessary to control land, it may not be sufficient since it may be there to keep animals or tennis balls inside and not to keep people out.[25] As an Australian court said in *Whittlesea City Council v Abbatangelo*:

> Plainly, fences serve multiple purposes. Some delineate title boundaries. Others are internal. Some are ornate. Others are minimalist and purely functional. The nature and purpose of a fence will be affected by the nature, location and characteristics of the land and the uses to which it is put.[26]

A wild animal is controlled by keeping it from escaping. In *Young v Hichens*,[27] the plaintiff was fishing in St Ives Bay. They were in the process of drawing their net in a circle around the fish when the defendant

---

23   [2002] UKHL 30 at para 40, [2003] 1 AC 419; see also *Bradford Investments (1963) Ltd v Fama* (2005), 257 DLR (4th) 347, 77 OR (3d) 127 at 147–48.

24   See, for example, *Johnston v Roode*, 2019 NSCA 98.

25   See *Clement v Jones*, [1909] HCA 11, 8 CLR 133; *Riley v Penttila*, [1974] VR 547.

26   [2009] VSCA 188, 259 ALR 56 at para 100.

27   (1844) 6 QB 606.

rowed through a gap in the circle and scooped up the fish. The plaintiff succeeded at trial against the defendant for wrongly taking the plaintiff's fish, but that was overturned on appeal. Lord Denman CJ said,

> It does appear almost certain that the plaintiff would have had possession of the fish but for the act of the defendant: but it is quite certain that he had not possession. Whatever interpretation may be put upon such terms as "custody" and "possession," the question will be whether any custody or possession has been obtained here. I think it is impossible to say that it had, until the party had actual power over the fish.[28]

This was approved by the Supreme Court of Canada in *Frederick Gerring Jr (Ship) v The Queen*,[29] in which an American schooner was seized and forfeited to the Crown for fishing illegally in Canadian waters. The Americans had completely enclosed their net around the fish while they were more than three miles off the coast of Nova Scotia, but they drifted inside the three-mile limit while they were still bailing fish out of the net and into their ship. A majority of the Court held that even if the Americans already possessed the fish inside the net, they were still "fishing" when they were taking them out of the net.

In *Popov v Hayashi*,[30] a California court decided that the plaintiff had acquired a property right to a baseball by attempting to catch it. The ball was hit into the stands as a record-breaking home run and later sold at auction for $517,500. The plaintiff's attempt to catch it was foiled by the crowd around him. The defendant was the first to pick up the ball, and, even though he had not interfered with the plaintiff in any way, he was required to share the net proceeds of sale equally with him. Justice McCarthy said, "Where an actor undertakes significant but incomplete steps to achieve possession of a piece of abandoned personal property and the effort is interrupted by the unlawful acts of others, the actor has a legally cognizable pre-possessory interest in the property."

That is clearly not the law in Canada. A failed attempt to obtain possession will not create a property right. The plaintiff might have had a claim against the crowd who assaulted him for damages for the lost opportunity to catch the ball, but the defendant was innocent of any wrongdoing, and there was no reason to deprive him of his right to possession. This is another example of the old saying that "hard cases make bad law."[31] Sympathy for the plaintiff produced a hollow victory.

---

28 *Ibid* at 611.
29 (1897) 27 SCR 271.
30 2002 WL 31833731 (Cal Super 2002).
31 See *Re Vandervell Trustees Ltd (No 2)*, [1974] EWCA Civ 7, [1974] Ch 269 at 322.

Although he did receive $225,000 from the sale of the ball, his lawyer then sued him for $473,530 in legal fees.

2) Intention to Possess

An intention to possess is different from an intention to own.[32] When you borrow something, you intend to control that thing and prevent others from using it even though you know you will have to return it to its owner.

We may think of the intention to possess as an intention to exclude others, but that does seem odd if you possess a café or shop and your business depends on inviting people to come inside. What you really intend is to control access to the premises to exclude people after hours and to ask disruptive customers to leave if necessary. People can and do possess spaces to which the public is routinely invited.

People often say "exclusive possession" when they mean possession. The two are really the same since a right to possession is a right to exclude others. However, on the breakdown of a marriage or similar relationship, a court may order that one spouse has exclusive possession of the family home. In addition to their normal right to exclude other people from the home, they now have the right to exclude the other spouse, who would otherwise share possession of the home.

Strangely, it is possible to intend to possess something even if you do not know that it exists. In *Flack v National Crime Authority*,[33] the police searched Mrs Flack's home and found a locked briefcase inside a cupboard. When they showed it to her, she said, "I have never seen it before. I don't know whose it is." They then forced open the lock and discovered that it contained $433,000 in cash. The police believed that it belonged to her son, who they suspected was involved in drug-related offences, and seized the cash, as they were entitled to do.

The police could not prove that the money was the proceeds of crime, and Mrs Flack successfully sued to get it back. She had a better right to possession than the police after their statutory right to retain it had expired because she had possession of the cash before the police took possession. She intended to possess it even when she was unaware of its existence because she had possession of her private home and therefore controlled and intended to possess everything inside it.

The same principle applies to things inside your car or backpack. Your intention to possess the car or backpack would mean that you also intend to possess the things inside it even if you are unaware of

---

32   See *JA Pye (Oxford) Ltd v Graham*, above note 23 at paras 42–43.
33   (1998) 156 ALR 501.

their existence. This does not mean that you would be guilty of a crime if those things turned out to be prohibited drugs or weapons or stolen goods. This is where property law and criminal law diverge. Whereas the property lawyer would say that you intend to possess those things, the criminal lawyer would say that you lack the necessary *mens rea* (or guilty mind) if you were not aware of their identity.[34]

3) Possession of Things in Public Places

Things found in a private home are usually possessed by the person who has possession of that home, but that is not true of things found in public places. In *Bridges v Hawkesworth*,[35] cash was found on the floor of a shop, and the finder had the right to keep it. Members of the public were routinely invited into the part of the shop where the cash was found. Although the shopkeeper possessed that space, they did not control or intend to possess everything brought into that space by their customers. The court came to the same conclusion in *Parker v British Airways Board*,[36] where the plaintiff found a gold bracelet on the floor of an executive lounge at Heathrow Airport. Access to the lounge was restricted to certain classes of passengers, but it was still a space to which some members of the public had access.

The court came to a different conclusion in *Waverley Borough Council v Fletcher*.[37] Mr Fletcher used a metal detector to find a medieval gold brooch twenty-three centimetres beneath the surface of the land in a public park owned by the council. Although members of the public were routinely invited to use the park, they were not permitted to dig into the soil. Therefore, the council had a better right to the brooch than the person who found it.

It is sometimes suggested that the landowner has a better right to things found in the soil because they are attached to the land and therefore part of it, but that is not the real reason. An owner of land has the right to possess the space both above the ground and below it. An essential fact in *Waverley* was that members of the public were invited to use only the space above ground. The outcome should have been the same if the brooch had been found lying on the ground in a section of the park to which the public was not invited, such as a fenced-off area where gardening equipment was kept. Conversely, if the brooch had been found buried in the sand on a public beach owned by the council,

---

34   *Beaver v The Queen*, [1957] SCR 531, 118 CCC 129.
35   (1851) 21 LJQB 75.
36   [1982] 1 QB 1004 (CA) [*Parker*].
37   [1995] 4 All ER 756 (CA) [*Waverley*].

the outcome should have been different because members of the public are routinely invited to dig into the sand and make sandcastles, etc.

4) Wrongdoing

It has also been suggested that the landowner should win if the finder is trespassing at the time. In *Parker*, Donaldson LJ said,

> Some qualification has also to be made in the case of the trespassing finder. The person vis à vis whom he is a trespasser has a better title. The fundamental basis of this is clearly public policy. Wrongdoers should not benefit from their wrongdoing. This requirement would be met if the trespassing finder acquired no rights.[38]

This is probably not the law. The common law does not normally care whether possession was acquired rightly or wrongly. Mr Parker won because British Airways did not have possession of the bracelet when he found it. That fact would not magically change if he had sneaked into the lounge. He did turn the bracelet over to British Airways to see if the owner could be found, but he still had a better right to possession because he had it first. Waverley Borough Council won because it possessed the brooch before Mr Fletcher found it, just as Mrs Flack had possession of the cash before it was found by the police. The essential question to ask in all of these cases is simply "Who had it first?"

In *Bird v Fort Frances*,[39] a twelve-year-old boy crawled under a building and found a can that contained $1,500. The police seized the money, and the boy sued to get it back. The owner of the land died, and his executor declined an invitation to join the proceedings. The executor had a better right to possession than the boy since the landowner had possession of the money before they boy found it, but that better right was not claimed. The boy won because he had possession before the police and therefore had a better right to possession than they did. The fact that he was trespassing was irrelevant. McCruer CJHC said that "it is not necessary for me to decide whether the taking was with felonious intent or not, as I think in this case the same result flows."[40]

In *Costello v Derbyshire Constabulary*,[41] the police seized a stolen car from Mr Costello (after a short chase), and it was clear that he knew that the car was stolen. The vehicle and engine registration numbers had been removed, and the owner was never found. Costello's claim to

---

38   *Parker*, above note 36 at 1009.
39   [1949] 2 DLR 791 (Ont).
40   *Ibid* at 799.
41   [2001] EWCA Civ 381, [2001] 1 WLR 1437.

have the car returned was successful in the English Court of Appeal. Lightman J said,

> In my view on a review of the authorities, (save so far as legislation otherwise provides) as a matter of principle and authority possession means the same thing and is entitled to the same legal protection whether or not it has been obtained lawfully or by theft or by other unlawful means. It vests in the possessor a possessory title which is good against the world save as against anyone setting up or claiming under a better title. In the case of a theft the title is frail, and of likely limited value, but nonetheless remains a title to which the law affords protection.[42]

One case that is inconsistent with these authorities is *Baird v British Columbia*.[43] Mr Baird checked into a Vancouver hotel with a large quantity of cash and traveller's cheques. The police were called, he was arrested, and he admitted that the money was stolen. However, he was never charged and sued to get the money back, but his claim failed. Gibbs JA said that "the conduct of Mr. Baird giving rise to his claim is so tainted with criminality or culpable immorality that as a matter of public policy the Court should not assist him to recover."[44]

The court applied the maxim *ex turpi causa non oritur action*, which means that "no right of action arises from a base cause."[45] There are several problems with this. First, Baird's involvement in the theft of the money was not an element of his cause of action. He needed only to prove that he had possession before the police to establish his better right to possession. How he obtained that possession should have been irrelevant. Second, the police succeeded not because they had a better right to possession than Baird but only because he was not allowed to enforce his right. Presumably, he would face the same obstacle regardless of whether the money had been seized from him lawfully or unlawfully or even if he was claiming against someone who had stolen the money from him. It cannot be right that property obtained illegally lies unprotected by the law and available to anyone who is able to take it away. Finally, the law with regard to illegality is changing, and courts are now willing to enforce claims even though the law relates to serious illegal conduct by the plaintiff.[46]

---

42 *Ibid* at para 31.
43 (1992) 77 CCC (3d) 365 (BCCA).
44 *Ibid* at para 24.
45 See *Hall v Hebert*, [1993] 2 SCR 159, 101 DLR (4th) 129.
46 See *Kim v Choi*, 2020 BCCA 98.

In *Thomas v Canada (Attorney General)*,[47] an envelope containing $18,000 had been delivered by mistake to Mr Thomas's post office box. He turned it over to the RCMP and successfully sued to get it back. Trussler J rejected the argument that his claim should fail because he wrongfully opened a package not addressed to him. She noted that the offence, if any, was minor and said,

> Even if Thomas' actions could be viewed as wrong or if the return of the money would trigger an offence, this should not disentitle him from asserting an interest in the money. The case law is not clear about the effect of acquiring possession of an item by a wrongdoing. However, I am more inclined to follow the reasoning in *Bird v. Fort Frances*. I reiterate the reasoning in *Baird* that the "wrongdoing" in *Bird v. Fort Frances*, as in the case at bar, was inadvertent and not tainted by a high level of "criminality and culpable immorality necessary to support an *ex turpi* cause plea."[48]

5) Rights to Possession

As discussed above, possession is different from ownership, and often the possessor is not the owner, as when land is leased to a tenant or a book is borrowed from the library. However, more important than the distinction between possession and ownership is the distinction between possession and a right to possession. Although the landlord and the library do not have possession, they have a right to possession in the future when the lease or loan comes to an end. They are also the owners, but they need not be. A tenant could sublet their apartment for the summer, in which case they would have a right to possession in the future without being the owner. Similarly, an interlibrary loan may involve the library lending a book that it does not own.

In many of the cases discussed above, neither party was the owner of the object of the dispute. That did not matter to the court, which was asked to decide who had the better right to possession. Although a right to possession is usually acquired when something is purchased or received as a gift, these cases (and many others) show that a right to possession can be acquired simply by taking possession. That is true for both goods and land. Possession of land is usually acquired with the permission of the owner, in which case a lease or tenancy is created (as discussed in the next chapter). Possession taken without permission is called *adverse possession* (as discussed below).

---

47   2006 ABQB 730, [2006] 12 WWR 742, 64 Alta LR (4th) 184.
48   *Ibid* at para 63.

Possession of goods with permission of the owner is called a *bailment*. The person in possession is the *bailee,* and the person with the right to possession in the future is the *bailor.* The bailor is usually the owner but need not be. In *Parker,* after Mr Parker found the bracelet in the defendant's lounge, he handed it over to one of the defendant's employees for the purpose of returning it to its owner. This created a bailment since he expected to get the bracelet back if its owner could not be located. Although Mr Parker was not the owner, he was a bailor since he had a right to possess the bracelet in the future. Of course, if the bracelet had been returned to its owner, the bailment would have been extinguished, but the bailment continued so long as the defendant had the bracelet and there was a possibility that it should be returned to Mr Parker.

A bailment normally occurs when the bailor agrees to let the bailee have possession of goods for a limited time. They may have a contract, but bailments also arise gratuitously. In either case, the bailee owes a duty to the bailor to take care of the bailed goods.[49] A bailment can arise even if the parties have not dealt with each other. If someone comes into possession of goods, by finding or otherwise, they become a bailee of those goods for the owner.[50] As Blanchard J said in *R v Ngan,* "At common law any person who finds an item of property and takes possession of it on behalf of the true owner as a temporary custodian is treated as a bailee of that property and is under an obligation to keep it safe and return it to the owner (if that is possible)."[51]

Once someone acquires a right to possession, that right normally continues even after they lose possession unless they choose to dispose of it by sale or gift. A right to possession will be lost if the item is consumed or destroyed. It may be lost if the claim to recover the item is barred because too much time has passed and a limitation period has expired. It is also possible that someone with an even better right to possession comes along to acquire the item.

The law makes an exception for wild animals. A person who captures a wild animal thereby acquires possession and the right to possession, but if the animal escapes and returns to the wild, the right to possession is lost.[52] Some animals, such as bees and pigeons, have a tendency to return home, and if so, the right to possession continues even while the animals are away unless they decide to make a new home

---

49 See, for example, *Punch v Savoy's Jewellers Ltd* (1986), 26 DLR (4th) 546, 54 OR (2d) 383 (CA).

50 *Gilchrist Watt & Sanderson Pty Ltd v York Products Pty Ltd*, [1970] 1 WLR 1262 (PC).

51 [2007] NZSC 105 at para 15, [2008] 2 NZLR 48 at 59.

52 See *Borwick Development Solutions Ltd v Clear Water Fisheries Ltd*, [2020] EWCA Civ 578.

elsewhere. Domestic animals (such as livestock and pets) are treated differently. If one escapes, the owner's right to possession continues even if the animal has no desire to go home again.

6) Relativity of Title

Title is a word that is commonly used in property law. We talk of land titles, title searches, and Aboriginal title. Although we often think of title as a synonym for ownership of land, it has a broader meaning. It is probably more accurate to think of title as equivalent to entitlement. People can acquire title to land or goods without being the owner merely by taking possession of them. Title obtained in this way is often called *possessory title*, but it is really no different from any other title. A person with possessory title has a right to possession that is enforceable generally against others, except for someone with a better title. The adjective refers to the mode of acquisition and not the nature of the rights acquired.

A key feature of the common law of property is *relativity of title*. Generally speaking, when two people have competing claims to the same thing, we do not care whether anyone has the best possible title, but only which of them has the better title. Both parties may have title, and it is only necessary to rank them relative to each other to resolve the dispute.

Relativity of title is demonstrated by one of the greatest (and shortest) cases in all of property law: *Armory v Delamirie*.[53] A piece of jewellery was found by a chimney sweeper's boy, who took it to a goldsmith to get it appraised. The goldsmith removed the gemstone from the jewellery and returned it to the boy with an empty socket. The goldsmith had committed the tort of conversion (then called *trover*),[54] which is the wrongful interference with someone's right to possess goods, and was liable to pay damages equal to the full market value of the gemstone.

The goldsmith had possession of the jewellery when the gemstone was converted. The boy had handed it over voluntarily, thereby creating a bailment. Although the boy no longer had possession, he still had a right to possession. The goldsmith also had a right to possession. Both of their rights to possession were enforceable generally against others except someone with a better right. Why did the boy have a better right? Simply because he had it first. It did not matter that he was not the owner or that he may have found the jewellery earlier that day. It did not matter that the owner of the jewellery might come along any day to

---

53   (1722) 1 Str 505, 93 ER 664.

54   See John Baker, *An Introduction to English Legal History*, 5th ed (Oxford: Oxford University Press, 2019) at 423–25.

claim it. As against the goldsmith, the boy's possessory title was just as good as a title acquired by purchase or gift.

7) Adverse Possession

There is a process by which possessory title can become ownership. When someone takes possession of goods or land, they thereby acquire a right to possession, which is enforceable generally against others, except someone with a better right to possession. Although there may be several people with better rights to possession, to keep things simple let us assume that the owner is the only one. If possession was taken without the owner's permission, it is called *adverse possession*. The owner will have a right to sue to recover possession, but that claim may be subject to a limitation period, which means that their right will be lost if they fail to bring their action in time.[55] If the owner's right to possession is extinguished, the possessor's title then becomes the best possible title. In other words, it becomes ownership.

Every jurisdiction has a statute that limits the time in which someone with a right to sue can commence their legal action.[56] It applies generally to all sorts of claims, with some important exceptions, and serves a useful purpose, as Plumer MR explained in *Cholmondeley v Clinton*:

> The statute is founded upon the wisest policy, and is consonant to the municipal law of every country. It stands upon the general principle of public utility. . . . The public have a great interest, in having a known limit fixed by law to litigation, for the quiet of the community, and that there may be a certain fixed period, after which the possessor may know that his title and right cannot be called in question. It is better that the negligent owner, who has omitted to assert his right within the prescribed period, should lose his right, than that an opening should be given to interminable litigation, exposing parties to be harassed by stale demands, after the witnesses of the facts are dead, and the evidence of the title lost. The individual hardship will, upon the whole, be less, by withholding from one who has slept upon his right, and never yet possessed it, than to take away from the other what he has long been allowed to consider as his own, and on the

---

55   See *Nelson (City) v Mowatt*, 2017 SCC 8 at para 17.

56   *Limitation Act*, SBC 2012, c 13; *Limitations Act*, RSA 2000, c L-12; *The Limitations Act*, SS 2004, c L-16.1; *Limitation of Actions Act*, CCSM c L150; *Limitations Act, 2002*, SO 2002, c 24; *Limitation of Actions Act*, SNB 2009, c L-8.5; *Limitation of Actions Act*, SNS 2014, c 35; *Statute of Limitations*, RSPEI 1988, c S-7; *Limitations Act*, SNL 1995, c L-16.1; *Limitation of Actions Act*, RSY 2002, c 139; *Limitation of Actions Act*, RSNWT 1988, c L-8.

faith of which, the plans in life, habits and expenses of himself and his family may have been . . . unalterably formed and established.[57]

Before systems were created to register title to land, limitation statutes helped establish certainty of title. For example, if you wish to buy my house, you will want to know that you will get good title to it when the transaction is complete. You would search the land title register to make sure that I have title to sell and that you will acquire good title when yours is registered. Before there was land title registration, you would need to investigate my *chain of title*. I would have good title only if I acquired it properly from a person with good title, who acquired it properly from a person with good title, and so on. The chain is only as good as its weakest link, and the worry is that there is someone out there with an older and better right to possession than me. How far back do you have to search, and how reliable will that search through old documents be?

A limitation statute can help provide a solution to this problem. If you could trace a good chain of title back beyond the limitation period, then you would know that, even if there was someone who did have a better right to possession, that right will have been extinguished by the limitation statute. Therefore, you can be satisfied with my title if the land has been possessed by me and my predecessors for the duration of the limitation period. Modern land title registration provides a different solution, which is a state guarantee that the person registered as owner is really the owner. This is why ownership can no longer be obtained by adverse possession in most parts of Canada where land title registration is used.[58]

Where limitation periods still apply to actions to recover possession of land, the typical limitation period is ten years.[59] They are often used to resolve boundary disputes, when a building or fence was constructed in the wrong place encroaching on neighbouring land.[60] When the problem is discovered years later, possession of the land encroached on may have become ownership through adverse possession.

---

57   (1820) 2 Jac & W 1, 37 ER 527 at 577.

58   *Limitation Act*, SBC 2012, c 13, s 28; *Land Titles Act, 2000*, SS 2000, c L-5.1, s 21; *Real Property Act*, CCSM, c R30, s 61; *Land Titles Act*, RSO 1990, c L.5, s 51; *Land Titles Act*, SNB 1981, c L-1.1, s 17; *Lands Act*, SNL 1991, c 36, s 36(1); *Land Titles Act, 2015*, SY 2015, c 10, s 44. See *Alberta Law Reform Institute, Adverse Possession and Lasting Improvements to Wrong Land: Final Report 115* (2020) at 107–9, online: www.alri.ualberta.ca/wp-content/uploads/2020/05/FR115.pdf.

59   *Limitations Act*, RSA 2000, c L-12, s 3; *Land Registration Act*, SNS 2001, c 6, ss 74 & 75; *Limitation of Actions Act*, RSNWT 1988, c L-8, s 18. It is twenty years in Prince Edward Island: *Statute of Limitations*, RSPEI 1988, c S-7, s 16.

60   See, for example, *Lutz v Kawa* (1980), 112 DLR (3d) 271; *Pepper v Brooker*, 2017 ONCA 532.

TITLE TO LAND

A. INTRODUCTION

As discussed in the previous chapter, ownership of goods is simply the best right to possess them for an unlimited period of time. The same is true of ownership of land except that a right to possess land is called an estate, and the right to possess land indefinitely is called a *fee simple estate*.

The word *estate* has two different meanings. When a person dies, they leave behind an estate, which is all of their property (using property in its widest sense to mean all of their assignable rights *in rem* and rights *in personam*). An estate in land is a right *in rem* to possess land for some period of time. Both meanings are commonly used, although people often refer to the latter as *real estate*.

Most of this chapter is concerned with estates in land, including the nature of an estate and the different kinds of estates that exist in Canada. The chapter begins with the concept of tenure, which is the relationship between the Crown and a person who holds an estate, and ends with Aboriginal title, which is another form of title to land.

B. TENURE

Most people think of tenure as holding an office, such as a political office or an appointment as a professor at a university. The word comes from the Latin *tenere*, which means to hold. In property law, tenure refers to holding an estate in land. In feudal England, the Crown would grant estates to tenants in chief, who would hold an office that involved more than just having possession of land.[1] They would owe duties to the Crown of loyalty and service, such as the duty to provide armed soldiers or agricultural produce. Tenants in chief might grant portions of their land to lesser tenants in exchange for loyalty and services from them, who in turn might grant estates to even lesser tenants. Goods and services would flow up the feudal pyramid in exchange for the use of the land and the landlord's protection. The process of a tenant granting an estate to a lesser tenant was called *subinfeudation*.

The landlords who held estates had relationships with the people who lived and worked on the land that went well beyond the relationships that exist between landlords and tenants today. Tenure provided what we would now regard as a form of local government, with executive and judicial decisions being made at the local level. Disputes would be resolved in local manor courts according to local laws and customs.[2]

We still have tenure today, which is why we say that someone holds an estate in land. However, it is only a vestige of what it once was. It no longer functions as a system of government, subinfeudation has been abolished, and feudal services are no longer required.

1) Subinfeudation

Subinfeudation was abolished in 1290 by the statute of *Quia Emptores*,[3] which also provided tenants with the right to transfer their land without the landlord's permission. That did not dismantle the feudal pyramid then in existence, but it was gradually reduced, so most freehold estates in England are now held directly from the Crown. The statute does not apply to life estates or leasehold estates, which is why private persons can still be landlords. *Quia Emptores* is part of the law of England that became the law of Canada when it became a British colony, and that statute still applies in Canada today.[4]

---

1   See John Baker, *An Introduction to English Legal History*, 5th ed (Oxford: Oxford University Press, 2019) at 241–49.

2   The common law of England was called the *common law* to distinguish it from these local laws. *Ibid*, ch 2.

3   18 Edw 1, c 1.

4   See, for example, *Hongkong Bank of Canada v Wheeler Holdings Ltd*, [1993] 1 SCR 167, 100 DLR (4th) 40.

2) Feudal Services

Tenures used to be classified according to the types of services that the tenants were required to provide to their landlord, such as agricultural, military, or spiritual services.[5] Most forms of tenure were abolished by the *Tenures Abolition Act 1660*[6] and converted into a form of tenure called *free and common socage*. Under socage tenure, the tenants' obligations (usually to provide some form of agricultural service or product) were fixed. As years passed, those obligations were exchanged for payments of fixed amounts, and as more years passed, those payments became trivial due to inflation and ceased to be collected.

In *Attorney General for Alberta v Huggard Assets Ltd*,[7] land in Alberta had been granted by the Crown subject to an obligation to pay royalties at variable rates for any petroleum and natural gas extracted from it: "TO HAVE AND TO HOLD the same unto the grantee in fee simple. Yielding and paying unto Us and Our Successors such royalty upon the said petroleum and natural gas, if any, from time to time prescribed by regulations of Our Governor in Council."[8]

A majority of the Supreme Court of Canada held that the obligation to pay royalties was invalid because it was not fixed and therefore contrary to the *Tenures Abolition Act 1660*, which limited tenure to free and common socage. This was reversed on appeal to the Judicial Committee of the Privy Council in London.[9] The Privy Council advised that socage tenure was not always completely fixed:

> A considerable degree of "uncertainty" in the consideration moving from the tenant is compatible with "free and common socage," notwithstanding the dicta of Littleton, Coke and Blackstone, to the contrary. One instance given by Littleton (Coke on Littleton 96A) of a tenure on "certain" services is where the tenure depends on the tenant shearing all sheep on the grantor's land: a service which can clearly be made more or less burdensome according as the grantor chooses to have upon his land few or many sheep.[10]

More importantly, the Privy Council advised that the *Tenures Abolition Act 1660* was just a statute that could be repealed or altered:

---

5   Baker, above note 1 at 245–47.
6   12 Car 2, c 24.
7   [1951] SCR 427, [1951] 2 DLR 305.
8   *Ibid* at 429.
9   [1953] UKPC 11, [1953] AC 420, [1953] 3 DLR 225 [cited to DLR].
10 *Ibid* at 235, Lord Asquith.

There can be no question that the Dominion Parliament was competent at all material times, after 1870, by clear enactment to repeal or vary any law as to land tenure prevailing in Rupert's Land before that region was in that year vested in the Dominion: even if this meant introducing forms of tenure unknown in the past to English law, or forbidden by it.[11]

Socage was the only form of tenure to come to Canada from England. If a grant of land subject to a variable royalty on oil and gas is inconsistent with socage tenure, then it is a change to the law that Parliament is entitled to make.

3) Radical Title

A vestige of tenure still exists in Canada, which means that people who own land are holding estates in land as tenants of the Crown. This implies that the Crown owns the land, but it is not ownership in the sense discussed in the previous chapter. The holder of the fee simple estate is the person who enjoys the standard incidents of ownership described by Professor Honoré.[12] The Crown's interest in that land exists as a kind of sovereignty called *radical title*.

In the important case of *Mabo v Queensland (No 2)*,[13] the High Court of Australia explained that the Crown has radical title to land when an estate has been granted or when that land is subject to Aboriginal title (called native title in Australia). It was argued that the Crown became the owner of the land in Australia when it became a British colony, and since the Crown's ownership was inconsistent with pre-existing native title, the latter was extinguished. That was rejected. Brennan J said,

> Recognition of the radical title of the Crown is quite consistent with recognition of native title to land, for the radical title, without more, is merely a logical postulate required to support the doctrine of tenure (when the Crown has exercised its sovereign power to grant an interest in land) and to support the plenary title of the Crown (when the Crown has exercised its sovereign power to appropriate to itself ownership of parcels of land within the Crown's territory). Unless the sovereign power is exercised in one or other of those ways, there is no reason why land within the Crown's territory should not continue to be subject to native title. It is only the fallacy of equating sovereignty

---

11   *Ibid.*

12   AM Honoré, "Ownership" in AG Guest, ed, *Oxford Essays in Jurisprudence* (Oxford: Oxford University Press, 1961) 107.

13   [1992] HCA 23, 175 CLR 1 [*Mabo No 2*].

and beneficial ownership of land that gives rise to the notion that native title is extinguished by the acquisition of sovereignty.[14]

When the Crown owns land for its own use, it has full ownership in the sense described by Honoré. There is no tenure relationship. The Crown does not have mere radical title to that land but has *allodial title* or an *allodium* (which means the entire property).

C. ESTATES

An estate in land is a right to possess it for some period of time. It is measured in four dimensions. Two horizontal dimensions define its area. When we look at a survey map or plan, that is what we see. The third, vertical dimension, gives it volume. The fourth dimension is time. Estates are classified by how long they last and are divided into two main categories: freehold estates measured in lives and leasehold estates measured in defined periods.

An estate entitles the holder to possession of some space measured relative to the surface of the earth. For many estates, such as those containing a house or farm, that space extends both up into the air and down below the surface. There are many other estates that do not intersect the surface of the earth, such as an apartment, a condominium, or an office located inside a building. That space is defined by floors, ceilings, and walls and may be located high above the earth.

When we think of owning land, we usually think of physical objects, such as a house with trees, gardens, and lawns. However, the estate is the space possessed and not the things within it. If the house was demolished and the trees were cut down, the estate would remain unchanged even though its market value may be significantly different. The right to possess that space would continue as before.

A change to an estate will occur if there is a change to any of its four dimensions. For example, a leasehold estate might be forfeited for nonpayment of rent, bringing it to a premature end. The area of an estate might be changed if some part of it was expropriated (e.g., to widen a public road) or additional land was acquired through adverse possession of a portion of the neighbour's land.[15] The area of an estate

---

14 *Ibid* at para 52, quoted by the BCCA in *Delgamuukw v British Columbia*, [1993] 5 WWR 97, 104 DLR (4th) 470 at para 46.

15 See, for example, *Bradford Investments (1963) Ltd v Fama* (2005), 257 DLR (4th) 347, 77 OR (3d) 127 at para 110.

can also change if a boundary is defined by a shoreline that is altered due to accretion or erosion.[16]

1) Air Space

The vertical dimensions of many estates are not clearly defined. The area of the estate will be marked with precision on a survey or plan and its duration will be identified (as a freehold or leasehold estate), but it is not entirely clear how high or low it goes. According to an old Latin maxim, estates reach up into the heavens and down to the centre of the earth. Monnin JA described the maxim as follows in *R v Air Canada* (in which the court rejected a claim by the Government of Manitoba that it had a right to tax the sale of liquor served in airplanes as they flew over the province):

> Counsel for the Province of Manitoba ... relied on the maxim *cujus est solum ejus est usque ad coelum et ad infernos*, which may be translated, though inadequately, by "ownership of the soil carries with it owner-ship of what is above and below it." The Latin phrase, much more picturesque than the English translation, speaks of "up to heaven and down to hell."[17]

In *Bernstein of Leigh v Skyviews & General Ltd*,[18] the plaintiff claimed that the defendants were trespassing when they flew over his land taking aerial photographs. Griffiths J rejected that claim, drawing a distinction between a permanent intrusion into air space (e.g., by an overhanging building or sign) and a temporary intrusion by aircraft. He said,

> The problem is to balance the rights of an owner to enjoy the use of his land against the rights of the general public to take advantage of all that science now offers in the use of air space. This balance is in my judgment best struck in our present society by restricting the rights of an owner in the air space above his land to such height as is necessary for the ordinary use and enjoyment of his land and the structures upon it, and declaring that above that height he has no greater rights in the air space than any other member of the public.[19]

---

16   *Southern Centre of Theosophy Inc v South Australia*, [1981] UKPC 41, [1982] AC 706.

17   [1978] 2 WWR 694, 86 DLR (3d) 631 at 635 (Man CA), aff'd [1980] 2 SCR 303, 111 DLR (3d) 513.

18   [1978] QB 479.

19   *Ibid* at 488.

In *Didow v Alberta Power Ltd*,[20] the Alberta Court of Appeal quoted this with approval and adopted the distinction between permanent and temporary intrusions. In that case, the defendant's power poles were on a road allowance next to the plaintiff's farm, with their crossbars and powerlines extending two metres into the air space above his land. The court held that this was a trespass. Haddad JA said:

> In my opinion, the balancing criterion formulated by Griffiths J is a logical compromise to the rights of the landowner and the general public. It is a test I adopt. I view this test as saying a land owner is entitled to freedom from permanent structures which in any way impinge upon the actual or potential use and enjoyment of his land. The cross arms constitute a low level intrusion which interferes with the appellant's potential, if not actual, use and enjoyment. This amounts to trespass.[21]

In response to this decision, Alberta law was amended by statute:

> (3) Notwithstanding anything in this Act, any structure that is part of a transmission line and is located on land comprising a public highway, street, lane, road allowance or other public place and any power line attached to or resting on the structure may project into the airspace over the property adjoining that land without the consent of the owners or occupants of the adjoining property . . . (4) No person is entitled to any remedy or damages or any other compensation or relief as a result of the existence of a projection described in subsection (3).[22]

2) Underground

An estate goes up to include potentially usable space above ground. A different approach is taken underground. The depth of an estate is not limited to potentially usable space.

In *Bocardo SA v Star Energy UK Onshore Ltd*,[23] there was an oil field under the plaintiff's land. The defendant drilled three wells diagonally from neighbouring lands to extract that oil at depths ranging from 250 to 900 metres below the surface. The plaintiff did not own the oil, which belonged to the Crown, and had no right to take it. The defendant did have a licence to drill for and extract oil but did not have permission to drill under the plaintiff's land. The Supreme Court of the United

---

20   [1988] 5 WWR 606, 60 Alta LR (2d) 212 (CA).

21   *Ibid* at para 40.

22   *Hydro and Electric Energy Act*, RSA 2000, c H-16, s 37.

23   [2010] UKSC 35, [2011] 1 AC 380.

Kingdom held that this was a trespass even though it did not interfere with any potential use by the plaintiff. Lord Hope said,

> In Canada, Griffiths J's approach in *Baron Bernstein of Leigh v Skyviews & General Ltd* [1978] QB 479 to the right to use air space above the land was described by the Alberta Court of Appeal as most persuasive in *Didow v Alberta Power Ltd* [1988] 5 WWR 606, 613. But we were not referred to any Canadian or Australian authority that extends that approach to ownership below the surface. In Todd, *The Law of Torts in New Zealand*, 5th ed (2009), p 426, it is stated that it appears to be generally accepted that any intrusion into the subsoil beneath the owner's land will constitute trespass, and that there appears to be no case in the Commonwealth where a plaintiff has failed on the basis that the area of subsoil invaded was so deep that the surface occupier's possessory rights did not extend that far....
>
> In *United States v Causby*, 328 US 256 the United States Supreme Court regarded the airspace as a public highway to which only the public had a just claim. The same cannot be said of the strata below the surface. As Aikens LJ said in the Court of Appeal [2010] Ch 100, para 61, it is not helpful to try to make analogies between the rights of an owner of land with regard to the airspace above it and his rights with regard to the strata beneath the surface. Although modern technology has found new ways of making use of it in the public interest, there is no question of it having become a public highway.[24]

The right to possess the space underground does not include a right to everything in that space. At common law, estates granted by the Crown did not include gold and silver unless they were expressly included:

> [A]ll mines of gold and silver within the realm, whether they be in the hands of the Queen, or of subjects, belong to the Queen by prerogative, with liberty to dig and carry away the ores thereof, and with other such incidents thereto as are necessary to be used for the getting of the ore.[25]

When granting estates, the Crown usually retains ownership of minerals, petroleum, and natural gas.[26]

---

24   *Ibid* at paras 24 and 26, [2011] 1 AC 380 at 397–98.

25   *Case of Mines* (1567), 1 Plowden 310, 75 ER 472 at 510. See also *Mines and Minerals Act*, RSA 2000, c M-17, s 10.

26   See *Land Act*, RSBC 1996, c 245, s 50; *Public Lands Act*, RSA 2000, c P-40, s 35; *Provincial Lands Act*, 2016, SS 2016, c P-31.1, s 2–8; *Crown Lands Act*, CCSM, c C340, s 4; *Public Lands Act*, RSO 1990, c P.43, ss 15, 60; *Ownership of Minerals*

D. FREEHOLD ESTATES

There are three different freehold estates. Land can be held in fee simple, in fee tail, or for life.

1) Fee Simple

The fee simple estate is the largest estate possible and is equivalent to ownership of land in a common law jurisdiction. The language is from a much earlier time. The term *fee* comes from the Latin *feodum*, which is used to refer to the grant of land as a reward to the tenant in exchange for loyalty and services.[27] It became so common for the tenant's heir to have a right to take over the estate when the tenant died that *fee* came to mean an estate that could be inherited.[28] It is a *fee simple* if the right to inherit it is not qualified or limited in any way.

A fee simple estate was created by granting it to a tenant and their heirs. On the death of the tenant, the estate would pass to the heir, who would take over as tenant. On their death, it would pass to their heir, and so on. So long as the dying tenant was survived by an heir, the estate would continue to exist and so might never end. However, if a tenant died without heirs, the estate would come to an end, and the right to possess the land would return to the Crown (or to a landlord if the estate had been created by subinfeudation). The end of an estate for lack of an heir is called *escheat*.

A grant to a tenant and their heirs did not give potential heirs any right to the estate. The identity of a tenant's heir could not be known until the tenant died. Any presumptive heir, however strong and healthy, might die before the tenant and not become the heir. Since the present tenant was the only person with any right to the estate, they were free to sell it or give it away during their lifetime. On transfer to the new tenant and their heirs, the fee simple estate would then be measured by the heirs of the new tenant and continue to exist so long as the new tenant had heirs. It would not matter if none of the heirs of the original tenant survived.[29]

If the fee simple estate had continued to be measured by the heirs of the original tenant to whom the estate was first granted, that would

---

Act, RSNB 2011, c 200; *Mineral Resources Act*, SNS 1990, c 18, s 4; *Mineral Resources Act*, RSPEI 1988, c M-7, s 2; *Petroleum and Natural Gas Act*, RSNL 1990, c P-10, s 3.

27   Baker, above note 1 at 243.
28   *Ibid* at 279.
29   *Ibid* at 281–83.

have created a serious practical difficulty. The estate might be sold and resold many times over the years, but the only way to know if it still existed would be to track the heirs of a person who owned it in a previous century. It was much easier to measure the estate by the heirs of the present tenant, whoever that might be. When that person died, it would normally be a simple matter to determine whether they had an heir.

When an estate was granted or transferred to a tenant and their heirs, the reference to the heirs was a formula used to indicate that the estate was held in fee simple. They were *words of limitation* used to indicate the duration of the estate, not *words of purchase*, which identify who is intended to receive the estate. Today, it is no longer necessary to use words of limitation. A grant or transfer to someone "in fee simple" will do the trick. It is usually assumed that a transfer of land is intended to transfer the entire estate held by the transferor unless some limitation is expressed. For example, the *Land Titles Act* in Northwest Territories and Nunavut states:

> No words of limitation are necessary in any transfer of land in order to transfer all or any title in the land, but every instrument transferring land operates as an absolute transfer of all such right and title that the transferor has in the land at the time of its execution, unless a contrary intention is expressed in the transfer.[30]

The tenant who held an estate in fee simple was free to sell it or give it away during their lifetime, but they could not give it away by will before that was made possible by the *Statute of Wills 1540*.[31] Before 1540, only personal property could be given away by will, and real property would go to their heir. We no longer have inheritance in common law jurisdictions. All of a person's property, including their fee simple estates, can be given away by will. This means that even if a tenant dies without heirs, the estate will continue to exist and be transferred according to the tenant's will.

If a person dies without leaving a valid will, they have died *intestate*. In that case, their property still does not go to an heir but is distributed among next of kin according to a statutory formula, normally to the surviving spouse and children, and if there are none, then to more

---

30   RSNWT 1988, c 8, s 77. See also *Land Title Act*, RSBC 1996, c 250, s 186; *Law of Property Act*, RSA 2000, c L-7, s 7; *Land Titles Act*, 2000, SS 2000, c L-5.1, s 157; *Law of Property Act*, CCSM, c L90, s 4; *Real Property Act*, CCSM, c R30, s 90; *Conveyancing and Law of Property Act*, RSO 1990, c C.34, s 5; *Property Act*, RSNB 1973, c P-19, s 12(3); *Conveyancing Act*, RSNS 1989, c 97, s 13; *Land Titles Act*, 2015, SY 2015, c 10.

31   32 Hen 8, c 1.

distant relatives.[32] If there are no relatives, then the property goes to the Crown.

The fee simple estate used to be measured in lives by reference to a succession of heirs, but that is no longer the case. It is now equivalent to permanent ownership. However, we continue to say that the landowner holds a fee simple estate even though almost every aspect of that phrase relates to conditions that no longer exist. Old habits die hard, especially in the law of property.

2) Fee Tail

A fee tail estate (sometimes called an *entailed estate* or *estate tail*) was created by a grant of land to a tenant and the heirs of their body. The term *fee tail* comes from the Latin *feodum talliatum*, which means cutdown fee. It is different from a fee simple in two important respects. First, the heirs of the body are the lineal descendants (i.e., children, grandchildren, etc.) of the tenant and do not include other relatives. It was also possible to create a fee tail male, which was restricted to the male heirs of the body. Second, a fee tail was not freely transferable because the heir of the tenant's body had the right to possess the land when the tenant died. Any other interests in the land created during the tenant's life (e.g., by lease, mortgage, or transfer) would be lost when the tenant died, either because the heir took possession or because there was no heir and the fee tail estate had come to an end.[33]

The fee tail was designed to keep land in the family, but it has fallen out of favour because it can tie up land that could be put to better use if sold or mortgaged. It became possible to *bar the entail* and thereby convert it to a fee simple estate.[34] The fee tail has been abolished in some jurisdictions,[35] and in others, it is no longer possible to create a new fee tail estate.[36]

---

32 *Wills, Estates and Succession Act*, SBC 2009, c 13, Part 3; *Wills and Succession Act*, SA 2010, c W-12.2, Part 3; *Intestate Succession Act, 2019*, SS 2019, c I-13.2; *Intestate Succession Act*, CCSM, c 185; *Succession Law Reform Act*, RSO 1990, c S.26, Part II; *Devolution of Estates Act*, RSNB 1973, c D-9, Part II; *Intestate Succession Act*, RSNS 1989, c 236; *Probate Act*, RSPEI 1988, c P-21, Part IV; *Intestate Succession Act*, RSNL 1990, c I-21; *Estate Administration Act*, RSY 2002, c 77, Part 10; *Intestate Succession Act*, RSNWT 1988, c I-10.

33 Baker, above note 1 at 292–94.

34 See, for example, *Reid v Whiteford* (1883), 1 Man R 19 (QB); *Baker*, above note 1 at 300–2.

35 *Property Act*, RSNB 1973, c P-19, s 19; *Real Property Act*, RSNS 1989, c 385, s 6.

36 *Property Law Act*, RSBC 1996, c 377, s 10; *Law of Property Act*, RSA 2000, c L-7, s 9; *Land Titles Act, 2000*, SS 2000, c L-5.1, s 157; *Law of Property Act*, CCSM, c L90, s 30; *Conveyancing and Law of Property Act*, RSO 1990, c C.34, s 4.

3) Life Estate

A life estate exists for the duration of the tenant's life. It is a permitted form of subinfeudation, which means that the holder of a fee simple estate can create one. The life tenant is entitled to possess the land until they die, at which time the right to possession belongs once again to the holder of the fee simple.

Life estates were often created by wills in which the deceased holder of a fee simple would create a new life estate for their surviving spouse and transfer their fee simple to their children.[37] In essence, the spouse enjoys the use of the land and any income it produces until they die, at which time the children receive the capital.

A life tenant can transfer their life estate to someone else, but it will still come to an end when the original life tenant dies. When a life estate is transferred, the new tenant holds it as a life estate *pur autre vie*, which means for the life of another. If the new tenant dies before the original tenant, the life estate will continue to exist and therefore could be given away by the new tenant's will or by intestacy.[38]

E. LEASEHOLD ESTATES

A leasehold estate is usually called a *lease* or *tenancy*. Leaseholds and freeholds are the same in one essential respect: they are both estates, which means that the tenant has a right to possession of a space on the earth for some period of time. They differ from each other in three significant ways. First, freeholds were originally measured in lifetimes by reference to the lives of the tenant and their heirs, whereas leaseholds are normally measured in defined periods, such as one month, one year, or twenty-five years. Second, feudal services were eliminated for freehold estates, but it is normal for leases to contain obligations that landlords and tenants must perform. Third, leases are not affected by the abolition of subinfeudation. Although the Crown often grants leases, the most common variety of lease is granted by a landlord who holds the fee simple estate.

---

37   See, for example, *Re Taylor Estate*, [1982] 6 WWR 109, 19 Sask R 361 (Surrogate Ct).

38   Baker, above note 1 at 283–85.

1) Possession

People can occupy spaces without possessing them. For example, a guest in a hotel has a licence to use a room for the duration of their stay but does not have a lease because they do not have possession of that room. Housekeeping services are provided daily. A lodger in a home also has only a licence to be there. Although they have exclusive use of a bedroom, they do not have possession because they share the kitchen and other spaces with the homeowner and access their bedroom through shared space in the home.

A hotel guest or lodger is different from a tenant in an apartment building, who has possession of their apartment and does not share their personal space with the other tenants in the building. All the tenants share the use of the hallways, elevators, and stairways and possibly also laundry facilities and recreation areas in and around the building. Each tenant has a lease of their own apartment coupled with a licence to use the common areas.

The distinction between a lease and a licence is important primarily because a lease is a right *in rem* that is enforceable generally against others (including the landlord), whereas a licence is (normally) only a right *in personam* that is enforceable (if at all) only against the person who granted it. Some licences are not even enforceable against the grantor. A guest invited over for dinner has a licence to be there but can be asked to leave at any time. So long as the licence continues, they simply have permission to do what would otherwise be a trespass.

It is not always easy to distinguish a lease from a licence. A person with a contractual licence to occupy premises may be paying rent and have a right to stay there for a defined period of time, just like a tenant. Whether an occupant has a lease or a licence depends on whether or not they have possession. In England, there was a time when landlords would get new tenants to sign agreements that stated that they had only a licence and no tenancy. This was done to avoid the statutory rights tenants then had to rent controls and protection from eviction. Courts would look through the wording of the agreement to see the substance of the arrangement. As Lord Templeman said in *Street v Mountford*, "Parties cannot turn a tenancy into a licence merely by calling it one. The circumstances and the conduct of the parties show that what was intended was that the occupier should be granted exclusive possession at a rent for a term with a corresponding interest in the land which created a tenancy."[39]

---

39   [1985] AC 809 at 821 (HL).

A tenant can have possession even if their use of the space is restricted by the terms of the lease. In many residential leases, the tenant is not allowed to carry on a business or keep pets. In *Metro-Matic Services Ltd v Hulmann*,[40] the owner of an apartment building in Toronto granted a five-year lease of the laundry room to a company that provided coin-operated washers and dryers. It was a term of the lease that the room would "be used only for the purpose of carrying on the business of an automatic laundry." The building was sold, and the new owner refused to honour the lease. The trial judge held that the company had only a licence to use the room, which was not binding on the new owner,[41] but that was overturned on appeal. Brooke JA said,

> While it is true that the appellant has by its own covenant restricted the use to which it will put the premises, such a covenant does not affect the demise any more than would be the case when a tenant covenants to use his apartment as a dwelling place only. This does not make his possession any the less exclusive.[42]

2) Certainty of Term

It is a requirement for most leases that the term (i.e., duration) of the lease is certain. There are two exceptions. First, it is possible to have a lease for life, although that might be regarded as "a species of freehold estate."[43] A life tenant can have either a life estate (as described above) or a lease for life. In either case, they have a right to possess the land for life, but the lease is likely to contain an obligation to pay rent.

Second, it is possible to have a tenancy at will, which either party can choose to end simply by giving reasonable notice to the other. In *Ocean Harvesters Ltd v Quinlan Brothers Ltd*, Dickson J said, "A tenancy at will is created when one person permits another to occupy lands on the agreement, express or implied, that the tenancy is determinable at the will of either."[44]

Most leasehold estates are either a *fixed-term lease* or a *periodic tenancy*. The start and end of a fixed-term lease must be specified at the outset. If there is any uncertainty over its term, then it is not valid as a fixed-term lease but will take effect instead as a tenancy at will or periodic tenancy. In *Prudential Assurance Co Ltd v London Residuary*

---

40   [1973] 4 OR (2d) 462, 48 DLR (3d) 326 (CA) [*Metro-Matic Services*].

41   (1970) [1970] 2 OR 707, 12 DLR (3d) 21.

42   *Metro-Matic Services*, above note 40 at 362. A *demise* is a grant of a leasehold estate.

43   *Berrisford v Mexfield Housing Co-operative Ltd*, [2011] UKSC 52, [2012] 1 AC 955 at para 36, Lord Neuberger.

44   [1975] 1 SCR 684 at 686, 44 DLR (3d) 687. See also Baker, above note 1 at 325.

Body,[45] London County Council leased a strip of land beside a road for £30 per annum until the land was needed by the council for the purpose of widening the road. Since the end of the lease was uncertain, all the tenant had was a yearly tenancy that could be terminated by giving six months' notice.

In *Black v Blair Athol Farms Ltd*, a lease was granted for "the term commencing on the 2nd day of January, 1992, and ending on the 31st day of December in the year of the Lessor's death."[46] It could not take effect as a lease for life since it did not end on death but only at the end of the year in which the landlord died. Since that date was uncertain when the lease was granted, it could not be a fixed-term lease. Lyon JA said, "The law is clear that if the lease created by the agreement is a fixed-term lease, it must have a certain beginning and a certain end. This is a principle of very long standing in Canada and in the Commonwealth."[47]

In *Lace v Chandler*,[48] the English Court of Appeal held that a lease until the end of the Second World War was not a valid fixed-term lease because its term was defined by an uncertain event. Many leases had been granted on the same basis but were converted by the *Validation of War-time Leases Act 1944* into ten-year leases, with either party having the option to terminate the lease when the war ended. It may seem odd that one lease was valid but not the other when they both achieved the same goal. However, so long as the maximum duration of a lease is fixed, it does not matter that it might end early as a result of an uncertain event. The landlord knows that they will once again have a right to possession of the land on a certain date (if not earlier), and so, too, would anyone interested in buying the landlord's estate.

The term of a lease can consist of a series of separate blocks of time, such as a lease of a lake cottage every July for the next five years.[49] Since the start and end dates of each block are certain when the lease is granted, it is a valid fixed-term lease.

Fixed-term leases often contain options for renewal, in which the tenant can choose to have one or more additional terms. Strangely, it is possible to have a lease that can be renewed perpetually. In *JE Gibson Holdings v Principal Investments*,[50] the tenant had a twenty-one-year lease

---

45 *Prudential Assurance Co Ltd v London Residuary Body*, [1991] UKHL 10, [1992] 2 AC 386.

46 [1996] 5 WWR 516 at 525, 110 Man R (2d) 84 (CA).

47 *Ibid*.

48 [1944] KB 368 (CA).

49 See, for example, *Cottage Holiday Associates Ltd v Customs and Excise Commissioners*, [1983] QB 735.

50 [1964] SCR 424, 44 DLR (2d) 673 [cited to SCR].

with an option to renew it, with rent to be determined by arbitration. If the tenant renewed the lease, then the landlord was required to grant an additional twenty-one-year lease on the same terms (other than rent), including another option to renew. If the tenant continues to renew, they might have possession of the land forever. This seems to contradict the requirement for certainty of term, but the Supreme Court of Canada rejected that argument:

> The further submission that this lease creates a term which is indefinite or infinite in time and is in effect a term in perpetuity also fails. This is a lease for twenty-one years. When that term expires a new lease is drawn on the same terms except as to rent and that lease, in turn, has a term certain of twenty-one years.[51]

A periodic tenancy is like a fixed-term lease that automatically renews when each period comes to an end unless the landlord or tenant gives notice to end the tenancy. Residential leases are commonly granted as monthly periodic tenancies, whereas agricultural leases are often granted as yearly tenancies to allow for planting and harvest. A fixed-term lease may be combined with a periodic tenancy, such as a fixed-term lease of an apartment for one year that will be followed by a monthly periodic tenancy unless the landlord or tenant gives notice to quit.

A periodic tenancy may continue indefinitely, but that does not offend the requirement for certainty. The landlord is free at any time to serve notice to bring the tenancy to an end, which means that the duration of the tenant's right to possession is known at any given moment. For example, if the landlord could serve notice today to end the lease on the last day of the next calendar month, then the tenant currently has a right to possess the land until the end of next month. Although the tenant might continue in possession indefinitely, the duration of their right to possession is always certain.

3) Leasehold Covenants

A covenant is a promise made in a deed. Since leases were normally granted by deed, the rights and obligations contained in a lease are called *leasehold covenants*. In addition to the covenants expressed in the written document, the law also imposes obligations on landlords and tenants. Shorter residential tenancies are heavily regulated by statute (as discussed below), but all leases are subject to covenants implied by the common law.

---

51 *Ibid* at 426, Judson J.

There are four main implied covenants: the tenant will have quiet enjoyment, the landlord will not derogate from the grant, the tenant will use the premises in a tenant-like manner, and the tenant will not commit waste. For leases of apartments or office space, there is also an implied covenant that the landlord will maintain the lobby, hallways, elevators, and other common areas in good repair.[52]

The covenant of quiet enjoyment is a covenant that the landlord will not interfere with the tenant's possession of the land. It is not about noise or joy, as demonstrated by *Southwark London Borough Council v Mills*.[53] Tenants in buildings owned by the council complained that the lack of sound insulation between flats meant that the noises made by their neighbours interfered with their quiet enjoyment. One tenant testified, "I can hear all the private and most intimate moments of [my neighbours'] lives—conversations, what television station they are viewing, when they go to the toilet, when they make love. Every light switched on, every door opened or closed, every pot or pan placed on the cooker, all these I hear."[54]

The House of Lords held that this did not breach the covenant of quiet enjoyment. Lord Hoffmann said:

> Read literally, these words would seem very apt. The flat is not quiet and the tenant is not enjoying it. But the words cannot be read literally. The covenant has a very long history. It has been expressed or implied in conveyances and leases of English land for centuries. It comes from a time when, in a conveyancing context, the words "quiet enjoyment" had a technical meaning different from what they would today signify to a non-lawyer who was unacquainted with their history. . . . The covenant for quiet enjoyment is therefore a covenant that the tenant's lawful possession of the land will not be substantially interfered with by the acts of the lessor or those lawfully claiming under him.[55]

The covenant that the landlord will not derogate from the grant is similar to the covenant for quiet enjoyment, except that it relates to the tenant's use of the land rather than their possession of it. In *Aussie Traveller Pty Ltd v Marklea Pty Ltd*,[56] a commercial building was divided into sections that were leased to different tenants. One tenant used their space to manufacture awnings, which required a relatively dust-free environment. The landlord later leased adjacent space to another

---

52   *Liverpool City Council v Irwin*, [1976] UKHL 1, [1977] AC 239.
53   [1999] UKHL 40, [2001] 1 AC 1 [*Southwark* cited to AC].
54   *Ibid* at 18.
55   *Ibid* at 10. See also *Stearman v Powers*, 2014 BCCA 206, 373 DLR (4th) 539.
56   [1997] QCA 2, [1998] 1 Qd R 1.

tenant who did carpentry and caused sawdust to spread throughout the building. This was an improper derogation from the first tenant's grant.

In *Firth v BD Management Ltd*,[57] several tenants leased offices with shared use of parking spaces. When the landlord reduced the number of parking spaces available, they claimed that this breached the covenants of quiet enjoyment and non-derogation, but that was rejected by the BC Court of Appeal:

> To establish a breach of the covenant of quiet enjoyment the appellant must show that the ordinary and lawful enjoyment of the demised premises is substantially interfered with by the acts of the lessor.... Mere temporary inconvenience is not enough — the interference must be of a grave and permanent nature. It must be a serious interference with the tenant's proper freedom of action in exercising its right of possession.... Similarly, when one considers whether a landlord's acts can be construed as a derogation from its grant, the appellant must demonstrate that there has been some act which renders the premises substantially less fit for the purposes for which they were let.[58]

At common law, there is no implied covenant to repair placed on either landlord or tenant. The tenant is under the implied obligations not to commit waste and to use the premises in a tenant-like manner, which Denning LJ described as follows:

> The tenant must take proper care of the place. He must, if he is going away for the winter, turn off the water and empty the boiler. He must clean the chimneys, when necessary, and also the windows. He must mend the electric light when it fuses. He must unstop the sink when it is blocked by his waste. In short, he must do the little jobs about the place which a reasonable tenant would do. In addition, he must, of course, not damage the house, wilfully or negligently; and he must see that his family and guests do not damage it: and if they do, he must repair it. But apart from such things, if the house falls into disrepair through fair wear and tear or lapse of time, or for any reason not caused by him, then the tenant is not liable to repair it.[59]

In *British Columbia (Director of Civil Forfeiture) v Onn*, the BC Court of Appeal described waste as "conduct by either a life tenant or a leasehold tenant which permanently alters the nature of the property they

---

57   (1990) 73 DLR (4th) 375 (BCCA).
58   *Ibid* at 379–80, Wallace JA.
59   *Warren v Keen*, [1954] 1 QB 15 at 20 (CA).

occupy."[60] In *Prince George (City) v Columbus Hotel Co (1991) Ltd,*[61] a hotel had been sold to the city because of unpaid taxes, and the previous owner remained in occupation. The hotel burned down, and the city claimed that the occupier was liable for waste. That was rejected by the BC Supreme Court:

> All types of waste require the participation of the tenant in the act or omission that affects the owner's interest in the property. The demolition and debris removal expense incurred in the case at bar was a consequence of fire. It cannot be said in this case that destruction of the occupied property by fire during the redemption period constitutes waste by the occupant.[62]

There is no implied covenant that the premises are in good condition or fit for the tenant's purposes unless the landlord provides furnished accommodation.[63] As Lord Hoffmann said in *Southwark,* "In the grant of a tenancy it is fundamental to the common understanding of the parties, objectively determined, that the landlord gives no implied warranty as to the condition or fitness of the premises. Caveat lessee."[64]

4) Residential Tenancies

As discussed above, the common law did little for tenants beyond protecting their right to possession. Any additional rights would depend on express covenants in the lease, but a person seeking a place to live where rental accommodation is in short supply has little bargaining power. The provinces and territories now have statutes that provide residential tenants with consumer protection.[65] The landlord has a duty to maintain the premises in a suitable condition, and there are provisions dealing with security deposits, rental increases, giving notices, and termination. It is not possible for landlords and tenants to avoid the rights and obligations imposed by statute.

---

60   [2009] 12 WWR 626, 312 DLR (4th) 739 at para 25, Garson J.
61   2010 BCSC 149.
62   *Ibid* at para 45, Willcock J.
63   *Smith v Marrable* (1843), 11 M & W 5, 152 ER 693.
64   *Southwark,* above note 53 at 12.
65   *Residential Tenancy Act,* SBC 2002, c 78; *Residential Tenancies Act,* SA 2004, c R-17.1; *Residential Tenancies Act, 2006,* SS 2006, c R-22.0001; *Residential Tenancies Act,* CCSM, c R119; *Residential Tenancies Act, 2006,* SO 2006, c 17; *Residential Tenancies Act,* SNB 1975, c R-10.2; *Residential Tenancies Act,* RSNS 1989, c 401; *Rental of Residential Property Act,* RSPEI 1988, c R-13.1; *Residential Tenancies Act, 2018,* SNL 2018, c R-14.2; *Residential Landlord and Tenant Act,* SY 2012, c 20; *Residential Tenancies Act,* RSNWT 1988, c R-5.

5) Privity of Estate

When a landlord grants a new lease or tenancy, they create a new estate. Typically, the landlord holds the fee simple, which is the right to possess the land indefinitely. By granting the lease, they give up their right to possession during the term of the lease. While the lease is in existence, the land is the subject of two estates: the landlord's fee simple (with the right to possession in abeyance) and the tenant's leasehold. The landlord has what is called the *reversion*, which consists of their right to possession at the end of the lease plus all of their rights under the terms of the lease, which correspond to the tenant's obligations.

The landlord and the tenant have a relationship called *privity of estate*, in which one party's obligations correspond to the other party's rights. The original landlord and the original tenant are probably also parties to a contract of lease and therefore also have privity of contract, but that is not required to enforce leasehold covenants. Privity of estate provides the basis for their enforcement.

If the landlord sells their reversion or gives it away, the new owner will acquire the landlord's fee simple estate and become the new landlord. They will not be a party to a contract with the tenant, but they will acquire the right to enforce the tenant's leasehold covenants and be required to perform the landlord's leasehold covenants. The new landlord and tenant have privity of estate but not privity of contract.

It has long been possible to assign contractual rights (as discussed in the first chapter), but, with few exceptions, it is not possible to assign obligations. Privity of estate provides a major exception to that rule. Although we can think of it as an exception to privity of contract, it should be noted that the concept of privity of estate predates the modern law of contract by centuries.

Just as the landlord might transfer their reversion, so might the tenant assign their leasehold estate, in which case the new tenant acquires the benefit of the landlord's covenants and becomes subject to the tenant's covenants. The current tenant and the current landlord will have privity of estate even if neither of them is a party to the original lease agreement.

The assignment of a lease (in which one tenant is replaced by another) is different from a sublease (which is similar to subinfeudation). A tenant who grants a sublease continues to be the tenant in privity of estate with their landlord. By subletting, they have created a new leasehold estate and become landlord to their subtenant. They still have privity of estate with their landlord but also have privity of (a different) estate with the subtenant. The landlord and subtenant do not have privity of estate with each other and have no direct legal relationship. The land is now the subject of three estates.

It is common for leases to contain a covenant that the tenant will not assign or sublet without the landlord's consent, which will not be refused unreasonably. Modern residential tenancy legislation contains a similar provision.[66]

F. FUTURE INTERESTS

Estates provide a way to allocate the possession of land among different people over time. For example, if I owned a fee simple estate and died leaving the land to my widow for life with the remainder to my daughter, my widow will have the right to possess it until she dies, at which time my daughter will have that right. My will has created a new life estate for my widow and transferred my fee simple estate to my daughter. While my widow lives, the land is the subject of two estates: one for life and one in fee simple. My widow's life estate is both *vested in interest* and *vested in possession* since she holds the estate and is currently in possession of the land. My daughter's fee simple is only vested in interest since she holds that estate but is not entitled to possession until my widow's life estate comes to an end.

My daughter's fee simple estate is vested in interest but not in possession because it is a right that she currently holds to possess the land in the future. She would be the registered owner of the fee simple and have a right to sell it or give it away to others (subject to my widow's life estate). Although not yet entitled to possession, she would have a legal right to complain if my widow committed acts of waste by destroying buildings or felling trees. In short, she has an existing and marketable interest in land, which is the right to possess it in the future.

---

66 *Residential Tenancy Act*, SBC 2002, c 78, s 34; *Residential Tenancies Act*, SA 2004, c R-17.1, s 22; *Residential Tenancies Act, 2006*, SS 2006, c R-22.0001, s 50; *Residential Tenancies Act*, CCSM, c R119, ss 42-50; *Residential Tenancies Act, 2006*, SO 2006, c 17, Part VI; *Residential Tenancies Act*, SNB 1975, c R-10.2, s 13; *Residential Tenancies Act*, RSNS 1989, c 401, s 9B; *Rental of Residential Property Act*, RSPEI 1988, c R-13.1, s 6(5); *Residential Tenancies Act, 2018*, SNL 2018, c R-14.2, s 10(3); *Residential Landlord and Tenant Act*, SY 2012, c 20, s 34; *Residential Tenancies Act*, RSNWT 1988, c R-5, ss 21–24.

1) Remainders

In the example above, my daughter's fee simple estate is called a *remainder* because it is what is left over after my widow's life estate comes to an end. It is possible to create a series of successive remainders, for example, to my widow for life, then to my daughter for life, and then in fee simple to my first grandchild to reach the age of twenty-one. In most jurisdictions, there is a *rule against perpetuities* that prevents people from using successive remainders to tie up land in perpetuity. That rule is discussed below.

A remainder can be vested or contingent.[67] It is vested if the identity of the person with the right to possession in the future is known and there are no conditions that might prevent them from acquiring that right. They are simply waiting for the termination of other estates. In the example above, my widow's life estate is vested in interest and possession and my daughter's life estate is vested in interest (but not possession while my widow lives). If there is no grandchild who is twenty-one or older, then the person entitled to the remainder in fee simple has not been identified. It will be a contingent remainder until a grandchild celebrates their twenty-first birthday or it becomes clear that no grandchild ever will.

The problem with contingent remainders is that no one knows who is going to be entitled to possession in the future until the contingency is resolved one way or another, and that might not happen for a very long time. In the above example, it might be unresolved until the last of my children has died, when it is finally known for sure that I will never have grandchildren. It might remain contingent even longer if the last child is survived by an infant grandchild of mine. Until the contingency is resolved, the fee simple estate will remain vested first in my executor and then in the person who will be entitled to it under my will, but the land is tied up. It is not freely marketable until a grandchild takes the fee simple estate at age twenty-one or it finally becomes certain that that will never happen.

2) Reversions

A reversion happens when someone grants an estate and the right to possession returns to them when that estate comes to an end.[68] When a lease is granted, the landlord holds the reversion (as discussed above), but reversions can also arise when freehold estates are granted. For

---

67   Baker, above note 1 at 295–96.
68   *Ibid* at 294–95.

example, if I granted a life estate to my daughter, the right to possession would revert to me when she died (or to the person entitled to my estate after my death). The reversion is vested in interest. It is not a new estate but the same fee simple that I had before I granted a life estate to my daughter.

In this example, it is certain that the right to possession will revert, even if that does not happen until long after my death. In some cases, it is not certain whether the reversion will occur. There will be uncertainty so long as a contingent remainder remains unresolved, as discussed above. It can also happen if an estate is granted in fee simple but is subject to a condition that might bring it to a premature end.

3) Defeasible and Determinable Estates

A condition that must be fulfilled before an estate can vest in interest (such as being the first grandchild to turn twenty-one) is a *condition precedent*. A condition that might cause a vested interest to come to an end is a *condition subsequent*. An estate subject to a condition subsequent is a *defeasible estate*.

In *Re North Gower Township Public School Board and Todd*,[69] a fee simple estate was sold to a school board subject to the condition "that should the said parcel or tract of land at any time hereafter cease to be used for the purposes for which it is hereby granted the said lands only and not the buildings or fences thereon shall revert to the [vendor]" on repayment of the purchase price of $75. The Ontario Court of Appeal held that this created a defeasible estate.

The law draws a distinction between *defeasible* and *determinable* estates. For example, a transfer of land *on condition that* it is used as a school will create a defeasible estate, whereas a transfer of land *for so long as* it is used as a school will create a determinable estate. These two transfers are treated very differently even though they do substantially the same thing. A defeasible estate is regarded as an ordinary fee simple estate that might come to an end prematurely if the condition subsequently occurs (e.g., the land ceases to be used as a school). A determinable estate is regarded as something less than a fee simple because the restriction on its use defines the duration of the estate.[70] The estate lasts only so long as it is used as a school. As Grant J said in *Re Tilbury West Public School Board and Hastie,* "The essential distinction appears to be that the determining event in a determinable fee itself sets the limit for

---

69   [1968] 1 OR 63, 65 DLR (2d) 421 (CA) [*Re North Gower*].
70   See *Westsea Construction Ltd v Land Title Office*, [1995] 4 WWR 725, 3 BCLR (3d) 56 [*Westsea*].

the estate first granted. A condition subsequent, on the other hand, is an independent clause added to a complete fee simple absolute which operates so as to defeat it."[71]

Unhappily, a minor variation in wording can lead to very different legal outcomes. There are three main ways in which defeasible and determinable estates are treated differently. First, a defeasible estate does not automatically come to an end if the condition subsequent occurs. The grantor has a *right of re-entry*, and the estate will continue until they choose to exercise that right. In contrast, a determinable estate ends when the determining event occurs since that is what defined the duration of the estate.

Second, if a condition subsequent is invalid for any reason, the defeasible estate is no longer defeasible but continues to exist free from that condition. If the limitation that defines a determinable estate is invalid, then the estate does not exist because its duration is not defined.

Third, the right of re-entry to end a defeasible estate is subject to the rule against perpetuities (discussed below).[72] The person who grants a determinable estate has a *possibility of reverter*, which is not subject to that rule at common law (but is by statute in some jurisdictions).[73]

Conditions and limitations can be invalid for various reasons. Some are contrary to public policy because they are used to interfere with the recipient's choice of religion or spouse or with their relations with members of their family.[74] Others are too vague to be enforceable. In *Sifton v Sifton*,[75] a father died leaving the income from his estate to be paid to his daughter "only so long as she shall continue to reside in Canada." The Privy Council (on appeal from Ontario) advised that the clause was a condition subsequent that was void for uncertainty. In *Re Gape*,[76] a woman in England made testamentary gifts to her American relatives on condition that they "take up permanent residence in England." The English Court of Appeal distinguished this from the clause in *Sifton v Sifton* on the basis that the concept of permanent residence was sufficiently certain to be a valid condition. In *Re Allen*, Evershed MR said,

> It has been long established that the courts (which are inclined against
> the divesting of gifts or estates already vested) will hold a condition

---

71   [1966] 2 OR 20 at 23–24, 55 DLR (2d) 407.

72   *Re North Gower*, above note 69.

73   *Perpetuity Act*, RSBC 1996, c 358, s 23; *Perpetuities Act*, RSA 2000, c P-5, s 19; *Perpetuities Act*, RSO 1990, c P.9, s 15; *Perpetuities Act*, RSY 2002, c 168, s 19; *Perpetuities Act*, RSNWT 1988, c P-3, s 16.

74   See *Eastern Trust Co v McTague* (1963), 39 DLR (2d) 743 (PEI SC AD).

75   [1938] AC 656 (PC). See also *Re McColgan*, [1969] 2 OR 152, 4 DLR (3d) 572.

76   [1952] Ch 743 (CA).

subsequent void if its terms are such that (apart from mere difficulties of construction of the language or of the ascertainment of the facts) it cannot be clearly known in advance or from the beginning what are the circumstances the happening of which will cause the divesting or determination of the gift or estate.[77]

A person who grants a defeasible or determinable estate in fee simple has a property right to that land. Since a defeasible estate is regarded as an ordinary fee simple subject to a condition that might bring it to a premature end, the grant of that estate is really a complete transfer of the fee simple, and the grantor's right of re-entry is a new interest that arises when the estate is transferred. This is conceptually different from the possibility of reverter that exists when a determinable estate is granted. The determinable estate is less than an ordinary fee simple, and the possibility of reverter is what is left behind and not included in the grant. However, the possibility of reverter is not itself an estate but a "special right."[78]

4) Rule Against Perpetuities

As discussed above, a contingent remainder can tie up land while everyone waits for the contingency to be resolved one way or another. A remainder that is vested in interest can be transferred, but a contingent remainder creates only a hope or expectation that it might vest. Since it is possible to make successive contingent remainders, it is possible to keep land tied up for a very long time. Left unchecked, people could control the use of their land for centuries after their death. The common law came up with a solution to this problem called the *rule against perpetuities*. However, the remedy turned out to be worse than the disease. Most jurisdictions have either amended or abolished the rule by statute.

According to the common law rule, a contingent remainder was void from the outset if there was any possibility, however unlikely, that it could remain contingent beyond the *perpetuity period*. It does not matter whether the remainder vests in interest or not, just so long as it is certain at the outset that the contingency will get resolved in time. In other words, when a contingent remainder is created, it must be absolutely certain that one of two things will happen within the perpetuity period: either the remainder will vest in interest, or it will become impossible for it to vest.

---

77   [1953] Ch 810 at 816.
78   *Westsea*, above note 70 at para 40, Boyle J.

The main difficulty with the common law rule against perpetuities was caused by its definition of the perpetuity period, which is a *life in being* plus twenty-one years.[79] A life in being is someone who is alive when the contingent remainder is created, even if they are an unborn fetus or embryo. The perpetuity period lasts for twenty-one years after the death of someone who was alive when the contingent remainder was created. This is best explained using examples.

Returning to a previous example, if I died leaving my land to my widow for life, then to my daughter for life, and then in fee simple to my first grandchild to reach the age of twenty-one, that would not offend the rule against perpetuities. The perpetuity period begins when a contingent interest is created, which was when I died and my will became operative. My widow and daughter have vested life estates created at that time. If I already had a grandchild who was twenty-one or older when I died, their fee simple would also be vested at that time. A potential perpetuity problem arises only if the remainder for the grandchild was contingent when I died, but that would be resolved within the perpetuity period, as follows.

Any of my children who survived me would count as lives in being since they would be alive when I died (even if they were an unborn fetus or embryo). It was not possible for me to have any more children (since modern reproductive technology did not exist when the rules were created). Similarly, any grandchildren I might have would be alive before the last of my children died. So if the remainder to a grandchild ever became vested at age twenty-one, it could only do so within the perpetuity period. It could not possibly happen more than twenty-one years after the death of the last life in being (my child) plus any gestation periods needed to connect the generations. The remainder cannot still be a contingent remainder beyond the perpetuity period. It will either vest or fail completely within that time.

If, instead of twenty-one years, I left the remainder in fee simple to my first grandchild to reach the age of twenty-five, and that remainder was contingent when I died, it would be void. That would be true even if I died leaving behind twelve healthy grandchildren, the oldest of whom was twenty-four. All of them might die before reaching the age of twenty-five, and another grandchild could be born after my death. When all of my children are dead, my oldest surviving grandchild might then be only three years old and might be the first grandchild to reach the age of twenty-five, which would occur more than twenty-one years after the death of the last life in being. Since that would fall outside the

---

79   Baker, above note 1 at 312.

perpetuity period, the remainder was void from the outset. When applying the rule against perpetuities, the common law cared nothing for realistic possibilities. If there was any theoretical, mathematical possibility that a remainder might still be contingent beyond the perpetuity period, it was void.

The rules made sense as a limit on the dynastic tendencies of landowners. As Lawson and Rudden explained, people were allowed some control over their lands after their death, but that control had to end when their grandchildren became adults (then at age twenty-one).[80] However, the rule against perpetuities was not limited to that context but applied to most contingent interests, even in commercial transactions. For example, in *Air Jamaica Ltd v Charlton*,[81] the terms of an employee pension plan violated the common law rule against perpetuities in Jamaica, leaving a surplus of $400 million that had to go back to the contributors.

In *Silver v Fulton*,[82] an option to purchase land in Nova Scotia at fair market value was granted to Mr Fulton in 1998, but no time limit was set for its exercise, so it was void. There was a remote possibility that it could be exercised more than twenty-one years after the parties had died. Justice Coady said,

> For many lawyers and judges, the rule against perpetuities is like a trip down Alice's rabbit hole to a land where things are not always what they seem. . . .
>
> While simple enough to state, the rule against perpetuities is harder to apply. Perhaps one of the more vexing aspects of the rule is that it can invalidate a gift or interest even where the parties' intentions are clear and even if it is highly probable that the transfer will occur within the perpetuities period.[83]

Legislatures have intervened to solve these problems in most jurisdictions. The rule against perpetuities has been abolished in Saskatchewan, Manitoba, and Nova Scotia (although not in time to save Mr Fulton's option to purchase).[84] In most other jurisdictions, the rule has been amended by statute. The most significant change is the introduction of a "wait and see" rule, which means that a contingent interest

---

80   FH Lawson & Bernard Rudden, *The Law of Property*, 3d ed (Oxford: Oxford University Press, 2002) at 190.

81   [1999] UKPC 20, [1999] 1 WLR 1399.

82   2011 NSSC 127.

83   *Ibid* at paras 18 and 20.

84   *Trustee Act, 2009*, SS 2009, c T-23.01, s 58; *Perpetuities and Accumulations Act*, CCSM, c P33, s 3; *Perpetuities Act*, SNS 2011, c 42, s 3.

is not void even if it might not get resolved within the perpetuity period. It is valid until the end of that period, and only then will it become invalid if it is still contingent.[85] This solves the vast majority of potential perpetuity problems. In British Columbia, people can choose a fixed perpetuity period of up to eighty years to avoid the complexities created by lives in being.[86]

G. ABORIGINAL TITLE

1) Aboriginal Title in Canadian Law

As discussed above, the dominant legal system in Canada is the common law imported from England when the land became part of the British Empire. Under that system, the Crown holds radical title to the land, which includes the power to take possession for its own use or to grant the right to possession to others. A right to possession of land is called an estate, and most estates are granted by the Crown or by a landlord who holds an estate granted by the Crown.

Aboriginal title to land operates differently. It is not a right granted by the Crown but is based on property rights that existed before the Crown acquired sovereignty and were then incorporated into the common law. As McLachlin CJ said in *Tsilhqot'in Nation v British Columbia*,

> At the time of assertion of European sovereignty, the Crown acquired radical or underlying title to all the land in the province. This Crown title, however, was burdened by the pre-existing legal rights of Aboriginal people who occupied and used the land prior to European arrival. The doctrine of *terra nullius* (that no one owned the land prior to European assertion of sovereignty) never applied in Canada, as confirmed by the *Royal Proclamation* of 1763.[87]

It is a feature of the common law that existing property rights are not destroyed by a change in sovereignty. As the High Court of Australia explained in *Mabo No 2*: "The strong assumption of the common law was that interests in property which existed under native law or customs were not obliterated by the act of State establishing a new British

---

85 *Perpetuity Act*, RSBC 1996, c 358, s 9; *Perpetuities Act*, RSA 2000, c P-5, s 4; *Perpetuities Act*, RSO 1990, c P.9, s 4; *Perpetuities Act*, RSY 2002, c 168, s 4; *Perpetuities Act*, RSNWT 1988, c P-3.

86 *Perpetuity Act*, RSBC 1996, c 358, s 7.

87 2014 SCC 44 at para 69 [*Tsilhqot'in* (2014)].

Colony but were preserved and protected by the domestic law of the Colony after its establishment."[88]

Property rights cannot exist without a system of property law. The property rights that existed before the common law came to Canada were defined and enforced by a different legal system or, more accurately, by a variety of different legal systems since the laws and customs of Aboriginal peoples are not uniform across the country. Those rights must be incorporated into the common law so that they can be enforced against the European settlers who did not observe the Aboriginal laws and customs on which they were based.

When pre-existing property rights are incorporated into the common law they become common law rights. They are placed in a category of property rights known as *Aboriginal title* in Canada and often called *native title* elsewhere. Aboriginal title is based on the property rights that exist pursuant to Aboriginal laws and customs but is different from them. The translation from one legal system to another produces a change. Aboriginal title is also different from other common law property rights, such as estates, easements, and *profits à prendre*, even though it is similar in many respects.

2) Content of Aboriginal Title

Aboriginal title is based on the occupation of land according to Aboriginal laws and customs. Occupation is similar to but different from possession at common law. As McLachlin CJ said in *Tsilhqot'in* (2014):

> In summary, what is required is a culturally sensitive approach to sufficiency of occupation based on the dual perspectives of the Aboriginal group in question—its laws, practices, size, technological ability and the character of the land claimed—and the common law notion of possession as a basis for title. It is not possible to list every indicia of occupation that might apply in a particular case. The common law test for possession—which requires an intention to occupy or hold land for the purposes of the occupant—must be considered alongside the perspective of the Aboriginal group which, depending on its size and manner of living, might conceive of possession of land in a somewhat different manner than did the common law.[89]

In that case, approximately 300 Tsilhqot'in people were living in the interior of British Columbia when the Crown acquired sovereignty in

---

88   *Mabo No 2*, above note 13 at 82, Deane & Gaudron JJ. See also *Adeyinka Oyekan v Musendiku Adele* (1957), 1 WLR 876 at 880 (PC).

89   *Tsilhqot'in* (2014), above note 87 at para 41.

1846.[90] They were a semi-nomadic people who used rivers, lakes, and trails over a very large area for hunting, fishing, trapping, and gathering.[91] This was sufficient occupation of the land to become Aboriginal title at common law.

Although similar to possession at common law, Aboriginal title is different in four important respects. First, it is not a form of private property held by individuals but is communal property belonging to the Aboriginal group as a whole.[92] Second, it belongs not just to the present members of the group but to future generations as well. Third, the land cannot be used in a way that would interfere too greatly with the rights of those who will enjoy it in the future:

> Aboriginal title confers ownership rights similar to those associated with fee simple, including: the right to decide how the land will be used; the right of enjoyment and occupancy of the land; the right to possess the land; the right to the economic benefits of the land; and the right to pro-actively use and manage the land.
>
> Aboriginal title, however, comes with an important restriction — it is collective title held not only for the present generation but for all succeeding generations. This means it cannot be alienated except to the Crown or encumbered in ways that would prevent future generations of the group from using and enjoying it. Nor can the land be developed or misused in a way that would substantially deprive future generations of the benefit of the land. Some changes — even permanent changes — to the land may be possible. Whether a particular use is irreconcilable with the ability of succeeding generations to benefit from the land will be a matter to be determined when the issue arises.[93]

Finally, Aboriginal title is non-transferable. It can be surrendered to the Crown but cannot be transferred to others.[94] King George III's *Royal Proclamation, 1763*[95] provided protection to the property rights of Aboriginal peoples in much of North America and banned the purchase of land from them by anyone other than the Crown:

---

90   *Tsilhqot'in Nation v British Columbia*, 2007 BCSC 1700 at paras 601–2 & 793 [*Tsilhqot'in* (2007)].

91   *Ibid* at paras 959–60.

92   *Delgamuukw v British Columbia*, [1997] 3 SCR 1010 at para 115, 153 DLR (4th) 193 [*Delgamuukw*].

93   *Tsilhqot'in* (2014), above note 87 at paras 73–74, McLachlin CJ.

94   *Delgamuukw*, above note 92 at para 113.

95   (UK), reprinted in RSC 1985, App II, No 1.

And whereas it is just and reasonable, and essential to our Interest, and the Security of our Colonies, that the several Nations or Tribes of Indians with whom We are connected, and who live under our Protection, should not be molested or disturbed in the Possession of such Parts of Our Dominions and Territories as, not having been ceded to or purchased by Us, are reserved to them, or any of them, as their Hunting Grounds. . . .

And whereas great Frauds and Abuses have been committed in the purchasing Lands of the Indians, to the great Prejudice of our Interests, and to the great Dissatisfaction of the said Indians; In order, therefore, to prevent such Irregularities for the future, and to the end that the Indians may be convinced of our Justice and determined Resolution to remove all reasonable Cause of Discontent, We do, with the Advice of our Privy Council strictly enjoin and require, that no private Person do presume to make any purchase from the said Indians of any Lands reserved to the said Indians, within those parts of our Colonies where, We have thought proper to allow Settlement; but that, if at any Time any of the Said Indians should be inclined to dispose of the said Lands, the same shall be Purchased only for Us, in our Name, at some public Meeting or Assembly of the said Indians, to be held for that Purpose.[96]

The Royal Proclamation explains why Aboriginal title is non-transferable in places where it applies. But Aboriginal title is non-transferable in other places as well, including Australia, where there was no equivalent proclamation. Brennan J said in *Mabo No 2* that "native title cannot be acquired from an indigenous people by one who, not being a member of the indigenous people, does not acknowledge their laws and observe their customs."[97] If someone acquires possession of land that used to be subject to Aboriginal title, they acquire an estate free of Aboriginal title and not the title itself.

In Canada, Aboriginal title is based on occupation of land. An Aboriginal right to use land without occupying it is called a *site-specific right*.[98] Although fishing, hunting, trapping, and gathering may amount to occupation of land and thus Aboriginal title, as in *Tsilhqot'in* (2007), the right to engage in one or more of these activities might be a site-specific right to land that is not occupied by that Aboriginal group.[99]

---

96 As quoted by McLachlin J (dissenting) in *Opetchesaht Indian Band v Canada*, [1997] 2 SCR 119 at para 82, 147 DLR (4th) 1.

97 *Mabo No 2*, above note 13 at 60.

98 *Delgamuukw*, above note 92 at paras 138–39; *R v Powley*, [2003] 2 SCR 207, 230 DLR (4th) 1 [cited to DLR] [*Powley*].

99 *R v Adams*, [1996] 3 SCR 101, 138 DLR (4th) 657.

Such a right is similar to but different from a *profit à prendre* at common law (which is discussed in Chapter 7).

In Australia, a site-specific right would be called native title, which is a broader concept than Aboriginal title in Canada. Native title in Australia may be the equivalent to full ownership, as in *Mabo No 2*, or it may be a limited right to fish, hunt, or use land for sacred ceremonies.[100]

3) Proof of Aboriginal Title

Proving the current existence of Aboriginal title can be a long and difficult process. The trial in *Tsilhqot'in* (2007) lasted for 339 days over five years, with proof of continuous occupation since the early nineteenth century provided by oral histories and historical documents.[101] A group that claims Aboriginal title today needs to prove that their right to occupy the land was in existence when the Crown acquired sovereignty over that land:

> In order to make out a claim for aboriginal title, the aboriginal group asserting title must satisfy the following criteria: (i) the land must have been occupied prior to sovereignty, (ii) if present occupation is relied on as proof of occupation pre-sovereignty, there must be a continuity between present and pre-sovereignty occupation, and (iii) at sovereignty, that occupation must have been exclusive.[102]

Proof of occupation before the Crown acquired sovereignty is essential. The common law will recognize and protect pre-existing property rights to land as Aboriginal title, but any new property rights can only be created under the new legal system. Normally, that requires a grant from the Crown.

The requirement that the property right was in existence before the change of sovereignty created a problem for Métis communities that were established soon afterwards. The Supreme Court of Canada held in *R v Powley* that their Aboriginal right to hunt for food would be protected if it arose before the Crown asserted effective control over the land in question:

> While the fact of prior occupation grounds aboriginal rights claims for the Inuit and the Indians, the recognition of Métis rights in s. 35 is not reducible to the Métis' Indian ancestry. The unique status of the Métis as an Aboriginal people with post-contact origins requires

---

100 See, for example, *Yanner v Eaton*, [1999] HCA 53, 201 CLR 351.
101 *Tsilhqot'in* (2007), above note 90.
102 *Delgamuukw*, above note 92 at para 143, Lamer CJ.

an adaptation of the pre-contact approach to meet the distinctive historical circumstances surrounding the evolution of Métis communities. . . .

The focus should be on the period after a particular Métis community arose and before it came under the effective control of European laws and customs. This pre-control test enables us to identify those practices, customs and traditions that predate the imposition of European laws and customs on the Métis.[103]

4) Constitutional Protection of Aboriginal Title

The Crown has the power to accept the surrender of Aboriginal title and to extinguish it through the exercise of radical title, subject to constitutional limits. The distribution of powers between the federal and provincial governments under the *Constitution Act, 1867*[104] provides one limit. Although much of the radical title in Canada is held by the Crown in right of a province,[105] and each province has the exclusive authority to makes laws concerning "Property and Civil Rights in the Province,"[106] the Parliament of Canada has the power to make laws concerning "Indians, and Lands reserved for the Indians."[107]

Other limits on the Crown's powers are provided by the *Canadian Charter of Rights and Freedoms*. Under section 15, everyone "is equal before and under the law and has the right to the equal protection and equal benefit of the law without discrimination and, in particular, without discrimination based on race." This requires the Crown to treat Aboriginal title no less favourably than other similar property rights[108] but does not prevent it being treated more favourably. Section 25 states,

> The guarantee in this Charter of certain rights and freedoms shall not be construed so as to abrogate or derogate from any aboriginal, treaty or other rights or freedoms that pertain to the aboriginal peoples of Canada including (a) any rights or freedoms that have been recognized by the Royal Proclamation of October 7, 1763; and (b) any rights or freedoms that now exist by way of land claims agreements or may be so acquired.

Section 35 provides special protection for Aboriginal rights:

---

103 *Powley*, above note 98 at paras 36–37.
104 (UK), 30 & 31 Vict, c 3, reprinted in RSC 1985, App II, No 5.
105 *Ibid*, s 109.
106 *Ibid*, s 92(13).
107 *Ibid*, s 91(24).
108 See *Mabo v Queensland*, [1988] HCA 69, 166 CLR 186.

(1) The existing aboriginal and treaty rights of the aboriginal peoples of Canada are hereby recognized and affirmed. (2) In this Act, "aboriginal peoples of Canada" includes the Indian, Inuit and Métis peoples of Canada. (3) For greater certainty, in subsection (1) "treaty rights" includes rights that now exist by way of land claims agreements or may be so acquired.

In *Tsilhqot'in* (2014),[109] the Province of British Columbia had granted a licence to a private company to cut trees on land occupied by the Tsilhqot'in people. Under the provincial *Forest Act*,[110] licences could be granted to cut trees on Crown land but not on private land. This meant that there was no authority to grant the licence once Aboriginal title was established and the land was no longer owned by the Crown. McLachlin CJ said:

> I conclude that the legislature intended the Forest Act to apply to lands under claims for Aboriginal title, *up to the time title is confirmed by agreement or court order.* To hold otherwise would be to accept that the legislature intended the forests on such lands to be wholly unregulated.... Once Aboriginal title is confirmed, however, the lands are "vested" in the Aboriginal group and the lands are no longer Crown lands.[111]

The Court went on to consider whether the province had the power to make laws regulating forestry on land that was confirmed to be subject to Aboriginal title. The trial judge had decided that the province did not have that power: "The *Forest Act*, an Act of general application, cannot apply to Aboriginal title land because the impact of its provisions all go to the core of Aboriginal title. The management, acquisition, removal and sale of this Aboriginal asset falls within the protected core of federal jurisdiction."[112] This was overturned by the Supreme Court of Canada:

> Broadly put, provincial laws of general application apply to lands held under Aboriginal title. However, as we shall see, there are important constitutional limits on this proposition.
>
> As a general proposition, provincial governments have the power to regulate land use within the province. This applies to all lands, whether held by the Crown, by private owners, or by the holders of Aboriginal title. The foundation for this power lies in s. 92(13) of the *Constitution Act, 1867*, which gives the provinces the power to legislate with respect to property and civil rights in the province.

109 *Tsilhqot'in* (2014), above note 87.
110 RSBC 1996, c 157.
111 *Tsilhqot'in* (2014), above note 87 at para 115.
112 *Tsilhqot'in* (2007), above note 90 at para 1031, Vickers J.

Provincial power to regulate land held under Aboriginal title is constitutionally limited in two ways. First, it is limited by s. 35 of the *Constitution Act, 1982*. Section 35 requires any abridgment of the rights flowing from Aboriginal title to be backed by a compelling and substantial governmental objective and to be consistent with the Crown's fiduciary relationship with title holders. Second, a province's power to regulate lands under Aboriginal title may in some situations also be limited by the federal power over "Indians, and Lands reserved for the Indians" under s. 91(24) of the *Constitution Act, 1867*.[113]

A law of general application that regulates the use of forests is very different from the grant of a licence that takes a right away from the Aboriginal group and transfers it to someone else:

> General regulatory legislation, which may affect the manner in which the Aboriginal right can be exercised, differs from legislation that assigns Aboriginal property rights to third parties. The issuance of timber licences on Aboriginal title land for example—a direct transfer of Aboriginal property rights to a third party—will plainly be a meaningful diminution in the Aboriginal group's ownership right and will amount to an infringement that must be justified in cases where it is done without Aboriginal consent.[114]

The Crown in right of Canada or a province can act in a way that adversely affects Aboriginal title, but only if it complies with section 35 of the *Charter*:

> To justify overriding the Aboriginal title-holding group's wishes on the basis of the broader public good, the government must show: (1) that it discharged its procedural duty to consult and accommodate; (2) that its actions were backed by a compelling and substantial objective; and (3) that the governmental action is consistent with the Crown's fiduciary obligation to the group.[115]

---

113 *Tsilhqot'in* (2014), above note 87 at paras 101–3, McLachlin CJ.
114 *Ibid* at para 124, McLachlin CJ.
115 *Ibid* at para 77, McLachlin CJ.

CHAPTER 4

EQUITY AND TRUSTS

A. EQUITY

Rights may be legal or equitable. This distinction is the product of the court system that existed in England before 1875. The common law was administered by the courts of Common Pleas, King's Bench, and Exchequer, whereas equity was administered by the Court of Chancery.[1] Those courts were merged into a single High Court of Justice in the 1870s, but common law and equity continue to exist as separate bodies of law administered by the unified court.

In most common law jurisdictions around the world, equity is no longer administered by a separate court of chancery but by a superior court that applies both common law and equity. For example, in Ontario, "[t]he Superior Court of Justice has all the jurisdiction, power and authority historically exercised by courts of common law and equity in England and Ontario."[2] Although it administers both common law and equity, they continue to exist as two separate bodies of law:

---

1   See John Baker, *An Introduction to English Legal History*, 5th ed (Oxford: Oxford University Press, 2019) chs 3 and 6.

2   *Courts of Justice Act*, RSO 1990, c C.43, s 11(2). See also *Law and Equity Act*, RSBC 1996, c 253, s 1; *Judicature Act*, RSA 2000, c J-2, s 5; *Queen's Bench Act, 1998*, SS c Q-1.01, s 51.1; *Court of Queen's Bench Act*, CCSM, c C280, s 32; *Judicature Act*, RSNB 1973, c J-2, s 9; *Judicature Act*, RSNS 1989, c 240, s 3; *Judicature Act*, RSPEI 1988, c J-2.1, s 2; *Judicature Act*, RSNL 1990, c J-4, s 3; *Judicature Act*, RSNWT 1988, c J-1, s 9; *Judicature Act*, SNWT (Nu) 1998, c 34, s 2.

Rules of law and equity

(1) Courts shall administer concurrently all rules of equity and the common law.

Rules of equity to prevail

(2) Where a rule of equity conflicts with a rule of the common law, the rule of equity prevails.[3]

It is not always easy to tell whether a right is legal or equitable. That depends on which court would have had jurisdiction if the proceedings took place in England prior to 1875. The right is legal if it would have been enforced in a court of common law and equitable if it could only be enforced in the Court of Chancery. This may seem like an odd way to tell them apart, but there is probably no better method. As Professor Maitland said,

> For suppose that we ask the question—What is Equity? We can only answer it by giving some short account of certain courts of justice which were abolished.... [W]e might have said "Equity is that body of rules which is administered only by those Courts which are known as Courts of Equity." The definition would not have been very satis- factory, but now-a-days we are cut off even from this unsatisfactory definition. We have no longer any courts which are merely courts of equity. Thus we are driven to say that Equity now is that body of rules administered by our ... courts of justice which, were it not for the operation of the Judicature Acts, would be administered only by those courts which would be known as Courts of Equity. This, you may well say, is but a poor thing to call a definition. Equity is a certain portion of our existing substantive law, and yet in order that we may describe this portion and mark it off from other portions we have to make reference to courts that are no longer in existence. Still I fear that nothing better is possible.[4]

You may wonder why it matters whether a right is legal or equitable if both rights are enforced in the same court. The distinction is import- ant in property law for two main reasons. First, the manner in which

---

3   *Courts of Justice Act*, RSO 1990, c C.43, s 96. See also *Law and Equity Act*, RSBC 1996, c 253, ss 4, 5, 7, 44; *Judicature Act*, RSA 2000, c J-2, ss 15, 16; *Queen's Bench Act, 1998*, SS c Q-1.01, s 52; *Court of Queen's Bench Act*, CCSM, c C280, s 33; *Judicature Act*, RSNB 1973, c J-2, s 26; *Judicature Act*, RSNS 1989, c 240, s 41; *Judicature Act*, RSPEI 1988, c J-2.1, s 39; *Judicature Act*, RSNL 1990, c J-4, ss 90, 107; *Judicature Act*, RSY 2002, c 128, ss 7, 29; *Judicature Act*, RSNWT 1988, c J-1, ss 22, 45; *Judicature Act*, SNWT (Nu) 1998, c 34, ss 21, 42.

4   FW Maitland, *Equity, Also the Forms of Action at Common Law: Two Courses of Lectures* (Cambridge: Cambridge University Press, 1929) at 1.

estates and other interests in land are created or transferred depends on whether they are legal or equitable. Generally speaking, more formality is required to create or transfer a legal interest than for an equitable interest. For example, the grant of a ten-year legal lease is achieved by execution or registration of a deed, whereas a ten-year equitable lease requires only an enforceable contract. This is discussed in Chapter 8.

Second, legal property rights tend to be more durable than equitable rights. In a competition between inconsistent property rights to the same thing, a legal right is more likely to prevail over an equitable right. It is true that a rule of equity will prevail if it conflicts with a rule of the common law, but rules are not the same as rights. Equitable rights are more fragile according to the rules of equity. This is discussed in Chapter 9.

Even though we must travel back to Victorian England to determine whether a right is equitable or legal, that does not mean that equity is frozen in time. Like the common law, it continues to evolve as judges modify the rules of equity in response to a changing world. Legislatures have also had an important role to play. Many equitable rules have been modified by statute. For example, most common law jurisdictions have a *Trustee Act* dealing with the rights and duties of trustees (discussed below). The Court of Chancery had exclusive jurisdiction over trusts, so any statutory rights conferred on trustees and trust beneficiaries are equitable. Chancery also had jurisdiction over companies and partnerships, and both areas of law have been heavily modified by statute.

B. EQUITABLE REMEDIES

Another reason why equity remains important today is the range of equitable remedies that are available. The term *remedy* is used in the law to refer to several different forms of relief. We are concerned here with *judicial* remedies, which are the orders that a court might make. They are different from *self-help* remedies, which are the steps people can take to enforce their rights without going to court. They are also different from *civil enforcement* remedies, which are the mechanisms available to enforce compliance with court orders.

Two main remedies are available at law to enforce private legal rights: a defendant can be ordered to pay a sum of money to the plaintiff (as payment of a debt or as damages for breach of contract or a tort) or to deliver possession of land or goods to the plaintiff.[5] In some cases,

---

5   There are also several other common law judicial remedies available when making claims against the government, including *certiorari*, *habeas corpus*, and *mandamus*.

an award of damages will be inadequate to achieve justice between the parties. In the days before the courts were merged, a plaintiff could go to the Court of Chancery to seek an equitable remedy.

Four equitable remedies are especially important in the law of property: injunctions, specific performance, rescission, and rectification. Injunctions are usually *prohibitive* (i.e., an order to stop doing something), but they can also be *mandatory* (i.e., an order to do something). They can also be *interim* (pending trial) or *permanent*. For example, a plaintiff might seek an injunction ordering a defendant to stop trespassing on their land or to stop violating a restriction on the use of land.[6]

If a defendant refuses to perform their contractual obligations to the plaintiff, a court might order specific performance of the contract if an award of damages for breach of contract would be inadequate. For example, if I made a contract to sell my house to you and refused to perform it, the damages may be relatively trivial if the purchase price was equal to market value, yet your disappointment may be significant if similar houses are not available on the market. In that case, a court may order me to perform the contract and transfer the house to you.[7]

Rescission is the process of undoing a transaction and restoring the parties to their previous positions, which is called *restitutio in integrum*. It is available at common law for a few reasons, most notably when the plaintiff entered into the transaction because of fraud or duress. Rescission is available in equity for a wider variety of reasons, including transactions induced by innocent misrepresentations or undue influence. Equitable rescission can also be used in cases of fraud or duress where rescission is not available at common law because *restitutio in integrum* is no longer possible. In *Alati v Kruger*, the High Court of Australia said,

> Equity has always regarded as valid the disaffirmance of a contract induced by fraud even though precise *restitutio in integrum* is not possible, if the situation is such that, by the exercise of its powers, including the power to take accounts of profits and to direct inquiries as to allowances proper to be made for deterioration, it can do what is practically just between the parties, and by so doing restore them substantially to the *status quo*.[8]

Rectification is the process of correcting errors in a written document. Normally, this requires a common mistake by both parties in which the document did not accurately record the transaction that they intended to

---

6   See, for example, *1465152 Ontario Ltd v Amexon Development Inc*, 2015 ONCA 86.

7   See, for example, *Raymond v Anderson*, 2011 SKCA 58.

8   [1955] HCA 64, 94 CLR 216 at 223–24, Dixon CJ, Webb, Kitto, & Taylor JJ. See also *Kellogg Brown & Root Inc v Aerotech Herman Nelson Inc*, 2004 MBCA 63.

make. Rectification is also available where one party is mistaken and the other party knows it. But if the other party was not aware of the mistake when the document was signed, then rectification is not available.[9]

C. TRUSTS

A trust is a relationship between trustees and beneficiaries in which the trustees are the owners of trust assets that they are required to use according to the terms of the trust for the benefit of the beneficiaries. The assets held in trust are the *subject* of the trust. The beneficiaries of the trust are its *objects*.

1) The Settlor

A person who creates a trust is called a *settlor*. That term comes from a time when most trusts were created as family settlements for the management and distribution of assets over several generations.[10] The creator of a trust is still called a settlor even if the trust is not a family settlement.

The settlor may also be a trustee or beneficiary of the trust, but they need not be. They might have no further connection with the trust they create (and that will always be the case when a trust is created by the will of a deceased settlor).

Some trusts do not have settlors but arise by operation of law when a trust is imposed on the owner of assets to compel them to use those assets for the benefit of another person. In essence, those assets should belong to that other person according to the rules of equity, and the trust is the mechanism employed to make that happen. This is discussed in Chapter 8.

2) Subject of the Trust

Almost any assignable rights *in rem* or *in personam* can be held in trust. Estates in land are often held in trust, but so are bank accounts, company shares, and contractual rights. There are some rights that cannot be held in trust because they are personal to the right holder, such as a right to vote in a parliamentary election, a driver's licence, or a licence

---

9   See *Riverlate Properties Ltd v Paul*, [1975] Ch 133 (CA); *Performance Industries Ltd v Sylvan Lake Golf & Tennis Club Ltd*, 2002 SCC 19.

10   Baker, above note 1 at 313–15.

to practise dentistry.[11] A commercial fishing licence can be held in trust because it is assignable.[12] Although the subject of a trust is often called the *trust property*, the term "assets" is used here because rights *in personam* (such as bank accounts) are often held in trust.

When a trust is created, the trustees will receive ownership of the trust assets (if they do not own them already). The trust does not take away that ownership or any of the rights and powers that go with it. The trustees have the rights and powers to sell the assets or give them away, lease or lend them out, receive the income or proceeds of sale, and sue others for wrongful interference with those assets. In short, the trustees still have all the incidents of ownership described by Professor Honoré (and discussed in Chapter 2).[13] However, the rules of equity prohibit the trustees from using those rights and powers for their own benefit (except for the rights to reimburse themselves for any legitimate trust expenses and to pay themselves remuneration for services as trustees). They are required to use their rights and powers of ownership for the benefit of the beneficiaries in accordance with the terms of the trust.

When something is held in trust, the subject of the trust is not that thing but the trustee's right to it. For example, if I held my house in trust for you, the subject of the trust is not the house. It is my fee simple estate. The physical space on the earth is the subject of my fee simple estate, and that fee simple estate (i.e., my legal right to possess that space) is the subject of the trust. Trusts operate in a parasitic way, attaching to the trustee's rights to things and not directly to the things themselves.[14]

In the same way, if I hold a bank account in trust for you, I am the bank's customer with the right to receive payment of the balance of the account, but I am required to use that right for your benefit. You have no legal relationship with the bank and will normally have no claims against it whatsoever.

3) The Beneficiaries

A trust may have many trustees and beneficiaries (such as a pension fund trust with a board of trustees and thousands of beneficiaries), but it can exist with only one trustee and one beneficiary. A trustee can also be a beneficiary, but a trust relationship requires at least two different people. Two people can be trustees for one of them or one person can be the sole

---

11   *Caratun v Caratun* (1992), 96 DLR (4th) 404, 10 OR (3d) 385 (CA).

12   *Saulnier v Royal Bank of Canada*, 2008 SCC 58; discussed in Chapter 1.

13   AM Honoré, "Ownership" in AG Guest, ed, *Oxford Essays in Jurisprudence* (Oxford: Oxford University Press, 1961) 107.

14   See *Pallot v Douglas*, 2017 BCCA 254 at para 32.

trustee and a beneficiary so long as there is at least one other beneficiary. One person cannot be the sole trustee and the sole beneficiary. People cannot be in relationships with themselves, owe duties to themselves, or enforce rights against themselves. Trusts are equitable relationships and cannot exist unless there is at least one beneficiary who can enforce their equitable rights against at least one trustee who is a different person. As Roxburgh J explained in *Re Astor's Settlement Trusts,*

> The typical case of a trust is one in which the legal owner of property is constrained by a court of equity so to deal with it as to give effect to the equitable rights of another. These equitable rights have been hammered out in the process of litigation in which a claimant on equitable grounds has successfully asserted rights against a legal owner or other person in control of property. *Prima facie*, therefore, a trustee would not be expected to be subject to an equitable obligation unless there was somebody who could enforce a correlative equitable right, and the nature and extent of that obligation would be worked out in proceedings for enforcement.[15]

This is called the *beneficiary principle*, and there is one major exception to it: trusts for charitable purposes do not have beneficiaries but are enforced on behalf of the Crown, as discussed below. A trust without beneficiaries for non-charitable purposes is invalid in most jurisdictions primarily because there is no one to enforce it. There are several "offshore" jurisdictions, such as the British Virgin Islands, the Cayman Islands, and Jersey, in which it is possible to create a trust for non-charitable purposes if someone is appointed as its *enforcer*.[16] This is a modification of the rules of equity by statute.

Trust beneficiaries must be legal persons (i.e., human beings or corporations) but need not have legal capacity. Trusts are often created for infants or other people who lack the capacity to manage their own affairs.[17]

Although beneficiaries may be identified by name, they are often identified as a class, such as a trust for the settlor's grandchildren or for the employees of a company.[18] When a trust is created for a class of beneficiaries, it is usually so that new beneficiaries may be added to the class automatically in the future (e.g., when grandchildren are born or employees are hired). A potential future beneficiary is not a beneficiary and can have no rights under the trust, but the trustees are required

---

15   [1952] Ch 534 at 541.

16   See, for example, *Trust (Jersey) Law 1984*, art 12.

17   See, for example, *SA v Metro Vancouver Housing Corp*, 2019 SCC 4.

18   See, for example, *McPhail v Doulton*, [1970] UKHL 1, [1971] AC 424.

to consider the potential rights of future beneficiaries when making decisions regarding the management and disposition of trust assets. For example, if I created a trust for my children and grandchildren but did not have any grandchildren, the trustees would still have to consider the potential claims of future grandchildren when investing the trust assets or making payments to my children.

4) Charitable Purposes

It is possible to create a trust for charitable purposes that has no beneficiaries at all. This is the main exception to the beneficiary principle that a trust cannot exist unless there is a beneficiary who can enforce it. Trusts for charitable purposes are enforced by the attorney general on behalf of the Crown. In practice, charities in Canada are overseen by the Canada Revenue Agency (CRA). As Samuel Singer said,

> Charities receive a hefty "double-barrelled" tax subsidy, benefitting from both their tax-exempt status and from the tax incentive that taxpayers receive for their donations. To obtain and maintain access to this subsidy, charities must conform to legal obligations about their activities, governance, and financial management, drawn primarily from the ITA and the Canadian common law. The CRA is the primary charity sector regulator in Canada, administering both the registration process and all oversight of activities related to maintaining charitable status.[19]

Most modern charities are non-profit corporations, but most law students encounter charity only when they study trusts. There are two main reasons for this. First, the law of charity developed at a time when most charities were trusts. Second, this exception to the beneficiary principle is a major anomaly that needs to be explained.

To be charitable, a purpose must be beneficial to the public and fall under one of the recognized heads of charity at common law. The heads of charity were divided into four main categories: "'Charity' in its legal sense comprises four principal divisions: trusts for the relief of poverty; trusts for the advancement of education; trusts for the advancement of religion; and trusts for other purposes beneficial to the community, not falling under any of the preceding heads."[20]

---

19   See Samuel Singer, "Charity Law Reform in Canada: Moving from Patchwork to Substantive Reform" (2020) 57 *Alta L Rev* 683 at 686. The *ITA* is the *Income Tax Act*, RSC 1985, c 1 (5th Supp).

20   *Income Tax Commissioners v Pemsel*, [1891] UKHL 1, [1891] AC 531 at 583, Lord Macnaghten.

This scheme is not that helpful since the fourth category contains a very large variety of purposes, such as the relief of old or disabled people, care for young people, public works, administration of justice, relief of prisoners, care for the sick, and animal welfare.

A trust that does not provide a benefit to the public will not be charitable even if its purpose falls under one of the recognized heads. For example, a trust for the education of the settlor's grandchildren is a trust for the advancement of their education and will provide a substantial benefit to them but does not provide a benefit to the public. It is a trust for a class of private persons. In *Oppenheim v Tobacco Securities Trust Co*,[21] a trust was created for the education of the children of more than 110,000 employees of a group of companies. Despite the large number of children who could benefit, it was not a benefit to the general public because eligibility was defined by a relationship to a specific person: the company that employed your parent.

Conversely, a purpose that does provide a genuine benefit to the public will not be charitable if it does not fall under one of the common law heads of charity. Trusts to promote sports are charitable only if they provide for the advancement of education, such as sports played in schools and universities.[22] The Supreme Court of Canada held that the Amateur Youth Soccer Association is not a charity even though its object is the promotion of amateur soccer in Ontario.[23] This is undoubtedly beneficial to the public, but it is not a head of charity. Rothstein J said, "While it may be desirable as a matter of policy to give sports associations the tax advantages of charitable status, it is a task better suited to Parliament than the courts."[24]

A trust for a charitable purpose does not have beneficiaries even if it is possible to identify a class of people who benefit from the performance of that purpose. For example, a trust to provide shelter for homeless people in Kamloops would be a charitable trust for the relief of poverty. Although the people who might benefit from that trust could be identified, they would not be beneficiaries. They would acquire no rights enforceable against the trustees and have no standing to sue them. Any claims of breach of trust would have to be brought on behalf of the Crown.

---

21 [1950] UKHL 2, [1951] AC 297.
22 *Re Nottage*, [1895] 2 Ch 649.
23 *AYSA v Canada (Revenue Agency)*, 2007 SCC 42.
24 *Ibid* at para 44.

5) Duties of Trustees

Most trustees have a number of duties to perform, which can be organized into four main categories: the duty to obey the trust, the duty to account to the beneficiaries, the duty to take reasonable care, and the fiduciary duty to exercise their powers only for proper purposes. First and foremost, the trustees must obey the terms of the trust and the rules of equity that apply to that trust. Trustees will be strictly liable for losses caused by their failure to obey the trust even if they acted honestly and reasonably. For example, in *Eaves v Hickson*,[25] the trustees were deceived by a forged document that caused them to pay trust money to people who were not beneficiaries. Romilly MR said,

> This is a very hard case on the trustees who were deceived by the forgery of the date in the marriage certificate, which had been altered in a manner which deceived them, and would have deceived anyone who was not looking out for forgery or fraud. The question is, where a forgery is committed, and a person wrongfully gets trust money which cannot be recovered from him, on whom is the loss to fall? I am of opinion, that it falls on the person who paid the money. Here the loss falls on the trustees, and the persons to whom the fund really belongs are not to be deprived of it. The trustee is bound to pay the trust fund to the right person.[26]

Second, the trustees must provide accounts to their beneficiaries (or to the CRA if the trust is for charitable purposes). As Plumer MR said in *Pearse v Green*, "It is the first duty of an accounting party, whether an agent, a trustee, a receiver, or an executor ... to be constantly ready with his accounts."[27] This requires the trustees to keep accurate records (including receipts), have the accounts ready for inspection, make the accounts and trust documents available to those who are entitled to see them, account at regular intervals as required by law or the terms of the trust, and provide final accounts when the trust comes to an end.

Third, the trustees owe a duty of care to preserve the trust assets from loss.[28] If they have a power to invest, they must take care to obtain an appropriate return from investments. They must also take reasonable care when selecting agents, such as stockbrokers or realtors, and

---

25   (1861) 30 Beav 136, 54 ER 840 [cited to ER].
26   *Ibid* at 842.
27   (1819) 1 J & W 135 at 140, 37 ER 327. See also *Sandford v Porter* (1889), 16 OAR 565 (CA).
28   *Fales v Canada Permanent Trust Co*, [1977] 2 SCR 302, 70 DLR (3d) 257.

monitor their performance.[29] So long as the trustees act with reasonable care (and obey the trust), they will not be in breach of trust even if their actions (or failure to act) cause a loss of trust assets or their value.

Finally, trustees normally owe a fiduciary duty to the beneficiaries. The term *fiduciary* comes from the Latin *fiducia*, which means trust. Trustees are not the only fiduciaries. The duty also applies to other people who manage the assets or affairs of others, such as agents, partners, company directors, guardians, and solicitors. The essence of the fiduciary duty is that discretionary powers should be exercised on behalf of others properly and only for the purposes for which they were conferred.

The problem in this area of law is knowing whether or not a discretion was exercised properly. It can be difficult to know exactly why someone made a decision. They may have acted properly in accordance with their fiduciary duty to be impartial and take only relevant factors into account, but often no one knows for sure (and that may include the decision maker, since we have unconscious biases). This problem is compounded in the law of trusts because (unlike many public officials) trustees are not required to give reasons for their decisions.[30]

The equitable rules regarding fiduciary duties address this problem by making it a breach of fiduciary duty to act in a way that might adversely affect the decision-making process regardless of whether or not that process is affected. The following can amount to a breach of fiduciary duty even if the trustees acted with complete honesty: (1) taking irrelevant factors into account or failing to take relevant factors into account when making a decision,[31] (2) failing to exercise a discretion and simply following orders,[32] (3) having personal interests or other duties that conflict with the duties to the beneficiaries unless those conflicts are authorized,[33] and (4) making unauthorized profits from the office.[34] Simply having a reason to prefer self-interest or other interests over the interests of the beneficiaries is a breach of fiduciary duty even if the trustee did not, in fact, yield to that temptation.

The office of trustee is onerous, and it is now common for trust instruments to contain broad exemption clauses that protect trustees from personal liability for breach of trust, so long as they acted honestly

29   *Wagner v Van Cleeff* (1991), 5 OR (3d) 477 (Div Ct).
30   *Re Londonderry's Settlement*, [1965] Ch 918 (CA).
31   See *Pitt v Holt*, [2013] UKSC 26, [2013] 2 AC 108.
32   *Turner v Turner*, [1984] Ch 100.
33   See *Cowan v Scargill*, [1985] Ch 270; *Strother v 3464920 Canada Inc*, 2007 SCC 24.
34   See *Boardman v Phipps*, [1966] UKHL 2, [1967] 2 AC 46; *ICBC v Lo*, 2006 BCCA 584.

and in good faith.[35] In addition, the court has a statutory power to relieve trustees from liability for breach of trust if they have "acted honestly and reasonably, and ought fairly to be excused for the breach of trust."[36]

6) Modern Discretionary Trusts

In a traditional family settlement, the interests of the beneficiaries are allocated by the settlor when the trust is created. For example, the settlor might create a trust in their will with the income paid to the surviving spouse for life and then to their children in equal shares until age thirty, at which time they become entitled to the capital. The trustees would normally be given some discretion, for example, to encroach on the capital to increase the income paid to the spouse or to advance part of a child's share to them at a younger age. The discretion allowed the trustees some freedom to deal with changing circumstances, but each beneficiary's interest was more or less fixed by the terms of the trust.

During the twentieth century, the standard forms of trust began to confer more and more discretion on the trustees, and it is now common for settlors to create *modern discretionary trusts*, in which the interests of the beneficiaries are not defined and the distribution of trust assets among them is left entirely to the trustees' discretion. The trustees decide whether to distribute income and capital and to whom it should be paid in which amounts for a number of years.[37] Anything left over is then paid to a named charity.

This modern discretionary trust has two main advantages. First, the trustees are better able to deal with changing circumstances, both among the beneficiaries and in the investment markets. Second, the beneficiaries do not have interests in the trust assets that can be taxed or taken to pay their creditors. Although a beneficiary might receive a

---

35 See *Armitage v Nurse*, [1997] EWCA Civ 1279, [1998] Ch 241.

36 *Trustee Act*, RSBC 1996, c 464, s 96. See also *Trustee Act*, RSA 2000, c T-8, s 41; *Trustee Act, 2009*, SS 2009, c T-23.01, s 45; *Trustee Act*, CCSM, c T160, s 81; *Trustee Act*, RSO 1990, c T.23, s 35; *Trustees Act*, SNB 2015, c 21, s 79; *Trustee Act*, RSNS 1989, c 479, s 64; *Trustee Act*, RSNL 1990, c T-10, s 32; *Trustee Act*, RSY 2002, c 223, s 33; *Trustee Act*, RSNWT 1988, c T-8, s 30. This provision was copied from England and is found in jurisdictions throughout the Commonwealth but not in Prince Edward Island.

37 In many jurisdictions, the duration of the trust is set according to the perpetuity period in that jurisdiction (e.g., eighty or 125 years). In Canada, the time limit is often set at twenty-one years because discretionary trusts are taxed on their deemed capital gains every twenty-one years: *Income Tax Act*, above note 19, s 104(4).

great deal of money from the trust over the years, they are not entitled to a single penny. It is up to the trustees to decide whether they will receive anything at all. A beneficiary's creditors can have no greater right to the trust assets than does the beneficiary. If the beneficiary had a fixed interest, their right to receive income or capital would be available to their creditors. Also, since the beneficiary of a modern discretionary trust does not have an interest in the trust assets, they may even be eligible for rent subsidies and other forms of social assistance that are not available to people with significant assets.[38]

7) Rights of Beneficiaries

The trustees' duties are owed to the beneficiaries, which means that the beneficiaries hold the rights that correspond to those duties. Every beneficiary has standing to bring a claim against the trustees, even if the beneficiary is an infant (in which case the claim would be brought on their behalf by a parent or guardian). A beneficiary has standing to sue even if they are unlikely to receive any benefit from the trust. For example, the beneficiary of a modern discretionary trust has a right to complain about a breach of trust even though they have no right to receive benefits from the trust.

One issue that has been debated for centuries is whether trust beneficiaries have rights *in personam* or rights *in rem*.[39] Their rights correspond to the trustees' duties and normally are enforced only against their trustees who have undertaken that office. For example, the beneficiaries' rights that the trustees take reasonable care and avoid conflicts of interest are rights enforceable only against the specific persons who have agreed to be trustees and so are rights *in personam*.

If that was all there was to it, there would be no debate. However, the beneficiaries can also enforce rights against strangers to the trust in certain circumstances. If trust assets are transferred to a stranger in breach of trust, the beneficiaries may be able to sue them to recover the trust assets or their value.[40] The stranger cannot be forced to carry out the trustee's duties to obey the terms of the trust, avoid conflicts of interest, and so on, but once they become aware that they hold assets transferred to them in breach of trust, they have a duty to preserve those assets and restore them to the proper trustees. In other words,

---

38   *SA v Metro Vancouver Housing Corp*, above note 17.

39   Baker, above note 1 at 328–29.

40   *BC Teachers' Credit Union v Betterly* (1975), 61 DLR (3d) 755 (BCSC); *Foskett v McKeown*, [2000] UKHL 29, [2001] 1 AC 102.

most of the beneficiaries' rights are rights *in personam* enforceable only against their trustees, but they do have one right that is enforceable generally against others, which is the right that the trust assets are held by persons who have been properly appointed as trustees. Although the stranger is not under a duty to perform the trust, those assets are trust assets in their hands. They cannot be used to pay the stranger's creditors because they belong in equity to the beneficiaries.

The beneficiaries' right to recover trust assets from a stranger probably developed slowly over time. What began as a right enforceable only against the trustee was extended to be enforceable against someone who received the trust assets knowing that they had been transferred in breach of trust. This was extended again to include someone who ought to have known about the breach and to anyone who received the assets as a gift, even if they had no reason to suspect a breach of trust. The donee of a gift can have no better right to it than the donor had.

Conceptually, this can be understood as a right *in personam* that was enforced against an ever-increasing group of people, but at some point our understanding of this flipped. We now regard the beneficiary's right to recover misapplied trust assets as a right that is enforceable against anyone who receives them except for someone who purchases them honestly, in good faith, and without any reason to suspect a breach of trust. In other words, the beneficiary has a right *in rem* enforceable generally against others but subject to the stranger's defence of bona fide purchase for value without notice. That defence is discussed in Chapter 9.

8) Beneficial Ownership

The trustees are the owners of the assets, but unless they are also beneficiaries, they are not allowed to use the rights and powers of ownership for their own benefit (except for reimbursement of trust expenses and remuneration for trustee services). Trustees who are not beneficiaries have *bare legal title*, whereas all the benefits of their ownership are enjoyed by the beneficiaries. The concept of *beneficial ownership* is a recognition of the fact that ownership and the benefits of ownership do not always belong to the same person.

Since trust beneficiaries have beneficial ownership of the trust assets according to the rules of equity, there is a common misperception that beneficial ownership is the same as *equitable ownership*. Most beneficial ownership has nothing to do with trusts or equity. Beneficial ownership simply means ownership for one's own benefit. Since most things are not held in trust, most beneficial ownership is legal ownership. We have legal title to most of the things we own and are free to use those legal rights for our own benefit. Unless a trust is created, there is no equitable ownership in existence. As Patten LJ said in *Swift 1st Ltd v Chief Land Registrar*, there are "limited circumstances in which the legal owner of property does not also enjoy full beneficial ownership. Absent a trust, the legal estate carries with it all rights to the property and equity has no role to play in separating legal from beneficial ownership."[41]

If there is more than one trust beneficiary, they share beneficial ownership of the trust assets, which can be distributed in many different ways. For example, the surviving spouse might be entitled to the income for life, after which the children share the capital equally. They have defined interests in the trust assets. In a discretionary trust, none of the beneficiaries has a defined share, yet, collectively, they are regarded as the beneficial owners of the trust assets. For example, suppose that trustees have the power to distribute the income and capital of the trust among the settlor's four children for twenty-one years, and if anything is left over, it will then be transferred to the Canadian Red Cross Society. No one can compel the trustees to pay them anything, yet, collectively, the children and the Red Cross are entitled to everything. All the assets will be distributed, one way or another, among the five of them.

There is a rule of equity that if all the beneficiaries are competent adults (or corporations), they can agree to end the trust and take the assets for themselves. This is called the rule in *Saunders v Vautier*,[42] after the most famous case in which it was applied. The Red Cross could agree with the children (if they were all competent adults) to divide the assets among themselves.[43] The trust was created entirely for their benefit, and they are the only persons with any right to compel the trustees to perform the trust. They are not bound to keep the trust going for their own benefit if they would rather do something else with the assets. The rule does not apply in Alberta,[44] Manitoba,[45] or the United States,[46] but even in those jurisdictions, the beneficial ownership of the trust assets belongs to the beneficiaries.

The concept of beneficial ownership will be encountered again in Chapter 6 concerning security interests. When a creditor acquires a property right to the debtor's property to secure payment of the debt, they do not acquire beneficial ownership even if they take legal title for

---

41   [2015] EWCA Civ 330, [2015] Ch 602 at para 41. See also *DKLR Holding Co (No 2) Pty Ltd v Commissioner of Stamp Duties*, [1982] HCA 14, 149 CLR 431.

42   (1841) Cr & Ph 240, 41 ER 482.

43   See *Tod v Barton*, [2002] EWHC 265 (Ch), 4 ITELR 715.

44   *Trustee Act*, RSA 2000, c T-8, s 42.

45   *Trustee Act*, CCSM, c T160, s 59.

46   *Claflin v Claflin*, 20 NE 454 (Mass 1889).

that purpose. The debtor is the beneficial owner. For example, if your house is mortgaged to the bank, you are the beneficial owner of the house and the bank holds a security interest, even if the amount owed to the bank equals the market value of the house.

One way to identify the person with beneficial ownership is to ask who has the hope of gain and bears the risk of loss. If your house goes up or down in value, that does not change the amount owed to the bank. You benefit from any rise in value and suffer any loss. The same is true for trust beneficiaries. Any increase in the value of the trust assets is for their benefit, and they will suffer any losses. The trustees are unaffected so long as the losses are not caused by their breach of trust.

CHAPTER 5

CO-OWNERSHIP

A. INTRODUCTION

As discussed in Chapter 3, rights can be allocated *successively* over time (e.g., to my widow for life and then to my daughter in fee simple). This chapter explains how rights can be shared *concurrently*, with two or more people sharing them at the same time. There are two main ways in which rights can be shared: *jointly* or *in common*. These are often called *joint tenancy* and *tenancy in common*, in reference to the tenants of freehold or leasehold estates, but all kinds of rights can be shared jointly or in common, including bank accounts and other rights *in personam*.

Joint and common ownership are not the only ways in which rights can be shared. As discussed in the previous chapter, the assets of a modern discretionary trust are distributed among the beneficiaries through the exercise of the trustees' discretion. As discussed below, condominiums allow people to divide up the possession of land, with some parts possessed individually and other parts collectively.

Two other forms of co-ownership are no longer in use. Prior to the *Married Women's Property Act 1882*[1] in the United Kingdom (and later in Canada), married women had only a limited capacity to own property because their legal property rights would be transferred to their husbands on marriage. If land was conveyed to a husband and wife, it

---

1   45 & 46 Vict, c 75.

would create a *tenancy by entireties*.[2] Back when real property would pass on the owner's death to their heir, a *co-parcenary* would be created if two or more daughters shared the property as heirs.[3]

This chapter deals first with the differences between joint and common ownership. It then explains *severance*, which is the process of changing joint ownership into common ownership, and *partition*, which is the process of bringing co-ownership to an end and dividing up the assets (or their sale proceeds). The chapter ends with a brief look at condominiums.

B. JOINT AND COMMON OWNERSHIP

There are two main differences between joint and common ownership. First, the interests of joint tenants must be identical, whereas the interests of tenants in common can differ from each other. Second, joint tenants have the *right of survivorship* (sometimes called the *jus accrescendi*), but tenants in common do not. When a joint tenant dies, their interest ceases to exist, and the surviving joint tenants keep the asset for themselves. If there is only one surviving joint tenant, then the joint tenancy has come to an end, and the survivor is the sole owner. When a tenant in common dies, their interest continues after their death and will be transferred by will or on intestacy to someone who will join the survivors as a tenant in common.

1) Four Unities

Joint tenancies must be identical in four different respects called the *four unities*: unity of possession, unity of interest, unity of title, and unity of time. Tenancies in common may have all four unities, but that is not required. The only unity required for a tenancy in common to exist is unity of possession.

Unity of possession means that all tenants share possession at the same time. If it is missing, then there is no co-ownership. The tenants will instead have possession at different times (e.g., a life estate followed by a remainder) or possession of different things (e.g., land subdivided into separate parcels).

---

2   See *Re Demaiter and Link*, [1973] 3 OR 140 (SC).
3   See John Baker, *An Introduction to English Legal History*, 5th ed (Oxford: Oxford University Press, 2019) at 287–88.

The requirement that tenants have unity of possession arose in the context of estates. Co-tenants share the same estate (i.e., the same right to possess the land), but other rights can also be shared. It is common for two people to have a joint bank account. It does not make much sense to talk of unity of possession when the right being shared is not a right to possession. When a non-possessory right is shared, unity of possession is satisfied if the right is held by two or more people at the same time.

Unity of interest means that each tenant has the same interest in the right they hold together. This is required for joint tenants, who hold the right collectively as if they were one person. There are no distinctions among them. Joint tenants do not have equal shares. Despite the language of shared rights (which is hard to avoid), there are no shares in a joint tenancy. Normally, joint tenants must act in unison if they want to deal with their right (e.g., to transfer, lease, or mortgage it). However, a joint tenant can act alone to sever the joint tenancy and turn it into a tenancy in common if they want to have a share that they can deal with on their own.

Tenancy in common is conceptually different from a joint tenancy. Each tenant has a share in the right they hold together. They are called *undivided shares* because the tenants have unity of possession; therefore, each tenant is entitled to possession of the whole regardless of the size of their share. Tenants in common may have equal shares but can also share unequally (as expressed in fractions or percentages). For a tenancy in common, unity of interest really means equality of interest.

Unity of title means that co-tenants derive their title from the same instrument, such as a transfer of land, will, or declaration of trust. *Unity of time* means that they acquired their interests at the same time. These two unities usually go together, but it is possible to have one without the other. For example, I might create a trust for my grandchildren, with grandchildren becoming beneficiaries at different times as they are born. They will all derive their interests from the same declaration of trust but will not have unity of time.

A joint tenancy normally requires both unity of title and unity of time, but there are exceptions. Trustees usually hold the trust assets as joint tenants, but trustees may be replaced from time to time. It is possible for retiring and continuing trustees to transfer all the assets to the new and continuing trustees as joint tenants to preserve the unities of title and time, but a simpler method is provided by statute. Every jurisdiction has a *Trustee Act* (or *Trustees Act*), which provides that the new and continuing trustees will be joint tenants without the need for a transfer.[4] Also, the beneficiaries of a trust can acquire joint ownership even though their interests arise at different times.[5]

2) Joint or Common?

When assets are acquired by more than one person, it is sometimes difficult to tell whether they are joint tenants or tenants in common. There is no co-ownership if there is no unity of possession. If they have unity of possession but no unity of interest, then it must be a tenancy in common. If those two unities are present but unity of title or time is missing, then it is normally a tenancy in common, but there are exceptions, as discussed above.

If all four unities are present, then it could be either joint or common ownership. That depends primarily on what was intended by the person who transferred or created the shared right. In an ideal world, the relevant document would simply say "as joint tenants" or "as tenants in common," but sometimes that information is missing or unclear or the document contains mixed messages.

The common law used to prefer joint tenancies over tenancies in common because it made things simpler when dealing with inheritance of real property. When a joint tenant died, there was no need to search for an heir. Their interest would cease to exist, and the surviving joint tenants would continue to hold the estate thanks to their right of survivorship. The need to search for an heir arose only on the death of the last surviving joint tenant (who was then the sole owner of the estate). In contrast, when each tenant in common died, their heir or heirs would take their place.

The problem was made worse when it became possible to give real property away by will. When property was inherited, there was usually only one heir, but wills enable tenants to leave their property to as many people as they wish. The number of tenants in common could grow exponentially, which provided another good reason to prefer joint tenancies.[6] As Holt CJ said in *Fisher v Wigg*, "joint-tenancies were favoured,

4   *Trustee Act*, RSBC 1996, c 464, s 29; *Trustee Act*, RSA 2000, c T-8, s 17; *Trustee Act, 2009*, SS 2009, c T-23.01, ss 19–21; *Trustee Act*, CCSM, c T160, s 13; *Trustee Act*, RSO 1990, c T.23, s 9; *Trustees Act*, SNB 2015, c 21, s 26; *Trustee Act*, RSNS 1989, c 479, s 18; *Trustee Act*, RSPEI 1988, c T-8, s 17; *Trustee Act*, RSNL 1990, c T-10, s 13; *Trustee Act*, RSY 2002, c 223, s 16; *Trustee Act*, RSNWT 1988, c T-8, s 13. See also *Property Act*, RSNB 1973, c P-19, s 21.
5   *Kenworthy v Ward* (1853), 11 Hare 196, 68 ER 1245.
6   See, for example, *Re Babour*, [1967] Qd R 10.

for the law loves not fractions of estates, nor to divide and multiply tenures."[7]

When the four unities were present but it was not clear whether a joint tenancy or tenancy in common was intended, the common law would assume it was joint. Over the years, courts became increasingly unhappy with this rule in which a person would lose their entire interest if they happened to die first. The winner-takes-all feature of the right of survivorship fell out of favour.

Courts began to lean in favour of tenancy in common when interpreting transactions that left the matter in doubt. The presumption of joint tenancy still applied if the document was silent on the matter, but if there was any indication that a tenancy in common was intended, the courts would use it as an excuse to avoid the presumption. These indications are called *words of severance*. Words such as "divided," "equally," "severally," or "share and share alike" do the trick because they reveal an intention that the co-tenants were meant to have shares, which is inconsistent with a joint tenancy.

The common law presumption in favour of joint tenancy has since been changed by statute in most jurisdictions to be a presumption in favour of tenancy in common. For example, in Ontario,

> Where by any letters patent, assurance or will, made and executed after the 1st day of July, 1834, land has been or is granted, conveyed or devised to two or more persons, other than executors or trustees, in fee simple or for any less estate, it shall be considered that such persons took or take as tenants in common and not as joint tenants, unless an intention sufficiently appears on the face of the letters patent, assurance or will, that they are to take as joint tenants.[8]

A document may contain mixed messages, such as "joint tenants in common," "jointly in equal shares," or "jointly and severally." This occurred in the Ontario case of *McEwen v Ewers and Ferguson*, where a testator left property to his two daughters "jointly and should they decide to sell the said property each of them is to have an equal share of the proceeds of the said sale."[9] Since Ontario has a statutory presumption in favour of tenancy in common, the judge had to decide whether

---

7   (1700) 1 Salk 391, 91 ER 339 at 340.

8   *Conveyancing and Law of Property Act*, RSO 1990, c C.34, s 13. See also *Property Law Act*, RSBC 1996, c 377, s 11; *Law of Property Act*, RSA 2000, c L-7, s 8; *Law of Property Act*, CCSM, c L90, s 15; *Property Act*, RSNB 1973, c P-19, s 20; *Real Property Act*, RSNS 1989, c 385, s 5; *Tenants in Common Act*, RSY 2002, c 216, s 1; *Tenants in Common Act*, RSNWT 1988, c T-1, s 1.

9   [1946] 3 DLR 494 at 495 (Ont HCJ).

it was sufficiently clear from the will that the daughters were intended to be joint tenants. Barlow J said, "It appears to me that not only does the testator not show an intention to create a joint tenancy, but in the use of the words 'equal share' he shows clearly an intention to create a tenancy in common."[10] The case would have been decided the same way in the absence of the statutory presumption.

Even if the parties are joint tenants at law, they may be tenants in common in equity. They may choose this arrangement, but it can also be presumed as a default rule in equity. In other words, there are circumstances in which the parties will be joint tenants at law holding the property in trust for themselves as tenants in common unless they choose joint beneficial ownership. This occurs in three main situations: where joint tenants contribute unequally to the purchase of property, where they acquire property as business partners, and where they are joint mortgagees.

If people buy property together as joint tenants but contribute unequally to the purchase price, it will be assumed that they are holding their joint tenancy in trust for themselves as tenants in common in proportion to their contributions.[11] The onus is on the tenant who contributed less to prove that the tenant who contributed more intended to make a gift. This is one application of a broader rule called the *presumption of resulting trust*, which applies to all apparent gifts that call for some explanation.

The presumption of resulting trust dates back to the fifteenth century, when it was common for the owner of an estate to transfer it to trusted friends as joint tenants to hold in trust for the owner (to avoid taxes and compulsory inheritance). The courts began to assume that an unexplained, gratuitous transfer of land was intended to be a trust for the transferor. The beneficial ownership of the land would result (i.e., spring back) to the transferor. This was once a fairly strong presumption, as Eyre CB said in *Dyer v Dyer*:

> The clear result of all the cases, without a single exception, is that the trust of a legal estate, whether freehold, copyhold, or leasehold; whether taken in the names of the purchasers and others jointly, or in the names of others without that of the purchaser; whether in one name or several; whether jointly or successive—results to the man who advances the purchase-money.[12]

---

10   *Ibid* at 496. See also *Watt v Watt Estate*, [1988] 1 WWR 534 at 539, 49 Man R (2d) 317 (CA).

11   *Lake v Gibson* (1729), 1 Eq Cas Abr 290, 21 ER 1052.

12   (1788) 2 Cox 92 at 93, 30 ER 42.

The presumption of resulting trust has weakened over time and can now be rebutted fairly easily by circumstantial evidence showing that it was more likely that a gift was intended.[13]

There is an exception to the presumption of resulting trust, which is called the *presumption of advancement*. Originally, it applied when a father made a large gift to help a son starting out on his own. The father's duty to advance his children in life provided an explanation for the transfer, so the presumption of resulting trust did not apply.[14] The presumption of advancement expanded to apply to gifts from husbands to wives (but not the other way around), but it no longer has much of a role to play. The Supreme Court of Canada held that the presumption of advancement applies equally to fathers and mothers but only to their gifts to minor children.[15] Since parents are unlikely to transfer legal ownership of significant assets to minor children, that presumption is more or less defunct. Legislation that provides for the distribution of family property on the breakdown of a marriage or similar relationship has displaced the presumptions between husbands and wives in many jurisdictions.[16] In any event, it rarely matters which presumption applies since courts are normally able to decide whether a gift was intended based on available evidence.

If business partners acquire property as joint tenants, it is assumed that they are holding it in trust for themselves as tenants in common even if they contribute equally to the purchase price. Joint tenancy at law means that the beneficiaries of a deceased partner's estate cannot acquire a legal interest in the partnership property, whereas the equitable tenancy in common ensures that partners do not lose their beneficial ownership when they die. The surviving partners will continue as legal joint tenants holding a share of the property in trust for the estate of the deceased partner.

---

13   See *Neazor v Hoyle* (1962), 32 DLR (2d) 131 (Alta SC AD); *Mehta Estate v Mehta Estate*, [1993] 6 WWR 457, 104 DLR (4th) 24 (Man CA); *Lohia v Lohia*, [2001] EWCA Civ 1691; *Pecore v Pecore*, 2007 SCC 17 [*Pecore*].

14   *Grey v Grey* (1677), 2 Swans 594 at 597, 36 ER 742.

15   *Pecore*, above note 13.

16   *Family Property Act*, RSA 2000, c F-4.7, s 36; *Family Property Act*, SS 1997, c F-6.3, s 50; *Family Law Act*, RSO 1990, c F.3, s 14; *Marital Property Act*, RSNB 2012, c 107, s 15; *Matrimonial Property Act*, RSNS 1989, c 275, s 21; *Family Law Act*, RSPEI 1988, c F-2.1, s 14; *Family Law Act*, RSNL 1990, c F-2, s 31; *Family Property and Support Act*, RSY 2002, c 83, s 7; *Family Law Act*, SNWT 1997, c 18, s 46. There are no equivalent provisions in British Columbia or Manitoba. See *Mehta Estate v Mehta Estate*, above note 13; *VJF v SKW*, 2016 BCCA 186; *McManus v McManus*, 2019 BCSC 123. See also *Clark, Drummie & Co v Ryan* (1999), 170 DLR (4th) 266 (NBCA).

The same assumption applies to people who become joint mortgagees. They have loaned money and have taken a mortgage of land from the debtor to secure repayment of the loan. Joint ownership of the mortgage is convenient since the debtor does not have to worry about who they should pay if a mortgagee dies. They can safely pay the surviving mortgagee or mortgagees thanks to the right of survivorship. However, the creditor should not lose their investment when they die, so it is assumed that the surviving mortgagees hold the mortgage in trust for themselves as tenants in common unless they say otherwise.

In *Malayan Credit Ltd v Jack Chia-Mph Ltd*,[17] two companies leased the seventh floor of a building in Singapore as joint tenants. There was no declaration of trust, but they paid rent and other expenses in proportion to the amount of space they each occupied. They had not contributed unequally to the purchase price (since the lease was not purchased with an upfront payment), they were not partners (since they had separate businesses), and they were not joint mortgagees. The Privy Council advised that they were holding the lease in trust for themselves as unequal tenants in common. The equitable assumption in favour of tenancy in common applied because the joint tenancy was part of a business arrangement even though it was not one of the three situations in which the assumption usually applied.

3) Survivorship

When someone becomes a joint tenant, they acquire a right of survivorship, which is a benefit they will enjoy if they outlive other joint tenants. When a joint tenant dies, their interest in the jointly owned property comes to an end, and the joint tenancy continues without them. The last surviving joint tenant is no longer a joint tenant because they became the sole owner when their fellow tenant died.

The right of survivorship does not operate by way of transfer. Nothing moves from the deceased joint tenant to the survivors. The deceased tenant's interest no longer exists, and the survivors continue to enjoy the same rights they had when they first became joint tenants.

A joint interest cannot be given away by will because it ceases to exist at the moment of death. It does not form part of the deceased joint tenant's estate. This is the main reason why married couples and people in similar relationships choose to be joint tenants with each other. Each wants the survivor to have the property. This happens automatically, without the need to probate the deceased tenant's estate and transfer

---

17   [1986] 1 AC 549 (PC).

assets according to a will or on intestacy. It can result in significant savings in taxes and probate fees based on the value of the estate since jointly owned property is excluded.

Parents and children may choose to be joint tenants for the same reason: when the parent dies, the child gets the property without the trouble and expense of administering the parent's estate. It is common for aged parents to hold joint bank accounts with their children, but this adds a complicating factor. One reason they might open a joint bank account is so that the child can help the parent manage their financial affairs. Was that the only reason, or did the parent also intend to use the right of survivorship to make a gift of the balance of the account when the parent died?

In *Pecore v Pecore*,[18] a father and daughter had several joint accounts that contained $1 million when the father died. The father had deposited all the money in the accounts, kept control over them, and wrote letters stating that he was "the 100% owner" of them in order to avoid capital gains tax. The daughter's ex-husband was a beneficiary of the father's will, so he argued that she was holding her interest in the accounts in trust for her father. As the sole surviving joint tenant, she became the sole legal owner of the accounts, but if she held them in trust for the father, his interest as trust beneficiary would form part of his estate, and the ex-husband would get a share.

The Supreme Court of Canada held that the presumption of resulting trust applied since the father had contributed all the money in the accounts but was rebutted by evidence that he had intended to make a gift to his daughter. Justice Rothstein talked about "gifting the right of survivorship,"[19] which may be confusing. It is not possible to separate the right of survivorship from a joint tenancy. The only way to make this sort of gift is for the donor and the donee to become joint tenants subject to a trust for the donor for life. The trust allows the donor to continue to enjoy full beneficial ownership of the jointly owned property for life. If the donor dies first, their equitable life interest comes to an end, and the surviving donee is the sole legal owner for their own benefit. If the donee dies first, the donor is the sole legal owner for their own benefit. The trust will cease to exist since the donor cannot be the sole trustee and the sole beneficiary (as discussed in the previous chapter).

A problem can arise if all the joint tenants die at the same time and there is no survivor. This happens surprisingly often because spouses tend to be joint tenants and travel together. The common law solution to this problem was to let the joint tenancy continue, with the deceased

---

18   *Pecore*, above note 13.
19   *Ibid* at para 68.

tenants being replaced by their heirs. Back when each tenant usually had only one heir, this was a simple solution, but it no longer functions well now that land may be given away by will or on intestacy to a group of people.

There are now two different statutory solutions to the problem. The first is to assume that the youngest tenant was the survivor. In Newfoundland and Labrador, for example, "[w]here 2 or more persons die at the same time or in circumstances making it uncertain which of them survived the other, the deaths are presumed to have occurred in the order of seniority and accordingly the younger is considered to have survived the older."[20]

The youngest joint tenant will be treated as the survivor and therefore become the sole owner of property, which will form part of their estate. It may not matter who survives if the joint tenants are spouses with both of their estates going to the same children, but that is not always true (especially for couples in subsequent marriages with different families for whom they wish to provide).

The second statutory solution is to treat joint tenants as if they are equal tenants in common, in which case, the estate of each joint tenant will receive an equal share. For example, in the Yukon,

[u]nless a contrary intention appears, if two or more persons hold legal title to property as joint tenants, or with respect to a joint account, with each other, and all of them die at the same time or in circumstances rendering it uncertain which of them survived the other or others, each person is . . . deemed to have an equal share with the other or with each of the others in that property.[21]

C. SEVERANCE

Severance is the process of converting a joint tenancy into a tenancy in common. It should not be confused with *words of severance*, which indicate that a tenancy in common was intended from the start. The main reason why joint tenants want to become tenants in common is to get rid of the right of survivorship. A tenant nearing the end of their life

---

20 *Survivorship Act*, RSNL 1990, c S-33, s 2. See also *Survivorship Act*, RSNS 1989, c 454, s 3; *Survivorship Act*, RSNWT 1988, c S-16, s 1.

21 *Survivorship Act*, RSY 2002, c 213, s 1. See also *Wills, Estates and Succession Act*, SBC 2009, c 13, s 5; *Wills and Succession Act*, SA 2010, c W-12.2, s 5; *Survivorship Act, 1993*, SS 1993, c S-67.1, s 8; *Survivorship Act*, CCSM, c S250, s 3; *Succession Law Reform Act*, RSO 1990, c S.26, s 55; *Survivorship Act*, RSNB 2012, c 116, s 3.

may decide that they want to give their interest in the property away by will and not let their fellow joint tenants keep it all.[22] Severance can also happen by operation of law contrary to the wishes of the joint tenants, as discussed below.

There are three main ways in which a joint tenancy can be severed: by the unilateral act of a joint tenant that causes their joint interest to be converted into a share, by mutual agreement, or by actions that indicate that the joint tenants are treating their joint tenancy as a tenancy in common. These methods are found in Page Wood VC's judgment in *Williams v Hensman*:

> A joint-tenancy may be severed in three ways: in the first place, an act of any one of the persons interested operating upon his own share may create a severance as to that share. The right of each joint-tenant is a right by survivorship only in the event of no severance having taken place of the share which is claimed under the *jus accrescendi*. Each one is at liberty to dispose of his own interest in such manner as to sever it from the joint fund—losing, of course, at the same time, his own right of survivorship. Secondly, a joint-tenancy may be severed by mutual agreement. And, in the third place, there may be a severance by any course of dealing sufficient to intimate that the interests of all were mutually treated as constituting a tenancy in common. When the severance depends on an inference of this kind without any express act of severance, it will not suffice to rely on an intention, with respect to the particular share, declared only behind the backs of the other persons interested.[23]

1) Unilateral Act

A tenant in common is normally free to deal with their share without the consent of their fellow tenants. They can sell it, give it away, leave it to someone in their will, mortgage it, and so on. Normally, joint tenants must act in unison to deal with jointly owned property. One of the reasons that trustees are joint tenants is to help protect the trust assets from being misappropriated by one of the trustees acting on their own.

Curiously, it is possible for a joint tenant to act alone to sever the joint tenancy and deal with their own share without the consent of the other joint tenants. It is doubly curious because joint tenants do not have shares. The act of transferring a non-existent share causes it to

---

22   See, for example, *Walker v Dubord* (1992), 92 DLR (4th) 257, 67 BCLR (2d) 302 (CA) [*Walker*].

23   (1861) 1 J & H 546 at 557–58, 70 ER 862.

come into existence as something that is capable of being transferred. This is a chicken-and-egg problem that the law ignores.

It is not enough to intend to sever even if that intention is announced to the other joint tenants.[24] Some action is required to give effect to that intention, and that must happen before the joint tenant dies. A will cannot sever a joint tenancy because it operates only when the testator (i.e., the person who made the will) dies. By then it is too late. Any interest they had as a joint tenant will have ceased to exist.

The most effective way to act on a share is to transfer it to someone else, who will receive it as a tenant in common. They cannot be a joint tenant because the unities of title and time will be missing. The size of their share will depend on the number of joint tenants. If there were only two joint tenants, they will become equal tenants in common. If there were more than two joint tenants, then the recipient will acquire a proportionate share: one-third if there were three tenants, one-quarter if there were four, and so on. How this affects the other tenants is discussed below.

Normally, a joint tenant who wants to sever the tenancy does not want to give up their interest in the property but wants to become a tenant in common. They can do this by transferring their share to a friend to hold it in trust for them. The friend would become a tenant in common at law, and the joint tenant would give up their legal interest in the property to become a tenant in common in equity.

Many jurisdictions have statutes that allow joint tenants to transfer their interests to themselves, so there is no need to involve a friend and create a trust. For example, in British Columbia, "[a] transfer by a joint tenant to himself or herself of his or her interest in land . . . has and is deemed always to have had the same effect of severing the joint tenancy as a transfer to a stranger."[25]

A transfer of legal title is not the only way to sever a joint tenancy. It is also possible to sever a joint tenancy in equity, in which case the joint tenants continue to be joint tenants at law but hold their joint tenancy in trust for beneficiaries who are equitable tenants in common. For example, if you and I were joint tenants and I declared that I held my interest in trust for my daughter, that would not affect our legal title, but we would become trustees for you and my daughter as equal tenants

---

24   *Walker*, above note 22.

25   *Property Law Act*, RSBC 1996, c 377, s 18. See also *Law of Property Act*, RSA 2000, c L-7, s 12; *Law of Property Act*, CCSM, c L90, s 17; *Conveyancing and Law of Property Act*, RSO 1990, c C.34, s 41; *Property Act*, RSNB 1973, c P-19, s 23; *Real Property Act*, RSPEI 1988, c R-3, s 13.

in common. If I died, you would become sole legal owner, but the trust would continue.[26]

There are two main criticisms of severance by unilateral act of a joint tenant. First, it seems odd to make a tenant jump through hoops to destroy the unities of title and time in order to sever the tenancy. Since tenancies at common can exist with all four unities present, why not allow a joint tenant to sever the tenancy simply by making a formal declaration of severance?

The second criticism is that it seems unfair to the other tenants that their joint tenancy can be severed without their knowledge. They might act differently if they knew that they had become tenants in common (e.g., by making or changing a will).[27] Why not require a joint tenant who severs to give their fellow tenants notice of the severance?

Some jurisdictions have responded to these criticisms. In England, a joint tenancy can be severed in equity by a joint tenant giving notice to the other tenants in writing.[28] In Tasmania,

> (1) A joint tenant of registered land may sever his joint tenancy by a declaration of severance in an approved form and registered under this Act.
>
> (2) On registering a declaration of severance in accordance with subsection (1), the Recorder shall notify every other joint tenant of the land by notice in writing.[29]

In Queensland and the Northern Territory, severance is still accomplished by registration of a transfer, but notice must be given to the other joint tenants.[30] The English and Tasmanian reforms address both concerns by providing a simple method of severance and ensuring that the other tenants receive notice of it. Law reform commissions in other jurisdictions have made similar recommendations.[31]

---

26   See *British Columbia (Public Trustee) v Mee*, [1972] 2 WWR 424, 23 DLR (3d) 491 (BCCA).

27   See also *McDonald v Eckert*, 2004 BCSC 323.

28   *Law of Property Act 1925* (UK), 15 & 16 Geo V, c 20, s 36.

29   *Land Titles Act 1980* (Tas), s 63.

30   *Land Title Act 1994* (Queensland), s 59; *Land Title Act 2000* (Northern Territory) s 59.

31   British Columbia Law Institute, *Report on Joint Tenancy* (2012), online: www.bcli.org/sites/default/files/report_66_joint_tenancy.pdf; New South Wales Law Reform Commission, *Unilateral Severance of a Joint Tenancy* (1994), online: www.lawreform.justice.nsw.gov.au/Documents/Publications/Reports/Report-73. pdf; Victorian Law Reform Commission, *Disputes Between Co-owners* (2001), online: www.lawreform.vic.gov.au/sites/default/files/Disputes%2Bbetween%2B Coowners%2Bfinal%2Brep.pdf; Law Reform Commission of Western Australian, *Report on Joint Tenancy and Tenancy in Common* (1994), online:

There is perhaps one further step, which is to require that notice always be given. In England and Tasmania, it is still possible to sever a joint tenancy in secret by unilateral act. It may not be practical, but perhaps a requirement to give notice should be required whenever a joint tenant wishes to sever by unilateral act, regardless of the method used.

2) Mutual Agreement and Course of Dealing

There is considerable overlap between these two categories. Severance by mutual agreement requires an express agreement among the tenants, whereas a course of dealing allows an agreement to be inferred from their actions. Both turn on an agreement by the tenants. The difference between them is how that agreement is proved.

In *Flannigan v Wotherspoon*,[32] two brothers (William and James) were joint owners of a house in Vancouver that they agreed to sell for $5,250. The couple buying it paid $800 up front and then $40 per month. This meant that the brothers would retain legal title until the purchase price was paid in full. William became ill and died, leaving his estate to his daughter Margaret, who argued that the joint tenancy had been severed in equity by a course of dealing between the brothers. The court agreed.

Their agreement to sell the house did not sever the joint tenancy, nor did the fact that they agreed to divide the sale proceeds equally. Three significant events led the court to "infer a mutual agreement to sever."[33] First, while William was ill, James arranged for the bank to collect $40 from the purchasers each month and deposit half in each brother's account. James told William that was so "neither of us has to worry about anything."[34] Justice Coady said, "This is strong evidence of a mutual agreement in relation to the division of the proceeds and not confined to payments made during the lifetime of either."[35]

Second, William told James that he was dying and had made a will leaving everything, including his interest in the Vancouver house, to Margaret. James made no objection and no mention of his right of survivorship. Finally, James indicated in a conversation with Margaret that she would be receiving William's share of the payments after he died.

---

www.lrc.justice.wa.gov.au/_files/P78-R.pdf. See also Ontario Law Reform Commission, *Report on Basic Principles of Land Law* (1996), online: https://archive.org/details/reportonbasicpri00onta/page/n3/mode/2up at 162–63.

32   [1953] 1 DLR 768, 7 WWR (NS) 660 (BCSC) [Cited to DLR].
33   *Ibid* at 769, Coady J.
34   *Ibid* at 770.
35   *Ibid* at 771.

An agreement to sever a joint tenancy, whether expressed or implied, does not alter the legal title. The severance takes effect in equity. When William and James agreed to sever their joint tenancy, they were still the registered owners of the fee simple estate as joint tenants, but they began to hold it in trust for themselves as equal tenants in common. When William died, James became the sole legal owner because of his legal right of survivorship, but the trust continued, with Margaret acquiring William's equitable share as the beneficiary of his estate.

3) Operation of Law

Severance by unilateral act, mutual agreement, or a course of dealing occurs because one or more tenants chooses to sever. Severance can also occur by operation of law without regard to the tenants' wishes.

When someone becomes bankrupt, most of their assignable rights are transferred by operation of law to their trustee in bankruptcy (as discussed in Chapter 1). This includes their interests as a joint tenant. Since the trustee in bankruptcy will not have unity of title or time with the other joint tenants, this will sever the joint tenancy, and the trustee will acquire a share as a tenant in common.[36]

In *R v Ford*,[37] a joint tenant was convicted of running an illegal marijuana grow operation on their jointly owned land. The court ordered the forfeiture of his interest in that land under the *Controlled Drugs and Substances Act*,[38] which caused a severance of the joint tenancy.

The murder of one joint tenant by another will also cause a severance. This happens surprisingly often since spouses tend to be joint tenants. Most of the cases involve a husband killing his wife. A trust is imposed to prevent the murderer from receiving a benefit from their crime. It does not strip the murderer of their entire interest in the property but severs the joint tenancy in equity to stop them from enjoying the right of survivorship.[39] That right still operates at law, so the murderer will become the sole legal owner, but as a constructive trustee for the murderer and the victim's estate as equal tenants in common.

---

36   *Re White*, [1928] 1 DLR 846, 8 CBR 544 (Ont SC); *Royal Bank of Canada v Oliver*, [1992] 1 WWR 320, 85 DLR (4th) 122 (Sask CA).

37   2010 BCCA 105.

38   SC 1996, c 19, s 16.

39   *Schobelt v Barber*, [1967] 1 OR 349, 60 DLR (2d) 519; *Re Gore*, [1972] 1 OR 550, 23 DLR (3d) 534 (SC); *Novak v Gatien* (1975), 25 RFL 397 (Man QB); *Re Dreger* (1976), 12 OR (2d) 371, 69 DLR (3d) 47 (SC).

This rule can also apply to manslaughter and similar crimes. In *Whitelaw v Wilson*,[40] a husband and wife formed a suicide pact and drank arsenic, but the husband survived. He was not allowed to benefit from his crime of aiding and abetting a suicide. In *Edwards v State Trustees Ltd*,[41] a woman was convicted in Australia of the crime of defensive homicide after she killed her abusive husband, and that also attracted the rule.

4) Effect of Severance

If there are two joint tenants, severance will always produce an equal tenancy in common. If there are more than two joint tenants, the effect of severance will depend on how many tenants have chosen to sever. If all the tenants agreed to sever, they will all be equal tenants in common. There is a different outcome if severance is the unilateral act of only one of three or more joint tenants. How this works is probably best explained by example.

Suppose that Anna, Barb, Cathy, and Deb were joint tenants of a fee simple estate and that Anna sold her interest to Eva. This will cause a severance of Anna's interest so that Eva will acquire a one-quarter share as tenant in common. The other three-quarters share will be held by Barb, Cathy, and Deb as joint tenants. Anna's unilateral act does not affect the relationship that the other three joint tenants have with each other. It did affect them by changing the co-ownership of the fee simple estate from a joint tenancy to an unequal tenancy in common. It also changed the subject of their joint tenancy, which used to be the entire estate and is now only a three-quarters share of that estate.

If Barb died, her interest would cease to exist. Cathy and Deb would enjoy their rights of survivorship and continue as joint tenants of their three-quarters share. If Cathy then died, Deb would become the sole owner of that share as the last surviving joint tenant. Their joint tenancy will have ended, and Deb and Eva would be tenants in common, with Deb having a three-quarters share and Eva one-quarter.

Let us change the example. We begin as before with Anna, Barb, Cathy, and Deb as joint tenants of a fee simple estate. Suppose that Anna did not sell her share to Eva but sold it to Barb instead. Perhaps surprisingly, this will have the same effect even though Barb is one of the joint tenants. She acquires a one-quarter share as tenant in common, whereas the other three-quarters share is held by Cathy, Deb, and

---

40   [1934] 3 DLR 554, [1934] OR 415 (SC). See also *Dunbar v Plant*, [1997] EWCA
       Civ 2167, [1998] Ch 412.
41   [2016] VSCA 28.

herself as joint tenants. Barb wears two hats: tenant in common of a one-quarter share and joint tenant of a three-quarters share. The fact that she has more of the estate than Cathy or Deb does not upset the unity of interest required for a joint tenancy. This is because Barb does not have a greater interest but has an additional interest. Barb, Cathy, and Deb all have identical interests in the three-quarters share.

If Barb died, her one-quarter share as tenant in common would continue to exist and be distributed by her will or on intestacy. Her joint interest in the three-quarters share would cease, and Cathy and Deb would continue to own it as the surviving joint tenants.

D. PARTITION

Partition is the process of ending co-ownership by ending the unity of possession. It usually happens by agreement, and it does not matter whether the co-owners are joint tenants or tenants in common. If it is practical to divide up the subject of their co-ownership, they might agree that each co-owner takes a portion of what they used to own together. A parcel of land might be subdivided. A collection of goods (such as a cellar of wine, library of books, flock of sheep, or silo of grain) might be divided among the co-owners. Each co-owner exchanges shared possession of every item in the collection for sole possession of some of those items.

The division of an asset might not be possible or practical. A boat, painting, or horse is much more valuable as a single thing. The subdivision of land is often not permissible or practical. In these cases, partition is achieved through sale. One co-owner might buy out the others, or the asset might be sold to someone else, and the co-owners will split the proceeds.

The reported cases are situations in which the co-owners could not agree on whether to end their co-ownership, how to end it, or both. One of the co-owners has applied to the court to resolve their dispute. Most jurisdictions have statutory provisions to deal with the partition or sale of land.[42] The English *Partition Act 1868* became part of the law of Sas-

---

42   *Partition of Property Act*, RSBC 1996, c 347; *Law of Property Act*, RSA 2000, c
      L-7, Part 3; *Law of Property Act*, CCSM, c L90, ss 19–26; *Partition Act*, RSO 1990,
      c P.4; *Rules of Court*, NB Reg 82-73, Rule 67; *Partition Act*, RSNS 1989, c 333; *Real
      Property Act*, RSPEI 1988, c R-3, Part III; *Conveyancing Act*, RSNL 1990, c C-34,
      ss 46–58. See *Pallot v Douglas*, 2017 BCCA 254; John Irvine, "A House Divided:
      Access to Partition and Sale under the Laws of Ontario and Manitoba" (2011) 35
      Manitoba Law Journal 217.

katchewan in 1870 and is still in force in that province.[43] The statutes authorize the court to exercise its discretion to resolve the situation, and it can order a sale if that is the most appropriate solution.

In *Cook v Johnston*,[44] the parties were joint owners of a summer cottage island in Ontario. One party applied to the court to have the island sold. The *Partition Act* states that "[a]ny person interested in land in Ontario … may take proceedings for the partition of such land or for the sale thereof under the directions of the court if such sale is considered by the court to be more advantageous to the parties interested."[45] The master refused and ordered a partition of the island instead, which was upheld on appeal:

> The evidence taken before the learned Master in this case reveals that there are very few similar islands in the area that are now available. The appellant urged that the island was not of such an area as permitted two families to enjoy the same in separate cottages. The last survey, however, indicated the island is slightly over two acres in area. It is between 500 and 600 ft. in length and probably 150 ft. in width. The Master was quite justified on the evidence in coming to the conclusion, as I think he did, that it was actually more advantageous to the parties to partition the property than take the chances as to what might develop if it was sold. Even if the parties received more than the actual value of the property from a stranger, neither of them could readily find another suitable summer island home in that district. If one of them was successful in buying the property at a sale, the other would be deprived entirely of his right to spend vacations in the area where he had enjoyed summer vacations for some 30 years. As it stands under the Master's report, each of the parties will have the privilege of enjoying one-half for the whole summer of what they formerly enjoyed for only one-half of the summer.[46]

This principle, that the court will order a sale only if it is more advantageous to the parties, was applied by the Ontario Court of Appeal in *Dibattista v Menecola*.[47] Four people were co-owners of land that was suitable for development. A developer purchased a parcel of adjoining land and then purchased the interests of two of the co-owners, hoping

---

43 Law Reform Commission of Saskatchewan, *Proposals for a New Partition and Sale Act* (2001), online: https://lawreformcommission.sk.ca/Partition_and_Sale_Proposals.pdf at 2–3.

44 [1970] 2 OR 1 (HCJ) [*Cook*].

45 RSO 1990, c P.4, s 3.

46 *Cook*, above note 44 at 2, Grant J.

47 (1990) 74 DLR (4th) 569, 75 OR (2d) 443 (CA).

to get the other two co-owners to sell their interests. When they refused, the developer applied to the court (as co-owner) for an order to sell the land. Although a sale would clearly be advantageous to one co-owner (the developer), it was not an advantage to the others, so the court ordered the partition of the land instead.

The most common situation in which co-owners turn to the courts to end their co-ownership is on the breakdown of their marriage or a similar relationship. These situations are no longer governed by the law relating to the partition of land in other contexts. Every jurisdiction has a statute that specifically addresses the division of family property and gives the court a wide discretion to deal with the use and disposition of the family home and other assets.[48]

E. CONDOMINIUMS

A condominium provides a way for people to share the use of land. Many people think of condos as units in high-rise apartment buildings, but condominiums take a variety of different forms, including walk-up apartments, townhouses, office buildings, and houses set in communal gardens.

Condominium is the preferred term in North America,[49] except in British Columbia, where it is now called *strata title*.[50] It is called *strata title* or *unit title* in Australia and New Zealand and *commonhold* in England. Despite differences in terminology, all follow the same basic principles: people have exclusive possession of their units as owners, the unit owners are collectively the owners of the common areas as tenants in common, there is a corporation that manages everything, and the unit owners are the shareholders of the corporation.

---

48   *Family Law Act*, SBC 2011, c 25; *Family Property Act*, RSA 2000, c F-4.7; *Family Property Act*, SS 1997, c F-6.3; *Family Property Act*, CCSM, c F25; *Family Law Act*, RSO 1990, c F.3; *Marital Property Act*, RSNB 2012, c 107; *Matrimonial Property Act*, RSNS 1989, c 275; *Family Law Act*, RSPEI 1988, c F-2.1; *Family Law Act*, RSNL 1990, c F-2; *Family Property and Support Act*, RSY 2002, c 83; *Family Law Act*, SNWT 1997, c 18.

49   *Condominium Property Act*, RSA 2000, c C-22; *Condominium Property Act, 1993*, SS 1993, c C-26.1; *Condominium Act*, CCSM, c C170; *Condominium Act, 1998*, SO 1998, c 19; *Condominium Property Act*, SNB 2009, c C-16.05; *Condominium Act*, RSNS 1989, c 85; *Condominium Act*, RSPEI 1988, c C-16; *Condominium Act, 2009*, SNL 2009, c C-29.1; *Condominium Act*, RSY 2002, c 36; *Condominium Act*, RSNWT 1988, c C-15.

50   The *Strata Property Act*, SBC 1998, c 43, replaced the *Condominium Act*, RSBC 1996, c 64.

This structure is designed to deal with the problem of maintaining and managing the rights and duties that people owe to each other when they live in close proximity and share common areas and facilities. The ordinary fee simple estate is not up to the task. Neighbours owe a limited range of duties toward each other, and those duties are negative (i.e., duties not to interfere with a neighbour's right to possession, etc.). There is no adequate mechanism for enforcing positive obligations, such as the duty to repair a common wall, fence, or roof or to maintain common areas and facilities in good condition.[51]

Leasehold estates can do this well because positive and negative leasehold covenants can be enforced against present and future landlords and tenants (as discussed in Chapter 3). Leases have two main limitations. First, people want to be owners, not tenants. Although a long leasehold estate is close to a fee simple, it is not the same. Second, tenants may worry about their landlord's ability and willingness to perform their obligations. The condominium addresses both issues. People can own their units and shares of the common areas in fee simple, and the condominium is managed on their behalf by a corporation that is owned by the unit owners.

Before the invention of the condominium, a similar result could be achieved using a corporation and leasehold estates. For example, an apartment building can be owned in fee simple by a corporation, which grants long leases (e.g., 125 years) of the apartments to tenants who are the shareholders of the corporation (with one share per apartment). They meet as shareholders to elect a board of directors to manage the affairs of the corporation and pay rent to the corporation to cover the costs of maintaining the common areas. If an apartment is sold, the lease is assigned to the new tenants, along with the share in the corporation. This is still the structure most commonly used in England.

The lease coupled with ownership of the corporate landlord is different from a condominium in two main respects. First, a long lease is not a fee simple estate. Second, the corporation is the sole owner of the common areas, whereas condo owners share ownership of the common areas as tenants in common.

Another advantage of a condominium is that the law provides a default structure. The registration of the condominium plan will bring the condominium corporation into existence, and the rights and duties of everyone involved are laid out in the statute. In contrast, leases and tenant-owned corporations are bespoke creations.

---

51 See *Rhone v Stephens*, [1994] UKHL 3, [1994] 2 AC 310.

CHAPTER 6

SECURITY INTERESTS

A. INTRODUCTION

As discussed in Chapter 1, debt is a relationship in which the debtor has an obligation to pay money to the creditor, who holds the corresponding right to be paid. The value of that right depends on the likelihood that the debtor will perform their obligation. If the debtor fails to pay, the creditor can take steps to enforce their right, first by going to court to get a judgment (and thus becoming a *judgment creditor*) and then by engaging the civil enforcement process to seize the debtor's assets (as an *execution creditor*). This can be slow, expensive, and disappointing.

If the debtor is unable to pay their debts, they may be bankrupt, in which case the creditor is not allowed to enforce their right against the debtor.[1] The creditor's only remedy is to make a claim in the bankruptcy. The debtor's trustee in bankruptcy will use the debtor's assets to raise money to pay the creditors, who hope to receive some portion of the money that is owed to them, after which those debts will be extinguished.[2]

A creditor can reduce the risk of non-payment by taking a security interest (and becoming a *secured creditor*). A security interest is a right *in rem* that exists for the purpose of making it more likely that a debt will be paid. Other personal obligations can be secured, but debt is by far the most common.

---

1 *Bankruptcy and Insolvency Act*, RSC 1985, c B-3, s 69.3.
2 *Ibid*, s 178(2).

Security interests take many different forms but share two common traits: they are property rights to one or more of the debtor's assets, and they exist for the limited purpose of securing payment of a debt (or some other personal obligation). The security interest with which most people are familiar is a mortgage of a home to secure the homeowner's obligation to pay back the money they borrowed in order to buy it. Once that obligation is performed, the mortgage has fulfilled its purpose, and the homeowner is entitled to have it discharged.

A secured creditor has several advantages over an *unsecured creditor*. If the debtor fails to pay, the secured creditor does not have to go through the process of becoming an execution creditor but can enforce their security and use the assets subject to their security interest to satisfy the debt. If the debtor becomes bankrupt, the secured assets cannot be used by the trustee in bankruptcy to pay the other creditors until the secured creditor has received what they are owed. The security interest also provides the debtor with an additional incentive to pay that debt. For example, if money is tight at the end of the month, most people will choose to make their mortgage payment before they pay their credit card debt. The consequences of failing to pay a secured debt are more severe.

Although security is designed to protect the creditor, it has an advantage for the debtor as well. The cost of borrowing is reduced if the debtor can offer security for the debt because interest rates reflect the risk taken by the creditor. For example, in 2020, typical mortgage interest rates in British Columbia were 3.5 percent, whereas interest on credit card debt was 20 percent (and interest on a "payday" loan was 400 percent).

This chapter looks first at the main forms of security. The common law provided two options: the creditor could take *possession* of the debtor's land or goods or take *legal title* to them. Equity allowed the creditor to have an *encumbrance* on the debtor's assets, which was neither possession nor legal title. That is now also possible by statute. This chapter then looks at mortgages of land and finishes with personal property security.

B. POSSESSION

1) Pawn or Pledge

The oldest form of security is called a *pawn* or *pledge*, in which the debtor transfers possession of goods or documents to the creditor to hold until the debt is repaid. It is simple and effective but has two main limitations: first, the debtor cannot make use of their goods until the debt is repaid, and, second, only tangible assets can be pledged. Both limitations can be avoided by using title as security.

2) Common Law Lien

A *common law lien* is like a pledge because both are rights to retain possession of goods or documents until a debt is paid. A pledge is created when the debtor transfers possession to the creditor to hold as security for the debt. A lien arises when the creditor obtains possession for some other purpose and is allowed to retain possession until a related debt is paid. All pledges are created by the intention to create them, but liens can arise by operation of law. Liens can be created by contract or excluded by contract, but a lien can arise even though no one intended to create it.

There are two kinds of common law liens: *general liens* and *particular liens*.[3] A general lien applies by custom in some professions and businesses. It allows the creditor to retain possession of the debtor's goods and documents as security for all of their debts, whether related directly to those things or not. For example, bankers, bookkeepers, solicitors, and stockbrokers have a lien on their client's documents as security for their fees and other debts owed by the client.[4]

A particular lien on goods arises to secure the payment of a debt that relates directly to those goods. These liens can be divided into two groups, as Stephen J explained in *Majeau Carrying Co Pty Ltd v Coastal Rutile Ltd*:

> There are two general categories of persons who have long been recognized by the common law as entitled to a particular lien not in any way dependent upon usage or custom: those whose quasi-public calling casts upon them a common law duty towards the public at large, such as innkeepers and carriers, and who in return are entitled to this special remedy for their charges, and those who in plying their trade improve the goods of others by the expenditure on those goods of skill and labour.[5]

Innkeepers and common carriers owed a duty to provide services to the public and owed a duty to care for the goods entrusted to them. The

---

3   See Alberta Law Reform Institute, *Report on Liens* (1992), online:
     www.alri.ualberta.ca/1992/09/report-on-liens-report-for-discussion-13.

4   See for example *Jones v Davidson Partners Ltd* (1981), 121 DLR (3d) 127, 31 OR
     (2d) 494 (SC); *Albion Securities Co Ltd v Nathanson*, 2003 BCSC 232.

5   [1973] HCA 22, 129 CLR 48 at 54.

common law gave them a lien over their customer's goods as security for the payment of their fees and charges.[6]

The other category of liens arose in favour of those who improved goods. These liens go by different names in different contexts, such as *repairer's lien*, *garage keeper's lien*, *artificer's lien*, and *artisan's lien*. At common law, it was not enough to preserve or care for goods. A lien would arise only if the creditor had improved them.[7] That was changed by statute to provide liens for creditors who store goods or take care of livestock.[8] In Saskatchewan, common law liens have been abolished and replaced by a statutory commercial lien.[9]

Lord Justice Diplock explained the nature of a common law lien in *Tappenden v Artus*,[10] in which a motor vehicle broke down on the motorway and was towed to a garage for repairs. The garage keeper had a lien on the vehicle:

> The common law lien of an artificer is of very ancient origin. . . . Because it arises in consequence of a contract, it is tempting to a twentieth-century lawyer to think of a common law lien as possessing the characteristics of a contractual right, express or implied, created by mutual agreement between the parties to the contract. But this would be to mistake its legal nature. Like a right of action for damages, it is a remedy for breach of contract which the common law confers upon an artificer to whom the possession of goods is lawfully given for the purpose of his doing work upon them in consideration of a money payment. . . .
>
> The common law remedy of a possessory lien, like other primitive remedies such as abatement of nuisance, self-defence or ejection of trespassers to land, is one of self-help. It is a remedy *in rem* exercisable upon the goods, and its exercise requires no intervention by the courts, for it is exercisable only by an artificer who has actual

---

6   See *R & R Cunningham Enterprises Ltd v Vollmers*, [1973] 4 WWR 339 (Alta QB).

7   *Re Southern Livestock Producers Ltd*, [1964] 1 WLR 24.

8   See *Livestock Lien Act*, RSBC 1996, c 272, s 2; *Warehouse Lien Act*, RSBC 1996, c 480, s 2; *Animal Keepers Act*, SA 2005, c A-40.5, s 2; *Possessory Liens Act*, RSA 2000, c P-19, s 4; *Warehousemen's Lien Act*, RSA 2000, c W-2, s 3; *Commercial Liens Act*, SS 2001, c C-15.1, s 3; *Stable Keepers Act*, CCSM, c S200, s 2; *Warehousemen's Liens Act*, CCSM, c W20, s 2; *Repair and Storage Liens Act*, RSO 1990, c R.25, s 4; *Liens on Goods and Chattels Act*, RSNB 2014, c 117, ss 5, 6; *Storer's Lien Act*, RSNB 2011, c 225, s 2; *Warehousemen's Lien Act*, RSNS 1989, c 499, s 3; *Warehousemen's Lien Act*, RSPEI 1988, c W-1, s 2; *Warehouser's Lien Act*, RSNL 1990, c W-2, s 3; *Warehouse Keepers Lien Act*, RSY 2002, c 226, s 2; *Warehouse Keepers Lien Act*, RSNWT 1988, c W-2, s 2.

9   *Commercial Liens Act*, SS 2001, c C-15.1, s 26.

10   [1964] 2 QB 185 (CA).

possession of the goods subject to the lien. Since, however, the remedy is the exercise of a right to continue an existing actual possession of the goods, it necessarily involves a right of possession adverse to the right of the person who, but for the lien, would be entitled to immediate possession of the goods. A common law lien, although not enforceable by action, thus affords a defence to an action for recovery of the goods by a person who, but for the lien, would be entitled to immediate possession.[11]

The common law lien was a passive security interest. The creditor was entitled to retain possession of the goods but was not allowed to sell them. In contrast, a creditor who receives goods as a pawn or pledge is entitled to sell them if the debt is not paid within a certain time. A problem with the passive nature of a common law lien is that it can leave the parties in a standoff if the debtor is unable or unwilling to pay. Most lien holders now have a statutory right to sell the goods.[12]

Common law liens should not be confused with *equitable liens, builders' liens,* or *mechanics' liens,* which have nothing to do with possession of goods or documents. An equitable lien is a form of encumbrance that is not a right to possession (as discussed below). A builder's lien and a mechanic's lien are different terms for the same thing, which is a statutory security interest in land that is given to contractors, subcontractors, and workers who do improvements to that land.[13] There are

---

11   *Ibid* at 194–95, Diplock LJ.

12   See *Hotel Keepers Act,* RSBC 1996, c 206, s 2; *Livestock Lien Act,* RSBC 1996, c 272, s 4; *Repairers Lien Act,* RSBC 1996, c 404, s 12; *Warehouse Lien Act,* RSBC 1996, c 480, s 4; *Animal Keepers Act,* SA 2005, c A-40.5, s 6; *Possessory Liens Act,* RSA 2000, c P-19, ss 10, 12; *Warehousemen's Lien Act,* RSA 2000, c W-2, s 6; *Commercial Liens Act,* SS 2001, c C-15.1, s 19; *Garage Keepers Act,* CCSM, c G10, s 9; *Hotel Keepers Act,* CCSM, c H150, s 4; *Stable Keepers Act,* CCSM, c S200, s 4; *Warehousemen's Liens Act,* CCSM, c W20, s 5; *Repair and Storage Liens Act,* RSO 1990, c R.25, ss 3, 4; *Liens on Goods and Chattels Act,* RSNB 2014, c 117, s 10; *Storer's Lien Act,* RSNB 2011, c 225, s 4; *Storage Warehouse Keepers Act,* RSNS 1989, c 447, s 3; *Warehousemen's Lien Act,* RSNS 1989, c 499, s 5; *Garage Keepers' Lien Act,* RSPEI 1988, c G-1, s 4; *Warehousemen's Lien Act,* RSPEI 1988, c W-1, s 4; *Warehouser's Lien Act,* RSNL 1990, c W-2, s 5; *Garage Keepers Lien Act,* RSY 2002, c 99, s 7; *Warehouse Keepers Lien Act,* RSY 2002, c 226, s 4; *Garage Keepers Lien Act,* RSNWT 1988, c G-1, ss 4–6; *Hotel Keepers Act,* RSNWT 1988, c H-5, s 3; *Warehouse Keepers Lien Act,* RSNWT 1988, c W-2, s 4.

13   *Builders Lien Act,* SBC 1997, c 45; *Builders' Lien Act,* RSA 2000, c B-7; *Builders' Lien Act,* SS 1984-85-86, c B-7.1; *Builders' Lien Act,* CCSM, c B91; *Construction Act,* RSO 1990, c C.30; *Mechanics' Lien Act,* RSNB 1973, c M-6; *Builders' Lien Act,* RSNS 1989, c 277; *Mechanics' Lien Act,* RSPEI 1988, c M-4; *Mechanics' Lien Act,* RSNL 1990, c M-3; *Builders Lien Act,* RSY 2002, c 18; *Mechanics Lien Act,* RSNWT 1988, c M-7.

a few other statutory liens that provide workers with non-possessory security interests in goods on which they have laboured.[14]

Non-possessory liens can arise in equity or by statute, but a common law lien is always a right to possession of goods and documents. It is not possible to have a common law lien over intangible assets. For example, in *Your Response Ltd v Datateam Business Media Ltd*,[15] a database management company claimed a common law lien over an electronic database of its customer's subscribers. That was rejected by the English Court of Appeal:

> As Diplock LJ observed in *Tappenden v Artus* [1964] 2 QB 185, the essential nature of a common law artificer's lien (which is the nearest analogy to the lien which the claimant sought to exercise in the present case) is a right to retain possession of goods delivered to him for the purpose of carrying out work on them. Although the right to exercise such a lien has been recognised in a wide variety of cases . . . , the claimant was unable to identify any case in which a right to exercise a lien over intangible property has been recognised. The reason is not difficult to find: whereas it is possible to transfer physical possession of tangible property by simple delivery, it is not possible to deal with intangible property in the same way. Although it is now possible by virtue of statutory provisions to transfer the legal title to choses in action, it is not possible to transfer possession of them in any physical sense. . . . Indeed, I do not think that the concept of possession in the hitherto accepted sense has any meaning in relation to intangible property.[16]

In *Fields of Athenry Resort Corporation v Grey*,[17] the Supreme Court of Newfoundland and Labrador gave effect to a "[b]ookkeeper's common law right to maintain a legal or possessory lien" over electronic accounting files, but without discussing the issue regarding possession of intangible property.

---

14   See *Tugboat Worker Lien Act*, RSBC 1996, c 466; *Woodworker Lien Act*, RSBC 1996, c 491; *Threshers' Lien Act*, RSS 1978, c T-13; *Woodmen's Lien Act*, RSS 1978, c W-16; *Threshers' Liens Act*, CCSM, c T60; *Woodmen's Liens Act*, CCSM, c W190; *Forestry Workers Lien for Wages Act*, RSO 1990, c F.28; *Woods Workers' Lien Act*, RSNB 1973, c W-12.5; *Woodmen's Lien Act*, RSNS 1989, c 507. The *Miners Lien Act*, RSY 2002, c 151, and *Miners Lien Act*, RSNWT 1988, c M-12, provide for liens over the mines (i.e., the land) and the minerals extracted from them.

15   [2014] EWCA Civ 281, [2015] QB 41.

16   *Ibid* at 49, Moore-Bick LJ.

17   2018 NLSC 230 at para 34, Khaladkar J.

C. TITLE

Instead of taking possession, a creditor can take legal title to the debtor's assets to hold as security. This has advantages for both parties. Since the debtor has possession of the assets, they can continue to use them while the debt is being repaid, and if the assets can be used to generate income, it will be easier to pay the debt. Since the creditor already has title to the assets, it can be easier to take steps to enforce their security if the debtor fails to pay the debt. Also, non-possessory rights can be used as security even though they cannot be pledged.

One disadvantage of title security is that other people who deal with the debtor can be misled to believe that the debtor is the owner of the goods in their possession. They might purchase the goods from the debtor or take a security interest in them without realizing that the creditor owns them. To address this problem, most security interests are registered if the creditor is not in possession (as discussed below and in Chapter 9).

There are two main ways in which creditors obtain legal title to hold as security. The first is when the debtor is buying something from the creditor and the parties agree that legal title will not be transferred to the debtor until the debt is paid in full. The second occurs when the debtor owns something and transfers title to the creditor to hold as security until a debt is paid.

1) Creditor Selling to the Debtor

Any asset can be sold on terms that title will not pass to the buyer until the purchase price is paid in fill. The creditor owns the asset before the debt arises and will continue to own them until the debt is extinguished. The debtor obtains possession and gets to use the asset while the debt is being paid and the creditor retains legal title as security for that debt. Even though the creditor's legal title does not change when the sale is agreed, they cease to be the beneficial owner and become a secured creditor.

An *agreement for sale* is a contract to sell land in which the vendor agrees to accept payments over a period of time and transfer legal title when the purchase price is paid in full. We saw an example of this in the previous chapter (concerning severance of a joint tenancy). In *Flannigan v Wotherspoon*,[18] the vendors agreed to sell a house in Van-

---

18   [1953] 1 DLR 768, 7 WWR (NS) 660 (BCSC).

couver for $5,250, with the purchasers paying $800 up front and $40 per month. The purchasers do not get legal title until payment is made in full, but they do acquire an equitable interest in the land when the contract is made.[19]

The vendors had been the legal and beneficial owners of the fee simple estate, but that changed when they made the agreement for sale, even though they continued to hold legal title. Consider the interests of the parties in light of Professor Honoré's description of ownership (discussed in Chapter 2).[20] The standard incidents of ownership belong to the purchasers. They have the rights to possess, use, and manage the land and to receive the income from it. They also have the right to the capital, although that may seem counterintuitive while the full purchase price has not yet been paid. The vendors have a right to be paid the purchase price set by the agreement for sale plus interest. The purchasers have the right to the capital value of the land. If the land goes up in value, that benefits the purchasers, and if it goes down, they suffer the loss. The amount they owe to the vendors stays the same regardless of what happens to the land's market value.

The only reason why the vendors retained legal title to the land was to secure their right to be paid the purchase price in full. If the purchasers fail to pay, the vendors might be able to cancel the agreement for sale and sell the land to others, but that is similar to the right of any secured creditor to realize their security if the debtor fails to pay. The purchasers might be entitled to relief from forfeiture or to receive a refund.[21]

While the agreement for sale continues, the vendors can transfer the fee simple estate (by sale, gift, or will), but the recipient will normally be in no better position than the vendors. They will receive the land subject to the purchasers' rights and become entitled to receive their payments. This is really no different from what happens when any secured creditor assigns their security interest to someone else.

Goods are often sold on terms that title will not pass until the purchase price is paid in full. These arrangements go by several different names depending on the context. A *hire-purchase* agreement is one in which the goods are leased to the buyer for a period of time, after which the buyer has the option to buy the goods for a specified price. Motor

---

19   *Church v Hill*, [1923] SCR 642, [1923] 3 DLR 1045.

20   AM Honoré, "Ownership" in AG Guest, ed, *Oxford Essays in Jurisprudence* (Oxford: Oxford University Press, 1961) 107.

21   See *March Brothers & Wells v Banton* (1911), 45 SCR 338; Francis CR Price, "Agreements for Sale to Corporations—The Remedy of Extra-Judicial Determination" (1981) 19 *Alta L Rev* 192.

vehicles are often sold on this basis.[22] A *conditional sale* is similar except that the buyer is obligated to buy at the end of the lease.[23] Both arrangements create a bailment followed by a transfer of legal title if the buyer chooses to buy or is obligated to do so.

A contract for the sale of goods may contain a "retention of title" clause, which is sometimes called a *Romalpa* clause after an English case that concerned its effect.[24] They have been used in contracts for the supply of raw materials to manufacturers and provide that title to those materials will not pass to the buyer until the buyer pays all of their debts to the seller or the goods are consumed in the manufacturing process.[25]

English law draws a sharp distinction between the cases in which the seller retains title until the purchase price is paid and the cases (discussed below) in which the creditor obtains title from the debtor. Canadian law does not. This is because England and Canada have different systems for registering security interests. In England, security interests are registered only if they are granted by the debtor.[26] That does not apply to legal title retained by the seller.[27] In Canada, registration requirements apply to all personal property security interests regardless of form. This is discussed below.

2) Debtor Transfers Title to the Creditor

The transfer of legal title from debtor to creditor takes different forms. The most famous of these is the *common law mortgage* of land, in which the debtor transfers their fee simple estate to the creditor to hold as security until the debt is repaid. That form of mortgage has been replaced in most jurisdictions by registration of a statutory encumbrance (which is still called a mortgage). Both forms of mortgage are discussed below.

A *chattel mortgage* is like a common law mortgage except that goods or other forms of personal property are transferred to the creditor instead of an estate in land.[28] A *bill of sale* can have the same effect by transferring legal title to goods to the creditor. Another method is called a *sale and lease back*, in which the debtor sells their goods to the creditor

---

22   See, for example, *Kerri (Guardian of) v Decker*, 2002 NFCA 11.

23   See *MEL Industries Ltd v Pioneer Machinery Co Ltd* (1981), 121 DLR (3d) 103, 15 Alta LR (2d) 140 (CA).

24   *Aluminium Industrie Vaassen BV v Romalpa Aluminium Ltd*, [1976] 1 WLR 676 (CA).

25   See *Clough Mill Ltd v Martin*, [1985] 1 WLR 111 (CA); *Coutinho & Ferrostaal GmbH v Tracomex (Canada) Ltd*, 2015 BCSC 787.

26   *Companies Act 2006* (UK), ss 859A, 859H.

27   *Clough Mill Ltd v Martin*, above note 25 at 122 (CA).

28   See, for example, *Dedrick v Ashdown* (1888), 15 SCR 227.

and leases them back.[29] Possession never changes hands, but the debtor goes from owner to bailee until the debt is paid. The sale price paid by the creditor is the loan, and the lease payments are calculated to provide repayment of the loan plus interest.

D. ENCUMBRANCE

At common law, a creditor can obtain security by taking possession of the debtor's goods or land or by taking legal title to them. The rules of equity provide for another kind of security interest that operates as an encumbrance on the debtor's assets. The debtor has both title and possession (if the assets are tangible things that can be possessed), and the creditor has a right of recourse to those assets if the debtor fails to pay the debt. An equitable security interest is similar to a *hypothec*, which is a security interest in civil law systems such as Quebec's.[30]

Equitable security interests may be divided into two categories: an *equitable charge* arises by intention, whereas an *equitable lien* (like a common law lien) arises by operation of law. There are also some statutory charges and liens that operate as encumbrances, such as the builder's lien and the mechanic's lien, discussed above. The modern form of land title mortgage (discussed below) is a statutory charge.

1) Equitable Charge

A debtor can grant an equitable charge over specific assets or over a shifting pool of assets. The equitable charge became popular because a company could borrow money and grant a charge over all of its present and after-acquired property. For many businesses, their two most valuable assets are their stock-in-trade (i.e., the goods they sell) and their book debts (i.e., the debts due from their customers when goods or services are supplied on credit). These are collections of assets that change daily. The ability to offer as security whatever happens to be in stock or owed to the company from time to time can make it easier to borrow money.

The ability to charge future property was confirmed by the important case of *Holroyd v Marshall*.[31] A cloth manufacturer borrowed money, and as security, they executed a deed that transferred title to the machinery

---

29 See, for example, *Yorkshire Railway Wagon Co v Maclure* (1882), 21 Ch D 309 (CA); *Westcoast Leasing Ltd v Westcoast Communications Ltd* (1980), 22 BCLR 285 (SC).

30 See, for example, *CIBC Mortgage Corp v Vasquez*, 2002 SCC 60.

31 (1862) 10 HLC 191, 11 ER 999 (cited to HLC).

currently in their mill and any machinery that they might acquire in the future. An execution creditor seized machinery that had been acquired after the deed had been executed. Did the security interest attach to that machinery?

The House of Lords decided that deed would transfer legal title to the machinery that the debtor owned when the deed was executed but could not affect the legal title to machinery acquired at a later date. However, the deed operated as a promise to transfer title to future machinery, which would give rise to an equitable charge over that machinery when it was acquired. Lord Westbury LC said,

> It is quite true that a deed which professes to convey property which is not in existence at the time is as a conveyance void at law, simply because there is nothing to convey. So in equity a contract which engages to transfer property, which is not in existence, cannot operate as an immediate alienation merely because there is nothing to transfer. But if a vendor or mortgagor agrees to sell or mortgage property, real or personal, of which he is not possessed at the time, and he receives the consideration for the contract, and afterwards becomes possessed of property answering the description in the contract, there is no doubt that a Court of Equity would compel him to perform the contract, and that the contract would, in equity, transfer the beneficial interest to the mortgagee or purchaser immediately on the property being acquired.[32]

The law drew a distinction between *floating charges* and *fixed charges*.[33] A charge was floating if the debtor was free to deal with the secured assets in the ordinary course of business. In other words, the debtor was free to sell them, consume them, or use them as security. The floating charge only mattered if the debtor failed to pay the debt and the creditor took steps to enforce their security. A fixed charge did not give the debtor any liberty to deal with the secured assets. That distinction has lost its importance under modern personal property security legislation (discussed below).

2) Equitable Lien

Equitable charges and liens are similar security interests that arise in different ways. A charge is created by intention, whereas a lien arises by operation of law (just as pledges are created by intention and common

---

32   *Ibid* at 210–11.
33   See Roderick J Wood, "The Floating Charge in Canada" (1989) 27 *Alta L Rev* 191.

law liens arise by operation of law). An equitable lien (like a charge) is an encumbrance that gives the creditor a right of recourse to assets owned (and possessed) by the debtor.

The most common equitable lien is the *unpaid vendor's lien*. When a vendor sells land and transfers legal title to the purchaser, they have an equitable lien on the land to secure the payment of the purchase price.[34] These liens arise routinely but rarely need to be enforced. Most purchasers need to borrow money to buy the land and will grant a mortgage over that land to secure the loan. To do this, the purchaser will need to acquire legal title to the land in order to grant a mortgage to the bank to obtain a loan to pay the vendor. So there will be a short period of time in which the purchaser has legal title and the vendor has not been paid in full. The unpaid vendor has a lien during that gap.

The corollary of the unpaid vendor's lien is the *purchaser's lien*. Typically, the purchaser will pay a hefty deposit when the contract is signed. If the transaction cannot proceed for any reason and the purchaser is entitled to a refund of some or all of the deposit, the purchaser's lien secures the vendor's obligation to pay that refund. It is an equitable interest in the land that the vendor had promised to sell.[35] The purchaser's lien matters only if the sale cannot proceed. In most cases, the purchaser will have the right to compel the vendor to complete the transaction.

The vendor's lien secures the purchaser's contractual obligation to pay the purchase price. Although that obligation is created by contract, the lien arises by operation of law. According to the rules of equity, it would be unjust for the purchaser to keep the land without paying for it.[36] The purchaser's lien seems to arise for a similar reason: it would be unjust for the vendor to keep the land and not refund the purchase price. The obligation to refund the money is not contractual but a duty that arises because the vendor has no contractual right to keep it. If the transaction does not proceed because of the purchaser's breach of contract, the vendor may be entitled to keep some or all of the deposit.[37]

Equitable liens can arise in other contexts, sometimes because the defendant acquired assets at the plaintiff's expense without the plaintiff's consent. In other words, the defendant has been *unjustly enriched* and must give the assets back to the plaintiff or pay for their value. This can happen when assets are misappropriated from the plaintiff or from

---

34   See *Mork v Bombauer* (1977), 4 BCLR 127 (SC); *Silaschi v 1054473 Ontario Ltd* (2000), 48 OR (3d) 313, 186 (4th) 339 (CA).

35   See *JAR Leaseholds Ltd v Tormet Ltd*, [1965] 1 OR 347, 48 DLR (2d) 97 (CA); *Lehmann v BRM Enterprises Ltd* (1978), 88 DLR (3d) 87, 7 BCLR 8 (SC).

36   *Leacock v Leacock*, 2009 ABQB 525 at para 7.

37   See *Kowbel v Marusiak* (1957), 7 DLR (2d) 424, 21 WWR (NS) 35 (Alta CA).

a trust for the plaintiff or when the plaintiff transfers assets by mistake. The plaintiff may claim that those assets are held in trust for them or that they have an equitable lien on those assets.[38] The lien secures the defendant's obligation to pay for the value of the assets received at the plaintiff's expense, whereas the trust is a claim to beneficial ownership of those assets.

E. MORTGAGES

The mortgage of land evolved over centuries from possessory security to title security. With the advent of land title registration in the nineteenth century, it has evolved further to become a form of encumbrance.

1) Common Law Mortgage

The mortgage began as a pledge of land called a *gage*. The debtor would transfer possession of the land to the creditor to hold as security for payment of the debt. While in possession, the creditor would receive the income from the land. If that income was credited toward repayment of the debt, the transaction was called a *vif-gage* (i.e., a living pledge). If the income did not reduce the debt, it was a *mortgage* (i.e., a dead pledge). According to canon law, mortgages were sinful because it was usury to charge interest on a loan, and the income was equivalent to interest. However, the arrangement was valid at common law.[39] We still use the term *mortgage* even though the transaction is not a pledge and the creditor does not receive the income from the land.

In the fourteenth century, two main forms of mortgage were used. The first was a lease to the creditor with the term of the lease equal to the term of the loan. If the loan was not repaid in time, the fee simple estate would be transferred to the creditor. This left the creditor with problems of enforcement in the event of default since the debtor held the title. Under the second method, the fee simple estate was transferred to

---

38 *Re Hallett's Estate* (1879), 13 Ch D 696 (CA); *BC Teachers' Credit Union v Betterly* (1975), 61 DLR (3d) 755 (BCSC); *Chase Manhattan Bank NA v Israel-British Bank (London) Ltd*, [1981] Ch 105; *Re Ontario Securities Commission and Greymac Credit Corp* (1986), 30 DLR (4th) 1, 55 OR (2d) 673 (CA), aff'd [1988] 2 SCR 172; *Foskett v McKeown*, [2000] UKHL 29, [2001] 1 AC 102; *BMP Global Distribution Inc v Bank of Nova Scotia*, 2009 SCC 15; *i Trade Finance Inc v Bank of Montreal*, 2011 SCC 26, at paras 29–32.

39 John Baker, *An Introduction to English Legal History*, 5th ed (Oxford: Oxford University Press 2019) at 330.

the creditor at the outset and transferred back to the debtor when the loan was repaid. Although the creditor was in a stronger position, this created other problems. If the creditor died, their heir would become entitled to the estate, and if the creditor died without heirs, the land would escheat to the Crown. Although there were advantages and disadvantages to both forms of mortgage, the second won out in popularity and became what we know today as the *common law mortgage*.[40]

Under a common law mortgage, the creditor has the right to possession of the land (since they hold the fee simple estate), but it became common for the debtor to remain in possession. Once creditors began to charge interest on the loan, they were not permitted to keep the income from the land as well. They were required to account for the income they received (or should have received), and there was no advantage to take possession unless the debtor failed to repay the loan. So the mortgage became a form of title security, with the creditor holding legal title and the debtor in possession (unless they default).

The debtor is the *mortgagor* because they grant the mortgage to the creditor, who receives it as the *mortgagee*. Lay people and law students often mix them up because of the popular notion that people go to the bank to get a mortgage. What they get is a loan. In return, they mortgage their land to the bank to hold as security.

2) Equity of Redemption

At common law, the mortgagor could lose their land if they failed to repay the loan on time, and the consequences could be harsh. The land might be worth much more than the debt. They may have made mortgage payments faithfully for years but missed a payment because of illness or other misfortune. The Court of Chancery began to intervene to provide relief. It would allow a mortgagor in default to redeem their right to recover the land if they could pay everything they owed to the mortgagee. This came to be known as the *equity of redemption*.[41]

The right to redeem could not last forever, so the Court of Chancery invented the decree of *foreclosure*. This is an order giving the mortgagor a period of time (e.g., six months) in which to pay their debt to the mortgagee. If they failed to pay, their right to redeem would be foreclosed, and the mortgagee would retain the fee simple estate free from any claims by the mortgagor.

The equity of redemption is fundamental to our modern understanding of security interests. It is a recognition that the mortgagee's

---

40 *Ibid* at 330–32.
41 *Ibid* at 332–33.

interest in the land is nothing more than security for the payment of a debt. If they receive everything they are owed, they have no cause for complaint and no further interest in the land because the only reason they held title was to make sure that they did get paid. Even though the mortgagee holds the fee simple estate, the mortgagor is the real beneficial owner of the land. The mortgagor holds all the standard incidents of ownership described by Honoré, including the right to the capital value of the land (as discussed above).[42] The mortgagor holds the hope of gain and bears the risk of loss if the land changes in value.

The equity of redemption evolved from a right to relief from forfeiture in the event of default to be understood as the mortgagor's beneficial ownership of the land in equity. It is similar to equitable beneficial ownership under a trust even though the relationship between mortgagee and mortgagor is very different from the relationship between trustee and beneficiary. The mortgagor, like a beneficiary, is the real owner of the land even though they do not have legal title. The mortgagee, like a trustee, does have legal title, but only for a limited purpose. However, the mortgagee does not owe a duty to look after the best interests of the mortgagor. They can act selfishly to preserve their own interests so long as they do so honestly and in good faith.[43] As Lord Templeman said in *Downsview Nominees Ltd v First City Corp Ltd*,

> Several centuries ago equity evolved principles for the enforcement of mortgages and the protection of borrowers. The most basic principles were, first, that a mortgage is security for the repayment of a debt and, secondly, that a security for repayment of a debt is only a mortgage. From these principles flowed two rules, first, that powers conferred on a mortgagee must be exercised in good faith for the purpose of obtaining repayment and secondly that, subject to the first rule, powers conferred on a mortgagee may be exercised although the consequences may be disadvantageous to the borrower.[44]

The term *equity of redemption* has been shortened to *equity* in common parlance. People think of someone's equity in the land as the market value of the land less what they owe on the mortgage. It is what they would have left if the land was sold and the mortgage debt repaid. If that debt is greater than the land's market value, they have *negative equity*.

---

42   Honoré, above note 20.
43   *J & W Investments Ltd v Black* (1963), 38 DLR (2d) 251 at 261–62 (BCCA).
44   [1993] AC 295 at 312 (PC).

3) Land Title Mortgage

Modern land title registration systems have created a new kind of mortgage in which the debtor retains legal title to their land and grants a registered charge to the creditor. This form of land registration is often called the *Torrens system* because it was first introduced in South Australia by Sir Robert Torrens.[45] A mortgage in this system is sometimes called a *Torrens mortgage*[46] but is often called a *land title mortgage* in Canada[47] because the land title registration statute in most provinces and territories is called the *Land Titles Act*.[48]

Land registration is discussed further in chapters 8 and 9. For now, it is enough to know that there are two different kinds of land registration systems in Canada: *title registration* and *deed registration*. Title registration uses a land title mortgage, whereas deed registration continues to use a common law mortgage. Title registration is the only system in British Columbia, Alberta, Saskatchewan, and the territories.[49] Manitoba, Ontario, New Brunswick, and Nova Scotia have both title registration[50] and deed registration.[51] Deed registration is the only system in Prince Edward Island and Newfoundland and Labrador.[52]

The switch from a common law mortgage to a land title mortgage has several benefits, but it is a practical necessity in a title registration system. Two key features of title registration are sometimes called the

---

45   See Robert Torrens, *The South Australian System of Conveyancing by Registration of Title* (Adelaide 1859).

46   See, for example, *Co-op Centre Credit Union Ltd v Greba*, [1984] 5 WWR 481, 10 DLR (4th) 449 (Alta CA) [*Co-op Centre*]; *Project Research Group Ltd v Acumen Investments Ltd* (1986), 33 DLR (4th) 118, 57 OR (2d) 332 (SC).

47   See, for example, *Canada (Director of Soldier Settlement) v Snider Estate*, [1991] 2 SCR 481 at 501, 81 DLR (4th) 161.

48   RSA 2000, c L-4; RSO 1990, c L.5; SNB 1981, c L-1.1; SY 2015, c 10; RSNWT 1988, c 8. It is called the *Land Title Act*, RSBC 1996, c 250, in British Columbia; the *Land Titles Act, 2000*, SS 2000, c L-5.1, in Saskatchewan, the *Real Property Act*, CCSM, c R30, in Manitoba; and the *Land Registration Act*, SNS 2001, c 6, in Nova Scotia.

49   *Land Title Act*, RSBC 1996, c 250; *Land Titles Act*, RSA 2000, c L-4; *Land Titles Act, 2000*, SS 2000, c L-5.1; *Land Titles Act, 2015*, SY 2015, c 10; *Land Titles Act*, RSNWT 1988, c 8.

50   *Real Property Act*, CCSM, c R30; *Land Titles Act*, RSO 1990, c L.5; *Land Titles Act*, SNB 1981, c L-1.1; *Land Registration Act*, SNS 2001, c 6.

51   *Registry Act*, CCSM, c R50; *Registry Act*, RSO 1990, c R.20; *Registry Act*, RSNB 1973, c R-6; *Registry Act*, RSNS 1989, c 392.

52   *Registry Act*, RSPEI 1988, c R-10; *Registration of Deeds Act, 2009*, SNL 2009, c R-10.01.

mirror principle and the *curtain principle*.[53] The mirror principle means that the land title register should provide an accurate reflection of legal title to land. The curtain principle means that purchasers should not have to look behind the register to search for unregistered interests but can acquire title free of those interests when they obtain registration. Trusts and other equitable interests in land do not get registered.

A common law mortgage would play havoc with both principles because the creditor obtains the legal fee simple estate and the debtor has only the equity of redemption. If a title registration system continued to use a common law mortgage, it would not provide an accurate reflection of title. A large number of fee simple estates would be owned by a few banks and other mortgage lenders, whereas the identities of the real owners in equity would be hidden behind the curtain.

For each parcel of land, there is a certificate of title that describes the parcel and who owns the fee simple estate. If the owner grants a mortgage, they continue to be the registered owner of that estate, and the mortgage gets recorded as a registered charge on their certificate of title.[54] Anyone searching the register will see the identity of the real owner and the fact that it is subject to a mortgage. This is an accurate reflection of title.

Another benefit of title registration is that it easily accommodates multiple mortgages. When a common law mortgage is granted, the first mortgagee gets the legal fee simple estate. The mortgagor has only an equity of redemption and therefore cannot grant anything more than an equitable interest to a second mortgagee. The second and all subsequent mortgagees will have equitable mortgages of the equity of redemption. In contrast, multiple land title mortgages can all be registered as legal charges on the mortgagor's certificate of title and take priority in order of registration.

Although the form of mortgage has changed from title security to encumbrance, much of the substance remains the same. We still regard the debtor as having an equity of redemption even though they hold the legal fee simple estate. As Clement JA explained in *Morguard Mortgage Investments Ltd v Faro Development Corp Ltd,*

---

53   *Durrani v Augier* (2000), 190 DLR (4th) 183, 50 OR (3d) 353 at para 42 (SC); *Stanbarr Services Ltd v Metropolis Properties Inc*, 2018 ONCA 244 at para 13; Marcia Neave, "Indefeasibility of Title in the Canadian Context" (1976) 26 *UTLJ* 173.

54   *Land Title Act*, RSBC 1996, c 250, s 231; *Land Titles Act*, RSA 2000, c L-4, s 103; *Land Titles Act, 2000*, SS 2000, c L-5.1, s 123; *Real Property Act*, CCSM, c R30, s 98; *Land Titles Act*, RSO 1990, c L.5, s 93; *Land Titles Act*, SNB 1981, c L-1.1, s 25; *Land Registration Act*, SNS 2001, c 6, s 51; *Land Titles Act, 2015*, SY 2015, c 10, s 123; *Land Titles Act*, RSNWT 1988, c 8, s 115.

We are concerned here with a statutory mortgage pursuant to the *Land Titles Act*, under which the security of the mortgage is afforded by a charge on the land, the title remaining in the name of the mortgagor. In this respect it differs from a common law mortgage in which the security is effected by a transfer of title from the mortgagor to the mortgagee; but the equitable jurisdiction of the Court of Chancery in England over mortgages generally, and the principles upon which it acted, are vested in this Court by virtue of ss. 15 and 16 of the *Judicature Act*, R.S.A. 1970, c. 193, and are exercisable in respect of a statutory mortgage.... The mortgagor is given an opportunity to redeem his land from the charge of the mortgage, as distinct from redemption of the title conveyed to the mortgagee by a common law mortgage.[55]

4) Enforcement

If the mortgagor fails to pay the debt, the mortgagee can enforce its security by taking possession of the land, foreclosing the mortgagor's interest, or selling the land.[56] The court controls the process and tries to maintain a balance between the rights of the parties.

Under a common law mortgage, the creditor has a right to possession of the land when the mortgage is granted. This is because they hold the fee simple estate, which is the right to possess the land for an indefinite period of time. They choose not to take possession but have a right to do so. As Harman J said in *Four-Maids Ltd v Dudley Marshall (Properties) Ltd*,

[T]he right of the mortgagee to possession in the absence of some contract has nothing to do with default on the part of the mortgagor. The mortgagee may go into possession before the ink is dry on the mortgage unless there is something in the contract, express or by implication, whereby he has contracted himself out of that right.[57]

A land title mortgage is a statutory charge and not a transfer of the estate, so whether it confers a right to possession depends on the statute that creates it. All statutes say that a mortgage operates as a charge and not a transfer, but in British Columbia, New Brunswick, and Nova Scotia, the statute goes on to say that it provides the same rights and remedies as a mortgage by transfer. According to the BC version,

---

55   [1975] 1 WWR 737, 50 DLR (3d) 426 at 433 (Alta CA).

56   *Co-op Centre*, above note 46 at para 5 (Alta CA). If the debtor is a corporation, the court might appoint a receiver to take over its management and sell the mortgaged assets for the benefit of the creditor.

57   [1957] Ch 317 at 320.

"the mortgagor and mortgagee are entitled to all the legal and equitable rights and remedies that would be available to them if the mortgagor had transferred the mortgagor's interest in the land to the mortgagee, subject to a proviso for redemption."[58]

It was argued in *Surrey Metro Savings Credit Union v West* that "the rights and remedies of the mortgagee under a mortgage registered under the *Land Title Act* are the same as those under the general law ... and that [the second mortgagee] is entitled to an order for possession."[59] The court did not decide the issue because the first mortgagee was seeking foreclosure and would be the person entitled to possession. In any event, whether the right to possession arises when the mortgage is granted or only later if the debtor is in default, the court has a discretion whether to order the transfer of possession to the creditor.[60] It is part of the overall process of enforcing a mortgage that is under the supervision of the court.

Foreclosure of an equity of redemption under a common law mortgage terminates the debtor's equitable interest and leaves the creditor in possession of the fee simple estate for their own benefit. For a land title mortgage, foreclosure causes a transfer of the fee simple estate from the debtor to the creditor. Foreclosure will not be ordered if the value of the land exceeds the mortgage debt. In that case, the land will be sold and the surplus will be paid to the debtor (or to subsequent mortgagees).

Sale of the land is the usual method of enforcement in most jurisdictions, but people often refer to this process as foreclosure. The creditor conducts the sale, which can place the debtor at a disadvantage because the creditor wants to sell quickly to raise enough money to pay off the debt. They have no incentive to get the best possible price since any surplus will go to the debtor or subsequent mortgagees. As Horsman J said in *0742848 BC Ltd v 426008 BC Ltd*,

> The equitable duties of a mortgagee exercising the power of sale on a mortgagor's default have evolved over time. Courts of equity have long recognized a mortgagor's vulnerability in such circumstances. A mortgagee wishes to recover on the debt and may have little interest in the increased effort and time that would be required to also realize a surplus on the sale. The mortgagor is vitally interested in generating a surplus on the sale but, absent judicial or statutory intervention, has no ability to control the conduct of sale. Left unsupervised, the

---

58   *Land Title Act*, RSBC 1996, c 250, s 231. See *Land Titles Act*, SNB 1981, c L-1.1, s 25(2); *Land Registration Act*, SNS 2001, c 6, s 52(1).

59   [1996] BCWLD 2468 at para 12 (BCSC), Joyce M.

60   *Devlin v Wilson*, [1936] 1 WWR 705 (Sask QB); *Co-op Centre*, above note 46.

mortgagee is free to pursue its self-interest at the expense of the interests of the mortgagor.[61]

To address this problem, the rules of equity require the creditor to act honestly and in good faith. They are entitled to look after their own best interests but cannot act in a way that is unfairly prejudicial to the debtor's interest.[62] In *Cuckmere Brick Co Ltd v Mutual Finance Ltd*,[63] the English Court of Appeal held that the creditor owes a duty of care as well as a duty to act in good faith. Salmon LJ said,

> It is impossible to pretend that the state of the authorities on this branch of the law is entirely satisfactory. There are some *dicta* which suggest that unless a mortgagee acts in bad faith he is safe. His only obligation to the mortgagor is not to cheat him. There are other *dicta* which suggest that in addition to the duty of acting in good faith, the mortgagee is under a duty to take reasonable care to obtain whatever is the true market value of the mortgaged property at the moment he chooses to sell it. . . .
>
> The proposition that the mortgagee owes both duties, in my judgment, represents the true view of the law. Approaching the matter first of all on principle, it is to be observed that if the sale yields a surplus over the amount owed under the mortgage, the mortgagee holds this surplus in trust for the mortgagor. If the sale shows a deficiency, the mortgagor has to make it good out of his own pocket. The mortgagor is vitally affected by the result of the sale but its preparation and conduct is left entirely in the hands of the mortgagee. The proximity between them could scarcely be closer. Surely they are "neighbours." Given that the power of sale is for the benefit of the mortgagee and that he is entitled to choose the moment to sell which suits him, it would be strange indeed if he were under no legal obligation to take reasonable care to obtain what I call the true market value at the date of the sale.[64]

Canadian courts have also concluded that the creditor owes a duty of care to the debtor, but with different views on the standard of care expected.[65] In *Canadian Imperial Bank of Commerce v Conrad*, the

---

61   2019 BCSC 1869 at para 38 [*0742848 BC Ltd*].

62   *South West Marine Estates Ltd v Bank of BC* (1985) 65 BCLR 328 (CA).

63   [1971] Ch 949 (CA).

64   *Ibid* at 966.

65   See *Canadian Imperial Bank of Commerce v Haley* (1979), 100 DLR (3d) 470, 25 NBR (2d) 304 (SC AD); *Re Whatmough and National Trust Co Ltd* (1979), 96 DLR (3d) 382, 23 OR (2d) 452 (SC); *Bank of Nova Scotia v Boisselle* (1985), 63 AR 283 (QB); *0742848 BC Ltd*, above note 61; *Canadian Imperial Bank of Commerce v Conrad*, 2019 NSSC 37 [*Conrad*]. See also *McHugh v Union Bank of Canada*, [1913] AC 299, 10 DLR 562 at 570 (PC).

Supreme Court of Nova Scotia said that the creditor was not expected to meet the standard of a prudent owner dealing with their own property but merely to act with "commercial reasonableness" in the circumstances.[66] In *Frost Ltd v Ralph*, the Newfoundland Supreme Court held that the duty of care was part of the creditor's duty to act in good faith:

> If I may attempt to express my own synopsis of these cases, I would say that a mortgagee is not a trustee except for the surplus after discharging the mortgage and the expenses of sale and, in the conduct of the sale, is bound to act in good faith. A mortgagor is not acting in good faith when the price realized is plainly and significantly short of the true value of the property sold, when the mortgagee acts wilfully and recklessly in the conduct of the sale with the result that the interests of the mortgagor are sacrificed, when he fails to take reasonable precautions to obtain a proper price, or fails to act in a prudent and business-like manner with a view to obtaining as large a price as may fairly and reasonably with due diligence and attention be under the circumstances obtainable.[67]

F. PERSONAL PROPERTY SECURITY

In every Canadian province and territory except Quebec, security interests in personal property are governed by a *Personal Property Security Act* (commonly called the *PPSA*).[68] These statutes were inspired by Article 9 of the American *Uniform Commercial Code*, but with significant differences. The *PPSA* in Saskatchewan was the model for the *PPSA* in New Zealand and Australia.[69] Most of the quotations below are from the Saskatchewan version.

The *PPSA* offers significant advantages over the previous patchwork of laws that governed various forms of personal property security. One advantage is the uniform treatment of all security interests regardless of form. Another is a simplified method of registration. One difficulty for law students (and lawyers) encountering the *PPSA* for the first time is that it uses language not found elsewhere in the law of property. This part of the chapter explains the fundamental concepts used in the *PPSA*.

---

66 *Conrad*, above note 65 at para 39, Smith J.

67 (1980) 115 DLR (3d) 612 at para 58, Goodridge J.

68 RSBC 1996, c 359; RSA 2000, c P-7; SS 1993, c P-6.2; CCSM, c P35; RSO 1990, c P.10; SNB 1993, c P-7.1; SNS 1995-96, c 13; RSPEI 1988, c P-3.1; SNL 1998, c P-7.1; RSY 2002, c 169; SNWT 1994, c 8.

69 Anthony Duggan, "A PPSA Registration Primer" (2011) 35 *Melbourne UL Rev* 865 at 866.

A discussion of its priority rules for dealing with competing security interests is saved for Chapter 9.

1) Security Interests

Most security interests need to be registered to be enforceable against the debtor's other creditors or against people who buy the secured assets from the debtor. Before the *PPSA*, whether a security interest needed to be registered and where it was registered depended on whether it was a bill of sale, charge, chattel mortgage, conditional sale, hire-purchase, and so on.[70] The *PPSA* solved this problem by making form irrelevant. It applies "to every transaction that in substance creates a security interest, without regard to its form and without regard to the person who has title."[71] Every type of security interest receives the same treatment. Form is now so unimportant that the parties need not choose a particular form but can make a security agreement that the creditor will have a "security interest" in the debtor's assets.[72]

There is a list of security interests that are excluded from the *PPSA*. The most significant (for a student of property law) are "a lien, charge or other interest given by statute or rule of law" and "the creation or transfer of an interest in land, including a lease."[73] The *PPSA* applies only to security interests in personal property that are created by intention. Interests that arise by operation of law (such as the repairer's lien, discussed above) are outside the scope of the Act. Interests in land are governed by the land registration systems in each province and territory.

In Ontario, the *PPSA* does not apply "to a transaction between a pledgor and a person who carries on the business of taking, by way of pawn or pledge, any article for the repayment of money lent on the basis of the pawn or pledge."[74] That exemption does not exist elsewhere in Canada.[75] It is an odd and seemingly unnecessary exemption. As discussed below, the creditor's security interest is fully protected so long as the creditor has possession of the secured asset, which is (by definition) what a pawn is. The problem in Ontario is that goods may be pawned that are already subject to a registered security interest. It is difficult to

---

70 Ronald Cuming, Catherine Walsh, & Roderick Wood, *Personal Property Security Law*, 2d ed (Toronto: Irwin Law, 2012) at 319–21.

71 *PPSA*, SS 1993, c P-6.2, s 3(1)(a).

72 Cuming, above note 70 at 116–17.

73 *PPSA*, above note 71, s 4.

74 *PPSA*, RSO 1990, c P.10, s 4(1)(d).

75 A similar exemption does exist in Australia: *Personal Property Securities Act 2009* (Cth), ss 8(1)(ja), 8(6).

understand why a pawnbroker should take priority over other secured creditors.[76] They would not take priority over the owner of stolen goods. The problem is similar.

The *PPSA* also applies to a few "deemed security interests."[77] There are some interests in personal property that are subject to the Act whether they create a security interest or not. The most important (again for a student of property law) is "a lease for a term of more than one year . . . that does not secure payment or performance of an obligation."[78] There are two good reasons for doing this. First, it is not easy to tell whether a lease is a normal lease (in which rent is paid for the use of goods) or a security lease (in which the rent is really payment of the purchase price or repayment of a loan plus interest). By deeming all leases for more than a year to be security interests, that issue is avoided, and the temptation to circumvent the *PPSA* by dressing up a security interest as a lease is removed.

The second reason is that the risk created by a lease is the same as the risk created by title security: the person in possession of goods appears to be the owner, and people may deal with them in the mistaken belief that they are the owner. Registration of the owner's interest, whether the bailment is an ordinary lease or a secured transaction, can alleviate that problem.

2) Registration

Another big advantage of the *PPSA* is the method of registration it provides. Before the *PPSA*, registers for personal property security interests were registers of the documents that created those interests. This was cumbersome to manage because those documents could be massively long debentures, mortgages, and so on. It also created the problem of a *registration gap*. A security document could not be registered until it was executed by the parties, and the registration process would take some time. This meant that there was a significant gap between the date when the security interest was created and the date when it would appear in the register. Someone dealing with the debtor during the gap might be adversely affected by a security interest that existed but was not yet registered.

The *PPSA* deals with both problems by providing a system of *notice registration*. The creditor does not register the security agreement but merely provides notice of its security interest by filling out a form

---

76 Cuming, above note 70 at 167.
77 *Ibid* at 13.
78 *PPSA*, above note 71, s 3(2).

online.[79] The data are much easier to manage, and the creditor can file their notice before the security agreement is executed. Also, one notice can cover several security agreements.[80] This does not eliminate the gap problem because the PPSA provides short grace periods in which to register in certain circumstances, such as when goods subject to a security interest in another jurisdiction are brought into a province or territory or when goods are sold on credit.[81]

3) Collateral and Proceeds

Under the PPSA, *collateral* "means personal property that is subject to a security interest."[82] Personal property is defined broadly and includes almost any sort of asset other than an interest in land. Goods are included (of course), but the definition of goods in the PPSA goes beyond the normal meaning of goods to include "fixtures, crops and the unborn young of animals."[83] These are not normally regarded as separate things subject to property rights. Fixtures are goods that are attached to land (as discussed in Chapter 9) and normally regarded as part of the estate in land and not as goods.[84] The same is true of growing crops, although they are treated as goods for some purposes. Unborn animals would normally be regarded as part of their mother.

Proceeds are assets that are acquired by the debtor in exchange for the collateral. For example, if goods subject to a security interest were sold, the money paid to the debtor for those goods would be their proceeds. If that money was deposited in the debtor's bank account, that account would be the proceeds, and if that account was used to buy other goods, they would become the proceeds.

The PPSA refers to proceeds as "identifiable or traceable personal property."[85] The process of identifying the product of an exchange is called *tracing*.[86] It can be difficult to trace when collateral or proceeds are mixed with other assets, which often happens when money gets paid in and out of bank accounts. The PPSA does not provide the rules used to sort out these difficulties but relies on common law and equity, which has a long history of dealing with that problem, most notably when

---

79   See Cuming, above note 70 at 332–34.
80   *Ibid* at 327–30.
81   *PPSA*, above note 71, ss 5, 34.
82   *Ibid*, s 2(1)(g).
83   *Ibid*, s 2(1)(u).
84   See Cuming, above note 70 at 590–600.
85   *PPSA*, above note 71, s 2(1)(hh).
86   See Lionel D Smith, *The Law of Tracing* (Oxford: Oxford University Press, 1997).

assets have been misappropriated from a trust and the beneficiaries are seeking to recover those assets or their traceable proceeds.[87]

4) Attachment and Enforceability

A security interest comes into existence when it *attaches* to the collateral. This occurs when "value is given" and "the debtor has rights in the collateral or power to transfer rights in the collateral to a secured party."[88] These two requirements relate to the very nature of a security interest, which is a property right to the debtor's assets to secure an obligation owed by the debtor to the creditor. It cannot exist until the debtor has something that can be the subject of the creditor's property right and there is an obligation to secure.

Those two requirements are sufficient to create a security interest that is enforceable against the debtor, but that interest will not be enforceable against anyone else until a third requirement is met. The "security interest is enforceable against a third party only where" the creditor has possession of the collateral or the debtor has signed a security agreement that creates a security interest and contains a description of the collateral.[89] Only tangible personal property can be possessed, so a security agreement is normally required for the enforcement of security interests in intangible property. However, the *PPSA* does allow enforcement against third parties if the creditor has *control* of certain types of intangible property (*investment property* and *electronic chattel paper*, which are defined in the Act).[90]

5) Perfection

An enforceable security interest is vulnerable unless it is *perfected* because an unperfected security interest is not enforceable against the debtor's trustee in bankruptcy.[91] A judgment creditor can also take priority over an unperfected security interest.[92] A security interest is perfected if the creditor has possession (or control) of the collateral or by registration of a financing statement.[93] A pawnbroker's security

---

87   See Cuming, above note 70 at 567–79.
88   *PPSA*, above note 71, s 12(1).
89   *Ibid*, s 10(1).
90   See Cuming, above note 70 at 24–37.
91   *PPSA*, above note 71, s 20(2); see *Re Giffen*, [1998] 1 SCR 91, 155 DLR (4th) 332.
92   See Cuming, above note 70 at 494–504.
93   *PPSA*, above note 71, ss 19, 24, 25; see Cuming, above note 70 at ch 5.

interest will be perfected because they have possession of the pawned goods. Most security interests are perfected by registration.

The priority of competing claims by secured creditors is normally determined by the order in which the security interests were perfected. This is discussed further in Chapter 9.

6) After-Acquired Property

A security agreement can contain "a statement that a security interest is taken in all of the debtor's present and after-acquired personal property."[94] This replaces the floating charge (discussed above). The security interest will attach to the collateral when it is acquired by the debtor, who is free to deal with the collateral if "the secured party expressly or impliedly authorizes the dealing."[95] In any event, if the debtor sells or leases goods in the ordinary course of their business, the buyer or bailee will take the goods free of any security interest in those goods unless they know it is a breach of the security agreement.[96]

---

94 *PPSA*, above note 71, s 10(1)(d)(iii).
95 *Ibid*, s 28(1).
96 *Ibid*, s 30(2); see Cuming, above note 70 at 383–93.

CHAPTER 7

OTHER INTERESTS IN LAND

A. INTRODUCTION

Much of the law of property applies generally to land, goods, and other things, all of which can be owned, shared, held in trust, subject to security interests, and so on. As discussed in Chapter 3, title to land is different from the ownership and possession of other things. This chapter deals with another way in which land is treated differently. There are property rights to make use of land that is owned and possessed by someone else that have no counterparts in other areas of property law.

Four types of property rights are discussed in this chapter: *rentcharges*, *profits à prendre*, *easements*, and *restrictive covenants*. A rentcharge (as the name implies) is a right to payments of money, a profit is a right to enter land and take away a natural resource (e.g., wood or minerals), an easement is a right to make some use of neighbouring land (e.g., a right of way to cross it), and a restrictive covenant is a right to restrict the use of neighbouring land (e.g., for residential purposes only). The first three have been part of the common law for many centuries, whereas the restrictive covenant was established by the rules of equity in the nineteenth century.

1) Incorporeal Hereditaments

Rentcharges, profits, and easements are classified as *incorporeal hereditaments*. Like many terms in the law of property, this is outdated and unhelpful. A hereditament was a right that could be inherited back when real property would descend to the heir on the death of its owner. It could be granted to a person and their heirs, just like a fee simple estate. We no longer have inheritance, so hereditaments form part of the estate of a deceased person and are given away by will or on intestacy (just like any other right *in rem* or right *in personam* that continues after death).

Hereditaments are either *corporeal* or *incorporeal*. These adjectives imply a distinction between tangible and intangible things, which sometimes finds expression in the cases. For example, the BC Court of Appeal quoted the leading English textbook on real property with approval: "Corporeal hereditaments are lands, buildings, minerals, trees and all other things which are part of or affixed to land—in other words, the physical matter over which ownership is exercised. Incorporeal hereditaments, on the other hand, are not things at all, but rights."[1]

However, all hereditaments are rights to land. The distinction is based on possession. An estate is a corporeal hereditament because it is a right to possess land. As discussed in Chapter 3, it is a right to possess a space on the earth regardless of the contents of that space. Most estates include the empty air space above the ground. If a house burns down, the estate remains unchanged: the owner still has the same right to possess the space where the house used to be.

In contrast, a *profit à prendre* is incorporeal because it is not a right to possession but a right to make some use of land possessed by another. A right to cut trees on someone's land can be a profit. It is a right to enter the land and remove trees. When it is exercised, the profit holder will remove physical objects from the land and obtain the right to possess them as goods.

We continue to classify property rights as corporeal hereditaments or incorporeal hereditaments even though both are rights to land, neither is inherited, and the terms do not reveal the real significance of the distinction, which is based on the right to possession. As Laskin J said (dissenting) in *Saskatchewan Minerals v Keyes*,

> The language of "corporeal" and "incorporeal" does not point up the distinction between the legal interest and its subject-matter. On this

---

1   *R v Esquimalt*, [1972] 5 WWR 362 at 365, Maclean JA, quoting the third edition of *Megarry and Wade on The Law of Real Property*; see Charles Harpum, Stuart Bridge, & Martin Dixon, *Megarry & Wade: The Law of Real Property*, 8th ed (London: Sweet & Maxwell, 2012) at 8 & 1359. See also *Pegg v Pegg* (1992), 1 Alta LR (3d) 249, 21 RPR (2d) 149 at para 15 (QB); *Bank of Montreal v Dynex Petroleum Ltd*, 2002 SCC 7 at para 8.

distinction, all legal interests are "incorporeal," and it is only the unconfronted force of a long history that makes it necessary in this case to examine certain institutions of property in the common law provinces through an antiquated system of classification and an antiquated terminology.[2]

Rentcharges, profits, and easements are not the only incorporeal hereditaments. There are other hereditaments that are significant in England (but not in Canada). For example, a *franchise* is a right to hold a public market in a specific place. The right to hold the market is different from the right to possess the land where the market is held. As Russell LJ said in *Oswestry Corp v Hudd*,

> In connection with a market there is a distinction to be drawn between the "market," in the sense of the right to hold a concourse of buyers and sellers, and the place where the concourse is held — the "market place." A market in the former sense is a local monopoly right in the nature of an incorporeal hereditament, commonly originating in a grant from the Crown.[3]

Another incorporeal hereditament is an *advowson*, which is the right of a patron to nominate someone to an ecclesiastical living when the office becomes vacant.[4] Land in England can be subject to a liability for *chancel repairs*, which requires the owners to contribute to the cost of repairing the chancel (i.e., the eastern half) of the local church.[5]

2) Limits on Property Rights to Use Land

There is a wide variety of ways in which people can have property rights to use land they do not possess, but the choice is not unlimited. Landowners are generally free to grant licences (i.e., rights *in personam*) to people to use the land as the parties see fit. However, a right to use land cannot be a right *in rem* that is enforceable generally against others unless it is recognized at law or in equity as an acceptable form of property.

In *Keppell v Bailey*,[6] the owners of three different ironworks got together with others to form a company for the construction of a railroad to be used to carry limestone from a quarry to their ironworks. The owners promised the company that they and their heirs, successors, and

---

2   [1972] SCR 703 at 722, 23 DLR (3d) 573.

3   [1966] 1 WLR 363 at 377 (CA).

4   *Sharpe v The Bishop of Worcester*, [2015] EWCA Civ 399 at para 16.

5   *Aston Cantlow and Wilmcote with Billesley Parochial Church Council v Wallbank*, [2003] UKHL 37, [2004] AC 546 at paras 97–109.

6   (1834) 2 My & K 517, 39 ER 1042 [cited to My & K].

assigns would obtain all of their limestone from that quarry and use the railroad to transport it at a rate of 5 pence per ton per mile. The owners of one of the ironworks sold it, and the court held that the new owners were not bound by that promise. The company had acquired rights *in personam* enforceable against the owners who made the promises but did not have any rights *in rem* concerning the use of their lands. Lord Brougham LC said,

> Consider the question first upon principle. There are certain known incidents to property and its enjoyment; among others, certain burthens wherewith it may be affected, or rights which may be created and enjoyed over it by parties other than the owner; all which incidents are recognised by the law.... But it must not therefore be supposed that incidents of a novel kind can be devised and attached to property at the fancy or caprice of any owner. It is clearly inconvenient both to the science of the law and to the public weal that such a latitude should be given. There can be no harm in allowing the fullest latitude to men in binding themselves and their representatives, that is, their assets real and personal, to answer in damages for breach of their obligations. This tends to no mischief, and is a reasonable liberty to bestow; but great detriment would arise and much confusion of rights if parties were allowed to invent new modes of holding and enjoying real property, and to impress upon their lands and tenements a peculiar character, which should follow them into all hands, however remote. Every close, every messuage, might thus be held in a several fashion; and it would hardly be possible to know what rights the acquisition of any parcel conferred, or what obligations it imposed.[7]

Another example is provided by *Hill v Tupper*.[8] The owner of a canal granted a lease of land beside the canal to the plaintiff to carry on the business of hiring out pleasure boats for use on the canal. The lease said that the plaintiff had "the sole and exclusive right or liberty to put or use boats on the said canal, and let the same for hire for the purpose of pleasure only."[9] The defendant was the landlord of a nearby inn that provided pleasure boats to their customers to use on the canal. The court held that the rights granted to the plaintiff by the canal owner could not be enforced against the defendant. Pollock CB said,

> This grant merely operates as a licence or covenant on the part of the grantors, and is binding on them as between themselves and the

---

7   *Ibid* at 535–36.
8   (1863) 2 H & C 121, 159 ER 51 [cited to H & C].
9   *Ibid* at 123.

grantee, but gives him no right of action in his own name for any infringement of the supposed exclusive right. . . . A new species of incorporeal hereditament cannot be created at the will and pleasure of the owner of property; but he must be content to accept the estate and the right to dispose of it subject to the law as settled by decisions or controlled by act of parliament. A grantor may bind himself by covenant to allow any right he pleases over his property, but he cannot annex to it a new incident, so as to enable the grantee to sue in his own name for an infringement of such a limited right as that now claimed.[10]

The right to use boats on a canal can be a perfectly valid easement (as discussed below). However, an easement to use land (including land covered by water) cannot confer the right to exclude others from that land. A person with an easement or other incorporeal hereditament can complain if someone interferes with their right to use the land. However, the defendant had not interfered with the plaintiff's right to put boats on the canal. The defendant was taking business away from the plaintiff by interfering with their exclusive right to do so. There are property rights that do create monopolies, such as intellectual property and a franchise to hold a market (mentioned above), but there is no property right to the kind of monopoly that the plaintiff claimed. The only person wronged by the defendant's activities was the canal owner, who was entitled to sue for wrongful interference with their right to possession.

In civil law jurisdictions (such as Quebec), there are strict limits on the variety of property rights less than ownership. This is based on the idea that one person should hold all the rights associated with ownership, which a civilian lawyer would describe as "the collective of the *usus* (right to use of the thing), *fructus* (right to its fruits) and *abusus* (right to alienate or destroy the thing)."[11] There is a *numerus clausus* (i.e., closed number) of permitted exceptions in which someone else can have a property right (which a civilian would call a *real right*) to use something without being its owner. As Paul Matthews said,

[T]he principle is that in relation to any particular thing there should be a single person who has all the rights. The fragmentation (or dismemberment) of property into different estates or interests of different values, each belonging to a different person, so characteristic of property law in the common law world (and especially in relation to land) finds no place in this system. It is true that societal necessity

---

10   *Ibid* at 127–28.
11   Daniel Clarry, "Fiduciary Ownership and Trusts in a Comparative Perspective" (2014) 63 *ICLQ* 901 at 907.

forces the civil law to provide for a limited number of real rights which are less than ownership. This so-called *numerus clausus* of lesser real rights includes rights such as the hypothec, the usufruct, the servitude and so on. But they are very much exceptions to the general principle. In the singular, they are usually each referred to as *ius in re aliena*: a right in a thing belonging to someone else.[12]

The common law does control the creation of new property rights (as discussed above), but it does not have a *numerus clausus*. There is no principle in favour of undivided and absolute ownership. The common law has always allowed the use and enjoyment of land to be distributed among many people holding different estates in the same land (as discussed in Chapter 3). It has enabled the creation of a wide variety of different ways in which people can make use of land possessed by others and continues to add new property rights to their number, which is never closed.

A recent addition is the *overriding royalty* used in the oil and gas industry. A right to take oil and gas from someone's land is a *profit à prendre* (discussed below). The person who holds that profit has a *working interest*. They would often grant shares of the royalties they hope to earn to others. The common law allows people to attach rentcharges to estates, but nothing similar was available for a *profit à prendre*. The profit was a property right to the land, but the right to receive a share of the money generated by that profit was not.[13] In *Bank of Montreal v Dynex Petroleum Ltd*,[14] the Supreme Court of Canada confirmed that an overriding royalty should be regarded as an interest in land. In other words, the common law evolved to keep up with the practice in the industry. Major J said,

> The oil and gas industry, which developed largely in the second half of the 20th century and continues to evolve, is governed by a combination of statute and common law. The application of common law concepts to a new or developing industry is useful as it provides the participants in the industry and the courts some framework for the legal structure of the industry. It should come as no surprise that some common law concepts, developed in different social, industrial

12   Paul Matthews, "The Compatibility of the Trust with the Civil Law Notion of Property" in Lionel Smith, ed, *The Worlds of the Trust* (Cambridge: Cambridge University Press, 2013) 313 at 320.

13   See WH Ellis, "Property Status of Royalties in Canadian Oil and Gas Law" (1984) 22 *Alta L Rev* 1.

14   [2002] 1 SCR 146, 208 DLR (4th) 155.

and legal contexts, are inapplicable in the unique context of the industry and its practices.

The appellant could not offer any convincing policy reasons for maintaining the common law prohibition on the creation of an interest in land from an incorporeal hereditament other than fidelity to common law principles. Given the custom in the oil and gas industry and the support found in case law, it is proper and reasonable that the law should acknowledge that an overriding royalty interest can, subject to the intention of the parties, be an interest in land.[15]

B. RENTCHARGES

The common law distinguished *rentcharges* from *rent services*.[16] The periodic payments due from a tenant to their landlord is a rent service, which we now just call *rent*. If land is charged with periodic payments of rent to someone other than a landlord, it is a rentcharge.

In *McDonald v Bode Estate*,[17] the owners of a fee simple estate granted a twenty-five-year lease to a tenant with rent paid annually. They then sold the fee simple to a purchaser who assigned the right to receive the rent back to them. The BC Court of Appeal held that their right to receive the rent was an interest in land even though they were no longer the tenant's landlords. In other words, what began as a rent service was converted by the assignment into a rentcharge.

In England, rentcharges are often used to compel the owners of fee simple estates to contribute to the cost of maintaining sewerage and other shared services. For example, in *Orchard Trading Estate Management Ltd v Johnson Security Ltd*,[18] a small industrial estate had a private sewage system. Fifteen separate units were sold, and each was subject to two rentcharges in favour of the company that owned the common areas: a fixed rentcharge of £1 per year plus a variable rentcharge to cover the costs incurred by the company to maintain the common areas. The sewage system broke down, and the company had to replace it at considerable expense. The unit owners were required to pay their share of the cost of this as a rentcharge.

---

15 *Ibid* at paras 17–18. See also *Third Eye Capital Corp v Dianor Resources Inc*, 2018 ONCA 253.

16 *Pickering Square Inc v Trillium College Inc*, 2014 ONSC 2629 at paras 29–36; *Toronto Standard Condominium Corp No 1487 v Market Lofts Inc*, 2015 ONSC 1067 at paras 57–59.

17 2018 BCCA 140.

18 [2002] EWCA Civ 406 [*Orchard Trading*].

Rentcharges are less common in Canada. The sharing of communal costs can be achieved by using a condominium instead. In a condominium (discussed in Chapter 5), the common areas are owned by the unit owners as tenants in common, and they are required to contribute to the cost of maintaining those areas through the payment of condo fees.

C. PROFITS

A *profit à prendre* is a right to enter land possessed by another and take away some part of the natural produce of the land.[19] This includes soil, minerals, natural vegetation, fish, and wild animals. For example, there are profits for sand and gravel,[20] minerals,[21] petroleum and natural gas,[22] hay,[23] timber,[24] fishing and hunting,[25] and trapping.[26] It is not possible to have a profit to take water since it is not regarded as the produce of the land,[27] but there are easements to take water from neighbouring land (as discussed below). There is no profit to take domestic animals or crops that are sown and harvested annually because they are regarded as the product of industry (sometimes called the *fructus industrials*) and not the natural produce of the land (i.e., the *fructus naturales*).[28] A right to harvest a sown crop is an *emblement*. A tenant who sows a crop has a right to harvest it if the tenancy ends prematurely.[29]

---

19   *R v Tener*, [1985] 1 SCR 533 at 540–42, 17 DLR (4th) 1 [*Tener*].
20   *Atlantic Concrete Ltd v Levatte Construction Co Ltd* (1975), 62 DLR (3d) 663, 12 NSR (2d) 179 (CA) [*Atlantic Concrete*]; *Siewert v Seward*, [1975] 3 WWR 584, 54 DLR (3d) 161 (Alta CA).
21   *Tener*, above note 19.
22   *Berkheiser v Berkheiser*, [1957] SCR 387, 7 DLR (2d) 721 [*Berkheiser*].
23   *Kirk v Ford*, [1920] 3 WWR 91, 53 DLR 644 (Sask CA) [*Kirk*].
24   *Anderson v Rolandi Brothers Logging Co* (1955), 17 WWR (NS) 119 (BCSC); *Cameron v Silverglen Farms Ltd* (1982), 132 DLR (3d) 505, 51 NSR (2d) 64 (SC) [*Cameron*]; *Robillard v Staaf*, 2008 BCSC 1266 [*Robillard*].
25   *Komari Inc v Feddema* (1988), 55 DLR (4th) 595, 67 OR (2d) 135 (SC).
26   *Bolton v Forest Pest Management Institute*, [1985] 6 WWR 562, 21 DLR (4th) 242 (BCCA).
27   See *Alfred F Beckett Ltd v Lyons*, [1967] Ch 449 at 481–82 (CA).
28   See *Fredkin v Glines* (1908), 9 WLR 393, 18 Man R 249 (CA); *Kirk*, above note 23.
29   *Cochlin v Massey Harris Co Ltd* (1915), 8 Alta LR 392 (CA); *F Moyer Boot & Shoe Co v Moellendorf*, [1930] 3 WWR 311, 25 Alta LR 76 (CA).

1) Profits in Gross and Profits Appurtenant

The land subject to a *profit à prendre* is called the *servient tenement*. A profit can exist *in gross*, meaning that it can belong to anyone (other than the owner of the servient tenement). A profit can also be granted for the benefit of nearby land, in which case it is a *profit appurtenant*.[30] This gives the owner of the nearby land (called the *dominant tenement*) the right to take some natural resource from the servient tenement. For a profit appurtenant, the amount that can be taken is limited either by the needs of the dominant tenement (e.g., wood for fuel) or by the terms of the grant.[31]

For example, a right to graze animals on the servient tenement can be a *profit à prendre*,[32] in which the animals enter the land and take away the natural produce by eating it. If it is a profit appurtenant, then the grant may specify the number of animals permitted to graze. If it does not, then the number of animals is limited by the capacity of the dominant tenement to support them through the winter. A profit appurtenant to graze without a specified limit cannot be separated from the dominant tenement because that could unfairly increase the burden on the servient tenement.

If the grant specifies a limit on the number of animals, then the profit can exist in gross and be transferred to others since the burden on the servient tenement would not be increased if someone other than a neighbour exercised the grazing right. In *Bettison v Langton*,[33] the House of Lords held that a profit appurtenant to graze ten head of cattle and thirty sheep could be severed from the dominant tenement and sold separately as a profit in gross.

2) Exclusive and Non-exclusive Profits

A profit can be an exclusive right to take something from the land, or it can leave the landowner free to take it as well. In *Duke of Sutherland v Heathcote*,[34] land was sold and the vendors reserved a profit for coal and other minerals. The court held that this was not an exclusive right; therefore, the new landowners were free to grant a right to take coal to someone else. Lindley LJ said,

---

30   See *Snyder v Chisholm*, 2015 NSCA 39.

31   *Ibid* at para 40.

32   See *R v Alexson*, [1989] 6 WWR 275, 68 Alta LR (2d) 255 (Prov Ct); *Patton v OH Ranch Ltd* (1996), 138 DLR (4th) 381, 43 Alta LR (3d) 445 (CA).

33   [2002] UKHL 24, [2002] 1 AC 27, aff'g [2000] Ch 54 (CA).

34   [1892] 1 Ch 475 (CA).

A *profit à prendre* is a right to take something off another person's land; such a right does not prevent the owner from taking the same sort of thing from off his own land; the first right may limit, but does not exclude, the second. An exclusive right to all the profit of a particular kind can, no doubt be granted; but such a right cannot be inferred from language which is not clear and explicit.[35]

3) Duration of the Profit

A profit can be granted for a limited time (like a lease or life estate) or indefinitely (like a fee simple).[36] In *Robillard v Staaf*,[37] land was sold but the vendors retained the timber on the property, with no time limit specified. The land had recently been logged and was then being used as a hayfield. The court construed this as a profit to harvest one crop of trees that may grow in the future. Williams J said,

> The contract is silent as to any duration. One possibility is that the right could be considered to have been granted in perpetuity. Frankly, that is not a compelling or especially reasonable conclusion. If that were to be the case, then the owner of the land is effectively limited in the use of his land forever. Its value to him is drastically curtailed. Presumably, by that analysis, his rights would be limited to looking after the property and paying taxes on it. In my view, for the right to be considered a perpetual one, the language would have to be clear and explicit to that effect. Alternatively, the right should be considered to extend to the harvest of one crop. Given the growth cycle of the crop involved, that makes the most practical sense.[38]

4) Profit or Sale of Goods?

It is not always easy to tell whether a right to take something from land is a *profit à prendre* or a sale of goods (coupled with a licence to enter the land and get the goods).[39] A profit is a property right to the land that arises when the profit is granted even though it might not be exercised for many years. A contract to sell the natural produce of the land as

---

35   *Ibid* at 484–85. See also *Cameron*, above note 24.

36   *Berkheiser*, above note 22.

37   *Robillard*, above note 24.

38   *Ibid* at paras 42–43. See also *Corporate Affairs Commission v ASC Timber Pty Ltd* (1989), 18 NSWLR 577 [*ASC Timber*].

39   See *Fredkin v Glines*, above note 28; *Kirk*, above note 23; *Atlantic Concrete*, above note 20.

goods cannot transfer any property rights to that produce until it is severed from the land and thereby converted into goods.

A person with a profit has a right *in rem* to the land that can be enforced against others who might acquire an interest in the land.[40] If the landowner becomes bankrupt, their trustee in bankruptcy will be entitled to take the land and sell it for the benefit of the landowner's creditors, but the profit will be enforceable against the trustee and anyone who buys the land.[41] In contrast, a person with a contract for the sale of future goods would not be able to enforce that right against a subsequent owner of the land but would have to be content with a claim against the seller for damages for breach of contract. If the seller is bankrupt, the buyer would be an unsecured creditor with the hope that they might receive some portion of what is owed to them when the bankrupt's estate is distributed.

In a perfect world, people would express clearly and in writing whether they are granting a *profit à prendre* or making a sale of goods. When they fail to do so, a court may be asked to decide what was intended, taking into account the language used and relevant circumstances. For example, a contract to sell hay or trees ready for harvest is likely to be a sale of goods, whereas a contract to sell natural produce that has yet to grow is more likely to be a profit.[42]

D. EASEMENTS

An easement is like a *profit à prendre* because both are common law property rights to make use of land (called a *servient tenement*) without possessing it. An easement differs from a profit in two respects. First, it is not a right to take something from the land but a right to use it in some other way. The best-known easement is a right of way to cross land (e.g., to access a beach or public road). It is possible to have an easement to take water, but that is not regarded as taking away part of the land.

Second, easements cannot exist in gross at common law. There are statutory easements in gross and public rights of way,[43] but a common law easement must have a dominant tenement. The person with possession of the dominant tenement has a right to make some use of the servient tenement.

---

40   *Kirk*, above note 23.
41   See *ASC Timber*, above note 38.
42   *Fredkin v Glines*, above note 28; *Kirk*, above note 23; *Robillard*, above note 24.
43   See *Nelson v 1153696 Alberta Ltd*, 2011 ABCA 203 [*Nelson*].

1) Positive and Negative Easements

Easements may be positive or negative. A *positive easement* is a right to do something that interferes with the possession or enjoyment of the servient tenement and would otherwise be a trespass or a nuisance.[44] A *negative easement* merely prevents the owner of the servient tenement from doing something they would normally be free to do. Schroeder JA provided a good description of these two categories in *Temma Realty Co Ltd v Ress Enterprises Ltd*:

> There is a sharp distinction between an affirmative easement such as a right of way and a negative easement such as a right to light or air. The former is one which entitles the dominant owner to make active use of the servient tenement, or to do some act which, in the absence of the easement, would be a nuisance or a trespass, whereas the latter is a right in the owner of the dominant tenement to restrict the owner of the servient tenement, in respect of the tenement, in the exercise of general and natural rights of property. It does not entitle the dominant owner to make any active use of the servient tenement.[45]

There are two negative easements: a right to light and air and a right to support for buildings. An easement for light and air prevents the owner of the servient tenement from obstructing the flow of light and air into windows and skylights on the dominant tenement.[46] If those windows are adjacent to the servient tenement, this easement can substantially limit the liberty to construct buildings on the servient tenement. There is no right to the flow of light and air generally from one parcel of land to another. The easement is limited to windows and skylights. An easement for light and air through a doorway was claimed and rejected in *Levet v Gas Light and Coke Co*[47] even though the owners were in the habit of leaving it open on nice days for the purpose of letting in light and air.

A right to lateral support from an adjoining building can be acquired as an easement.[48] The owner of the building on the servient tenement must take care when renovating or demolishing it to avoid damage to the adjoining building caused by removing the support. However, they

---

44   See *Ross v Hunter* (1882), 7 SCR 289 at 315–16.

45   [1968] 2 OR 293, 69 DLR (2d) 195 at para 28 (CA).

46   *Tapling v Jones* (1865), 11 HL Cas 290, 20 CBNS 166; *Easton v Isted*, [1903] 1 Ch 405 (CA). See also *Earl Putnam Organization Ltd v Macdonald* (1978), 91 DLR (3d) 714, 21 OR (2d) 815 (CA).

47   [1919] 1 Ch 24.

48   *Dalton v Henry Angus & Co* (1881), 6 App Cas 740.

do not have an obligation to keep their building in good repair (since an easement does not impose a positive obligation to do something). This easement should not be confused with the natural right every land-owner has to support for their land in its natural state.[49] Excavation that causes a neighbour's land to subside is actionable without the need for an easement.

The law draws a "sharp distinction" between positive and negative easements because of the manner in which easements are created. As discussed below, most easements are created by intention, in which the owner of the servient tenement agrees to grant an easement to the owner of the dominant tenement. However, in some jurisdictions, ease-ments can also arise by *prescription* without the consent of the owner of the servient tenement. This can occur if an easement is exercised without permission for a sufficiently long period of time (e.g., twenty years). The exercise of a positive easement (before it exists) is a trespass or nuisance, and the landowner can take legal action to stop it. The enjoyment of a negative easement (before it exists) involves no wrong-doing. There is no interference with the landowner's rights.

Because easements can arise by prescription in England and else-where, the law is reluctant to allow new forms of negative easements to be created. The worry is that a landowner may lose the right to make full use of their land if they choose not to do so for a long period of time. If your neighbours have long enjoyed the view across your land, should you be prevented from building on it and blocking their view? If they enjoyed the shade from your tree, could they stop you from cutting it down?[50]

This problem was addressed by the English Court of Appeal in *Phipps v Pears*.[51] Two houses in Warwick had been constructed next to each other. The owner of one house pulled it down, which left a wall of the other house exposed to weather. The wall had never been properly weatherproofed and never needed to be while the other house stood next to it. The exposed wall was severely damaged by the weather, and its owner sued their neighbour, claiming an easement by prescription to be protected from the weather. That was rejected by the court. Lord Denning MR said,

> There are two kinds of easements known to the law: positive ease-
> ments, such as a right of way, which give the owner of land a right
> himself to do something on or to his neighbour's land: and negative

---

49   See *Morris v Redland Bricks Ltd*, [1970] AC 652.
50   See *Zbarsky v Lukashuk*, [1992] 1 WWR 690, 61 BCLR (2d) 349 (CA).
51   [1964] EWCA Civ 3, [1965] 1 QB 76.

easements, such as a right of light, which gives him a right to stop his neighbour doing something on his (the neighbour's) own land. . . . [A] right to protection from the weather (if it exists) is entirely negative. It is a right to stop your neighbour pulling down his own house. Seeing that it is a negative easement, it must be looked at with caution. Because the law has been very chary of creating any new negative easements. . . .

    [I]f we were to stop a man pulling down his house, we would put a brake on desirable improvement. Every man is entitled to pull down his house if he likes. If it exposes your house to the weather, that is your misfortune. It is no wrong on his part. Likewise every man is entitled to cut down his trees if he likes, even if it leaves you without shelter from the wind or shade from the sun. . . . There is no such easement known to the law as an easement to be protected from the weather. The only way for an owner to protect himself is by getting a covenant from his neighbour that he will not pull down his house or cut down his trees. Such a covenant would be binding on him in contract: and it would be enforceable on any successor who took with notice of it. But it would not be binding on one who took without notice.[52]

It is possible to acquire the right to restrict a neighbour's use of their land by getting a covenant from them not to use their land in a certain way. Since covenants are always express promises and never arise by prescription, they can be used to create restrictions that are not allowed to take effect as negative easements. Covenants are discussed below.

Positive easements are treated differently from negative easements. As Perell J said in *1832732 Ontario Corp v Regina Properties Ltd,*

The types of easements are not closed, and new examples may be created. However, there are few negative easements, and the law is reluctant to grant new ones. The work of negative easements is, practically speaking, more often performed by equity through its recognition of restrictive covenants.[53]

New positive easements have developed to keep up with the changing ways in which people use land. The New South Wales Court of Appeal said in 2002, "Novelty alone is insufficient as bar to the recognition of

---

52 *Ibid* at 82–84.

53 2018 ONSC 7643 at para 42. See also *Attorney-General of Southern Nigeria v John Holt & Co (Liverpool) Ltd,* [1915] AC 599 at 617 (PC); *Mulvaney v Jackson,* [2002] EWCA Civ 1078, [2003] 4 All ER 83 at para 20; *Regency Villas Title Ltd v Diamond Resorts (Europe) Ltd,* [2017] EWCA Civ 238, [2017] Ch 516 at para 51, varied [2018] UKSC 57, [2019] AC 553.

the creation of an easement."[54] Lord St Leonards LC said back in 1852: "The category of servitudes and easements must alter and expand with the changes that take place in the circumstances of mankind. The law ... frequently moulds its practical operation without doing any violence to its original principles."[55]

There is a surprisingly wide variety of positive easements, including easements to wander in a garden,[56] plant a flower garden,[57] use a beach for swimming and recreation,[58] use a playground,[59] use a golf course and swimming pools,[60] park cars,[61] use an airfield,[62] use a lavatory,[63] and use a pew in church.[64] There are easements for pipelines that run through the land.[65] There are rights of way to cross land, which may be restricted to footpaths,[66] may allow motor vehicles,[67] or may even include a right to drive cattle.[68]

There are numerous easements related to water, including the right to take water from ponds and wells on the servient tenement to supply the dominant tenement,[69] the right for cattle to enter the servient tenement to drink water,[70] and the right to discharge water onto the servient

54   *Clos Farming Estates v Easton*, [2002] NSWCA 389 at para 41, Santow JA.

55   *Dyce v Lady James Hay* (1852), 1 Macq 305 at 312–13.

56   *Re Ellenborough Park*, [1955] EWCA Civ 4, [1956] Ch 131 [*Ellenborough Park* cited to Ch]; *Beyer v Clarke*, 2010 BCSC 1190.

57   *Mulvaney v Jackson*, above note 53.

58   *Wells v Mitchell*, [1939] 3 DLR 126, [1939] OR 378 (CA); *Dukart v District of Surrey*, [1978] 2 SCR 1039, 86 DLR (3d) 609.

59   *Blankstein v Walsh*, [1989] 1 WWR 277, 55 Man R (2d) 125 (QB), aff'd [1989] 4 WWR 604, 58 Man R (2d) 269 (CA).

60   *Regency Villas Title Ltd v Diamond Resorts (Europe) Ltd*, [2018] UKSC 57, [2019] AC 553; see *Grant v MacDonald*, [1992] 5 WWR 577, 68 BCLR (2d) 332 (CA).

61   *Depew v Wilkes* (2002), 216 DLR (4th) 487, 60 OR (3d) 499 (CA); *Moncrieff v Jamieson*, [2007] UKHL 42, [2007] 1 WLR 2620.

62   *Dowty Boulton Paul Ltd v Wolverhampton Corp (No 2)*, [1976] Ch 13 (CA).

63   *Miller v Emcer Products Ltd*, [1956] Ch 304 (CA); *Hedley v Roberts*, [1977] VR 282.

64   *Phillips v Halliday*, [1891] AC 228.

65   *Vannini v Public Utilities Commission of Sault Ste Marie*, [1973] 2 OR 11, 32 DLR (3d) 661 (HCJ); *Husky Oil Operations Ltd v Shelf Holdings Ltd*, [1989] 3 WWR 692, 56 DLR (4th) 193 (Alta CA); *Carter v Sigmund* (1996), 75 BCAC 93; *Mihaylov v 1165996 Ontario Inc*, 2017 ONCA 116 [*Mihaylov*].

66   *Arbutus Bay Estates Ltd v Canada*, 2017 BCCA 374; *Klippstein v Kapasiwin (Summer Village)*, 2020 ABCA 32.

67   *Grant v Lowres*, 2018 BCCA 311.

68   *Myers v Johnston*, [1923] 4 DLR 1152, 52 OLR 658 (CA).

69   *Cargill v Gotts*, [1981] 1 WLR 441 (CA); *Nordin v Faridi*, [1996] 5 WWR 242, 17 BCLR (3d) 366 (CA).

70   *Canada Cement Co v Fitzgerald* (1915), 9 OWN 79 (Ont CA); *Thomson v Neil* (1974), 7 OR (2d) 438.

tenement.[71] These easements should not be confused with the natural rights that landowners have in relation to water flowing naturally in a defined channel. The owners downstream have a right that the flow will not be unduly impeded by owners upstream, whereas the owners upstream have a right that drainage will not be unduly impeded by owners downstream.[72] These are not easements but are *riparian rights* enjoyed by landowners with water flowing naturally through or next to their land.

2) Four Requirements for a Valid Easement

There are four requirements for a valid easement, which were set out in the important case of *Re Ellenborough Park*:

> They are (1) there must be a dominant and a servient tenement, (2) an easement must "accommodate" the dominant tenement, (3) dominant and servient owners must be different persons, and (4) a right over land cannot amount to an easement, unless it is capable of forming the subject-matter of a grant.[73]

Ellenborough Park is on the English coast of the Bristol Channel. The Court of Appeal held that the people who owned homes around the park had an easement to use it for recreation. The first and third requirements were easily satisfied: the homes are the dominant tenements, the park is the servient tenement, and they are owned by different persons. The real questions were whether the right to use the park accommodated the homes around it and could be the subject matter of a grant.

3) Accommodate the Dominant Tenement

An easement accommodates the dominant tenement if it provides a benefit that enhances the use and enjoyment of the dominant tenement. The benefit must be connected to that land in some way. This was satisfied in *Ellenborough Park* because the park provided an extension to the small garden (which a Canadian might call a yard) that each homeowner had behind their house. Evershed MR said,

---

71   *West Flamborough v Pretuski*, [1931] 1 DLR 520, 66 OLR 210 (CA).
72   *McCartney v Londonderry & Lough Swilly Railway Co Ltd*, [1904] AC 301; *Watson v Jackson* (1914), 19 DLR 733 (Ont CA); *Lockwood v Brentwood Park Investments Ltd* (1970), 10 DLR (3d) 143, 1 NSR (2d) 669 (CA); *Palmer v Bowman*, [2000] 1 WLR 842 (CA).
73   *Ellenborough Park*, above note 56 at 163, Evershed MR.

The park became a communal garden for the benefit and enjoyment of those whose houses adjoined it or were in its close proximity. Its flower beds, lawns and walks were calculated to afford all the amenities which it is the purpose of the garden of a house to provide; and, apart from the fact that these amenities extended to a number of householders, instead of being confined to one (which on this aspect of the case is immaterial), we can see no difference in principle between Ellenborough Park and a garden in the ordinary signification of that word. It is the collective garden of the neighbouring houses, to whose use it was dedicated by the owners of the estate and as such amply satisfied, in our judgment, the requirement of connexion with the dominant tenements to which it is appurtenant.[74]

When someone purchased a house, they acquired a fee simple estate to the house plus an easement to use the park. The easement enhanced the value of the house, but as Evershed MR said, "[I]t is not sufficient to show that the right increased the value of the property conveyed, unless it is also shown that it was connected with the normal enjoyment of that property."[75] That connection was easier to establish because each house was sold subject to a restrictive covenant that it could only be used as a residential dwelling and not "for any purpose of trade or commerce other than a lodging-house or private school or seminary."[76] The permitted commercial uses also involve someone residing on the dominant tenement, even if only temporarily. Without that covenant, it might have been difficult to show that the use of the park "was connected with the normal enjoyment of that property." How would the right to use a park for recreation provide a benefit to land being used as a quarry, factory, shop, or farm?

In *Moody v Steggles*,[77] a sign was hung on a building on a busy street advertising a public house located nearby down a small side street. That was a valid easement. Fry J said,

It is said that the easement in question relates, not to the tenement, but to the business of the occupant of the tenement, and that therefore I cannot tie the easement to the house. It appears to me that that argument is of too refined a nature to prevail, and for this reason, that the house can only be used by an occupant, and that the occupant only uses the house for the business which he pursues, and therefore

---

74   *Ibid* at 174–75.
75   *Ibid* at 173.
76   *Ibid.*
77   (1879) 12 Ch D 261.

in some manner (direct or indirect) an easement is more or less connected with the mode in which the occupant of the house uses it.[78]

In *Clapman v Edwards*,[79] a tenant of a petrol station was granted the right to use a wall next to the station for advertising purposes. They assigned that right to someone else. The landlord objected and argued that the right was an easement that could not be separated from the dominant tenement. The court held that it was not an easement because it was not restricted to advertising the business carried out on the dominant tenement. In other words, it was not sufficiently connected to the use of the dominant tenement as a petrol station to meet the requirement for accommodation. Since it was not an easement, it was a licence to use the wall, which could be assigned to anyone.

4) Subject Matter of a Grant

The requirement that an easement must be "capable of forming the subject-matter of a grant" is somewhat cryptic and circular. Easements are normally granted by deed. Most of the cases that grapple with this issue are cases in which the terms of the easement were set out in a deed. In other words, the easement was the subject matter of a grant. Evershed MR said that this really means that the easement must not be "too wide and vague,"[80] but that also requires explanation.

All easements limit the use and enjoyment of the servient tenement by its owner to some extent. An easement is too wide if it interferes too greatly with their right to possess it. If it does, that right is not capable of being granted as an easement but must be granted as an estate. Rights to park cars can run into this problem. A right to park two cars in a parking lot that holds ten cars could be granted as an easement, but if there were only two parking spaces, the right to use both spaces would really be possession of them and therefore an estate.[81]

An easement is too vague if it is not clearly defined. The owner of the servient tenement (and any subsequent owners) must be able to know how the use of their estate is limited, just as the owners of the dominant tenements (and their successors) must be able to know what they are entitled to do with the servient tenement.

---

78 *Ibid* at 266.
79 [1938] 2 All ER 507.
80 *Ellenborough Park*, above note 56 at 164 and 175.
81 See *Sturgeon Hotel Ltd v St Albert (City)* (2010), 504 AR 202 (QB); *Batchelor v Marlow*, [2001] EWCA Civ 1051, [2003] 1 WLR 764; *Moncrieff v Jamieson*, above note 61.

The problem with the easement in *Ellenborough Park* was that it appeared to be both too wide and too vague. The homeowners were granted "the full enjoyment ... at all times hereafter in common with the other persons to whom such easements may be granted of the pleasure ground."[82] The full enjoyment of land seems a lot like possession, and if not, what are the limits of that right?

This easement was valid because the park was also subject to a restrictive covenant that its owners would not

> erect or permit to be erected any dwelling-house and other building (except any grotto bower summer-house flower-stand fountain music-stand or other ornamental erection) within or on any part of the said pleasure ground ... but that the same shall at all times remain as an ornamental garden or pleasure ground.[83]

Without this covenant, the easement should have been invalid because a right to the full enjoyment of someone else's land does not leave them with much that they can do with it. However, if they are already bound to maintain it as a garden, then allowing their neighbours to use and enjoy it is not too great an interference. As Evershed MR said, "We see nothing repugnant to a man's proprietorship or possession of a piece of land that he should decide to make it and maintain it as an ornamental garden, and should grant rights to a limited number of other persons to come into it for the enjoyment of its amenities."[84]

The covenant to maintain it as a garden also provided the context that gave meaning to the words "full enjoyment." They are not too vague because they meant full enjoyment of a garden:

> The enjoyment contemplated was the enjoyment of the vendors' ornamental garden in its physical state as such—the right, that is to say, of walking on or over those parts provided for such purpose, that is, pathways and (subject to restrictions in the ordinary course in the interest of the grass) the lawns; to rest in or upon the seats or other places provided; and, if certain parts were set apart for particular recreations such as tennis or bowls, to use those parts for those purposes, subject again, in the ordinary course, to the provisions made for their regulation; but not to trample at will all over the park, to cut or pluck the flowers or shrubs, or to interfere in the laying out or upkeep of the park. Such use or enjoyment is, we think, a common and clearly understood conception, analogous to the use and

---

82 *Ellenborough Park*, above note 56 at 134.
83 *Ibid*.
84 *Ibid* at 176.

enjoyment conferred upon members of the public, when they are open to the public, of parks or gardens such as St. James's Park, Kew Gardens or the Gardens of Lincoln's Inn Fields. In our judgment, the use of the word "full" does not import some wider, less well understood or less definable privilege.[85]

5) Dominant and Servient Tenements

At common law, every easement must have a dominant tenement.[86] As Lord Cairns LJ said in *Rangeley v Midland Railway Co*,

> There can be no such thing according to our law, or according to the civil law, as what I may term an easement in gross. An easement must be connected with a dominant tenement. In truth, a public road or highway is not an easement, it is a dedication to the public of the occupation of the surface of the land for the purpose of passing and repassing, the public generally taking upon themselves (through the parochial authorities or otherwise) the obligation of repairing it.[87]

There are now many statutes that allow some types of easements to exist without dominant tenements.[88] For example, many jurisdictions allow for the creation of conservation easements for the preservation of natural habitats or places of archaeological significance. They can be granted to the Crown, municipalities, and other non-profit organizations even though there is no dominant tenement that would benefit from the easement. Although these easements are designed to benefit

---

85 *Ibid* at 168–69, Evershed MR.
86 *Miller v Tipling* (1918), 43 OLR 88, 43 DLR 469 at 477 (CA); *Hutchings v Campbell, Wilson and Horne Ltd*, [1924] 1 WWR 1070, [1924] 2 DLR 299 at 300–1 (Alta CA); *Willman v Ducks Unlimited (Canada)*, [2005] 2 WWR 1, 245 DLR (4th) 319 (Man CA); *Harbour Authority v Simpson Aqua*, 2016 PECA 20.
87 (1868) LR 3 Ch App 306 at 311.
88 See *Land Act*, RSBC 1996, c 245, s 40; *Land Title Act*, RSBC 1996, c 250, s 218; *Alberta Land Stewardship Act*, SA 2009, c A-26.8, s 34; *Conservation Easements Act*, SS 1996, c C-27.01, s 11.21; *Public Utilities Easements Act*, RSS 1978, c P-45, s 2; *Real Property Act*, CCSM, c R30, s 111.1; *Conservation Land Act*, RSO 1990, c C.28, s 3; *Ontario Heritage Act*, RSO 1990, c O.18, s 22; *Ontario Trails Act, 2016*, SO 2016, c 8, s 12(15); *Conservation Easements Act*, RSNB 2011, c 130, s 2; *Property Act*, RSNB 1973, c P-19, s 26; *Community Easements Act*, SNS 2012, c 2, s 6; *Conservation Easements Act*, SNS 2001, c 28, s 6; *Land Registration Act*, SNS 2001, c 6, s 61A; *Museum Act*, RSPEI 1988, c M-14, s 11; *Wildlife Conservation Act*, RSPEI 1988, c W-4.1, s 18; *Historic Resources Act*, RSNL 1990, c H-4; *Environment Act*, RSY 2002, c 76, s 79; *Land Titles Act, 2015*, SY 2015, c 10, s 114; *Land Titles Act*, RSNWT 1988, c 8, s 76.

the public, they do not confer rights on members of the public (like a public right of way).

Many of these easements go even further to impose positive obligations on the owner of the servient tenement. That is not possible at common law. The parties to a transaction that creates an easement can agree on who is responsible for its construction (e.g., to create a road or footpath or to install water pipes and a pumping system), but positive obligations (e.g., to repair or maintain) cannot be imposed on subsequent owners of either tenement. The owner of the dominant tenant is entitled to enter the servient tenement to make necessary repairs but is not obliged to do so. In *Jones v Pritchard*, Parker J said,

> [I]t appears to me that, apart from any special local custom or express contract, the owner of a servient tenement is not bound to execute any repairs necessary to ensure the enjoyment or convenient enjoyment of the easement by the owner of the dominant tenement. The grantor of a right of way over a bridge is not by common law liable, nor does he impliedly contract, to keep the bridge in repair for the convenience of the grantee. . . .
>
> [T]he grant of an easement is *prima facie* also the grant of such ancillary rights as are reasonably necessary to its exercise or enjoyment. Thus the grantee of an easement for a watercourse through his neighbour's land may, when reasonably necessary, enter his neighbour's land for the purpose of repairing, and may repair, such watercourse.[89]

The obligation to pay for repairs can be imposed as a rentcharge (as discussed above). In *Orchard Trading Estate Management Ltd v Johnson Security Ltd*,[90] the owners of units on an industrial estate had easements to use a private sewer but were required to pay for its upkeep because their units were subject to a rentcharge for that purpose.

At common law, the dominant and servient tenements must be possessed by different persons. This is an application of the general rule that people cannot have rights enforceable against themselves. As owner of the dominant tenement, I cannot sue myself as owner of the servient tenement. Also, my right to use the servient tenement is subsumed in my ownership of it. For example, if I own two adjacent parcels of land, I may cross over one to get to the other. My right to cross over one of my parcels is not an easement since I possess it and have the right to use it as I wish. My right to cross over that parcel is just one of the many liberties I enjoy as its owner in fee simple.

---

89   [1908] 1 Ch 630 at 637–38.
90   *Orchard Trading*, above note 18.

There are now statutes in many jurisdictions that allow the dominant and servient tenements to be owned and possessed by the same person and allow people to grant easements to themselves.[91] This solves a problem that can occur when an easement exists and the dominant and servient tenements come to be owned by the same person. The easement can continue to exist since it might be needed again if ownership of the tenements gets separated. Also, people can subdivide their land and create easements between the separate parcels before they are sold.

6) Creation of Easements

The creation and transfer of property rights are the subject of Chapter 8. As discussed there, most rights are created by intention: the parties intend to create a right and do what is necessary to give effect to their intention. However, rights can also arise by operation of law whether or not the parties to create them. This is also true of easements. Most are created by intention, but they can also arise in other ways. There are *implied* easements, easements arising by *prescription*, and easements arising by *estoppel*.

An easement can be created when the owner of the servient tenement chooses to grant it to the owner of the dominant tenement. For example, when the owner of Ellenborough Park (discussed above) sold the homes around the park, they transferred a fee simple estate to each homeowner and granted an easement to use the park.

Problems can arise if it is not clear what the parties intended. A right to use land might be a licence (i.e., a personal right) and not an easement even it satisfies all four requirements for a valid easement. It depends on what was intended. As Gillese JA said in *Mihaylov v 1165996 Ontario Inc*,

> The right to do something on land belonging to another can be a licence or an easement. A right to walk over a path on another's land is a good example of this. If I give you the right to walk along a path on my land so that you can reach the lake in front of it, that right may be a licence or an easement. In its simplest terms, it depends upon whether I gave you alone the right to walk along the path or whether I agreed that the right to walk along the path was to bind my land and

---

91   *Property Law Act*, RSBC 1996, c 377, s 18; *Land Titles Act*, RSA 2000, c L-4, s 68; *Land Titles Act, 2000*, SS 2000, c L-5.1, s 147; *Land Registration Act*, SNS 2001, c1486, s 61; *Land Titles Act, 2015*, SY 2015, c 10, s 113; *Land Titles Act*, RSNWT 1988, c 8, s 76.

benefit yours. The former is a personal right known as a licence. The latter is a proprietary right, known as an easement.[92]

In a perfect world, the landowner would always state clearly and in writing whether they are granting an easement or a licence to their neighbour, but we do not live in that world. There are times when the court is called on to decide what was intended based on the language used and surrounding circumstances.[93] This is like the problem of trying to distinguish between a *profit à prendre* and a sale of goods (discussed above).

Easements can be granted to the owner of the dominant tenement but can also be reserved by the owner of the dominant tenement when they transfer the servient tenement to another person. This can happen when someone subdivides their land and sells a portion. The buyer receives an estate subject to an easement. Ideally, the terms of this arrangement would be stated clearly and in writing, but people sometimes forget to do so. In that situation, a court may be asked to declare that an easement can be implied.

The rules relating to implied easements are a bit messy.[94] They can be divided into three groups: easements of *necessity*, the rule in *Wheeldon v Burrows*,[95] and other implied easements. Easements of necessity were described by Welsh JA in *Atlantic Developments Inc v Fowler*:

> To summarize principles relevant in the instant case, an easement of necessity may arise where a property is "landlocked" such that there is no other way, including inconvenient means, by which the owner can access the land. Such an easement is restricted to circumstances where the landlocked property and the land over which the easement is claimed were in the common ownership of one person prior to creation of the two tenements. The easement cannot exist over the land of a stranger. The grantor of the easement has the right to select the location of the easement, and need not choose the location most convenient to the grantee.[96]

---

92   *Mihaylov*, above note 65 at para 48.
93   See, for example, *Gypsum Carrier Inc v The Queen*, [1978] 1 FC 147, 78 DLR (3d) 175; *Parker v Parker* (1989), 100 NBR (2d) 361, 252 APR 361 (QB); *Imperial Oil Ltd v Young* (1996), 142 Nfld & PEIR 280, 445 APR 280 (Nfld SC).
94   See British Columbia Law Institute, *Report on the Doctrine of Implied Grant: The Rule in Wheeldon v. Burrows* (2012), online: www.bcli.org/sites/default/files/report_65_implied_grant.pdf.
95   (1872) 12 Ch D 31 (CA) [*Wheeldon*].
96   2013 NLCA 58 at para 19.

In *Toronto-Dominion Bank v Wise*, the Ontario Court of Appeal held that an easement of necessity will not arise if the land can be accessed by water, even if the "water access was, and probably remains, inconvenient or impractical."[97] In contrast, the Alberta Court of Appeal declared that an easement of necessity existed in *Nelson v 1153696 Alberta Ltd*, even though the dominant tenement was surrounded on three sides by a large river: "It is doubtful whether access by water in these circumstances can operate to disallow an easement of necessity. . . . In any event, the trial judge found that 'while frozen the North Saskatchewan River is not by any standards a navigable body of water.'"[98]

In *Hirtle v Ernst*, the Supreme Court of Nova Scotia also held that access by water does not prevent an easement of necessity from arising:

> The cases which have been cited indicate that the doctrine of right of way of necessity has been continuing to evolve over the years and has evolved to the stage where a number of statements of principle can be added to the traditional conception of the doctrine:
> 1. The doctrine of right of way of necessity is based on public policy — that land should be able to be used and not rendered useless. . . .
> 2. Although there can be no right of way of necessity where there is an alternative inconvenient means of access, the requirement of an absolute necessity or a strict necessity has developed into a rule of practical necessity. . . .
> 3. Water access is not considered to be the same as access over adjacent land.[99]

The Ontario Court of Appeal expressly rejected these statements of principle in *Toronto-Dominion Bank v Wise*. Huscroft JA said,

> The necessity test has not been reduced to a requirement of "practical necessity," as the Nova Scotia Supreme Court held in *Hirtle*. . . . [T]he test for easements of necessity in Ontario is "strict necessity." In my view, *Hirtle* is not sound authority for the proposition that easements of necessity are creatures of public policy. Although there is no doubt that easements of necessity have the salutary effect of allowing land to be used, rather than rendered useless, easements of necessity flow from the intentions of the parties to a grant, not from public policy.[100]

97 2016 ONCA 629 at para 29, Huscroft JA [*Toronto-Dominion Bank*].
98 *Nelson*, above note 43 at para 44, Paperny JA.
99 (1991), 110 NSR (2d) 216, 299 APR 216 (SC) at para 50, Nathanson J.
100 *Toronto-Dominion Bank*, above note 97 at paras 32–33.

The second category of implied easements is known unhelpfully as the rule in *Wheeldon v Burrows*.[101] In that case, a workshop and the vacant land next to it were both owned by Tetley, who sold the vacant land to Wheeldon and later sold the workshop to Burrows. When the vacant land was sold to Wheeldon, Tetley did not reserve an easement for the flow of light and air into the windows in the workshop that over-looked the vacant land. Wheeldon later put up boarding on their land to block the windows of the workshop. Burrows knocked them down, claiming an easement. The court held that there was no easement and that Burrows was liable for trespass.

The flow of light and air into the workshop windows was not a necessity. If Tetley had wanted to reserve an easement when they sold the vacant land, they should have reserved it expressly. A seller cannot *derogate from the grant* (i.e., take anything away from the estate trans-ferred) to the buyer by implication. It can only be done expressly.

If the transactions had occurred in reverse order, with Burrows buying the workshop from Tetley before Wheeldon bought the vacant land, the result may have been different. A grant of a fee simple estate normally includes any easements attached to that estate as the domin-ant tenement. The right to the flow of light and air into the windows of the workshop could not exist as an easement over the vacant land while both parcels were owned by Tetley. However, it would be apparent to anyone interested in buying the workshop that the flow of light and air into the windows was a benefit that Tetley enjoyed while they owned both parcels. That benefit was called a *quasi-easement*, which could become a real easement when the parcels were separated. This is also based on the principle of non-derogation: the sale of the fee simple will include any associated benefits unless they are expressly excluded.

The process by which a quasi-easement can turn into a real ease-ment if land is subdivided by sale of the dominant tenement is called the rule in *Wheeldon v Burrows* even though it does not apply if the land is subdivided by sale of the servient tenement, as in *Wheeldon v Burrows* itself. Thesiger LJ explained it as follows:

> We have had a considerable number of cases cited to us, and out of them I think that two propositions may be stated as what I may call the general rules governing cases of this kind. The first of these rules is, that on the grant by the owner of a tenement of part of that tenement as it is then used and enjoyed, there will pass to the grantee all those continuous and apparent easements (by which, of course, I mean *quasi* easements), or, in other words, all those easements which are

---

101 *Wheeldon*, above note 95.

necessary to the reasonable enjoyment of the property granted, and which have been and are at the time of the grant used by the owners of the entirety for the benefit of the part granted. The second proposition is that, if the grantor intends to reserve any right over the tenement granted, it is his duty to reserve it expressly in the grant. Those are the general rules governing cases of this kind, but the second of those rules is subject to certain exceptions. One of those exceptions is the well-known exception which attaches to cases of what are called ways of necessity; and I do not dispute for a moment that there may be, and probably are, certain other exceptions.[102]

The probable existence of "certain other exceptions" was relied on by the Ontario Court of Appeal in *Barton v Raine*.[103] The court held that an easement can be implied if that is what the parties actually intended, even if it is not necessary and cannot be based on the rule in *Wheeldon v Burrows*. A father owned two houses on adjoining lots. They were less than four metres apart with a paved driveway running between them to access the garages behind the houses. The father sold one of the houses to his son. They both continued to use the driveway, but there was no easement reserved or granted when the estate was transferred to the son. The son later sold the house, and the buyers built a fence on the property line between the houses, which prevented access to the garages. There were no easements of necessity since it was not strictly necessary to access the garages by car. However, the court held that easements were implied because the parties must have had a common intention that they would each have an easement to use the portion of the driveway on the other's land.

An easement can arise by *prescription* in some jurisdictions if the owner of the dominant tenement has made use of the servient without permission for twenty years.[104] This is no longer possible in British Columbia, Alberta, Saskatchewan, and the territories,[105] nor is it possible for land registered in the land title registration systems in Ontario,

---

102 *Ibid* at 49.

103 (1980) 114 DLR (3d) 702, 29 OR (2d) 685 (CA).

104 See, for example, *Stall v Yarosz* (1964), 43 DLR (2d) 255, 47 WWR (NS) 113 (Man CA); *Caldwell v Elia* (2000), 129 OAC 379, 30 RPR (3d) 295; *Wylie v McCarron*, 2020 NBCA 28; *Mason v Partridge*, 2005 NSCA 144; *Franklin v St John's (City)*, 2012 NLCA 48.

105 *Land Title Act*, RSBC 1996, c 250, s 24; *Law of Property Act*, RSA 2000, c L-7, s 69; *Land Titles Act, 2000*, SS 2000, c L-5.1, s 150; *Land Titles Act, 2015*, SY 2015, c 10, s 43; *Limitation of Actions Act*, RSY 2002, c 139, s 49; *Limitation of Actions Act*, RSNWT 1988, c L-8, s 48.

New Brunswick, and Nova Scotia.[106] For land elsewhere, a *prescriptive easement* can be acquired at common law, except for easements for light and air, which cannot arise by prescription in Manitoba, Ontario, and New Brunswick.[107] Most of the cases are about rights of way.

At common law, a prescriptive easement is based on a legal fiction called a *lost modern grant*. This is the idea that someone who makes use of land as if they had an easement must be doing so because that easement was granted at some point in a deed that was lost. It is pure fiction, so it is no defence to prove that a grant was never made. It is called a *lost modern grant* in England to distinguish it from the presumption that an easement was granted if the land has been used from *time immemorial*, which is set artificially at 3 September 1189 (when Richard I became king).[108] There is no need to draw this distinction in Canada, but the term *lost modern grant* is still used in the provinces that allow easements to arise by prescription.

In Manitoba, Ontario, New Brunswick, and Nova Scotia, a prescriptive easement can also arise by statute.[109] The Canadian statutes are patterned after the English *Prescription Act 1832*,[110] which applies in Manitoba but was not yet part of English law when it was received in the Atlantic provinces. The common law and statutory methods of acquiring an easement by prescription are similar. As Cory JA said in *Henderson v Volk*:

> It should be emphasized that the nature of the enjoyment necessary to establish an easement under the doctrine of lost modern grant is exactly the same as that required to establish an easement by prescription under the *Limitations Act*. Thus, the claimant must demonstrate a use and enjoyment of the right-of-way under a claim of right which was continuous, uninterrupted, open and peaceful for a period of 20 years. However, in the case of the doctrine of lost modern grant,

---

106 *Land Titles Act*, RSO 1990, c L.5, s 51; *Land Titles Act*, SNB 1981, c L-1.1, s 17; *Land Registration Act*, SNS 2001, c 6, s 74.

107 *Law of Property Act*, CCSM, c L90, s 29; *Real Property Limitations Act*, RSO 1990, c L.15, s 33; *Easements Act*, RSNB 2011, c 143, s 8. Prescriptive easements for wires and cables are also abolished in Ontario and New Brunswick: *Real Property Limitations Act*, RSO 1990, c L.15, s 35; *Easements Act*, RSNB 2011, c 143, s 9.

108 John Baker, *An Introduction to English Legal History*, 5th ed (Oxford: Oxford University Press, 2019) at 32.

109 *Real Property Limitations Act*, RSO 1990, c L.15, ss 31–41; *Easements Act*, RSNB 2011, c 143; *Real Property Limitations Act*, RSNS 1989, c 258, ss 32–37.

110 2 and 3 Will 4, c 71.

it does not have to be the 20-year period immediately preceding the bringing of an action.[111]

The acquisition of an easement by prescription seems like the acquisition of a fee simple estate by adverse possession, but they are based on different principles. Adverse possession depends on relativity of title (discussed in Chapter 2). Someone who obtains possession of land thereby acquires a right to possession, which is enforceable generally against everyone else in society except someone with a better right to possession. The owner has a better right to possession, but that may be lost if they do not sue to recover possession before the limitation period expires. The adverse possessor's estate arises at the outset when they take possession of the land and becomes ownership when the owner's estate is lost. In contrast, a person making use of land without permission does not acquire any right to do so at the outset. If they continue to use the land continuously for twenty years, they will then acquire a new easement by prescription.

Finally, it is also possible for an easement to be created by *estoppel*.[112] This can occur when someone has a reasonable expectation that they will be granted an easement and rely on that expectation to their detriment. This method of acquiring an easement is not unique to easements but is a general principle that can apply to all property rights to land. It is called *proprietary estoppel* and is discussed in Chapter 8.

E. COVENANTS

A covenant is a promise made in a deed. Like contractual promises, most covenants only create rights *in personam*: the right to enforce the promise is enforceable only against the person who made it. However, some covenants relating to land create rights *in rem* that can be enforced against subsequent landowners.

As discussed in Chapter 3, leasehold covenants create obligations owed by the landlord to the tenant and vice versa. They can be enforced against subsequent landlords (if the landlord's estate is transferred) and subsequent tenants (if the lease is assigned). This creates a major exception to *privity of contract*, which allows contractual rights to be assigned

---

111 (1982) 132 DLR (3d) 690, 35 OR (2d) 379 at para 14 (CA).
112 See *Crabb v Arun District Council*, [1975] EWCA Civ 7, [1976] Ch 179; *Hill v Nova Scotia (Attorney General)*, [1997] 1 SCR 69, 142 DLR (4th) 230; *Hoyl Group Ltd v Cromer Town Council*, [2015] EWCA Civ 782, [2015] HLR 43.

but not contractual obligations. Landlords and tenants do not need privity of contract because they have *privity of estate*.

Some covenants between neighbours can be enforced against subsequent landowners under the rules of equity even though they have neither privity of contract nor privity of estate. This was established in the mid-nineteenth century by the important case of *Tulk v Moxhay*,[113] which concerned the use of Leicester Square in London. The plaintiff owned the square and several houses around it. They sold the square to a purchaser who made a covenant to the plaintiff that they would "keep and maintain the said piece or parcel of ground and square garden, and the iron railing round the same, in its present form, and in sufficient and proper repair as a square garden and pleasure ground, in an open state, uncovered with any buildings, in a neat and ornamental order." The square was sold to the defendant, who intended to build on it. The Court of Chancery granted an injunction to the plaintiff to stop the defendant from violating the covenant. Lord Cottenham LC said,

> Here there is no question about the contract: the owner of certain houses in the square sells the land adjoining, with a covenant from the purchaser not to use it for any other purpose than as a square garden. And it is now contended, not that the vendee could violate that contract, but that he might sell the piece of land, and that the purchaser from him may violate it without this Court having any power to interfere. If that were so, it would be impossible for an owner of land to sell part of it without incurring the risk of rendering what he retains worthless. It is said that, the covenant being one which does not run with the land, this Court cannot enforce it; but the question is, not whether the covenant runs with the land, but whether a party shall be permitted to use the land in a manner inconsistent with the contract entered into by his vendor, and with notice of which he purchased. Of course, the price would be affected by the covenant, and nothing could be more inequitable than that the original purchaser should be able to sell the property the next day for a greater price, in consideration of the assignee being allowed to escape from the liability which he had himself undertaken.[114]

These covenants are often called *restrictive covenants* because they will only be enforced against subsequent landowners if they restrict the use of the land and not if they impose positive obligations. They are also known as *freehold covenants* to distinguish them from leasehold covenants. Neither term is ideal for two reasons. First, leases often contain

113 (1848) 2 Ph 774, 41 ER 1143 [*Tulk* cited to Ph].
114 *Ibid* at 777–78.

restrictive covenants (e.g., not to use the leased premises for commercial purposes or to keep pets). Second, people who have leasehold estates can enforce covenants regarding the use of nearby land.[115] They are not enforced as leasehold covenants since the neighbours do not have privity of estate, but neither are they freehold covenants. The principles are the same whether the neighbours have freehold or leasehold estates.

1) Positive and Negative Covenants

A restrictive covenant is similar to a negative easement. They both restrict the use of a servient tenement for the benefit of a dominant tenement. Easements are part of the common law, whereas restrictive covenants are permitted by the rules of equity. Negative easements are strictly limited (as discussed above), but covenants can impose a wide range of restrictions on the use of land so long as they are not contrary to public policy (such as a restriction limiting the use of land to people of certain races).[116]

Positive covenants are not like positive easements. A positive covenant creates an obligation to do something (e.g., to repair or pay rent). A positive easement does not impose an obligation to do anything but confers a right to do something that would otherwise be a trespass or nuisance. The corresponding obligation on the owner of the servient tenement is negative: they cannot interfere with the exercise of the easement. In other words, the adjective *positive* refers to the obligation imposed by a covenant and to the right conferred by an easement.

The common law has long allowed the benefit of covenants to run with land and be enforced by subsequent owners if the covenant touches and concerns the land. It does not matter whether the covenant is positive or negative. In *Smith and Snipes Hall Farm Ltd v River Douglas Catchment Board*,[117] the defendant made an agreement with eleven landowners to carry out works to prevent their land from being flooded, but the land flooded again because the defendant had done the work poorly. The plaintiffs sued for damages but were not parties to the agreement. They were a subsequent landowner and their tenant. The trial judge

---

115 *Russo v Field*, [1973] SCR 466, 34 DLR (3d) 704 [*Russo*]; *Canada Safeway Ltd v Thompson (City)*, [1996] 10 WWR 252 at 271–72, 112 Man R (2d) 94 (QB), aff'd [1997] 7 WWR 565, 118 Man R (2d) 34 (CA) [*Canada Safeway*].

116 See *Re Drummond Wren*, [1945] 4 DLR 674 (Ont HC); *Noble v Alley*, [1951] SCR 64, [1951] 1 DLR 321; *Land Title Act*, RSBC 1996, c 250, s 222; *Law of Property Act*, CCSM, c L90, s 7; *Conveyancing and Law of Property Act*, RSO 1990, c C.34, s 22; *Human Rights Act*, RSPEI 1988, c H-12, s 4; *Land Titles Act, 2015*, SY 2015, c 10, s 95.

117 [1949] 2 KB 500 (CA).

held that they had no right to sue, but that was overturned by the Court of Appeal. Denning LJ said, "If a successor in title were not allowed to sue it would mean that the covenantor could break his contract with impunity, for it is clear that the original owner, after he has parted with the land, could recover no more than nominal damages for any breach that occurred thereafter."[118]

The agreement imposed positive obligations on the defendant that corresponded to rights *in personam* held by the landowners. Those rights could only be enforced against the defendant who made the promise, but the benefit of that promise touched and concerned the land and was enforceable at law by subsequent landowners.

The common law did not allow the burden of covenants to be enforced against subsequent landowners (unless they were leasehold covenants and the parties had privity of estate). It was the Court of Chancery that allowed that to happen in *Tulk*.[119] This created another exception to privity of contract. An obligation can be imposed on a subsequent landowner if it restricts what they can do with their land but not if it compels them to do something positive, such as spend money, make repairs, or perform maintenance.

In *Rhone v Stephens*,[120] the owner of a house sold the cottage attached to it. The roof of the house extended over a bedroom in the cottage, and the owner made a covenant to the purchaser to maintain that part of the roof "in wind and water tight condition." The house was sold, and the owner of the cottage sued the subsequent owner of the house for breach of that covenant. The claim was dismissed because the burden of a positive covenant cannot be enforced on a subsequent landowner even if they acquired the land with knowledge of it. Lord Templeman said,

> My Lords, equity supplements but does not contradict the common law. When freehold land is conveyed without restriction, the conveyance confers on the purchaser the right to do with the land as he pleases provided that he does not interfere with the rights of others or infringe statutory restrictions. The conveyance may however impose restrictions which, in favour of the covenantee, deprive the purchaser of some of the rights inherent in the ownership of unrestricted land....
>
> Restrictive covenants deprive an owner of a right which he could otherwise exercise. Equity cannot compel an owner to comply with a positive covenant entered into by his predecessors in title without flatly contradicting the common law rule that a person cannot be

---

118 *Ibid* at 516.
119 *Tulk*, above note 113.
120 [1994] UKHL 3, [1994] 2 AC 310 [cited to AC].

made liable upon a contract unless he was a party to it. Enforcement of a positive covenant lies in contract; a positive covenant compels an owner to exercise his rights. Enforcement of a negative covenant lies in property; a negative covenant deprives the owner of a right over property.[121]

This accords with the nature of property rights generally. We are content to allow them to be enforced generally against other members of society because they do not impose positive obligations. A property right corresponds to a general duty of non-interference. Some good reason is needed before a person can be compelled to pay money or perform some other positive duty. The most common reason is that they promised to do it, but there are others. They may have committed a tort or other wrong and become liable to pay damages, they may have a statutory duty to pay (e.g., taxes), or they may have a duty to refund money paid to them by mistake. Generally speaking, positive obligations are not imposed on people at common law or in equity unless they agreed, did something wrong, or were unjustly enriched.

The rule that positive covenants cannot be enforced against subsequent landowners has been criticized, and there are calls to reform this area of law.[122] However, that is not a step that courts are willing to take, as Charron JA said in *Durham Condominium Corp No 123 v Amberwood Investments Ltd*:

> The rule that positive covenants do not run with the land has been a settled principle of the English common law for well over a century and it is undisputed that it has clearly been adopted in Canada: *Parkinson v. Reid*, [1966] S.C.R. 162, 56 D.L.R. (2d) 315. It appears to be equally undisputed that the rule at times causes inconvenience, that its application in some cases may even result in unfairness, and that the present state of the law should be modified to meet the needs of modern conveyancing. However, it is my view that the call for reform is not one for the courts to answer but for the legislature. Any change in the law in this area could have complex and far-reaching effects that cannot be accurately assessed on a case-by-case basis. The

---

121 *Ibid* at 317–18.
122 See British Columbia Law Institute, *Report on Restrictive Covenants* (2012), online: www.bcli.org/sites/default/files/report_67_restrictive_covenants.pdf; Law Commission, *Making Land Work: Easements, Covenants and Profits à Prendre* (2011), online: https://s3-eu-west-2.amazonaws.com/lawcom-prod-storage-11jsxou24uy7q/uploads/2015/03/lc327_easements_report.pdf; Ontario Law Reform Commission, *Report on Covenants Affecting Freehold Land* (1989), online: https://archive.org/details/reportoncovenant00onta.

need to preserve certainty in commercial and property transactions requires that any meaningful reform be achieved by legislation that can be drafted with careful regard to the consequences.[123]

Whether a covenant is positive or negative depends on the substance of what is required and not the form of the words. For example, a covenant to maintain land as a garden implies a positive duty of maintenance, but it can be enforced as a negative duty not to use the land for any other purpose. Covenants may contain a mix of positive and negative obligations (like the covenant in *Tulk*), in which case the negative obligations can usually be enforced against a subsequent landowner even though the positive obligations are not. As Megarry J said in *Shepherd Homes Ltd v Sandham (No 2)*,

> First, the question is not whether a covenant is negative in wording but whether it is negative in substance. . . . Second, what is worded or set out in the instrument as a single covenant may give rise to more obligations than one; and if one obligation is positive, that is no reason why another obligation should not be negative, and be enforced as such.[124]

In *Aquadel Golf Course Ltd v Lindell Beach Holiday Resort Ltd*,[125] the BC Court of Appeal held that a covenant to use land as a golf course was in substance a positive obligation. A landowner named Whitlam had made covenants "(1) not to use the land for any purpose other than as a golf course; (2) to maintain the golf course to an acceptable standard; and (3) to give certain persons a preferential rate for use of the golf course."[126] The trial judge held that the second and third covenants were positive and unenforceable, but the first covenant was negative and could be severed from the others. The Court of Appeal held that they were all unenforceable. Finch CJ said,

> If the first paragraph were interpreted to mean that Whitlam did not have to use the lands as a golf course, and could allow it to return to wilderness, the remaining paragraphs of the Agreement would be meaningless and unenforceable. Whitlam could hardly maintain the golf course in a proper and acceptable manner and give preferential rates to certain golfers for its use if he failed to use the land as a golf course at all.[127]

---

123 (2002) 211 DLR (4th) 1, 58 OR (3d) 481 at para 17 (CA).
124 [1971] 1 WLR 1062 at 1067 (Ch D).
125 2009 BCCA 5.
126 *Ibid* at para 15, Finch CJ.
127 *Ibid* at para 18.

2) Use of the Servient Tenement

To be enforceable against subsequent landowners, a covenant must restrict the use of the servient tenement. For example, a covenant might state that the land can only be used for residential purposes,[128] or it might limit the height of buildings.[129] A covenant that merely restricts the transfer of land is not a covenant regarding its use and does not qualify as a restrictive covenant.[130]

A restriction on transfer might also be unlawful as a *restraint on alienation*.[131] In *Blackburn v McCallum*,[132] a father died leaving land to his son subject to a restriction that the son could not dispose of it for twenty-five years. The Supreme Court of Canada held that this restriction was void. This rule can be traced back to the statute of *Quia Emptores 1290*, which abolished subinfeudation and gave tenants the right to transfer their land without their lord's permission (as discussed in Chapter 3). Mills J said,

> All this was changed by the statute *quia emptores*, enacted in the eighteenth year of Edward I., and which, while it authorised the tenant to sell his estate in the land, forbade subinfeudation. . . . The holder of the fee has, by law, since then, the right to convey away his tenure, and any attempt to restrain him and to limit his exercise of powers which are incident to the estate, are repugnant to it, and therefore void.[133]

The rule against restraint on alienation can also be justified on the basis of public policy. According to Howland JA in *Stephens v Gulf Oil Canada Ltd*,

> The objections in principle to restraints on alienation are twofold. They keep property out of commerce and have a tendency to result in a concentration of wealth. They also tend to prevent improvement of property, since a landowner will be reluctant to make improvements when he cannot sell the property.[134]

This rule or policy can influence the interpretation of restrictive covenants that operate as anti-competition clauses. As McLachlin JA

---

128 See, for example, *Re Community Youth Services Inc*, 2011 NBQB 19.
129 See, for example, *Hofer v Guitonni*, 2011 BCCA 393.
130 *Noble v Alley*, above note 116; *White v Lauder Developments Ltd* (1975), 60 DLR (3d) 419, 9 OR (2d) 363 (CA); *Edmonton Regional Airports Authority v Canada Life Assurance Co*, [2004] 4 WWR 192, 24 Alta LR (4th) 251 (QB).
131 *Re Drummond Wren*, above note 116.
132 (1903) 33 SCR 65.
133 *Ibid* at 83.
134 (1975) 65 DLR (3d) 193 at 220, 11 OR (2d) 129 (CA).

said in *Nylar Foods Ltd v Roman Catholic Episcopal Corp of Prince Rupert*, "The policy of the courts to favour competition and alienability leads to a strict construction of restrictive covenants."[135] In that case, the defendant granted a lease that contained a covenant that the landlord would not lease nearby land to someone who might compete with the tenant's business. Some of that land was sold to the plaintiff, who obtained a declaration from the BC Court of Appeal that the covenant was not binding on them. The covenant was construed strictly. It could stop the landlord from leasing land to their tenant's competitors but did not stop them from selling it to someone who wanted to operate a competing business. Therefore, the covenant was personal and did not run with the land.

In *Russo v Field*,[136] the owner of a shopping centre in Toronto leased a shop to the plaintiffs to be used as a hairdressing and beauty salon. The lease contained a covenant that the landlord would "not suffer or permit any of the other stores in the Shopping Centre to carry on the business of a hairdresser and Beauty Salon."[137] The landlord then let the shop next door to a tenant who sold and serviced wigs. The Supreme Court of Canada held that this was a violation of their leasehold covenant to the defendants. However, the court also ordered the tenant next door to pay damages to the plaintiffs. The plaintiffs had an equitable interest in all the other shops in the shopping centre created by the landlord's leasehold covenant. Each of the other shops became a servient tenement subject to a restriction that they would not be used as a business that would compete with the plaintiffs. The plaintiffs' leasehold estate was the dominant tenement.

This was followed in *Canada Safeway Ltd v Thompson (City)*.[138] In 1971, Woolworth owned a shopping centre in Thompson, Manitoba, and leased one of the shops to Safeway for twenty years with five options to renew the lease for five years each. Woolworth had an option to purchase adjoining land. The lease contained a covenant that Woolworth would not lease land in the shopping centre or the adjoining land to anyone who would carry on a competing business. Woolworth purchased the adjoining land in 1975, sold the shopping centre in 1982, and sold the adjoining land to the city in 1995. The city argued that the covenant in the lease was a restriction on alienation and not a restriction on use, but that was rejected by the court, which held that the city was bound by the covenant.

---

135 (1988) 48 DLR (4th) 175 at para 6 (BCCA).
136 *Russo*, above note 115.
137 *Ibid* at 469.
138 *Canada Safeway*, above note 115.

The court held that the Safeway's leasehold estate was the dominant tenement, which means that the covenant ends when the lease ends because a restrictive covenant cannot exist without a dominant tenement. One issue that was not addressed by the court was the status of the renewals. As the Supreme Court of Canada held in *JE Gibson Holdings v Principal Investments*,[139] each renewal is a new lease granted on the same terms. When the lease was renewed in 1991, Woolworth no longer owned the shopping centre, so the covenant was granted by the new landlord, who did not have an interest in the adjoining land. When the lease was renewed again in 1996, Woolworth no longer owned the adjoining land. On what basis did a covenant made by the new landlord affect land that they did not own?

3) Benefit to the Dominant Tenement

A restrictive covenant cannot exist without a dominant tenement.[140] The covenant must provide some benefit to that land. As Farwell J said in *Rogers v Hosegood*,

> Covenants which run with the land must have the following characteristics: (1.) They must be made with a covenantee who has an interest in the land to which they refer. (2.) They must concern or touch the land. . . . [T]he covenant must either affect the land as regards mode of occupation, or it must be such as per se, and not merely from collateral circumstances, affects the value of the land.[141]

In that case, the famous painter Sir John Millais bought land in Kensington that had the benefit of a covenant that neighbouring plots of land could only be used as private residences with one dwelling house per plot. This provided a clear benefit to the use and value of the land, and his successors in title were able to prevent the construction of a block of residential flats on land burdened by the covenant.

As discussed above, an anti-competition clause can qualify as a restrictive covenant. It can enhance the value of a business operating on the dominant tenement by attracting more customers to that location and can enhance the market value of the dominant tenement should its owner choose to sell it.[142] However, anti-competition was taken too far in *880682 Alberta Ltd v Molson Breweries Properties Ltd*.[143] Molson sold

139 [1964] SCR 424 at 426, 44 DLR (2d) 673; discussed in Chapter 3.
140 *Galbraith v Madawaska Club Ltd*, [1961] SCR 639, 29 DLR (2d) 153.
141 [1900] 2 Ch 388 at 395.
142 See *Canada Safeway* (1996), above note 115.
143 [2003] 2 WWR 642, 4 RPR (4th) 271 (Alta QB) [*Molson*].

a disused brewery in Calgary subject to a covenant that it would not "be used for the purposes of either the brewing and packaging of malt based beverages or the production of alcoholic beverages in any manner and to any extent whatsoever." The dominant tenement was Molson's brewery, located 300 kilometres away in Edmonton. The covenant did not bind a subsequent owner of the land in Calgary because it did not touch and concern the land in Edmonton.

The covenant could benefit Molson by stopping a competitor from using its old brewery to make beverages that would compete for sales in Alberta. However, that benefit had no direct connection to the land in Edmonton. Most anti-competition covenants enhance the value of the land by attracting more customers to that location because there are no competing businesses nearby. There was nothing about the location of the Edmonton brewery that was enhanced by the covenant.

In *Re Bowes Co Ltd and Rankin*,[144] Dominion Canners Ltd owned three canneries in the village of Bloomfield, Ontario. It sold one cannery subject to a covenant that it not be used for "the manufacturing and dealing in canned fruits, vegetables, or meats." The dominant tenements were its other two canneries. The court held that this was a valid restrictive covenant that provided a benefit to the dominant tenement and not just personally to the company that owned them. The trial judge said,

> It is said in one of the affidavits that the population of Bloomfield is small, and that operatives for even two factories, run to their full capacity, are not available; also that the produce of the district round about is less than the existing factories could handle. If these statements are true, it is apparent that the Dominion Canners, in exacting the covenant in question, were seeking to protect their interests as the owners of the two canneries; and, while the covenant would not have any physical effect on the canneries, or any considerable effect upon the character of the district, it is apparent that it must have an effect upon the value of the canneries as canneries, no matter who owns them. . . .
>
> The circumstances make it plain that, even if they would like to see the end of all competition, their primary object in exacting this covenant must have been to some extent to protect themselves and their successors as owners of the Bloomfield factories — to do something towards making sure of a supply of fruits and vegetables, and so towards making their factory more valuable as a factory. This seems to me to be something different from an endeavour to secure

---

144 [1924] 4 DLR 406, 55 OLR 601 (CA) [cited to DLR].

some benefit for themselves, as the Dominion Canners, operating at Bloomfield or elsewhere.[145]

In the *Molson* case, the court held that a restrictive covenant required "the existence of a dominant tenement proximately situated to the servient tenement."[146] Molson argued that "proximity is 'not limited to spatial relationships, but includes the concept of causation or a causal connection.'"[147] The court disagreed and held that the covenant required physical proximity. Rooke J said,

> [M]odern "business realities" do not change the fundamental nature of property law, and that is what I find Molson seeks to do in this case. While the law needs to adapt to modern issues, it does not throw out basic principles just because times change. Indeed, I would say that, while some of the authorities are old, and there is perhaps a need to consider the law applicable to the current day having regard to more modern methods of transportation and communication, I do not find that there is any issue with respect to the basic principles for which these old cases stand.[148]

---

145 *Ibid* at 409–10, Rose J.

146 *Molson*, above note 143 at para 28, quoting Rawlins J in *Crump v Kernahan* (1995), 32 Alta LR (3d) 192 at para 11 (QB).

147 *Molson*, above note 143 at para 30, quoting *Black's Law Dictionary*, 6th ed, sub verbo "proximity."

148 *Ibid* at para 41.

SOURCES OF RIGHTS

A. INTRODUCTION

This chapter is about the ways in which property rights can be created or transferred. It is divided into six main parts: gifts, trusts, wills and estates, land contracts, proprietary estoppel, and sale of goods. As you read, it is helpful to keep several important distinctions in mind.

1) Intention or Operation of Law

The creation or transfer of property rights is usually done intentionally: a person chooses to create or transfer a particular right and does what is necessary to give effect to their intention. Most of this happens simply and informally. We can acquire ownership of a bag of groceries at a self-checkout without speaking a word. Some transactions are more complicated, such as buying a house or making a will.

Property rights can also arise by operation of law even though no one intended to create them. Some have been discussed in previous chapters, such as a repairer's lien (in Chapter 6), a trust that arises when one joint tenant murders the other (in Chapter 5), or a prescriptive easement (in Chapter 7). Although most of this chapter is about rights created or transferred by intention, rights arising by operation of law will also be encountered.

2) Creation or Transfer

The creation of a new right is different from the transfer of an existing right. For example, I can create a new leasehold estate by granting a lease to a tenant. They might then transfer that estate to someone by assigning the lease, or they might create another new estate by subletting the premises. If I find someone's lost umbrella and pick it up, I thereby acquire a new right to possession, which is subject to the owner's better right to possession. I can transfer my right by giving the umbrella to a friend, or I can create a new right by loaning it to them (as a bailment). The rules that apply to the creation of a right can be different from those that apply to its transfer.

3) *Inter Vivos* or Testamentary

A transaction is *inter vivos* if it occurs during life. It is testamentary if it takes effect on death. Although the term *testamentary* normally refers to something in a will (*testamentum* in Latin), that term is used more broadly here to refer to any transaction that takes effect on death. This distinction matters because different rules apply depending on whether a transaction is *inter vivos* or testamentary. Generally speaking, more formalities must be observed to make a gift on death than during life.

The death of a person can have proprietary consequences that are not testamentary. A life estate ends on the death of the life tenant, and someone else becomes entitled to possession, but that is not a testamentary disposition. Similarly, when a joint tenant dies, the other tenants will enjoy their rights of survivorship, but that is not a testamentary disposition. Those are just the inherent features of those property rights, however they are created. A life estate or joint tenancy may be created by will and so begin as a testamentary disposition, but the end of a life or joint tenant's interest is not testamentary.

4) Gift or Contract

Most property rights are acquired pursuant to contracts. We buy food, clothes, furniture, homes, and so on. Of course, giving is a big part of life, with gifts for birthdays, for weddings, or to say thank you and donations to charity. Giving is also a huge part of death, when everything we own will be given away.

There are significant differences between the status of a buyer and the status of a donee. People who make contracts to buy things acquire rights to receive them. In contrast, little can be done to help someone hoping to receive a gift. Also, as discussed in the next chapter on competing rights, the law offers greater protection to someone who acquires something for value than to someone who receives it for free.

5) Law or Equity

The rules for creating property rights depend on whether the right is legal or equitable. Some property rights are necessarily equitable because they do not exist at common law, such as the interest of a beneficiary under a trust (discussed in Chapter 4) or a restrictive covenant over land (discussed in Chapter 7). Other rights can be legal or equitable depending on the manner of their creation. For example, a long leasehold estate is created at law by deed or registration (depending on its location), but an equitable lease can be created by contract. This is discussed below.

It can matter whether a property right is legal or equitable when people make competing claims to the same thing. As discussed in the next chapter, legal rights usually receive greater protection than equitable rights.

B. GIFTS

The normal way to make a gift is to transfer legal title to the intended donee. It is also possible to give them the benefits of ownership by creating a trust for them, with someone else holding legal title. A gift or trust may be *inter vivos* or testamentary. *Inter vivos* gifts are discussed here. Trusts and testamentary gifts are discussed separately below.

How one transfers legal title depends on the subject matter being transferred. Goods and cash are normally transferred by delivery, whereas land is normally transferred by deed or registration. Goods can also be transferred by deed, but that is less common. Intangible things (such as copyrights, patents, debts, and company shares) cannot be delivered and so are transferred by document or registration.

1) Delivery of Goods

Two things are needed to make a gift by delivery: the donor intends to give, and the donee obtains possession. One without the other is not sufficient. For example, you can buy a book as a gift for a friend, write a nice message inside, gift-wrap it, and even tell them about it, but the gift will not be complete until they get possession. Wanting it badly enough will not make it happen.

Conversely, if you handed a book to a friend, that will not complete a gift unless that is what you intended. If you were intending to loan the book, then you created a bailment instead. The same action can have different legal consequences depending on the intention of the actor.

In *Day v Harris*,[1] the English Court of Appeal was asked to decide whether a delivery of goods was a gift or a bailment. When the composer Sir Malcolm Arnold moved from a house to a flat, he had several boxes of goods (including his Oscar for the score of the 1957 film *The Bridge on the River Kwai* and original manuscripts of his compositions) delivered to his daughter Katherine's house unannounced. He also sent a postcard to his son Robert (in another city), which said: "All the books, pictures, sculptures etc are for you and Katherine to share and keep, or sell if you like! Dad."[2] The court held that he intended to make a gift of everything in the boxes because of the word "etc" on the postcard.

When people make a contract, the relevant intention is based on the agreement of both parties, but the effect of a gift depends solely on the donor's intention. As Lloyd LJ said, "if the governing intention is that of a single party, the deliverer of the goods, the issue depends on the intention of that party, and again not his subjective intention but rather his intention objectively ascertained from his words and conduct."[3] Of course, the recipient can reject the gift, but they need not know that it is intended as a gift for the gift to be complete.

Most gifts are achieved by an act of delivery. The donor may present the gift in person (e.g., when a guest hands a bottle of wine to their host on arrival) or may arrange for someone else to make the delivery (as Sir Malcom Arnold did). They may purchase the item online and arrange for delivery by the seller. In each case, the gift is complete when the donee obtains possession.

Although an act of delivery is common, it is not required. If the donee has possession when the donor intends to give, the gift is complete. It does not matter which happens first so long as the donee's possession and the donor's intention coincide at some point. This is demonstrated nicely by two English cases: *Re Stoneham*[4] and *Thomas v The Times Book Co Ltd*.[5]

---

1   [2013] EWCA Civ 191, [2014] Ch 211.
2   *Ibid* at para 53.
3   *Ibid* at para 69.
4   [1918] 1 Ch 149 (Ch D) [*Re Stoneham*].
5   [1966] 1 WLR 911 (Ch D) [*Thomas*].

In *Stoneham*, a grandson was living in a house owned by his grandfather, who would come to visit from time to time. On one of his visits, he told his grandson that he could keep the furniture and other things in the house as a gift. After the grandfather died, it was argued that the gift was incomplete because there had been no act of delivery, but that was rejected by the court. Lawrence J said,

> In principle I can see no distinction between a delivery antecedent to the gift and a delivery concurrent with or subsequent to the gift. Nor can I see any reason in principle why the rule should not apply to a case where chattels have been delivered to the donee before the gift as bailee or in any other capacity, so long as they are actually in his possession at the time of the gift to the knowledge of the donor.[6]

In *Thomas*, the poet Dylan Thomas lost the original manuscript to his play *Under Milk Wood* in one of the many pubs he had visited in London over the weekend before he was due to fly to New York on Monday morning. Fortunately, a producer at the BBC named Cleverdon had arranged for stencil copies to be made, and he gave three copies to Thomas at the air terminal. Thomas was grateful and told Cleverdon that he could keep the original manuscript if he could find it. Cleverdon found it the next day, and Thomas died three weeks later. The manuscript was sold a few years later, and Thomas's widow sued the buyer to recover it. She argued unsuccessfully that the gift to the producer was incomplete because there had been no act of delivery. Plowman J said,

> It is then said on behalf of the plaintiff that even if Dylan Thomas intended to give this manuscript to Cleverdon, he did not succeed in giving effect to that intention because there was no delivery of the subject-matter of it to Cleverdon by Dylan Thomas. I feel bound to reject that argument. The fact is that Cleverdon got possession of this manuscript from the Soho public-house in which it had been left by Dylan Thomas and that he got that possession with the consent of Dylan Thomas. That, in my judgment, is sufficient delivery to perfect a gift in Cleverdon's favour.[7]

In *Re Cole*,[8] the English Court of Appeal held that it is not enough for the donee to obtain possession; it is also necessary for the donor to give up possession. This can create a problem when they both live together and share possession of the home where the goods are kept. In *Cole*, a husband bought a large house in London in the summer of 1945 and

---

6   *Re Stoneham*, above note 4 at 153–54.
7   *Thomas*, above note 5 at 919.
8   [1964] Ch 175 (CA).

spent £20,000 furnishing it. When his wife joined him in December, he showed her around all the rooms and said, "It's all yours."[9] He became bankrupt in 1961 and argued that his trustee in bankruptcy could not take the furniture because it had been given to his wife in 1945. That was rejected by the court.

The problem was that the husband remained in possession of the furniture, so there was no change of possession when his wife moved into the home. Harman LJ said, "It is, I think, trite law that a gift of chattels is not complete unless accompanied by something which constitutes an act of delivery or a change of possession."[10] The court acknowledged that symbolic delivery is possible if the goods are bulky, citing *Rawlinson v Mort*,[11] where a church organ had been given by the donor to the donee when both were standing next to it in the presence of witnesses. The court also said that a deed can be used to make a gift of goods if delivery is impractical. A deed would provide certainty that a gift had been made even though the donor remained in possession.

The Alberta Court of Appeal cited *Cole* and came to a similar conclusion in *Nicholls Estate v Nicholls Estate*.[12] A husband paid to rent a safety deposit box in his wife's name and used a power of attorney from her to access the box and place valuable items inside it. He died two years before she did, and the court was asked to decide whether the contents of the safety deposit box belonged to his estate or hers. The trial judge held that she had exclusive possession of the items (after he died) and that the *presumption of advancement* applied,[13] which is the assumption that a transfer of legal title from husband to wife is intended as a gift in the absence of evidence to the contrary (as discussed in Chapter 5). Therefore, the gift to her was complete.

There are two problems with the trial judge's approach. First, the wife did not have exclusive possession until the husband died, at which point he was no longer capable of intending anything. Therefore, his intention to give (if it existed) did not coincide with her exclusive possession. Second, the presumption of advancement applies only when there has been a transfer of legal title and it is not clear whether a gift was intended. The issue before the court was whether a transfer had occurred.

The Court of Appeal held that there had been no gift to the wife. At no point during her husband's life did she have exclusive possession of

---

9   *Ibid* at 184.
10   *Ibid* at 185.
11   (1905) 21 TLR 774, 93 LT 555.
12   [1972] 5 WWR 99 (Alta CA) [*Nicholls*].
13   *Ibid* at para 5.

the contents of the safety deposit box. Their shared possession of the box was insufficient to perfect a gift.

In *Langer v McTavish Bros Ltd*,[14] the BC Court of Appeal came to a different conclusion, but that was thirty years before *Cole*. The facts in both cases are surprisingly similar. In *Langer*, a husband was negotiating the purchase of a furnished house in Vancouver in 1926. He brought his wife to see the furniture before he bought it, she was pleased with it, and he said, "This is all yours."[15] His creditors seized the furniture in 1931, and the couple argued that the furniture had been given to her. A majority of the Court of Appeal agreed. Macdonald JA said,

> The donee was in physical possession of the furniture if not concurrently with the gift, at least subsequently thereto, in the sense that she occupied as of right or with the consent of her future husband the home where the furniture was installed.... It is immaterial that it is a joint occupation of the premises. When the words of gift were uttered, *qua* the furniture, the subject of the gift, the donee was either already in possession or subsequently acquired it.[16]

The dissenting judge (Macdonald CJBC) said,

> Of course, in the case of a gift there must be delivery—must be possession on the part of the donee. There was nothing of that kind in this case. She was simply told by the husband, who was not the owner, and I do not think it would have made any difference if he had been the owner, "This is all yours." There was no handing over or giving her actual possession of the furniture. He simply took her there to live as his wife, and they enjoyed the furniture together.[17]

Whether the donee's shared possession with the donor should be sufficient to complete a gift by delivery is a debatable issue. More troubling is this statement by Macdonald JA:

> Physical delivery, dependant upon circumstances, the nature of the chattel and the relationship of the parties may be, *as part of the evidence*, a necessary element to establish a completed gift. In other instances (as in the case at Bar) where physical delivery is unnecessary or would be an idle or purely artificial act, as where from the nature of the gift and the position of the parties the chattels *ex necessitate* remain in the same place before and after the gift it is sufficient

---

14   [1932] 4 DLR 90 (BCCA) [*Langer*].
15   *Ibid* at 91.
16   *Ibid* at 95–96.
17   *Ibid* at 91.

if we find, "Two contemporaneous acts, which at once complete the transaction, so that there is nothing more to be done by either party. The act done by the one is that he gives; the act done by the other is that he accepts. These contemporaneous acts being done, neither party has anything more to do."[18]

The difficulty is that delivery is not evidence that a gift was made. It is how a gift is made. Intention alone will not perfect a gift even if it is absolutely certain that a gift was intended. Something must be done to give effect to that intention. For a gift of goods, this requires either a transfer of possession to the donee or the execution of a deed. As McDermid J said in *Nicholls*, "Actual delivery is not mere evidence of the gift but is part of the gift itself."[19]

In *Hatch v Mackedie*,[20] a father had five paintings by Archibald Thorburn in his possession when he died in 1997. His son Graeme successfully claimed that he was the owner of the paintings, which had been transferred to him as *inter vivos* gifts on his birthdays from 1969 to 1973. On each birthday, a painting was gift wrapped, handed to the son, who unwrapped it, and then rehung on the wall in the father's home. The mother had written on the back of each painting "Happy Birthday Graeme" along with the date and his full name. The father also told his solicitor that the paintings had been given to his son as birthday gifts. After quoting the passage from *Langer*,[21] Hunter J said,

> After careful consideration I am satisfied that the presentation of the paintings as birthday gifts, and wrapped as such, constitutes delivery even though they remained in the possession of the father. If I am wrong in concluding that physical delivery took place then I am satisfied that in all the circumstances it is not necessary given the factual circumstances including the "writings" on the back of the paintings and the deceased's statement to his solicitor, Wilson, in 1992.[22]

The ruling that the paintings were given to the son by delivery is perfectly consistent with the law. Legal title would be transferred to the son when he took hold of each painting, and the father would become a bailee when it was placed back on the wall. However, the suggestion that a gift could be made without delivery to the son is unorthodox.

---

18 *Ibid* at 95 [emphasis added], quoting Lord Esher MR in *Cochrane v Moore* (1890), 25 QBD 57 at 76. See also *Re McLeod Estate*, 2012 ABQB 384.

19 *Nicholls*, above note 12 at para 8, quoting *Halsbury's Laws of England*, 3rd ed (London: Butterworths, 1957) vol 18 at 382.

20 1998 CanLII 1080 (BCSC).

21 *Langer*, above note 14.

22 *Ibid* at paras 27–28.

Although *Langer* may be inconsistent with *Cole* and *Nicholls*, the wife did obtain shared possession of the furniture. If the son never obtained possession of the paintings, then there was nothing that could have perfected the gift. The writing on the back of the painting would not count as a deed, nor would the statement to the solicitor. They provide convincing evidence that gifts were intended, but intention alone is not enough.

2) Transfer of Land

This section deals with grants and transfers of legal interests in land. These can occur as gifts or pursuant to contracts. The issues discussed here apply equally to both. Land contracts and trusts of land give rise to equitable interests in land. They are discussed separately below.

At one time, legal title to land was transferred by delivery. The transfer of a freehold estate was called a *feoffment*. In a ceremony called *livery of seisin*, the feoffor would present the feoffee with a twig or piece of sod in the presence of witnesses as a symbolic act to deliver possession. A *charter of feoffment* was used as a record of the event. The document did not cause title to pass but provided documentary evidence that it had passed.

This was changed in England, first to require writing and then to require a deed to transfer legal title to land. The writing requirement was imposed by the *Statute of Frauds 1677*.[23] Land was still transferred by livery of seisin, but the transfer would be ineffective unless it was put in writing and signed by the grantor or their agent. The *Real Property Act 1845*[24] made it necessary to use a deed. Ordinary signed writing was no longer sufficient. Both statutes have since been replaced in England by the *Law of Property Act 1925*, which states that feoffment and livery of seisin are abolished and that legal interests in land can only be granted by deed.[25] All three statutes preserved an exception for leases of up to three years, which can be made informally by putting the tenant into possession.

The *Real Property Act 1845* was received as part of English law in the territories and western provinces but not in Ontario or the Atlantic provinces, which received English law before 1845.[26] Most of the provinces that did not receive the *Real Property Act 1845* have enacted

---

23   29 Car 2, c 3.

24   8 and 9 Vic, c 119.

25   15 and 16 Geo V, c 20, ss 51–54.

26   See JE Cote, "The Introduction of English Law into Alberta" (1964) 3 *Alta L Rev* 262 at 262–63. The relevant dates are 1758 in New Brunswick and Nova Scotia,

a similar version of their own. For example, the *Real Property Act* in Prince Edward Island states, "A feoffment shall be void at law, unless evidenced by deed; and a partition and an exchange of any tenements or hereditaments, and a lease required by law to be in writing, of any tenements or hereditaments, shall be void at law unless made by deed."[27]

A deed is also required in Ontario and New Brunswick.[28] In Nova Scotia, feoffment and livery of seisin are abolished, and the transfer of legal title to land is accomplished by a *conveyance*, which is defined as "an instrument which expresses an intention to convey thereby a property right."[29]

There is no equivalent statute in Newfoundland and Labrador, where transfers of land are still subject to the English *Statute of Frauds 1677*.[30] According to *Butt v Humber*,[31] it is possible to transfer legal title to land in the province in three different ways: (1) by deed, (2) by livery of seisin, and (3) by signed document plus transfer of possession. The owner of a house signed a document that declared that he transferred his title to that house to his stepdaughter when they were both living in it. This was a gift and not a land contract. She then sued to evict him, and the court had to decide whether the transfer was valid. The document was not a deed because it was not under seal. There was no livery of seisin in which the stepdaughter was given vacant possession by symbolic delivery. Goodridge J held that legal title had been transferred by the third method:

> I am of the opinion therefore that where an instrument duly signed by the grantor, purporting to convey a present interest in land to the grantee, delivered to the grantee, accompanied by the delivery of possession (vacant or otherwise) to the grantee if he is not then already in possession, the interest which is purported to be thereby conveyed, (or the present interest of the grantor therein if that is less than what he purports to convey) passes thereby to the grantee notwithstanding that the instrument is not sealed and was not executed for good or valuable consideration.[32]

1763 in Prince Edward Island, 1792 in Ontario, 1832 in Newfoundland, 1858 in British Columbia, and 1870 in the rest of Canada.

27 RSPEI 1988, c R-3, s 5.

28 *Conveyancing and Law of Property Act*, RSO 1990, c C.34, s 3; *Property Act*, RSNB 1973, c P-19, s 11.

29 *Conveyancing Act*, RSNS 1989, c 97, ss 9, 10.

30 See *Hollett v Hollett* (1993), 334 APR 271, 106 Nfld & PEIR 271 (Nfld SC).

31 (1976) 46 APR 92, 17 Nfld & PEIR 92 (Nfld SC).

32 *Ibid* at para 72.

Newfoundland's third method is similar to its first and second methods. It is different from transfer by deed because the instrument does not need to be sealed; instead, the donee must get possession of the land. However, the instrument must be signed and delivered, just like a deed. It is different from livery of seisin because there is no need for a ceremony to put the donee into vacant possession of the land. Shared possession is good enough. It is otherwise just like livery of seisin because that also requires signed writing to comply with the *Statute of Frauds 1677.*

A deed is a document that is signed, sealed, and delivered. Delivery of the deed, rather than delivery of the land, causes title to pass, but physical delivery of the deed is often not required. Although it may seem odd, a deed will be treated as having been delivered if the grantor clearly intends that it should be effective at once. As Schroeder JA explained in *Carson v Wilson,*

> It is, as a rule, essential to the validity of a deed that there should be a delivery of the instrument: If the grantor clearly manifests his intention that the deed shall presently become operative and effectual; if he by words or conduct expressly or impliedly acknowledges his intention to be immediately and unconditionally bound by its provisions that will constitute a sufficient delivery in law. The controlling factor is the intention of the grantor which may be inferred from his acts or declarations at the time of delivery, or from all the circumstances surrounding the transaction. If this intention is made clearly apparent by other means, then manual delivery of the deed or instrument to the grantee, which affords cogent evidence of the grantor's intention, is not requisite to the consummation of the gift. But where, as here, the instruments are physically delivered to a third party there must be evidence to establish that they were delivered to the third party for the use of the grantees and the delivery will not be effectual unless it amounts to proof—and clear proof—that the grantor intended to part with his dominion and control over the instruments and thereupon to vest such right, dominion and control in the grantees and to create an interest *in praesenti* in their favour.[33]

A deed can be executed and then transferred to a third party, who holds it in *escrow* pending the fulfillment of certain conditions.[34] Delivery will occur when the conditions are met because the third party holds the deed on behalf of the grantor until that occurs and then on

---

33 [1961] OR 113, 26 DLR (2d) 307 at para 14 (CA). See also *Chase v Chase* (1962), 36 DLR (2d) 351 (NBCA); *Re Sammon* (1979), 94 DLR (3d) 594, 22 OR (2d) 721 (CA).

34 See *Foundling Hospital Governors and Guardians v Crane*, [1911] 2 KB 367 (CA).

behalf of the grantee. If the condition is the death of the grantor, then it is a testamentary disposition to which different rules apply (as discussed below).[35]

In most of Canada, legal title to land is no longer transferred by deed. It is transferred by registration. As discussed in Chapter 6, there are two main types of land registration systems: *deed registration* and *title registration*. In a deed registration system, title is transferred by deed. Registration of that deed helps protect that title (as discussed in the next chapter). In a title registration system, legal title is transferred only when the appropriate document is registered. Deed registration is the only system in Prince Edward Island and Newfoundland and Labrador.[36] Title registration is the only system in British Columbia, Alberta, Saskatchewan, and the territories.[37] Manitoba, Ontario, New Brunswick, and Nova Scotia have both systems.[38]

One of the limitations of a deed registration system is that registration does not confirm that the deed is valid or that the grantor had good title to begin with. There is a principle of the common law called *nemo dat quod non habet*, which means that no one can give what they do not have. A person who acquires land by deed cannot get a better title than their grantor had. This means that a prudent person buying land in a deed registration system will conduct searches to determine whether the grantor has good title. They will need to establish a good chain of title since a chain is only as strong as its weakest link. Did the grantor acquire their title in a valid transaction from someone who had good title? How did that person get their title? What about the person before them?

Land title registration alleviates this problem because title is acquired by registration and not by deed. Subject to numerous exceptions, a person who obtains a registered estate for value has good title even if registration is based on a flawed or forged document. The document itself has no legal effect (although it may give rise to equitable rights, as discussed below). For example, the Alberta *Land Titles Act* states,

---

35 *Ibid; Chase v Chase*, above note 33; *Carson v Wilson*, above note 33.

36 *Registry Act*, RSPEI 1988, c R-10; *Registration of Deeds Act, 2009*, SNL 2009, c R-10.01.

37 *Land Title Act*, RSBC 1996, c 250; *Land Titles Act*, RSA 2000, c L-4; *Land Titles Act, 2000*, SS 2000, c L-5.1; *Land Titles Act, 2015*, SY 2015, c 10; *Land Titles Act*, RSNWT 1988, c 8.

38 *Registry Act*, CCSM, c R50; *Real Property Act*, CCSM, c R30; *Registry Act*, RSO 1990, c R.20; *Land Titles Act*, RSO 1990, c L.5; *Registry Act*, RSNB 1973, c R-6; *Land Titles Act*, SNB 1981, c L-1.1; *Registry Act*, RSNS 1989, c 392; *Land Registration Act*, SNS 2001, c 6.

[N]o instrument is effectual to pass any estate or interest in that land
(except a leasehold interest for 3 years or for a less period) ... unless
the instrument is executed in accordance with this Act and is registered under this Act, but on the registration of any such instrument
in the manner hereinbefore prescribed the estate or interest specified
in the instrument passes.[39]

The strength of a title in a title registration system depends on the
exceptions provided by that system. That is discussed in the next chapter. An important exception is made for leases of up to three years if
the tenant is in possession.[40] There is no need for tenants to incur the
expense to register short leases and no need to clog up the registration
system with them. The consequences are relatively minor for anyone
who acquires the land subject to the tenant's rights.

Leases of up to three years do not need to be in writing. They can be
created informally by putting the tenant into possession if rent is being
paid. The *Statute of Frauds 1677* (and its exception for short leases) still
applies in Alberta, Saskatchewan, Prince Edward Island, Newfoundland
and Labrador, and the territories.[41] Manitoba and New Brunswick have
repealed the *Statute of Frauds*,[42] so they have no need for the exception.
British Columbia, Ontario, and Nova Scotia have created an exception for
leases of up to three years in their own statutes.[43] In Nova Scotia,

[e]very estate, or other interest in land not put in writing and signed
by the person creating or making the same, or his agent thereunto
lawfully authorized by writing, shall have the force of a lease or estate

---

39 RSA 2000, c L-4, s 53. See also *Land Title Act*, RSBC 1996, c 250, ss 20, 22; *Land
Titles Act, 2000*, SS 2000, c L-5.1, s 25; *Real Property Act*, CCSM, c R30, s 66;
Land Titles Act, RSO 1990, c L.5, s 66; *Land Titles Act*, SNB 1981, c L-1.1, ss 15,
16; *Land Registration Act*, SNS 2001, c 6, s 45; *Land Titles Act, 2015*, SY 2015, c 10,
ss 38, 39; *Land Titles Act*, RSNWT 1988, c 8, ss 65, 66.

40 *Land Title Act*, RSBC 1996, c 250, ss 20(3), 23(2)(d); *Land Titles Act*, RSA 2000,
c L-4, ss 32, 61(1)(d), 95; *Land Titles Act, 2000*, SS 2000, c L-5.1, ss 18(1)(d), 139;
Real Property Act, CCSM, c R30, s 58(1)(d); *Land Titles Act*, RSO 1990, c L.5,
s 44(1); *Land Titles Act*, SNB 1981, c L-1.1, ss 17(4)(b), 27; *Land Registration Act*,
SNS 2001, c 6, s 55(5); *Land Titles Act, 2015*, SY 2015, c 10, ss 59(e), 104; *Land
Titles Act*, RSNWT 1988, c 8, ss 69(d), 107.

41 See *Le Corporation Episcopale Catholique Romane of St Albert v RJ Sheppard &
Co* (1913), 9 DLR 619, 3 WWR 814 (Alta QB); *Shamac Country Inns Ltd v 412765
Alberta Ltd* (1994), 18 Alta LR (3d) 396 (QB).

42 *An Act to Repeal the Statute of Frauds*, CCSM, c F158; *An Act to Repeal the Statute
of Frauds*, SNB 2014, c 47.

43 *Law and Equity Act*, RSBC 1996, c 253, s 59(2); *Property Law Act*, RSBC 1996,
c 377, s 5(2); *Statute of Frauds*, RSO 1990, c S.19, s 3; *Statute of Frauds*, RSNS
1989, c 442, s 3.

at will only, except a lease not exceeding the term of three years from the making thereof, whereupon the rent reserved amounts to two thirds at least of the annual value of the land demised.[44]

The exception applies if the rent is two-thirds or more of "the annual value of the land," which is market rent. Ontario's *Statute of Frauds* copied the wording of the *Statute of Frauds 1677* and states that rent must be "at least two-thirds of the full improved value of the thing demised." In *Hoj Industries Ltd v Dundas Shepard Square Ltd*,[45] the court held that this means two-thirds of market rent and not two-thirds of the land's sale value.

C. TRUSTS

As discussed in Chapter 4, a trust is a relationship between trustees and beneficiaries in which the trustees hold title to the trust assets and are required to use them according to the terms of the trust for the benefit of the beneficiaries. A trust for charitable purposes does not have beneficiaries but is enforced by the attorney general on behalf of the Crown, with the Canada Revenue Agency having oversight of the trustees' activities.

1) Express, Resulting, and Constructive Trusts

Trusts are often classified as *express, resulting,* or *constructive.* It is not apparent from those labels, but those categories are based on how trusts are created. An express trust arises because someone (called the *settlor*) chose to create it. In other words, they expressed an intention that a trust should arise and did what was necessary to give effect to their intention (as discussed below).

Resulting and constructive trusts arise by operation of law (or, more accurately, by operation of the rules of equity). They do not depend on an intention to create a trust but are imposed on the owner of assets to compel them to use those assets for the benefit of someone else.

Resulting trusts were encountered in Chapter 5. A resulting trust can arise when someone receives an asset gratuitously and it is presumed or proven that the transaction was not intended as a gift.[46] It can also arise when someone receives assets as an express trustee, but the

---

44   *Statute of Frauds*, RSNS 1989, c 442, s 3.
45   (1978) 95 DLR (3d) 354, 23 OR (2d) 295.
46   *Madsen Estate v Saylor*, 2007 SCC 18.

express trust fails or comes to an end, leaving them with an unexpected surplus.[47] In both situations, someone has received assets at another person's expense, they were not meant to keep those assets as a gift, and the resulting trust compels them to give the assets back to that other person.

Constructive trusts were also encountered in Chapter 5. If one joint tenant murders the other, a trust is imposed on them to prevent them from profiting from their crime. The murderer becomes the sole legal owner as the surviving joint tenant but is compelled to hold the legal title in trust for the victim's estate as an equal tenant in common.[48] Constructive trusts respond to other forms of wrongdoing as well. For example, if someone in a fiduciary position receives a bribe or makes an unauthorized secret profit, they will hold that asset on constructive trust for their principal.[49] Although many constructive trusts arise to strip people of wrongful gains, most have nothing to do with wrong-doing. They more commonly arise to fulfill expectations or to perfect intentions to benefit others. Some of these trusts are discussed below.

2) The Settlor

The creation of an express trust depends on the intention of the settlor, who provides the assets that will be held in trust and sets the terms of the trust. In many trusts, the settlor drops out of the picture once the trust is created. The trustees must obey the terms of the trust imposed by the settlor, but their duties are owed to the beneficiaries and not to the settlor. Unless the settlor becomes a trustee or beneficiary or expressly reserves some powers (such as the power to revoke the trust or to appoint trustees), they have no further say in the matter.

A settlor can become a beneficiary if they transfer assets to a trustee to hold in trust for them. Legal title to those assets is transferred from settlor to trustee, and the settlor immediately acquires an equitable interest in them as the beneficiary of the trust. We might say that the settlor continues to be the *beneficial owner* of the assets because they enjoyed all the benefits of ownership as legal owner before the trust was created and still enjoy those benefits as trust beneficiary. However, their equitable rights under the trust are new rights that did not exist

---

47   *Vandervell v Inland Revenue Commissioners*, [1966] UKHL 3, [1967] 2 AC 291; *Parkland Mortgage Corp v Therevan Development Corp*, [1982] 1 WWR 587, 130 DLR (3d) 682 (Alta QB).

48   *Schobelt v Barber*, [1967] 1 OR 349, 60 DLR (2d) 519.

49   *Soulos v Korkontzilas*, [1997] 2 SCR 217, 146 DLR (4th) 214; *ICBC v Lo*, 2006 BCCA 584.

before the trust was created. Previously, they held legal title for their own benefit. Equity did not get involved until the trust arose.

A settlor can become a trustee by declaring that they hold assets in trust for a beneficiary. The settlor continues to hold legal title to those assets but is no longer allowed to use them for their own benefit. Although the legal title has not changed, the settlor has given up their beneficial ownership of the assets. The beneficiary acquired a new equitable interest in those assets when the trust was created.

3) Three Certainties

It is often said that the creation of an express trust requires three certainties: *certainty of intention, certainty of subject matter*, and *certainty of objects*.[50] In other words, an express trust will not be created unless the settlor intended to create a trust, identified the trust assets, and identified the beneficiaries. The phrase *three certainties* is encountered only in the law of trusts, but the same issues arise in other areas of property law as well. As Judge Paul Matthews said in *Legg v Burton*,

> [T]he so-called "three certainties" rule is not a rule about trust law at all. Instead it is a rule about property law, and, trusts being part of property law, they follow that rule too. If A is to make a gift to B of some asset valid at common law, it is obvious that A must intend a gift and not a loan (or some other legal construct), that it must be clear exactly what it is that is being given, and that it must be clear to whom it is being given. A failure in any respect causes the gift to fail. So too with trusts.[51]

a) Certainty of Intention

A settlor can create a trust without ever using the word "trust." It is sufficient if they manifest an intention to create a relationship in which one person is under a duty to use some asset for the benefit of another. This can make it difficult to determine whether a trust was actually intended, especially when a gift in a will is followed by a request concerning its use. This happened in *Johnson v Farney*.[52] The testator left everything to his widow and made several requests in his will (including

---

50   *Knight v Knight* (1840), 3 Beav 148 at 172, 49 ER 58; *Renehan v Malone* (1897), 1 NB Eq 506 at para 4; *Re Jessop Estate* (1987), 55 Sask R 18 at para 9 (CA); *Lewis v Alliance of Canadian Cinema Television and Radio Artists*, [1996] 6 WWR 588, 18 BCLR (3d) 382 at paras 21–22 (CA); *Henry v Henry* (1999), 126 OAC 372 at paras 14–15; *White v Gicas*, 2014 ONCA 490.

51   [2017] 4 WLR 186 at para 68 (Ch D) [*Legg*].

52   (1913), 14 DLR 134 (Ont CA).

requests that she should live with her mother or a lady companion and not remarry). The will went on to say, "I also wish if you die soon after me that you will leave all you are possessed of to my people and your people equally divided between them, that is to say your mother and my mother's families."[53]

The Ontario Court of Appeal held that this did not create a trust after considering the language used in the entire will. Also, the request referred to all her property and not just the property left to her by her husband. Since he could only create a trust of the property he gave to her in his will, this provided a good indication that his request just expressed a wish and did not impose a trust.

In *Paul v Constance*,[54] an *inter vivos* trust was created by informal language. A man was separated from his wife and living with the plaintiff. He was injured at work and received a payment of damages of £950, which he deposited in his bank account. He often told the plaintiff that the "money is as much yours as mine."[55] The man died intestate, and his wife was entitled to his entire estate. The plaintiff claimed that his statements to her had amounted to a declaration of express trust for the two of them; therefore, she was entitled to half of the money. The Court of Appeal agreed. Although he did not use the word "trust," he had intended a trust relationship in which he had legal title to the bank account, with the benefit of it belonging to both of them.

The issue of certainty of intention can arise in a commercial context as well, but the issue is not whether the parties intended a gift or a trust but whether they intended a trust or some other legal relationship. In *Ontario Hydro-Electric Power Commission v Brown*,[56] the defendant Brown was an agent for the plaintiff power company. He collected money due from the plaintiff's customers and deposited it in his safe. The money was stolen, and the plaintiff sued him for that amount. He argued that he was not liable because he was a trustee of the money and had taken reasonable care of it. The Ontario Court of Appeal held that there was no trust because Brown had no duty to keep the money separate from his own. His obligation was to pay the plaintiff an amount equal to what he had collected less his commission. He was a debtor and not a trustee and therefore still liable to pay his debt. The court quoted from *Henry v Hammond* with approval:

---

53   *Ibid* at para 9.
54   [1977] 1 WLR 527 (CA) [*Paul*].
55   *Ibid* at 532.
56   [1960] OR 91, 21 DLR (2d) 551 (CA).

It is clear that if the terms upon which the person receives money are that he is bound to keep it separate, either in a bank or elsewhere, and to hand that money so kept as a separate fund to the person entitled to it, then he is a trustee of that money and must hand it over to the person who is his *cestui que* trust. If on the other hand he is not bound to keep the money separate, but is entitled to mix it with his own money and deal with it as he pleases and when called upon to hand over an equivalent sum of money, then in my opinion, he is not a trustee of the money. All the authorities seem to me to be consistent with that statement of the law.[57]

Trustees can be given the authority to mix trust assets with their own, and that will not negate a trust if the intention to create it is clear.[58] However, if it is not clear whether a trust was ever intended, then the right to mix money received with one's own is a good indication that there is no trust, and "a direction that moneys are to be kept separate and apart is a strong indication of a trust relationship being created," as McGillivray CJA said in *R v Lowden*.[59]

b) Certainty of Subject Matter

Certainty of subject matter requires that the settlor identifies the assets that will be held in trust. A trust often begins with a small amount placed in trust, and substantial contributions are made afterwards. That is not a problem. Each contribution is essentially a trust settlement on the same terms as the original. The trust attaches to each contribution when it is made. Pension fund trusts operate by receiving regular contributions from employers on behalf of their employees. The subject matter is always certain.

Certainty of subject matter is lacking if the assets that are supposed to be held in trust cannot be identified when the trust is created. In *Re Beardmore Trusts*,[60] a husband and wife separated and the husband declared a trust for his wife and their daughters. The subject matter of the trust was defined as "an amount, sum or other assets equal to three-fifths of the husband's net estate" when he died. The court declared that the trust was void for two reasons. First, it was testamentary since it would become effective only on the husband's death and did not comply with the formalities required to make a valid will (discussed below).

---

57 [1913] 2 KB 515 at 521, Channell J. See also *MA Hanna Co v Provincial Bank of Canada*, [1935] SCR 144; [1935] 1 DLR 545. A *cestui que* trust is a trust beneficiary.

58 *Air Canada v M & L Travel Ltd*, [1993] 3 SCR 787, 108 DLR (4th) 592.

59 (1981) 15 Alta LR (2d) 250, 27 AR 91 at 101 (CA).

60 [1952] 1 DLR 41, [1951] OWN 728.

Second, the subject matter was uncertain. It would become certain when the husband died and his estate was administered, so it could have been valid as a testamentary trust. It could not take effect as an *inter vivos* trust because it was impossible to identify the subject matter while the husband was still alive.

The problem of certainty of subject matter is not exclusive to the law of trusts. It is a potential problem throughout the whole of the law of property, including gifts and sales of goods. A problem can arise if the settlor (or donor or seller) has several assets that match the description of the subject matter, but only some of them are intended to be the subject of the trust (or gift or sale). The trust cannot arise unless we can identify which of those assets are intended to be held in trust.

This problem does not prevent a trust from arising over some of the money in a bank account. For example, I can declare that I hold $50 in a specific bank account in trust for you even if I have $950 in that account. The account does not hold 950 dollars or 95,000 cents. It is a single debt due to me from the bank, and I am required by the terms of the trust to use that right so that you will receive the benefit of $50 (and any interest earned on that amount).

In *Hunter v Moss*,[61] the English Court of Appeal held that the same principle applied to shares in a company. Moss owned 950 shares in a company and declared that he held fifty of those shares in trust for Hunter. The court held that intangibles should be treated differently from goods, so a trust of fifty of 950 company shares is valid, but a trust of fifty of 950 bottles of wine would be invalid unless those fifty bottles were set aside and identified. Although some of the reasoning in the case has been criticized, it makes more sense when we understand the nature of a share in a company. There is only one company, and if it has issued 1,000 shares (as in *Hunter v Moss*), ownership of fifty shares is not ownership of fifty different bits of the company. It is ownership of 5 percent of the company. A trust of fifty of 950 shares is really no different from a trust of $50 in a bank account with a balance of $950.

If there is more than one beneficiary, it is not enough to identify the subject matter of the trust. Those assets must also be allocated among the beneficiaries (e.g., in equal shares or to one beneficiary for life with the remainder to another). In modern trusts, the most common way to do this is by giving the trustees the discretion to decide how to distribute the income and capital among the beneficiaries. A trust can fail if the settlor does not either allocate the assets among the beneficiaries or provide a mechanism for doing so.

---

61   [1993] EWCA Civ 11, [1994] 1 WLR 452.

In *Boyce v Boyce*,[62] a testator left four houses in trust for his daughters Maria and Charlotte. Under the terms of the trust, Maria was entitled to choose one of the houses for herself, and the other three would go to Charlotte. Unfortunately, Maria died without making her choice. The trust failed because the mechanism for allocating the houses between the beneficiaries died with Maria. It is likely that Charlotte would have been much happier with the three worst houses than none at all. The settlor should have provided an alternate mechanism for allocating the houses if Maria failed to make a choice.

Surprisingly, the same problem with the allocation of four houses happened again in *Asten v Asten*.[63] A father built four new houses on the same street in Colchester. He made a will giving one house to each of his four sons, but the houses had not yet been numbered when the will was made, so it was not known which house was given to which son. The gifts failed. No doubt the sons would have been happy coming to an agreement about the allocation of the houses or selling them and splitting the proceeds, but that was not an option. Romer J said,

> If a will shews that a testator intends to give a particular property to a legatee, and, owing to the testator having several properties answering the description in the will of the particular property given you are unable to say, either from the will itself or from extrinsic evidence, which of the several properties the testator referred to, then on principle the gift must fail for uncertainty, and the Court cannot, in order to avoid an intestacy, change the will, or construe it as giving to the legatee the option of choosing any one of the properties.[64]

c) Certainty of Objects

The test for certainty of objects depends on the mechanism for allocating the trust assets among the beneficiaries. If it is fixed by the terms of the trust (e.g., equally among the members of my family), then the trustees must make a complete list of those beneficiaries in order to perform the trust. This is called *list certainty*. If it is impossible to compile a complete list (e.g., because we do not know what the settlor meant by family), then the trust will fail.

If the trustees have a discretion to distribute the assets among the class of beneficiaries, then they are not required to make a complete list. Since they can choose who receives payments from the trust, they need only be sure that they do not pay someone who is not a beneficiary. If

---

62   (1849) 16 Sim 476, 60 ER 959.
63   [1894] 3 Ch 260.
64   *Ibid* at 263.

they can be sure that anyone who receives benefits from the trust falls within the settlor's criteria for being a beneficiary, then the trust is valid. This is called *criteria certainty*.

The case that established these rules is *McPhail v Doulton*.[65] In 1941, Bertram Baden created a trust for the employees of his company (in the days before pension fund trusts were common). The trustees had the discretion to distribute the income from the trust as they saw fit among the current and former employees and officers of the company and their relatives and dependants. Baden died in 1960, and his executors began litigation in 1963 claiming that the trust was invalid because it lacked certainty of objects: it was impossible to make a list of all the relatives and dependants. If they were successful, the trust funds would be held on resulting trust for Baden's estate.

The case went to the House of Lords once and the Court of Appeal twice before it was finally resolved in 1972. The trust was valid. There was no need to list all the beneficiaries. The inclusion of dependants and relatives was problematic, but there was sufficient criteria certainty. The trustees could pay money to a person if they were sure they were a beneficiary but not if they were in doubt.

4) Constitution

Another requirement for the creation of a trust is *constitution*, which is the transfer of the trust assets to the intended trustees. This is not a problem when settlors declare themselves to be trustees because they already have title to the trust assets. It is also not a problem for testamentary trusts because the executors or administrators of the settlor's estate have a duty to transfer the trust assets to the intended trustees. The problem occurs only when a settlor creates an *inter vivos* trust and is not one of the trustees.

In *T Choithram International SA v Pagarani*,[66] a wealthy man executed a trust deed to create a foundation for charitable purposes. He was the settlor and one of the trustees. Shortly before he died, he said he was giving all of his wealth to the foundation. Members of his family argued that his oral declaration of gift was not effective to transfer his assets to the foundation. The Privy Council advised that the trust was constituted because the settlor was one of the trustees. Lord Browne-Wilkinson said,

---

65 [1970] UKHL 1, [1971] AC 424. See also *Lewis v Alliance of Canadian Cinema Television and Radio Artists*, above note 50 at paras 29–33 (CA).

66 [2000] UKPC 46, [2001] 1 WLR 1 (on appeal from the British Virgin Islands) [*Choithram* cited to WLR].

The foundation has no legal existence apart from the trust declared by the foundation trust deed. Therefore the words "I give to the foundation" can only mean "I give to the trustees of the foundation trust deed to be held by them on the trusts of foundation trust deed." Although the words are apparently words of outright gift they are essentially words of gift on trust. . . .

There can in principle be no distinction between the case where the donor declares himself to be sole trustee for a donee or a purpose and the case where he declares himself to be one of the trustees for that donee or purpose. In both cases his conscience is affected and it would be unconscionable and contrary to the principles of equity to allow such a donor to resile from his gift. . . . In their Lordships' judgment in the absence of special factors where one out of a larger body of trustees has the trust property vested in him he is bound by the trust and must give effect to it by transferring the trust property into the name of all the trustees.[67]

The valid transfer of assets from settlor to trustee depends on the nature of the assets involved: goods are transferred by delivery or deed, land is transferred by deed or registration, and so on. The issues are no different from those discussed above in relation to gifts.

In *Watt v Watt Estate*,[68] a man named Richard Watt owned a boat called *Thunderbird*, which was worth $40,000. He signed a written declaration "that the boat commonly known as the Thunderbird is now owned jointly by myself R J Watt and Mrs Shirley Watt."[69] The Manitoba Court of Appeal held that there was no valid gift to her because the document was not a deed and there was no delivery. She had a duplicate set of keys and used the boat, but so did several other people. The court decided that the document was a written declaration of trust, which was constituted because Richard Watt was both settlor and trustee.

5) Formality

For some express trusts, certain formalities must be observed in order to create them. Testamentary trusts are usually created by the settlor's will, as discussed below. In some jurisdictions, a trust of an interest in land cannot be proved unless the terms of the trust are in writing and signed by the settlor. There are no formalities required to create an *inter vivos* trust of anything other than land. A settlor can simply manifest

---

67 *Ibid* at 12.
68 [1988] 1 WWR 534, 49 Man R (2d) 317 (CA) [*Watt*].
69 *Ibid* at 537.

an intention to create the trust, and it will arise if there is certainty of subject matter and objects and a trustee has title to the trust assets. This is true even if the assets are worth millions.

If the settlor is not one of the intended trustees, then constitution of the trust will require the transfer of assets to the trustees (as discussed above). The transfer of those assets may require formalities that are different from the formalities required to declare the trust. For example, if the subject matter of the trust is a fee simple estate, the transfer of legal title to the trustees will require a deed or registration (as discussed above). Depending on the jurisdiction, the declaration of the trust may be informal or may require proof in signed writing but does not require a deed or registration.

The formalities required for an express trust of land were introduced by the *Statute of Frauds 1677*, which states that a declaration of a trust of an interest in land is void unless it is "manifested and proved by some writing signed by the [settlor]."[70] That provision is still in force in Alberta, Saskatchewan, Prince Edward Island, Newfoundland and Labrador, and the territories. It is also found in Ontario's *Statute of Frauds*.[71] Nova Scotia's version is worded differently. It does not say that the declaration must be manifested and proved by signed writing but states that "[n]o declaration or creation of any trust in land shall be valid unless it is *in writing*."[72] There is no writing requirement for an *inter vivos* trust of land in British Columbia, Manitoba, or New Brunswick.

Except in Nova Scotia, there is no requirement that a trust of land be declared in writing. The existence of the trust and its essential terms must be proved by signed writing. This is a limit on the evidence that can be admitted to prove the existence of the trust. An oral declaration of trust can be proved by subsequent written correspondence signed by the settlor.[73] Also, the court will admit other evidence to prove the trust in order to prevent fraud. This was established by the English Court of Appeal in the important case of *Rochefoucauld v Boustead*.[74]

In *Rochefoucauld*, the defendant agreed to purchase land in Ceylon and hold it in trust for the plaintiff, subject to a lien for his expenses. Years later, the plaintiff sued the defendant in England for breach of that trust. He relied on the *Statute of Frauds 1677* as a defence. The plaintiff

---

70 29 Car 2, c 3, s 7.

71 RSO 1990, c S.19, s 9.

72 *Statute of Frauds*, RSNS 1989, c 442, s 5 [emphasis added].

73 *Ong v Ping*, [2017] EWCA Civ 2069; see *Rochefoucauld v Boustead*, [1897] 1 Ch 196 at 206 (CA) [*Rochefoucauld*].

74 *Rouchefoucauld*, above note 73.

argued that the English statute could not apply to foreign land, but that was rejected. Lindley LJ said,

> Counsel for the plaintiff contended that the Statute of Frauds had no application to lands in Ceylon. But, having regard . . . to the language of s. 7 of the Statute of Frauds, we are unable to see why the defendant should not be able to rely on that statute as a defence to any proceedings in this country having for their object the proof and enforcing of a trust, even of lands abroad. The statute relates to the kind of proof required in this country to enable a plaintiff suing here to establish his case here.[75]

However, the court would not allow the defendant to use the *Statute of Frauds* to commit a fraud by denying the existence of the trust:

> It is further established by a series of cases, the propriety of which cannot now be questioned, that the Statute of Frauds does not prevent the proof of a fraud; and that it is a fraud on the part of a person to whom land is conveyed as a trustee, and who knows it was so conveyed, to deny the trust and claim the land himself. Consequently, notwithstanding the statute, it is competent for a person claiming land conveyed to another to prove by parol evidence that it was so conveyed upon trust for the claimant, and that the grantee, knowing the facts, is denying the trust and relying upon the form of conveyance and the statute, in order to keep the land himself.[76]

It has been suggested that this "amounts to a judicial repeal of the statute."[77] If it is always fraud to deny the existence of a trust, then the statute can never be used as a defence. However, it is only fraud if the defendant is "a person to whom land is conveyed as a trustee, and who knows it was so conveyed." There is an important difference between someone who agreed to be a trustee and later denies the existence of the trust and someone who did not undertake any trust but faces a claim that land they acquired is held in trust. The innocent landowner should be free to rely on the *Statute of Frauds* and insist on proof by signed writing.

---

75   *Ibid* at 207.

76   *Ibid* at 206, Lindley LJ. See also *Morris v Whiting* (1913), 15 DLR 254 at 257–58 (Man KB); *Beemer v Brownridge*, [1934] 1 WWR 545 at 556 (Sask CA); *MacDonald v MacDonald*, 2003 NSSC 8.

77   *MacDonald v MacDonald*, *ibid* at para 11, Moir J. See also Law Reform Commission of British Columbia, *Report on the Statute of Frauds*, part C(2)(c), online: www.bcli.org/sites/default/files/LRC33-Status_of_Frauds.pdf.

6) Incomplete Gifts

When an intended gift is incomplete, there is a temptation to save it as a trust for the intended donee. The donor holds legal title and intends to benefit the donee. It is not that different from someone who declares that they hold something in trust for another. However, a court will not construe a failed attempt to make an outright gift as a declaration of trust for the intended donee.[78] As Professor Maitland said, "The two intentions are very different — the giver means to get rid of his rights, the man who is intending to make himself a trustee intends to retain his rights but to come under an onerous obligation. The latter intention is far rarer than the former."[79]

There are cases when something that looks like a gift can properly be construed as a trust, as in *Choithram*,[80] where gifts were made to trustees to hold in trust, or *Paul*,[81] where there was no attempt to transfer legal title to a bank account but simply a declaration that it was "as much yours as mine." *Watt*[82] might be close to the borderline. The written declaration that a boat "is now owned jointly" might have been intended as a gift but can reasonably be construed as a declaration of trust.

Some gifts must be completed by registration. A gift of shares in a private company will be complete when a transfer of those shares is received by the company and its register of shareholders is updated to list the new shareholder in place of the old. A gift of land in a land title system will be complete when a transfer is accepted by the land titles office and the land titles register is changed accordingly. In these situations, there is a gap between the execution of the transfer document by the donor and its registration by the company or the land titles office. Courts have held that a trust can arise during that gap. The donor will hold the shares or land in trust for the donee pending the transfer of legal title.

The main case is *Re Rose*.[83] On 30 March 1943, a husband executed the forms to transfer 10,000 company shares to his wife as a gift and another 10,000 shares to her and the company's secretary to hold in

---

78   *Milroy v Lord* (1862), 4 De G F & J 264, 45 ER 1185 (CA); *Richards v Delbridge* (1874), LR 18 Eq 11.

79   FW Maitland, *The Forms of Action at Common Law* (Cambridge: Cambridge University Press, 1909) at 74.

80   *Choithram*, above note 66.

81   *Paul*, above note 54.

82   *Watt*, above note 68.

83   [1952] EWCA Civ 4, [1952] Ch 499. A different case also called *Re Rose*, [1949] Ch 78 (Ch D), came to the same conclusion on this issue.

trust for her and her son. The transfers were registered by the company on 30 June 1943. The husband died in 1947, and estate duty was payable not just on the value of his estate but also on the value of any gifts he made after 10 April 1943. The English Court of Appeal decided that the husband held the shares in trust for the transferees from 30 March until 30 June; therefore, no estate duty was payable on them because he was only a bare trustee on 10 April.

This seems to contradict the rule that a court will not complete an attempted gift by construing it as a declaration of trust. However, the trust is not express. It is constructive. It does not arise because the donor intended to create a trust. It arises because the donee has the power to complete the gift without the donor's help. This was explained best in *Mascall v Mascall*,[84] in which a father intended to give a house to his son and gave him a registrable transfer of the fee simple estate. The transfer was held up pending the payment of stamp duty, the father and son had a falling out, and the father sued the son to stop the registration of the transfer. The court applied *Rose* and held that the father was a trustee of the estate for his son, who therefore had a right to receive the legal title. Browne-Wilkinson LJ said,

> The basic principle underlying all the cases is that equity will not come to the aid of a volunteer. Therefore, if a donee needs to get an order from a court of equity in order to complete his title, he will not get it. If, on the other hand, the donee has under his control everything necessary to constitute his title completely without any further assistance from the donor, the donee needs no assistance from equity and the gift is complete. It is on that principle, which is laid down in *Re Rose*, that in equity it is held that a gift is complete as soon as the settlor or donor has done everything that the donor has to do, that is to say, as soon as the donee has within his control all those things necessary to enable him, the donee, to complete his title.[85]

The rule in *Rose* has been accepted in Canada.[86] Although the issue in *Rose* was tax, the rule is most often used to allow a donee to achieve completion of a gift, as in *Mascall*. It can operate to complete a gift or constitute a trust (or both, as in *Rose* itself).

---

84   [1984] EWCA Civ 10, 50 P & CR 119 [*Mascall*].
85   *Ibid* at 126.
86   *Sanderson v Halstead*, [1968] 1 OR 749, 67 DLR (2d) 567 (HCJ); *Re Amland Estate* (1975), 10 NBR (2d) 285 (QB); *MacLeod v Montgomery Estate*, [1980] 2 WWR 303, 108 DLR (3d) 424 (Alta CA); *Mordo v Nitting*, 2006 BCSC 1761; *Shkuratoff v Shkuratoff*, 2007 BCSC 1061.

D. WILLS AND ESTATES

There was a time when people were not permitted to give their real property away by will. On the death of the tenant, it would be transferred to their heir, and if there was no heir, it would escheat to the Crown or the lord from whom they held tenure. The power to give real property away by will was introduced by the *Statute of Wills 1540*. Today, we no longer have heirship. All transferable property can be given away by will. If a person dies without leaving a will, their property is distributed according to the rules of *intestate succession*.

When a person dies, their assets are transferred to their *executor* if one is appointed by their will. If there is no executor, the court will appoint an *administrator*, who performs the same functions. An executor or administrator is known as the *personal representative* of the deceased. Anything said about an executor in this part applies also to an administrator. A female executor is sometimes called an *executrix*, just as a female administrator may be called an *administratrix* and a female *testator* may be called a *testatrix*. The terms *executor, administrator,* and *testator* are used here to refer to a person of any gender.

As discussed in Chapter 1, some rights are not transferable, such as a university degree, licence to practise law, or driver's licence. These are not transferred to the executor. A life estate or the interest of a joint tenant will come to an end when the tenant dies. It is not transferred to the executor because it no longer exists. Everything else will be transferred to the executor and forms the *estate* of the deceased person. The executor will have no better right to the assets in the estate than the deceased had. Anything that was the subject of a trust, a security interest, a lease, an easement, and so on, will still be subject to those rights.

The executor has a duty to distribute the estate according to law. They must gather in the assets that belonged to the deceased, including debts due to them, and pay their debts and the taxes due on the estate. Anything that remains is distributed according to the terms of the will or the rules of intestacy.

The executor has a right to custody of the body of the deceased and the duty to dispose of it properly. If there is no executor or administrator, that task falls to the spouse, parents, or next of kin. As Richards JA said in *Mason v Mason*,

> In provinces that have not legislated otherwise, the common law obliges either the executor, the administrator, the surviving spouse, the parents or the next of kin, in that order, as the case may be, to properly dispose of the remains of a deceased person. To that end, a

right of custody and possession is recognized until the obligation has been fulfilled.[87]

1) Wills

A *will* contains instructions by the person who makes it (the *testator*) about what to do with their estate after their death. It usually appoints an executor and may contain instructions about burial or cremation. If a person wishes to change their will, they may revoke it and make a new one, or they may make a *codicil*, which amends a will without revoking it.

Normally, wills are made in writing and signed by the testator in the presence of two witnesses, who also sign the will.[88] Since the testator will be dead when the will takes effect, having two witnesses present at the signing reduces the possibility of fraud. The witnesses usually execute *affidavits of execution* after they sign the will to confirm that they were present at the same time to witness the testator's signature.[89] After the testator dies, the will and affidavits of execution will be submitted to the court to *probate* the will, which is confirmation that it is valid.

In most jurisdictions, a testator can make a *holograph will*, which is valid without witnesses if it is written entirely in the testator's own handwriting and signed by the testator.[90] British Columbia and Prince Edward Island do not provide for holograph wills, but a court in British Columbia can declare that any document or record (including data stored electronically) is a valid will even if it does not comply with the

---

87 2018 NBCA 20 at para 1. See also *Miner v CPR* (1910), 18 WLR 476, 3 Alta LR 408 (CA); *Edmonds v Armstrong Funeral Home Ltd*, [1931] 1 DLR 676 (Alta CA); *Hunter v Hunter*, [1930] 4 DLR 255, 65 OLR 586 (SC); *Waldman v Melville (City)*, [1990] 2 WWR 54, 65 DLR (4th) 154 (Sask QB); *Saleh v Reichert* (1993), 104 DLR (4th) 384 (Ont).

88 *Wills, Estates and Succession Act*, SBC 2009, c 13, s 37; *Wills and Succession Act*, SA 2010, c W-12.2, s 15; *Wills Act, 1996*, SS 1996, c W-14.1, s 7; *Wills Act*, CCSM, c W150, s 4; *Succession Law Reform Act*, RSO 1990, c S.26, s 4; *Wills Act*, RSNB 1973, c W-9, s 4; *Wills Act*, RSNS 1989, c 505, s 6; *Probate Act*, RSPEI 1988, c P-21, s 60; *Wills Act*, RSNL 1990, c W-10, s 2; *Wills Act*, RSNWT 1988, c W-5, s 5; *Wills Act*, RSY 2002, c 230, s 5.

89 See, for example, *Wallbridge Estate*, 2010 ONSC 3409.

90 *Wills and Succession Act*, SA 2010, c W-12.2, s 16; *Wills Act, 1996*, SS 1996, c W-14.1, s 8; *Wills Act*, CCSM, c W150, s 6; *Succession Law Reform Act*, RSO 1990, c S.26, s 6; *Wills Act*, RSNB 1973, c W-9, s 6; *Wills Act*, RSNS 1989, c 505, s 6(2); *Wills Act*, RSNL 1990, c W-10, s 2; *Wills Act*, RSNWT 1988, c W-5, s 5(2); *Wills Act*, RSY 2002, c 230, s 5(2). See *Re Tachibana* (1968), 66 DLR (2d) 567, 63 WWR (ns) 99 (Man CA).

usual formalities.[91] There are rules that allow wills to be made with less formality by members of the armed forces on active service and mariners at sea (and members of the RCMP in Yukon).[92]

A will does not take effect until the testator dies. They are free to revoke it or change it at any time. Therefore, a person does not normally acquire any rights by being named as a will beneficiary. When a testator dies leaving a valid will, the beneficiaries will acquire rights enforceable against the executor but still might not receive what was given to them in the will. The creditors and taxes must be paid first.

A testamentary gift may fail if it *abates, adeems,* or *lapses.* It abates if all or some of it is needed to pay creditors or taxes. A gift of a specific asset will adeem if the testator no longer owned it when they died. A gift lapses if the beneficiary dies before the testator.

Testamentary gifts commonly bear different names depending on the subject matter of the gift. A gift of land is called a *devise,* and a gift of personal property is a *bequest,* although a gift of a sum of money is often called a *legacy.* Anything left over is the *residue of the estate* or the *residuary estate.* The will should contain a clause that provides for the effective distribution of the residue even if the main beneficiaries die before the testator.

2) Intestate Succession

If a person dies without leaving a valid will, they have died *wholly intestate.* If they have a valid will, but it fails to dispose of their entire estate, then they are *partially intestate.* Every jurisdiction provides for *intestate succession* with a comprehensive set of instructions for distributing the estate.[93] Typically, the estate is divided between the surviving spouse and the children. If there are none, then it goes to other relatives listed

---

91   *Wills, Estates and Succession Act,* SBC 2009, c 13, s 58. See also *Wills and Succession Act,* SA 2010, c W-12.2, s 37.

92   *Wills, Estates and Succession Act,* SBC 2009, c 13, s 38; *Wills and Succession Act,* SA 2010, c W-12.2, s 17; *Wills Act, 1996,* SS 1996, c W-14.1, s 6; *Wills Act,* CCSM, c W150, s 5; *Succession Law Reform Act,* RSO 1990, c S.26, s 5; *Wills Act,* RSNB 1973, c W-9, s 5; *Wills Act,* RSNS 1989, c 505, s 9; *Probate Act,* RSPEI 1988, c P-21, s 62; *Wills Act,* RSNL 1990, c W-10, s 2(2); *Wills Act,* RSNWT 1988, c W-5, s 6; *Wills Act,* RSY 2002, c 230, s 5(3).

93   *Wills, Estates and Succession Act,* SBC 2009, c 13, Part 3; *Wills and Succession Act,* SA 2010, c W-12.2, Part 3; *Intestate Succession Act, 2019,* SS 2019, c I-13.2; *Intestate Succession Act,* CCSM, c I85; *Succession Law Reform Act,* RSO 1990, c S.26, Part II; *Devolution of Estates Act,* RSNB 1973, c D-9, Part II; *Intestate Succession Act,* RSNS 1989, c 236; *Probate Act,* RSPEI 1988, c P-21, Part IV; *Intestate Succession Act,* RSNL 1990, c I-21; *Estate Administration Act,* RSY 2002, c 77, Part 10; *Intestate Succession Act,* RSNWT 1988, c I-10.

in order of priority: descendants, parents, siblings, grandparents, and so on, and if there are no relatives, then it goes to the Crown.

Some jurisdictions now recognize that there may be two or more surviving spouses or people who were in equivalent relationships with the deceased. British Columbia and Alberta provide a mechanism for dividing the spouse's share of the estate.[94] In Yukon, a court may order that some or all of the estate be used for the benefit of a "common law spouse" even if there is a surviving spouse.[95] Saskatchewan and Manitoba have rules to determine which person gets the spouse's share.[96] Statutes in other jurisdictions do not address the issue, except in Nova Scotia, where a husband or wife "living in adultery" at the time of their spouse's death has no claim on the estate.[97]

The Nova Scotia statute was considered recently in *Jackson Estate v Young*.[98] A man and a woman lived together in a common law relationship from 2004 until she died intestate in 2017. They were not living in adultery, but the statutory provision relating to adultery was a factor that led the court to conclude that the spouse's share could go only to someone who was legally married to the deceased.

3) Adequate Provision for Families

In civil law jurisdictions, some of the assets of a deceased person must go to their heirs, with a portion for the surviving spouse, a portion for the children, and a portion that may be given away by will. This is sometimes called *forced heirship*. The common law took a different approach. It began to allow people to give their real property away by will in 1540 (as discussed above) and eventually got rid of heirship altogether. *Freedom of testation* is important in common law jurisdictions, but since the early twentieth century, it has been limited by statutes that require testators to make provision for their families.

Every common law jurisdiction in Canada has a statute that allows spouses, children, and sometimes other relatives of the deceased to apply to the court to receive benefits from their estate.[99] Who is eligible

---

94   *Wills, Estates and Succession Act*, SBC 2009, c 13, s 22; *Wills and Succession Act*, SA 2010, c W-12.2, s 62.

95   *Estate Administration Act*, RSY 2002, c 77, s 74.

96   *Intestate Succession Act, 2019*, SS 2019, c I-13.2, s 15; *Intestate Succession Act*, CCSM, c 185, s 3(3).

97   *Intestate Succession Act*, RSNS 1989, c 236, s 17.

98   2020 NSSC 5.

99   *Wills, Estates and Succession Act*, SBC 2009, c 13, s 60; *Wills and Succession Act*, SA 2010, c W-12.2, s 88; *Dependants' Relief Act, 1996*, SS 1996, c D-25.01; *Dependants Relief Act*, CCSM, c D37; *Succession Law Reform Act*, RSO 1990, c S.26, s 58;

to apply varies across the country. In Alberta, children can apply if they are under eighteen, a full-time student under twenty-two, or "unable to earn a livelihood by reason of mental or physical disability."[100] Similar limits are found in Saskatchewan, Manitoba, Prince Edward Island, and the territories. In contrast, any child can apply in British Columbia, Ontario, New Brunswick, Nova Scotia, and Newfoundland and Labrador, including independent adults.

The basis for granting relief also varies across Canada from a purely needs-based approach to one that takes into account the moral obligations of testators to provide for their families. The leading case is *Tataryn v Tataryn Estate*,[101] in which the Supreme Court of Canada applied the BC legislation, which then stated,

> Notwithstanding any law or statute to the contrary, if a testator dies leaving a will which does not, in the court's opinion, make adequate provision for the proper maintenance and support of the testator's wife, husband or children, the court may, in its discretion, in an action by or on behalf of the wife, husband or children, order that the provision that it thinks adequate, just and equitable in the circumstances be made out of the estate of the testator for the wife, husband or children.[102]

Alexander Tataryn died leaving a widow (Mary) and two adult sons (John and Edward). His estate was valued at $315,265, including the matrimonial home (which he owned), a rental property next door, and $122,630 in the bank. Mary had $25,000 of her own. Alexander disliked John since he was six years old, and his will was designed to keep him from getting anything. It stated, "I HAVE PURPOSELY excluded my son, JOHN."[103] He gave Mary a life interest in the family home and the benefit of a discretionary trust of other assets (with Edward as trustee) and gave everything else to Edward.

The court ordered that Mary was entitled to the matrimonial home, a life interest in the rental property, and the residue of the estate after payment of $10,000 each to John and Edward. On her death, one-third

---

Provision for Dependants Act, RSNB 2012, c 111; *Testators' Family Maintenance Act*, RSNS 1989, c 465; *Dependants of a Deceased Person Relief Act*, RSPEI 1988, c D-7; *Family Relief Act*, RSNL 1990, c F-3; *Dependants Relief Act*, RSY 2002, c 56; *Dependants Relief Act*, RSNWT 1988, c D-4.

100 *Wills and Succession Act*, SA 2010, c W-12.2, s 72.

101 [1994] 2 SCR 807, 116 DLR (4th) 193 [*Tataryn* cited to SCR].

102 *Wills Variation Act*, RSBC 1979, c 435, s 2; replaced by *Wills, Estates and Succession Act*, SBC 2009, c 13, s 60.

103 *Tataryn*, above note 101 at 811.

of the rental property would go to John and the other two-thirds to Edward. McLachlin J said,

> The two interests protected by the Act are apparent. The main aim of the Act is adequate, just and equitable provision for the spouses and children of testators. . . .
>
> The other interest protected by the Act is testamentary autonomy. The Act did not remove the right of the legal owner of property to dispose of it upon death. Rather, it limited that right. The absolute testamentary autonomy of the 19th century was required to yield to the interests of spouses and children to the extent, and only to the extent, that this was necessary to provide the latter with what was "adequate, just and equitable in the circumstances." And if that testamentary autonomy must yield to what is "adequate, just and equitable," then the ultimate question is, what is "adequate, just and equitable" in the circumstances judged by contemporary standards. Once that is established, it cannot be cut down on the ground that the testator did not want to provide what is "adequate, just and equitable." . . .
>
> If the phrase "adequate, just and equitable" is viewed in light of current societal norms, much of the uncertainty disappears. Furthermore, two sorts of norms are available and both must be addressed. The first are the obligations which the law would impose on a person during his or her life were the question of provision for the claimant to arise. These might be described as legal obligations. The second type of norms are found in society's reasonable expectations of what a judicious person would do in the circumstances, by reference to contemporary community standards. These might be called moral obligations, following the language traditionally used by the courts. Together, these two norms provide a guide to what is "adequate, just and equitable" in the circumstances of the case.[104]

The extent to which this approach applies elsewhere in Canada depends on differences between the BC statute and those found elsewhere.[105] Blair JA said in *Cummings v Cummings*, "I see no reason why the principles of *Tataryn* should not apply equally in Ontario,"[106] despite the differences between the BC and Ontario statutes. The Manitoba statute states, "If it appears to the court that a dependant is in financial need, the court, on application by or on behalf of the dependant, may order

---

104 *Ibid* at 815–16 and 820–21 [emphasis in the original].
105 See *Currie v Currie Estate* (1995), 425 APR 144, 166 NBR (2d) 144 (CA); *Lawen Estate v Nova Scotia (Attorney General)*, 2019 NSSC 162; *Lutz Estate v Lutz*, 2020 SKCA 14.
106 (2004) 235 DLR (4th) 474, 69 OR (3d) 398 at para 40 (CA).

that reasonable provision be made out of the estate of the deceased for the maintenance and support of the dependant."[107]

In *McAuley v Genaille*,[108] the Manitoba Court of Appeal held that the emphasis on financial need made all the difference. Pfuetzner JA said, "Given the different legislative focus of the Act, it is therefore not surprising that *Tataryn* and the cases that apply its principles ... have not been embraced by the Manitoba courts."[109]

4) *Donatio Mortis Causa*

A *donatio mortis causa* is a gift that is conditional on the donor's death. The donee receives control over the subject matter of the gift, which is perfected when the donor dies. It does not have to comply with the formalities for making a valid will (discussed above).

Courts often quote Lord Russell CJ in *Cain v Moon* concerning the three requirements for making a *donatio mortis causa*:

> [F]or an effectual *donatio mortis causa* three things must combine: first, the gift or donation must have been made in contemplation, though not necessarily in expectation, of death; secondly, there must have been delivery to the donee of the subject-matter of the gift; and, thirdly, the gift must be made under such circumstances as shew that the thing is to revert to the donor in case he should recover. This last requirement is sometimes put somewhat differently, and it is said that the gift must be made under circumstances shewing that it is to take effect only if the death of the donor follows; it is not necessary to say which way of putting it is the better.[110]

a) Conditional Gift

It is not enough that a gift is conditional on death because that is true of all testamentary gifts. A *donatio mortis causa* is made when the donor is facing something more than the usual risk of death, such as an illness or a risky adventure. In *Thompson v Mechan*,[111] the Ontario Court of Appeal held that commercial air travel was not an extraordinary risk (in the 1950s). The deceased was afraid of flying and said that his friend could have his car if he did not make it back from a business trip. That did not count as a valid *donatio mortis causa*. The court also said that

---

107 *Dependants Relief Act*, CCSM, c D37, s 2.
108 2017 MBCA 69.
109 *Ibid* at para 57.
110 [1896] 2 QB 283 at 286.
111 [1958] OR 357, 13 DLR (2d) 103 (CA) [*Thompson*].

the impending peril must place the donor *in extremis*, but that has not been followed by courts in other jurisdictions.[112]

The court in *Thompson* also said that the donor must die from the peril that induced them to make the gift and not from some other cause. Even if air travel could count as an unusual risk, the deceased did not die in a plane crash but suffered a coronary thrombosis on arrival at his destination (which, ironically, we now recognize as a risk of air travel). However, this is not a requirement elsewhere. In *Wilkes v Allington*,[113] a man made a *donatio mortis causa* after he was diagnosed with cancer. He caught a chill on a bus trip and died from pneumonia. Lord Tomlin said, "If a man, in contemplation of death within the meaning of the phrase, as used by Lord Russell, in fact dies from some cause other than the disorder which was present to his mind when he made the gift, I have a difficulty in seeing why the gift is not operative."[114]

A gift can be conditional on death even if the donor knows that death is certain. As Lord Tomlin said in *Wilkes*, "[W]hen a man is smitten with a mortal disease, he may know, in fact, that there cannot be any recovery; yet I apprehend that a man in that situation, in point of law, is capable of creating a good *donatio mortis causa*."[115] The gift is still conditional while the donor lives because the donee may die first. However, a person with no hope of survival may choose instead to make an outright gift. In *Re Bayoff Estate*,[116] Peter Bayoff was diagnosed with terminal cancer. He made a will appointing Antoinette Simard as his executor. He then gave her the key to his safety deposit box and said, "[E]verything there is yours." The court concluded that this was not intended as a *donatio mortis causa*. Krueger J said,

> The essence of a *donatio mortis causa* is that the property will revert to the donor if the imminent death does not occur. Two difficulties arise here. Bayoff was terminally ill when he made the gift; recovery was not a possibility. And by his words he indicated that he wished Simard to have immediate ownership of the contents of the safety deposit box. Bayoff did not, either by words or actions, suggest that the gift was to take effect only if he died. He had just finished signing a Will in contemplation of his death. It is likely that any gifts which he intended to take effect on death were included in his Will. The gift

112 *Lumsden v Miller*, [1980] 4 WWR 143, 110 DLR (3d) 226 (Alta QB); *Saulnier v Anderson* (1987), 43 DLR (4th) 19, 83 NBR (2d) 1 (QB); *Slagboom v Kirby*, 1993 CanLII 449 (BCSC).
113 [1931] 2 Ch 104 (Ch D) [*Wilkes*].
114 *Ibid* at 110.
115 *Ibid* at 111.
116 2000 SKQB 23 [*Bayoff*].

of the contents of the safety deposit box, in my opinion, was intended to be a gift *inter vivos*.[117]

b) Delivery

Lord Russell's second requirement is delivery of the subject matter to the donee. This is clearly satisfied if the donee obtains possession of the subject matter, in which case they will be a bailee of those items pending the death of the donor, when the gift will be complete and they become the legal owner. However, a transfer of possession is not required. It is sufficient if the donee obtains control over the subject matter.

When Bayoff gave the key to his safety deposit box to Simard, he also signed a paper authorizing her to have access to the box. She was denied access because Bayoff had not signed the bank's prescribed form. The court held that the attempted *inter vivos* gift failed because Simard had not obtained possession of the box. However, there was a sufficient transfer of control over the box to be a *donatio mortis causa* (if that had been intended):

> Bayoff gave up the only means he had of getting to the contents of the safety deposit box. Therefore, he parted with control over the contents. . . . I find that care and control over the contents of the safety deposit box had been transferred to Simard notwithstanding that the appropriate and necessary paperwork had not been completed prior to Bayoff's death.[118]

Cash and negotiable instruments (e.g., cheques) can be transferred by delivery, and in many of these cases, the donee obtained possession of them pending the donor's death. It is also possible to make a *donatio mortis causa* of money in a bank account because it is only necessary to transfer control to the donee. It is sufficient if the donee receives a deposit receipt, a passbook, or another document that must be presented to the bank to make a withdrawal.[119] If the document is not needed to access the account, then it will not transfer control to the donee and will not be a valid *donatio mortis causa*.[120]

---

117   *Ibid* at para 10. See also *Snitzler v Snitzler*, 2015 ONSC 2539 [*Snitzler*].

118   *Bayoff*, above note 116 at para 8, Krueger J.

119   *Re Dillon* (1890), 44 Ch D 76 (CA); *Re Weston*, [1902] 1 Ch 680 (Ch D); *McDonald v McDonald* (1903), 33 SCR 145; *Kendrick v Dominion Bank* (1920), 58 DLR 309, 48 OLR 539 (CA); *Birch v Treasury Solicitor*, [1951] Ch 298 (CA); *Saulnier v Anderson*, above note 112.

120   *Cusack v Day*, [1925] 3 DLR 1028, [1925] 2 WWR 715 (BCCA); *Delgoffe v Fader*, [1939] Ch 922 (Ch D); *Brown v Rotenberg*, [1946] OR 363 (CA).

c) Land

In England, land can be the subject of a *donatio mortis causa*, but that has not been approved in Canada. In *Sorensen (Estate) v Sorensen*, McDermid JA said (in the Alberta Court of Appeal), "[R]eal property cannot be the subject of a *donatio mortis causa*. That it cannot appears to be a historical anomaly, and it has been questioned why it cannot, but I have found no case in Canada or England where it has been held that land could be given *mortis causa*."[121]

This was cited with approval in *Dyck v Shingle Estate*,[122] where the Alberta Court of Appeal held that a dying uncle had not intended to make a *donatio mortis causa* of his house when he gave the keys to his nephew. Haddad JA said that "the weight of judicial opinion is that real property cannot be the subject of a *donatio mortis causa*" and explained why:

> The issue of delivery provides a bar to a *mortis causa* gift of land. The roots of the principle are historical. As land in earlier times presented a difficulty of delivery transfer was accomplished by the method of feoffment with livery of seisin. This consisted of a formal ceremony whereby the donor presented the donee with a clump of dirt to symbolize transfer and delivery. That formality was replaced in modern times with a deed of conveyance. In Alberta passing title is accomplished by the use of an instrument of transfer with delivery of a duplicate certificate of title followed by registration.[123]

In *Danicki v Danicki*,[124] the Ontario Superior Court came to the same conclusion in a case where an elderly mother had transferred her fee simple estate to her son by deed, subject to a life interest for herself. The court held that the gift had not been made in contemplation of death but also that "the *donatio mortis causa* must be a gift of personal property."[125]

These cases were decided in 1977, 1984, and 1995. At that time, there were two English cases in which a mortgage was the subject of a valid *donatio mortis causa* when the mortgagee delivered the mortgage deeds to the donees,[126] but no case had decided that the ownership of the land could be given in that way. The English Court of Appeal has since decided that a fee simple estate can be given as a *donatio mortis causa*.

---

121 (1977) 90 DLR (3d) 26 at 38, 3 AR 8 (CA).
122 1984 ABCA 185, 54 AR 382.
123 *Ibid* at para 11.
124 [1995] OJ No 3995, 59 ACWS (3d) 1097.
125 *Ibid* at para 36, Cumming J.
126 *Duffield v Elwes* (1827), 1 Bli NS 497, 4 ER 959 (HL); *Wilkes*, above note 113.

In *Sen v Headley*,[127] the owner of a house was dying in hospital. He said to his friend, "The house is yours, Margaret. You have the keys. They are in your bag. The deeds are in the steel box."[128] This gave her control of the title deeds and therefore control over the ownership of the fee simple estate because the land was unregistered and the title deeds would be needed in order to transfer or mortgage it. The court compared this to a *donatio mortis causa* of a bank account by giving a document needed to access the account. In neither case does the document transfer ownership or possession, but the transfer of control is sufficient for a *donatio mortis causa*. Nourse LJ said,

> Let it be agreed that the doctrine is anomalous. Anomalies do not justify anomalous exceptions. If due account is taken of the present state of the law in regard to mortgages and choses in action, it is apparent that to make a distinction in the case of land would be to make just such an exception. A *donatio mortis causa* of land is neither more nor less anomalous than any other. Every such gift is a circumvention of the *Wills Act 1837*. Why should the additional statutory formalities for the creation and transmission of interests in land be regarded as some larger obstacle?[129]

In *Snitzler v Snitzler*,[130] the Ontario Superior Court decided in 2015 that land cannot be transferred as a *donatio mortis causa*, citing the earlier Canadian cases but with no reference to *Sen*. A woman with terminal liver cancer was the sole owner of the family home. She transferred it to her husband and two children as joint tenants shortly before her death. Dunphy J decided that it was intended as an absolute gift and not conditional on her death (and therefore not included in the value of her estate). He went on to say,

> Secondly, I cannot ignore the line of cases which suggests that the entire doctrine of gifts *mortis causa* is of no application to real estate. In the case of *Sorenson's Estate v Sorenson*, the Alberta Court of Appeal concluded that to be the case. In this province, Cumming J. in *Danicki v Danicki* also concluded that the doctrine is restricted to personal property. None of the cases shown to me where *donatio mortis causa* was invoked by the courts involved real estate and the *Sorenson* and *Danicki* cases seem to suggest that that is no accident. Personal property is generally transferred with a minimum of ceremony by

---

127 [1991] EWCA Civ 13, [1991] Ch 425 [*Sen* cited to Ch].
128 *Ibid* at 431.
129 *Ibid* at 440.
130 *Snitzler*, above note 117.

mere delivery and parties seldom do so through the intermediary of solicitors. Real estate, on the other hand, is subject to registration requirements, land transfer tax obligations and the like and is almost invariably subject to considerable formality and the intervention of a solicitor. In such transactions, any conditional intent can be both ascertained and recorded in an enforceable way.[131]

d)   *Inter Vivos* or Testamentary?

One last issue to consider before leaving this part is whether a *donatio mortis causa* is an *inter vivos* or testamentary gift. In *Re Beaumont*, Buckley J said, "A *donatio mortis causa* is a singular form of gift. It may be said to be of an amphibious nature, being a gift which is neither entirely *inter vivos* nor testamentary. It is an act *inter vivos* by which the donee is to have the absolute title to the subject of the gift not at once but if the donor dies."[132]

There are good arguments in favour of a *donatio mortis causa* being regarded as testamentary. It only takes effect on death and is revocable until then, just like a will. Although the donor must take action during their life to put the donee in control of the subject matter, the formal execution of a will is also an action that the testator must take during their life. If there are insufficient funds in the estate to pay the creditors, a *donatio mortis causa* can be taken and used for that purpose.

In *Re Korvine's Trust*,[133] a *donatio mortis causa* was held to be an *inter vivos* gift for the purpose of the conflict of laws. Admiral Korvine fled the Russian revolution in 1917 and died two years later in London. He had made a *donatio mortis causa* of money, jewellery, and bonds that he had brought with him to London. If it was an *inter vivos* gift, then English law applied (as the law of the place where the gift was made), and it was valid. If it was a testamentary gift, Russian law applied (as the law of the deceased's domicile), and it was invalid. Eve J held that it was *inter vivos*:

> No doubt the gift is consummated by the death of the donor, but it is not a legacy or a testamentary act—it is I think a gift, though an incomplete gift, *inter vivos*—a gift subject to revocation by the act of the donor himself or by his recovery from his illness. If he dies without revoking the gift the donee's title is derived from the act of the donor in his lifetime and relates back to the date of that act. On these grounds, and notwithstanding that the subject matter of the *donatio*

---

131 *Ibid* at para 26 [citations omitted].
132 [1902] 1 Ch 889 at 892 (Ch D).
133 [1921] 1 Ch 343.

is liable to the donor's debts upon a deficiency of assets and is also subject to legacy and estate duty, I think the law to be applied is that applicable to gifts *inter vivos* and not that applicable to testamentary dispositions, and I so hold.[134]

5) Incomplete Gifts to Executors

If a donor intends to make an *inter vivos* gift but fails to transfer legal title to the donee, it may be completed when the donor dies if the donee is appointed as their executor or administrator. When appointed, the donee becomes the owner of all the donor's assets, including the subject matter of the intended gift. The gift is then complete, although not in the way that the donor had intended. The donee is permitted to keep the gift for their own benefit.

This method of completing gifts is sometimes called the rule in *Strong v Bird*,[135] after the case that made it possible. A woman loaned £1,100 to her stepson and later forgave the debt. Her forgiveness did not discharge the debt at law because there was no consideration for it and no deed under seal. She died four years later, and the stepson was appointed as her executor. He thus acquired the legal claim against himself for payment of the debt. That discharged the debt.

In *Re Stewart*,[136] the court held that this principle is not limited to the forgiveness of debts but also applies to the completion of *inter vivos* gifts. A husband had purchased several bonds as a gift for his wife but died before he could transfer them to her. She was appointed as one of his executors, and that was sufficient to complete the gift. Neville J said,

> [W]here a testator has expressed the intention of making a gift of personal estate belonging to him to one who upon his death becomes his executor, the intention continuing unchanged, the executor is entitled to hold the property for his own benefit. The reasoning by which the conclusion is reached is of a double character—first, that the vesting of the property in the executor at the testator's death completes the imperfect gift made in the lifetime, and, secondly, that the intention of the testator to give the beneficial interest to the executor is sufficient to countervail the equity of beneficiaries under the will, the testator having vested the legal estate in the executor. The whole of the property in the personal estate in the eye of the law vesting in each executor, it seems to me immaterial whether the donee is the

---

134   *Ibid* at 348.
135   (1874) LR 18 Eq 315.
136   [1908] 2 Ch 251 (Ch D).

only executor or one of several; nor do I think the rule is confined to cases of the release of a debt owing by the donee. The intention to give, however, must not be an intention of testamentary benefaction, although the intended donee is the executor, for in that case the rule cannot apply, the prescribed formalities for testamentary disposition not having been observed.[137]

In *Re James*,[138] the principle was extended to cover gifts of real property and to cases in which the donee was appointed as the administrator of the donee's estate. A man died intestate in 1924, and his son was entitled to his entire estate, including his house and furniture. The son gave the title deeds and furniture to his father's housekeeper, who continued to live in the house with her husband. The gift of the furniture was completed by delivery, but the son was still the legal owner of the house when he died intestate in 1933. The housekeeper was appointed as his administrator, and this completed his gift of the house.

In *Re Gonin*, Walton J felt bound to follow *James* even though he was unhappy extending the rule from executors to administrators:

> [B]y appointing the executor, the testator has by his own act made it impossible for the debtor to sue himself. . . . The appointment of an administrator, on the other hand, is not the act of the deceased but of the law. It is often a matter of pure chance which of many persons equally entitled to a grant of letters of administration finally takes them out. Why, then, should any special tenderness be shown to a person so selected by law and not the will of the testator, and often indifferently selected among many with an equal claim? . . . This appears to me to treat what ought to be a simple rule of equity . . . as something in the nature of a lottery. I cannot think that equity is so undiscriminating.[139]

However, it must be remembered that the donor does not appoint the donee as their executor for the purpose of completing the gift. The rule applies only to *inter vivos* gifts that were intended to take effect when they were made. The donor believes that the gift is complete. The appointment of the donee as executor operates to complete the gift because it transfers legal title to the donee and not because it reveals an intention to make a gift. The appointment of the donee as an administrator has the same effect.

---

137 *Ibid* at 254–55.
138 [1935] Ch 449 (Ch D).
139 [1979] Ch 16 at 35 (Ch D).

The rule in *Strong v Bird* has been adopted in Canada.[140] In *Bayoff Estate* (discussed above), a gift of the contents of a safety deposit box failed as a *donatio mortis causa* because the donor intended to make an *inter vivos* gift, which failed because the donee did not obtain possession of the box. However, the donee was appointed as the donor's executor, and that completed the gift. Krueger J said,

> An unfulfilled gift will be treated as complete if the donee becomes an executor under the Will of the donor. See *Strong v. Bird*, (1874) 80 All E.R. 230. So long as the intent to make the gift continues until death, by administering the estate, the donee receives control over the donor's property and can perfect the gift. That constitutes delivery of the gift.[141]

6) Secret Trusts

Normally, testamentary trusts must comply with the formalities for making a valid will (discussed above). However, it is possible to avoid those formalities by making a *secret trust*. This occurs when the testator makes an arrangement with a will beneficiary that they will use all or some of the assets they receive from the testator's estate for the benefit of someone else. The trust is *fully secret* if it appears from the terms of the will that the gift to the will beneficiary is for their own benefit. The trust is *half-secret* if the will indicates that the gift is made on trust but does not reveal the identity of the trust beneficiaries.

A will that has been probated is a public document. The early cases of secret trusts involve men who wanted to make a testamentary gift to a mistress or illegitimate child secretly. They would confide in a trusted friend and make a testamentary gift to that friend on the understanding that the mistress or child would receive the benefit. Of course, the secrecy was lost if the matter came before the court, but the question would sometimes arise whether the friend was permitted to carry out the trust despite the failure to comply with the formalities required for making a testamentary disposition.

To create a valid secret trust, it is necessary for the testator to obtain the agreement of the secret trustee that they will carry out the trust when the time comes. This is different from the creation of an ordinary express trust (whether *inter vivos* or testamentary), which requires no

---

140 See *Re Barnes* (1918), 42 OLR 352; *Dickson v Chamberland* (1926), 22 Alta LR 270 (CA); *Re Harvey* (1932), 41 OWN 420 at 422; *Rennick v Rennick* (1962), 33 DLR (2d) 649 (Sask CA); *Re Hogg Estate* (1987), 83 AR 165 at para 25 (QB); *Hilliard v Lostchuk*, [1993] OJ No 2204, 42 ACWS (3d) 1097; *Bayoff*, above note 116 at para 17.

141 *Bayoff*, *ibid.*

previous arrangement with the trustees. If they choose not to accept
the trust, it does not fail. Other trustees will be appointed. For a fully
secret trust, the secret trustee must agree to the arrangement before the
testator dies. For a half-secret trust, that arrangement must be in place
by the time the will is made.

In *Re Boyes*,[142] the testator George Boyes left all of his property to
his friend Fred Carritt and appointed him as the executor of his estate.
Boyes's brother challenged the grant of probate to Carritt, who was the
solicitor who drafted the will. When Boyes signed the will, he asked
Carritt to act as trustee "to provide for a certain lady and child, whose
names he did not wish to appear in his will."[143] Carritt agreed but did
not receive further instructions before Boyes died. Two letters from
Boyes to Carritt were found among Boyes's papers. They both asked
Carritt to keep £25 for himself and give everything else to Nell Brown.
The secret trust failed because communication of the terms of the trust
did not happen in time. Kay J said,

> If the trust was not declared when the will was made, it is essential
> in order to make it binding, that it should be communicated to the
> devisee or legatee in the testator's lifetime and that he should accept
> that particular trust. It may possibly be that he would be bound if
> the trust had been put in writing and placed in his hands in a sealed
> envelope, and he had engaged that he would hold the property given
> to him by the will upon the trust so declared although he did not
> know the actual terms of the trust.[144]

Carritt was not allowed to keep the property for himself because it
was given to him as a trustee and not for his own benefit. Therefore, he
held it on resulting trust for Boyes's brother, who was his next of kin.

A testator can communicate the terms of the trust by giving a sealed
envelope to the secret trustee and asking them to open the envelope
when the testator dies and follow the instructions inside. In *Re Keen*,[145]
the testator's will stated that he was giving £10,000 to his nephew and
a friend "upon trust to be disposed of by them among such person, persons or charities as may be notified by me to them or either of them during my lifetime."[146] Before the will was signed, he gave a sealed envelope
to his friend that contained the terms of the trust. Wright MR said, "[A]
ship which sails under sealed orders, is sailing under orders though the

---

142 (1884) 26 Ch D 531 [*Re Boyes*].
143 *Ibid* at 532.
144 *Ibid* at 536.
145 [1937] Ch 236 (CA).
146 *Ibid* at 239.

exact terms are not ascertained by the captain till later."[147] Communication was in time for a half-secret trust, but, unfortunately, the will referred to future communication of the terms of the trust. Communications before the will was made were inadmissible because that would contradict the terms of the will. Therefore, the half-secret trust failed.[148]

It is not always easy to tell whether or not a gift in a will is made in trust. This is a problem of certainty of intention to create a trust (discussed above). When the gift is made to the solicitor who drafted the will and was appointed as executor, it seems more likely that it was intended as a trust, and the terms of the will may be construed accordingly. In *Re Freud*,[149] the painter Lucian Freud died leaving an estate worth £96 million, including a residue worth £42 million. He gave the residue to his executors, who were his solicitor who drafted the will and one of his children. Another child argued that it must be implied from the circumstances and other terms in the will that they held the residue in trust, and they admitted that they were secret trustees. The court held that the gift of the residue was not made in trust according to the terms of the will, so they were fully secret trustees and not half-secret trustees.

In *Jankowski v Perpetual Trustee Co Ltd*,[150] the testator left the residue of her estate to her "Executor to deal with as he may in his discretion decide upon." The executor was the solicitor who drafted her will. After the will was signed, she provided him with instructions for a secret trust. Huband JA said (in dissent),

> In my opinion, the correct interpretation of the residuary clause, standing alone, is that the executor receives the residue in his capacity as executor, and holds the property as trustee for others. The clause, on its face, should not be construed as a power which the executor might exercise in his own favour. However, there may well be ambiguity about the capacity in which the executor receives the legacy—either individually or *virtute officii*. Extrinsic evidence on that issue clearly confirms that the executor was intended to take only in his capacity as executor, and to distribute the residue to others.[151]

In Huband JA's opinion, there was an invalid half-secret trust because the instructions were given after the will was signed. The

---

147   *Ibid* at 242.
148   See also *Re Mihalopulos* (1956), 5 DLR (2d) 628, 19 WWR 118 (Alta SC); *Jankowski v Perpetual Trustee Co Ltd*, [1996] 2 WWR 457, 131 DLR (4th) 717 (Man CA) [*Jankowski*].
149   [2014] EWHC 2577 (Ch).
150   *Jankowski*, above note 148.
151   *Ibid* at para 14.

majority of the Manitoba Court of Appeal construed the clause as an absolute gift to the executor; therefore, the fully secret trust was valid.

It is sometimes questioned why communication to the trustees must occur before the testator's death for a fully secret trust and before the will is made for a half-secret trust. The usual answer is that it would contradict the statutory formality requirements for making wills and codicils if the testator could vary their instructions by informal communications made afterwards. In *Blackwell v Blackwell*, Viscount Sumner said,

> A testator cannot reserve to himself a power of making future unwitnessed dispositions by merely naming a trustee and leaving the purposes of the trust to be supplied afterwards, nor can a legatee give testamentary validity to an unexecuted codicil by accepting an indefinite trust, never communicated to him in the testator's lifetime. To hold otherwise would indeed be to enable the testator to "give the go-by" to the requirements of the *Wills Act*, because he did not choose to comply with them.[152]

The difficulty with this explanation is that every secret trust ignores the formalities normally required to make a testamentary disposition. There may be good reasons to insist on communication and acceptance before the testator dies. The testator's reliance on the secret trustee's undertaking provides a justification for enforcing the trust (as discussed below) and reduces the risk of fraud if the secret trustee receives instructions directly from the testator (and not, for example, from a forged document placed among the testator's papers). However, that does not explain why half-secret trusts are treated differently from fully secret trusts. Perhaps there is a worry that if testators were allowed to communicate the terms of a half-secret trust after the will was made, they would just leave everything to their executors in trust with instructions to follow and thus avoid the expense and bother of updating their wills or making codicils.

Another question is why we allow secret trusts at all. The standard explanation is fraud. As Huband JA said in *Jankowski*,

> The court will enforce the trust in order to avoid the fraud on the part of the legatee were he to keep the legacy as his own in defiance of his undertaking. The legatee cannot plead the *Wills Act* and thus avoid the obligation which has motivated the gift. The *Wills Act* cannot be used

---

152 [1929] UKHL 1, [1929] AC 318 at 339 [citations omitted] [*Blackwell*].

as an instrument of fraud, and evidence is therefore permitted even though the trusts were not created in proper testamentary form.[153]

This treats a secret trust like an informal express trust of land and adopts the approach taken in *Rochefoucauld*.[154] As discussed above, the defendant in that case had agreed to be a trustee of land and was not allowed to rely on the *Statute of Frauds 1677* to deny the existence of that trust. There are two significant differences between that situation and a secret trust. First, in none of the secret trust cases do the trustees deny the existence of the trust. They are honest people who want to carry out the testator's wishes if the court will let them. No one is trying to commit a fraud.

Second, the statutory requirement that trusts of land be "manifested and proved by some writing signed by the [settlor]" is a rule of evidence. The trust does not have to be made in writing, and the court can admit other evidence to prove the existence of the trust in order to prevent fraud. The formalities required by the *Wills Act* are not rules of evidence but are the means by which testamentary dispositions are made. If those rules are not followed, then normally there is no trust (and it cannot be fraud to deny the existence of a non-existent trust). The law regarding secret trusts provides another way to make a testamentary trust.

A secret trust can be justified as a response to the testator's detrimental reliance on the secret trustee's undertaking to perform it. If the trustee had declined, the testator could have made alternate arrangements, but it is too late to do so once they are dead. At that point, a trust arises to give effect to the testator's expectations. Although the cases speak of fraud, they also make reference to the testator's reliance on the secret trustee's undertaking. As Kay J said in *Re Boyes*,

> There is another well-known class of cases where no trust appears on the face of the will, but the testator has been induced to make the will, or, having made it, has been induced not to revoke it by a promise on the part of the devisee or legatee to deal with the property, or some part of it in a specified manner. In these cases the Court has compelled discovery and performance of the promise, treating it as a trust binding the conscience of the donee, on the ground that otherwise a fraud would be committed, *because it is to be presumed that if it*

---

153 *Jankowski*, above note 148 at para 50. See also *Re Boyes*, above note 142 at 535–36; *Blackwell*, above note 152 at 334–35; *Keen*, above note 145; *Re Riffel Estate* (1987), 64 Sask R 190 at para 9 (QB); *Rufenack v Hope Mission*, [2003] 3 WWR 161, 10 Alta LR (4th) 172 at para 125 (QB); *Bergler v Odenthal*, 2020 BCCA 175 at para 1.

154 *Rouchefoucauld*, above note 73.

had not been for such promise the testator would not have made or would have revoked the gift.[155]

Lord Warrington said much the same thing in *Blackwell*:

It has long been settled that if a gift be made to a person or persons in terms absolutely but in fact upon a trust communicated to the legatee and accepted by him, the legatee would be bound to give effect to the trust, on the principle that *the gift may be presumed to have been made on the faith of his acceptance of the trust*, and a refusal after the death of the testator to give effect to it would be a fraud on the part of the legatee.[156]

The trustee's undertaking separates secret trusts from express trusts. There are two different ways to create a testamentary trust. First, the terms of the trust can be expressed in a will or other document that complies with the formalities for making a testamentary disposition. If so, there is no need for a previous undertaking from anyone that they will perform the trust. A trustee will be appointed. Second, the trust can be created informally if the intended trustee undertakes to the testator that they will perform the trust. Both are testamentary. The testator is free to revoke or change their mind at any time. The trust is constituted and takes effect only once the testator is dead, the estate has been distributed, and the trustee has received the trust assets. If the testator wishes to revise the terms of a half-secret trust, they will need to make a new will or a codicil, but they are free to do so.

7) Mutual Wills

Normally, testators are free to revoke their wills at any time. However, it is possible to make a contract not to revoke or change a will. Spouses (or people in similar relationships) may make an agreement about the distribution of their estates and make their wills together as part of a common estate plan. Typically, both wills leave everything to the surviving spouse and otherwise to a common set of beneficiaries.

Spouses often make wills together on the same terms. These are called *reciprocal wills*. Nothing prevents a testator from changing a reciprocal will. Less commonly, spouses make contracts in which they agree not to change their wills. These are called *mutual wills*. As Reid J said in *Rammage v Roussel Estate*,

---

155 *Re Boyes*, above note 142 at 535–36 [emphasis added].
156 *Blackwell*, above note 152 at 341 [emphasis added].

Reciprocal wills contain terms that are mirror images of each other. By definition, they represent the wishes of the two testators at the date of signing. . . . However, the simple fact that the wills were made in that form simultaneously is not enough, by itself, to establish that they are mutual wills. Mutual wills are reciprocal wills that the makers have agreed cannot be changed, at least as to their effect, without the consent of the other. Once one of the testators has died, it is not possible for the surviving testator to receive such consent, and therefore the terms cannot be altered.[157]

The parties can agree to cancel their contract not to change their wills while both are still alive and competent to do so. Once the first party dies or loses mental capacity,[158] the survivor is bound by the contract. The survivor will breach that contract if they die and their estate is not distributed according to the terms of the mutual wills. Their executor or administrator will hold the estate on constructive trust for the beneficiaries of the mutual wills.[159] If they have already distributed the estate contrary to the terms of the mutual wills, the beneficiaries have a claim to recover the assets from the recipients.[160]

In most mutual wills contracts, the obligation imposed on the survivor is to leave their estate to the agreed set of beneficiaries. In that case, the constructive trust would arise when the survivor died, which is when the subject matter of that trust would be ascertained.[161] In some cases, the parties agreed that a specific asset (e.g., a house) would be left to the beneficiaries, in which case the trust will arise when the first party dies, subject to the survivor's life estate.[162] The survivor might also breach the contract if they sought to avoid it by making substantial *inter vivos* gifts.[163] As Judge Paul Matthews said in *Legg v Burton*,

Lastly, it is clear that the idea of not changing or revoking your will carries with it the notion that everything that you leave at your death shall pass to the ultimate beneficiaries. So the subject matter of this trust is everything which is left at the death of the survivor. And that is the point at which usually the constructive trust is imposed, to the

157 2016 ONSC 1857 at paras 17–18.
158 *Hall v McLaughlin Estate* (2006), 25 ETR (3d) 198 (Ont SC).
159 *University of Manitoba v Sanderson Estate*, [1998] 7 WWR 83, 155 DLR (4th) 40 (BCCA) [*University of Manitoba*].
160 *Hall v McLaughlin Estate*, above note 158.
161 See *Birmingham v Renfrew* (1937), 57 CLR 666 at 689–91; *Re Goodchild*, [1996] 1 All ER 670 at 676.
162 *In re Hagger*, [1930] 2 Ch 190; *Re Green*, [1951] Ch 148; *Fisher v Mansfield*, [1997] 2 NZLR 230.
163 See *Birmingham v Renfrew*, above note 161 at 689.

extent that the provision then made by the will of the survivor, or the intestacy rules so far as they are applicable, or a combination of both, is or are inconsistent with the original agreement.

There is no trust imposed on the death of the first to die, unless that is so agreed. How far the survivor may deal with the assets which come from the first testator and with the assets which remain in the second testator's estate is a matter of construction of the agreement (or other binding promise) between them. In the ordinary case, one may imagine that their agreement would allow for the survivor to spend capital (or some agreed amount or fraction of the capital) on herself if that should prove necessary, but, on the other hand, not to give it away to third parties during her life. It may be that, if the survivor attempts to give away (or otherwise deal with) such property in breach of the agreement, that too is an event which would justify the imposition of a constructive trust on the purported gift.[164]

In *University of Manitoba v Sanderson Estate*,[165] a husband and wife made mutual wills in which everything went to the survivor and otherwise to the University of Manitoba to fund student bursaries. She died in 1985, but her will was never probated because all of her significant assets were owned jointly with her husband. He changed his will that year and died in 1994. The beneficiaries of his new will argued that he was not bound by the mutual wills contract because he never received any benefits from her will. He acquired all the assets as surviving joint tenant. This was accepted at trial but rejected by the BC Court of Appeal. There is no requirement that the survivor benefits from the other party's will. The constructive trust was imposed to give effect to their agreement that he would leave his entire estate to the university, not just the assets he received from his wife.[166]

As with secret trusts, the constructive trust that arises to give effect to a mutual wills contract is often justified on the basis of fraud. However, the parties made their contract in good faith, and it is only later that the survivor changed their mind. It seems odd to say that a person commits fraud if they breach a contract honestly made, even if they do it intentionally. It is possible to breach a mutual wills contract unintentionally. In many jurisdictions, a person's will is revoked automatically if they get married.[167] The survivor could remarry and not

---

164 *Legg*, above note 51 at paras 69–70.
165 *University of Manitoba*, above note 159.
166 *Ibid* at 57.
167 *Wills Act*, CCSM, c W150, s 17; *Succession Law Reform Act*, RSO 1990, c S.26, s 16; *Wills Act*, RSNB 1973, c W-9, s 15.1; *Wills Act*, RSNS 1989, c 505, s 17; *Probate Act*, RSPEI 1988, c P-21, s 68; *Wills Act*, RSNL 1990, c W-10, s 9; *Wills Act*,

realize that they revoked their mutual will.[168] They may die intestate honestly believing that they kept their promise.

A better explanation is detrimental reliance on expectations. The first party to die relied on the survivor's promise to keep their agreement. They could have made alternate arrangements if they had known that the survivor might change their mind. As Rowles JA said in *University of Manitoba*,

> Equity considers it a fraud upon the deceased, *who has acted upon and relied upon the mutually binding nature of the agreement*, for the survivor to change the will and break the agreement. As the deceased cannot intervene to enforce the obligation, equity will enforce the survivor's obligation, despite the survivor's subsequent intentions.[169]

E. LAND CONTRACTS

A *land contract* is a contract to grant or transfer an interest in land, such as a contract to sell a house or grant a mortgage. A contractual licence to use land (e.g., to enter a theatre or music venue) is not normally regarded as a land contract. Land contracts are subject to the normal rules that apply to all contracts but are different in two important respects. First, a land contract is not normally enforceable in most jurisdictions unless the essential terms are in writing and signed. Second, a land contract can give rise to equitable interests in land if it is specifically enforceable.

1) Formalities

A writing requirement for land contracts was first introduced by section 4 of the *Statute of Frauds 1677*, which states,

> [N]o Action shall be brought ... to charge any person ... upon any Contract or Sale of Lands Tenements or Hereditaments or any Interest in or concerning them ... unless the Agreement upon which such Action shall be brought or some Memorandum or Note thereof shall be in Writing and signed by the party to be charged therewith or some other person thereinto by him lawfully authorized.

RSY 2002, c 230, s 10; *Wills Act*, RSNWT 1988, c W-5, s 11. Marriage no longer revokes a will in British Columbia, Alberta, or Saskatchewan.

168 See TG Youdan, "The Mutual Wills Doctrine" (1979) 29 UTLJ 390 at 405.

169 *University of Manitoba*, above note 159 at 51 [emphasis added].

This section of the *Statute of Frauds 1677* still applies in Alberta, Saskatchewan, Prince Edward Island, Newfoundland and Labrador, and the territories. Similar requirements are found in British Columbia, Ontario, and Nova Scotia.[170] The writing requirement has been abolished in Manitoba and New Brunswick.[171]

The formalities required to make an enforceable land contract are different from the formalities required to perform that contract. The contract does not need to be made in writing, but it will not be enforceable in most jurisdictions unless there is an agreement, a memo, or a note in writing that is signed by the party against whom it is being enforced or their agent. In *Leoppky v Meston*,[172] the Alberta Court of Queen's Bench held that those formalities were satisfied by email correspondence and an email signature. The performance of a land contract will require the transfer or grant of an interest in land, which normally requires a deed or registration, as discussed above.

If the writing requirement is not satisfied, a land contract is not void. It is unenforceable.[173] An unenforceable contract does exist and can still be used as a defence.[174] For example, in *Thomas v Brown*,[175] the plaintiff agreed to buy the defendant's shop and paid a deposit. They changed their mind and sued to get their money back. Although the contract may have been unenforceable, the defendant was entitled to raise it as a defence. Quain J said, "Now where, upon a verbal contract for the sale of land, the purchaser pays the deposit and the vendor is always ready and willing to complete, I know of no authority to support the purchaser in bringing an action to recover back the money."[176]

The effect of an oral land contract is different from the effect of an oral trust of land (discussed above). The contract is unenforceable, and the trust is unprovable. A contract that cannot be enforced can still have legal consequences, but a trust that cannot be proved does not exist as far as the court is concerned. If the trustee accepted the trust

---

170 *Law and Equity Act*, RSBC 1996, c 253, s 59; *Statute of Frauds*, RSO 1990, c S.19, s 4; *Statute of Frauds*, RSNS 1989, c 442, s 7.

171 *An Act to Repeal the Statute of Frauds*, CCSM, c F158; *An Act to Repeal the Statute of Frauds*, SNB 2014, c 47.

172 2008 ABQB 45.

173 *Maddison v Alderson* (1883), 8 App Cas 467 (HL) [*Maddison*].

174 *Frith v Alliance Investment Co* (1914), 49 SCR 384, 20 DLR 356; *Switzer's Investments Ltd v Burn* (1964), 47 DLR (2d) 280 (Alta QB); *Wauchope v Maida*, [1972] 1 OR 27, 22 DLR (3d) 142 (CA); *MacIntyre v Spierenburg* (1979), 41 NSR (2d) 584, 76 APR 584 (SC); *Barber v Glen*, [1987] 6 WWR 689, 59 Sask R 49 (CA); *Sadaka v Saleh*, 2011 SKQB 416.

175 (1876) 1 QBD 714.

176 *Ibid* at 723. See also *Switzer's Investments Ltd v Burn*, above note 174.

and then later denied its existence, then other evidence is admissible to prove the trust under the fraud exception explained in *Rochefoucauld*.[177]

There is a different exception that allows for the enforcement of oral land contracts. An oral land contract can be enforced in Canada on the basis of *part performance*.[178] This exception came to us from England,[179] but it has been abolished there.[180] If the contract has been partly performed by the parties, that may be accepted as sufficient proof that it exists without signed writing.[181] Part performance can also amount to detrimental reliance on the contract, which can provide another justification for its enforcement.[182] As Tallis JA said in *Lensen v Lensen*,

> There are two theoretical bases for the doctrine of part performance. The more orthodox approach to the doctrine is that of regarding it as a theory that some writers call "alternative evidence." Under this approach acts of part performance are viewed as being evidence sufficiently cogent to allow a court of equity to enforce the contract even though it could not be enforced at common law because of non-compliance with the statute. Under this approach, it is necessary that the "acts" of part performance be adduced as a pre-condition to the introduction of parol evidence to prove the contract. However, this raises the question as to what are sufficient acts of part performance to enable the court to consider parol evidence of the contract. Must the acts prove the precise terms of the alleged contract or only that there is *a* contract? The second theoretical basis of the doctrine emphasizes the acts of part performance not so much for their evidentiary value but as raising equities in the plaintiff's favour which render it unjust not to enforce the contract.[183]

Detrimental reliance on a land contract can also give rise to an equitable interest in the land on the basis of proprietary estoppel (discussed below).[184] These two approaches to part performance have been given a statutory basis in British Columbia:

---

177 *Rouchefoucauld*, above note 73.
178 See, for example, *Thompson v Guaranty Trust Co*, [1974] SCR 1023, 39 DLR (3d) 408 [cited to SCR] [*Thompson*]; *Lensen v Lensen*, [1984] 6 WWR 673, 14 DLR (4th) 611 (Sask CA) [*Lensen*]; *Booth v Knibb Developments Ltd*, 2002 ABCA 180; *Erie Sand and Gravel Ltd v Tri-B Acres Inc*, 2009 ONCA 709.
179 See *Maddison*, above note 173.
180 *Law of Property (Miscellaneous Provisions) Act 1989*, s 2, sch 2; see *Firstpost Homes Ltd v Johnson*, [1995] 1 WLR 1567 (CA).
181 *McNeil v Corbett* (1907), 39 SCR 608.
182 *Hill v Nova Scotia (Attorney General)*, [1997] 1 SCR 69, 142 DLR (4th) 230.
183 *Lensen*, above note 178 at paras 26–27; rev'd [1987] 2 SCR 672, 44 DLR (4th) 1.
184 See, for example, *Cowper-Smith v Morgan*, 2017 SCC 61 [*Cowper-Smith*].

A contract respecting land or a disposition of land is not enforceable unless (a) there is, in a writing signed by the party to be charged or by that party's agent, both an indication that it has been made and a reasonable indication of the subject matter, (b) the party to be charged has done an act, or acquiesced in an act of the party alleging the contract or disposition, that indicates that a contract or disposition not inconsistent with that alleged has been made, or (c) the person alleging the contract or disposition has, in reasonable reliance on it, so changed the person's position that an inequitable result, having regard to both parties' interests, can be avoided only by enforcing the contract or disposition.[185]

What counts as part performance has changed over the years. In *Maddison v Alderson*,[186] Thomas Alderson owned a farm in Yorkshire. His housekeeper, Elizabeth Maddison, worked for him from 1845 until he died intestate in 1877. He ran into financial difficulties, so she worked without wages for the last twenty years of his life in reliance on his promise to give her a life estate in the farm. He signed a will giving her that life estate, but it was invalid because it had not been witnessed properly. The House of Lords held that the oral contract could not be enforced because the acts of part performance were not sufficiently connected to the contract. Lord Selborne LC said that "the acts relied upon as part performance must be unequivocally, and in their own nature, referable to some such agreement as that alleged."[187]

In *Thompson v Guaranty Trust Co*,[188] Dick Copithorne owned a farm in Saskatchewan. Gus Thompson began to work for him as a farm labourer in 1922 and stayed there until Dick died intestate in 1970. Gus was paid for the first two years, but Dick had health and financial problems and could not afford to pay him. Gus continued to work in reliance on Dick's promise to leave the farm to him when he died. Gus eventually took over the management of the farm and made substantial improvements to it. The Supreme Court of Canada held that these were sufficient acts of part performance. Spence J said,

I am personally of the opinion that practically every act of part performance as to which evidence was given, and I have read the record carefully, were acts which were unequivocally referable to a contract in reference to the very lands in question, that is the farm consisting of five one-quarter sections which had been the property of the

---

185 *Law and Equity Act*, RSBC 1996, c 25, s 59(3).
186 *Maddison*, above note 173.
187 *Ibid* at 479.
188 *Thompson*, above note 178.

deceased. The appellant was no mere farm hired man and had not been since about 1924.[189]

Gus was able to enforce the oral contract and obtain title to the farm. Although part performance has been abolished in England, an English court would reach the same result today on the basis of proprietary estoppel.[190]

2) Specific Performance

A court can order a defendant in breach of contract to perform the contract or to pay damages as a substitute for performance and as compensation for loss. The most common breach of contract is the failure to pay a debt, and courts routinely order defendants to perform that obligation. For most other breaches of contract, the normal remedy is an award of damages. Land contracts are different because courts will often order the performance of an obligation to grant or transfer an interest in land.

An order for *specific performance* of a contract is justified when an award of damages will fail to achieve its purpose, which is to put the plaintiff in the position they would have been in if the contract had been performed. For most contracts to sell goods, an award of damages is an adequate remedy because the plaintiff can use the money to buy the same goods from someone else. If similar goods are not readily available, then a court will order specific performance of the contract.[191] For many land contracts, an adequate substitute is not readily available on the market.

An order for specific performance is a discretionary equitable remedy, but for centuries it was routinely available for land contracts. This was not because a different rule applied to land but because it was assumed that damages would be inadequate. Similar land might be available, but it would not be the same and might not meet the purchaser's needs and desires. As Leach VC said in *Adderley v Dixon*,

> Courts of Equity decree the specific performance of contracts, not upon any distinction between realty and personality, but because damages at law may not, in the particular case, afford a complete remedy. Thus a Court of Equity decrees performance of a contract for land, not because of the real nature of the land, but because damages at law, which must be calculated upon the general money value of

---

189 *Ibid* at 1034.
190 *Thorner v Major*, [2009] UKHL 18, [2009] 1 WLR 776 [*Thorner*].
191 See, for example, *Behnke v Bede Shipping Co Ltd*, [1927] 1 KB 649; *Dougan v Ley* [1946] HCA 3, 71 CLR 142.

land, may not be a complete remedy to the purchaser, to whom the land may have a peculiar and special value.[192]

The purchaser was not required to prove that the land had "a peculiar and special value" to them. It was enough that it might. That is still the rule in other common law jurisdictions, but the law in Canada took an unfortunate turn in 1996. In *Semelhago v Paramadevan*,[193] the vendor breached a contract to sell a house in the Toronto area for $205,000. The purchaser claimed specific performance but elected to take damages instead at the trial four years later, when the market value of the house was $325,000. The case concerned the appropriate measure of damages. The parties had assumed that specific performance had been available, and that was not the issue before the Supreme Court of Canada, but Sopinka J said,

> It cannot be assumed that damages for breach of contract for the purchase and sale of real estate will be an inadequate remedy in all cases.... Specific performance should, therefore, not be granted as a matter of course absent evidence that the property is unique to the extent that its substitute would not be readily available.... In future cases, under similar circumstances, a trial judge will not be constrained to find that specific performance is an appropriate remedy.[194]

This comment had major, unintended consequences for the law of property in Canada. In order to get specific performance of a contract to buy land, it is now necessary for the purchaser to prove that they have a good personal reason for wanting that land and that no similar land is available. As Caldwell JA said in *Raymond v Anderson*,

> Until 1996 it had long been a tenet of our law that each parcel of real property was inherently unique. Given this inherent uniqueness, our courts made the equitable remedy of specific performance readily available to a plaintiff purchaser who claimed the vendor had breached a contract for the sale of real property. In 1996, Sopinka J.'s majority decision in *Semelhago v. Paramadevan* ... questioned these longstanding, rudimentary elements of our law of real property. His comments, although *obiter*, were thereafter generally accepted as law....
>
> In practical terms, this means the prospective purchaser bears the burden of adducing evidence that the subject property is specially suited to the purchaser and that a comparable substitute property is not readily available.... [O]n the basis of the evidence, the prospective

---

192 (1824) 1 Sim & St 607, 57 ER 239 at 240.
193 [1996] 2 SCR 415, 136 DLR (4th) 1 [*Semelhago*].
194 *Ibid* at 10–11.

purchaser must discharge the overall burden of persuading the judge that the subject property is so different from others that damages is an inadequate remedy and that justice dictates the purchaser should have the subject property. The judge, in turn, must conduct a critical inquiry on the evidence as to the nature and function of the subject property in relation to the prospective purchaser.[195]

Semelhago introduced a great deal of uncertainty and complexity into an area of law that had long been settled. A purchaser can no longer be sure whether they are entitled to enforce their contract without asking a judge to "conduct a critical inquiry." Far worse is the effect this has had on the law of property. Land contracts create equitable interests in the land when the contract is made, but only if the contract is specifically enforceable.[196] As Lord Westbury LC said in *Holroyd v Marshall*,

> A contract for valuable consideration, by which it is agreed to make a present transfer of property, passes at once the beneficial interest, provided the contract is one of which a Court of Equity will decree specific performance.... [T]he vendor becomes a trustee for the vendee; subject, of course, to the contract being one to be specifically performed. And this is true, not only of contracts relating to real estate, but also of contracts relating to personal property, provided that the latter are such as a Court of Equity would direct to be specifically performed.[197]

If a contract of sale is specifically enforceable, the vendor holds the land on constructive trust. As Lord O'Hagan said in *Shaw v Foster*, "By the contract of sale the vendor in the view of a Court of Equity disposes of his right over the estate, and on the execution of the contract he becomes constructively a trustee for the vendee."[198]

Beneficial ownership is shared by the parties pending completion of the transaction. The vendor is entitled to possession of the land and to receive the income from it, but the purchaser is entitled to its capital value. The purchaser is bound to pay the agreed purchase price regardless of what happens to the market value and so has the hope of gain and risk of loss associated with beneficial ownership. As Lord Walker said in *Jerome v Kelly*,

> Neither the seller nor the buyer has unqualified beneficial ownership. Beneficial ownership of the land is in a sense split between the seller

---

195 2011 SKCA 58 at paras 7 and 15.
196 *Lysaght v Edwards* (1876), 2 Ch D 499 (CA).
197 (1862) 10 HLC 191 at 209, 11 ER 999.
198 (1872) LR 5 HL 321 at 349.

and buyer on the provisional assumptions that specific performance is available and that the contract will in due course be completed, if necessary by the Court ordering specific performance. In the meantime, the seller is entitled to enjoyment of the land or its rental income.... If the contract proceeds to completion the equitable interest can be viewed as passing to the buyer in stages, as title is made and accepted and as the purchase price is paid in full.[199]

All of this depends on the contract being specifically enforceable. "It is axiomatic that if specific performance is not available, there is no interest in the land," as Berger JA said in *1244034 Alberta Ltd v Walton Int Group Inc.*[200] This is true not just of contracts of sale but of all land contracts. Under an *agreement for sale* (discussed in Chapter 6), the vendor retains title while the purchaser pays the purchase price in instalments over a period of time. It was long understood that the purchaser acquires beneficial ownership of the land in equity when the agreement is made but only because it is specifically enforceable.

A contract to grant a lease creates an equitable lease if the contract is specifically enforceable, and the rights of the landlord and tenant are really no different whether the lease is legal or equitable.[201] It was common for tenants to be content with a contract and not bother with the grant of a legal leasehold estate by deed or registration. However, a lease contract will no longer give rise to an equitable lease unless the premises are especially suited to the tenant and no similar rental properties are available. If not, the tenant will only be a tenant at will or a periodic tenant.

It is a general principle in the law of property that a person has an equitable interest in an asset if they have the power to acquire it. This explains why a constructive trust arises when a donor provides the donee with the power to obtain legal title without further help from the donor (as discussed above). The right to specific performance of land contracts has the same effect because the purchaser or tenant has the power to obtain legal title. The loss of that right has had profound consequences. The Alberta Law Reform Institute recommended that legislation should be passed that "will restore the law as it existed before *Semelhago* and will thus confer on the purchaser an interest in land."[202]

---

199 [2004] UKHL 25, [2004] 1 WLR 1409 at para 32.
200 2007 ABCA 372.
201 *Walsh v Lonsdale* (1882), 21 Ch D 9 (CA); *R (Von Goetz) v Tower Hamlets LBC,* [1998] EWCA Civ 1507, [1999] QB 1019.
202 Alberta Law Reform Institute, *Contracts for the Sale and Purchase of Land: Purchasers' Remedies* (2009), online: www.alri.ualberta.ca/wp-content/uploads/2020/05/fr97.pdf at 25.

Another difficulty is created by the requirement that the land must be "specially suited to the purchaser."[203] In *Holden v Tanase*,[204] the Alberta Court of Queen's Bench held that a contract to sell a house near Commonwealth Stadium in Edmonton was specifically enforceable because the purchaser was a "huge football fan" and it was one of very few houses in the area with an extra wide lot and finished basement. It seems bizarre that a football fan would have a right to specific performance and an equitable interest in the land, whereas a hockey fan or movie buff would have to settle for damages.

A person's legal and equitable rights should not depend on irrelevant personal characteristics. Would a Roman Catholic have a right to specific performance if the house was near the basilica or a Mormon if it was near the temple? Would atheists and people of other faiths have to settle for damages? We are supposed to be equal before the law.

In a case prior to *Semelhago*, Gushue JA said,

> The question here is whether damages would have afforded ... an adequate remedy, and I have no doubt that they could, and would, have. There was nothing whatever unique or irreplaceable about the houses and lots bargained for. They were merely subdivision lots with houses, all of the same general design, built on them. ... It would be quite different if we were dealing with a house or houses which were of a particular architectural design, or were situated in a particularly desirable location, but this was certainly not the case.[205]

This was quoted in *Semelhago* with apparent approval. Houses with special architectural features in desirable locations tend to be purchased by wealthier members of society. It seems unacceptable that they would have rights to specific performance, whereas a working class family that skimps and saves to buy an average home is entitled only to damages.

Normally, property rights are not linked to the personal characteristics of the right holder. As Mummery LJ said in *Dear v Reeves*, "A distinguishing feature of a right of property, in contrast to a purely personal right, is that it is transferable: it may be enforced by someone other than the particular person in whom the right was initially vested."[206] Professor James Penner said,

> What distinguishes a property right is not just that they are only contingently ours, *but that they might just as well be someone else's*. ...

---

203 *Raymond v Anderson*, above note 195 at para 15, Caldwell JA.
204 2002 ABQB 1025.
205 *Chaulk v Fairview Construction Ltd* (1977), 14 Nfld & PEIR 13 at 21 (Nfld CA).
206 [2001] EWCA Civ 277, [2002] Ch 1 at para 40.

The contingency of our connection to particular items of property is such that, in theory, there is nothing special about *my* ownership of a particular car — the relationship the next owner will have to it is essentially identical. "In theory" is there to point out that it is of course true that we may become emotionally or otherwise "attached" to specific pieces of property, but while these attachments may have moral or political significance, or even legal significance in a secondary way, these attachments are utterly irrelevant if, or to the extent that, the object is treated as property. The converse proposition is that, to the extent that an individual personal relationship is the legally recognized essence of the relationship between a person and the putative object of property, that relationship fails to be a property relationship.[207]

If the existence of the purchaser's right to the land depends on the personal characteristics of the right holder, then it seems to lack an essential attribute of property. If they have an equitable property right because they are a football fan, what happens to that right if they assign it to an art lover? The fact that the right depends on the needs or desires of the right holder would seem to suggest that it is not property.

3) Options to Purchase and Rights of First Refusal

An *option to purchase* land is a contractual right to buy it without the obligation to do so. The owner who grants the option is making an offer to sell that is irrevocable for the duration of the option contract. An option to obtain or renew a lease is really no different, except that it confers the right to acquire a leasehold estate instead of the fee simple.

A *right of first refusal* is sometimes called a *right of pre-emption* or *pre-emptive right*. It is similar to an option to purchase. The owner agrees that they will not sell the land unless they first offer it to the right holder on those terms. It is different from an option because the owner cannot be compelled to sell.

It has long been understood that an option is an equitable interest in land. As Jessel MR said in *London and South Western Railway Co v Gomm*,

> The right to call for a conveyance of the land is an equitable interest or equitable estate. In the ordinary case of a contract for purchase there is no doubt about this, and an option for repurchase is not different in its nature. A person exercising the option has to do two things, he has to give notice of his intention to purchase, and to pay the purchase

207 JE Penner, *The Idea of Property in Law* (Oxford: Clarendon Press, 1997) at 112 [emphasis in the original].

money; but as far as the man who is liable to convey is concerned, his estate or interest is taken away from him without his consent, and the right to take it away being vested in another, the covenant giving the option must give that other an interest in the land.[208]

The option holder has the power to acquire the legal title, but only if the exercise of the option will give rise to a specifically enforceable contract. As Martland J said in *Canadian Long Island Petroleums Ltd v Irving Industries Ltd*, "[F]orthwith upon the granting of the option, the optionee upon the occurrence of certain events solely within his control can compel a conveyance of the property to him."[209] After *Semelhago*, many options are not interests in land because the contract of sale or lease that would be created by the exercise of the option would not be specifically enforceable. The option holder has no power to compel conveyance but will only have a claim for damages.

In *Canadian*,[210] the Supreme Court of Canada held that a right of first refusal was not an interest in land. The English Court of Appeal came to the same conclusion in *Pritchard v Briggs*.[211] The right holder does not have the power to compel conveyance even if it might possibly lead to a specifically enforceable contract of sale. Lord Justice Goff said,

> [A] right of pre-emption gives no present right, even contingent, to call for a conveyance of the legal estate. So far as the parties are concerned, whatever economic or other pressures may come to affect the grantor, he is still absolutely free to sell or not. The grantee cannot require him to do so, or demand that an offer be made to him.[212]

British Columbia and Alberta have declared by statute that a right of first refusal is an equitable interest in land. The *Property Law Act* in British Columbia states, "A right of first refusal to land, also known as a right of refusal or right of pre-emption, created before or after this section comes into force is an equitable interest in land."[213] Ironically, this makes it clear that a right of first refusal is a property right but leaves the status of an option to purchase in doubt.

---

208 (1881) 20 Ch D 562 at 581 (CA), quoted with approval in *Canadian Long Island Petroleums Ltd v Irving Industries Ltd*, [1975] 2 SCR 715 at 730, 50 DLR (3d) 265 [*Canadian*]. See also *Mountford v Scott*, [1975] Ch 258.

209 *Canadian*, above note 208.

210 *Ibid*. See also *2123201 Ontario Inc v Israel Estate*, 2016 ONCA 409.

211 [1980] Ch 338 (CA).

212 *Ibid* at 389.

213 RSBC 1996, c 377, s 9; see also *Law of Property Act*, RSA 2000, c L-7, s 63.

F. PROPRIETARY ESTOPPEL

The are several different kinds of estoppel, most of which involve detrimental reliance on assumptions. Estoppel at common law (which also works in equity) is a rule of evidence. If one party represents to another that a fact is true, and the other party arranges their affairs in reliance on that fact, then in subsequent litigation between them, the party who made the representation may be estopped from denying it is true if that would cause a detriment to the other party. This can affect the legal rights and obligations between the parties if that fact is an essential element of a claim or defence.

Equitable estoppel is different because it involves representations about future intentions, not existing facts. There are two different types: *promissory* and *proprietary*. Promissory estoppel occurs when one party to a contract represents to the other that a right under the contract will not be enforced. The party making the representation may later be estopped from enforcing that right.[214] This is similar to waiver.

We are concerned here with proprietary estoppel, which is the most far-reaching estoppel because it can operate as an independent source of equitable property rights.[215] Oliver J described it as follows in *Taylors Fashions Ltd v Liverpool Victoria Trustees Co Ltd*:

> If under an expectation created or encouraged by B that A shall have a certain interest in land, thereafter, on the faith of such expectation and with the knowledge of B and without objection by him, acts to his detriment in connection with such land, a Court of Equity will compel B to give effect to such expectation.[216]

The expectation can be generated by an express promise, but that is not required. In *Thorner v Major*,[217] David Thorner worked for thirty years without pay on a farm in Somerset that was owned by his father's cousin, Peter Thorner, who died intestate in 2005. Peter never expressly promised David that he would inherit the farm, but David's hope gradually became an expectation. The trial judge found that this expectation was reasonable and that David was entitled to the farm on the basis of proprietary estoppel.[218] This was reversed by the Court of Appeal because

---

214 See *John Burrows Ltd v Subsurface Surveys Ltd*, [1968] SCR 607, 68 DLR (2d) 354; *Maracle v Travellers Indemnity Co of Canada*, [1991] 2 SCR 50, 80 DLR (4th) 652.
215 *Crabb v Arun District Council*, [1976] Ch 179 at 187.
216 [1982] QB 133 at 144.
217 *Thorner*, above note 190.
218 [2007] EWHC 2422 (Ch), [2008] WTLR 155.

Peter never made "a clear and unequivocal representation" to David.[219] The House of Lords restored the trial judgment. Lord Walker said,

> In this case the context, or surrounding circumstances, must be regarded as quite unusual. The deputy judge heard a lot of evidence about two countrymen leading lives that it may be difficult for many city-dwellers to imagine—taciturn and undemonstrative men committed to a life of hard and unrelenting physical work, by day and sometimes by night, largely unrelieved by recreation or female company.[220]

In *Inwards v Baker*,[221] a father owned six acres of land in Buckinghamshire. His son wanted to buy land and build a bungalow, and the father suggested that he build it on the father's land. The son built it in 1931, doing most of the labour and spending half of the £300 it cost to build. He lived there until his father died in 1951. The father left the land to his common law partner and their two children. The son continued to live there until 1963, when they sued to evict him. The Court of Appeal held that the son was entitled to live there as long as he wished. Lord Denning MR said,

> So in this case, even though there is no binding contract to grant any particular interest to the licensee, nevertheless the court can look at the circumstances and see whether there is an equity arising out of the expenditure of money. All that is necessary is that the licensee should, at the request or with the encouragement of the landlord, have spent the money in the expectation of being allowed to stay there. If so, the court will not allow that expectation to be defeated where it would be inequitable so to do.[222]

This was followed in *Stiles v Tod Mountain Development Ltd*,[223] where the plaintiff built a house near the ski resort on Tod Mountain (now Sun Peaks) with the expectation that the land would be subdivided and he would acquire legal title to a newly created lot. The subdivision never occurred, and the BC Supreme Court declared that he had an irrevocable licence to occupy the land that he had expected to acquire. In both this case and *Inwards*, the court declared that the person had acquired a licence, which suggests that they had only a right *in personam*. However,

---

219 *Thorner v Major*, [2008] EWCA Civ 732 at para 74, Lloyd LJ.

220 *Thorner*, above note 190 at para 59.

221 [1965] 2 QB 29 (CA) [*Inwards*].

222 *Ibid* at 37.

223 (1992) 88 DLR (4th) 735, 64 BCLR (2d) 366 (SC).

in both cases, that licence was a right to possession of land that was enforceable against subsequent owners, so it must have been an estate.

In some cases, the plaintiff relied on an express promise that would have been a valid land contract if it had been in writing and signed by the defendant. In *Yaxley v Gotts*,[224] Keith Yaxley was a builder. Brownie Gotts and his son Alan owned several rental properties in Norfolk. Keith and Brownie made a "gentleman's agreement" that Brownie would buy a house, Keith would convert it into six flats to rent, Keith would act as his agent and building manager, and Keith would own the two ground-floor flats. Alan bought the house instead of Brownie. Keith did the work, let the flats, and managed the building for three years until Alan excluded him from the premises.

The agreement between Keith and Brownie did not satisfy the formalities required in England, where oral land contracts are now void and part performance has been abolished. The Court of Appeal ordered that Keith was entitled to a ninety-nine-year lease of the two ground-floor flats, free of rent, on the basis of proprietary estoppel. In other words, he obtained exactly what was promised to him under the void land contract.

In *Cowper-Smith v Morgan*,[225] a sister convinced her brother to move from England back to their mother's home in Victoria, British Columbia, to look after her. They agreed that if the brother did this, he could buy the sister's share of the home after the mother died. They both expected that she would leave the home to them in equal shares. The Supreme Court of Canada held that this promise was enforceable on the basis of proprietary estoppel. The promise was an unwritten land contract to grant an option to purchase.

It may seem strange that estoppel can be used to enforce land contracts that do not comply with the usual formalities. Although contract is the normal way in which to make an enforceable promise, it is not the only way. Long before the modern law of contract, promises were made by deed under seal, and they can still be made that way. In the sixteenth century, promises could be enforced without a deed if there was consideration for the promise, and the modern law of contract was born.[226] In the twentieth century, we began enforcing promises relating to land if there was sufficient detrimental reliance.

This leads to the question why the enforcement of promises by estoppel is limited to proprietary estoppel. It operates only when the

---

224 [1999] EWCA Civ 3006, [2000] Ch 162.

225 *Cowper-Smith*, above note 184.

226 See John Baker, *An Introduction to English Legal History*, 5th ed (Oxford: Oxford University Press, 2019) at 358–68.

plaintiff reasonably expects to acquire an interest in the defendant's land. In *Thorner v Major*, Lord Walker said that "it is a necessary element of proprietary estoppel that the assurances given to the claimant . . . should relate to identified property owned (or, perhaps, about to be owned) by the defendant."[227]

In *Cowper-Smith v Morgan*,[228] the Supreme Court of Canada held that proprietary estoppel can operate even though the defendant does not own the land when the plaintiff relies on their promise. If both parties reasonably expect that the defendant will acquire that land in the future, the plaintiff can acquire an interest in that land by estoppel if and when that occurs. McLachlin CJ said,

> An equity arises when the claimant reasonably relies to his detriment on the expectation that he will enjoy a right or benefit over property, whether or not the party responsible for that expectation owns an interest in the property at the time of the claimant's reliance. Proprietary estoppel may not protect that equity immediately. It may not protect the equity until considerable time has passed. If the party responsible for the expectation never acquires a sufficient interest in the property, proprietary estoppel may not arise at all; where there is proprietary estoppel, there must be an equity, but not vice versa. When the party responsible for the expectation has or acquires a sufficient interest in the property, however, proprietary estoppel attaches to that interest and protects the equity. Ownership at the time the representation or assurance was relied on is not a requirement of a proprietary estoppel claim.[229]

Estoppel has been carried further in Australia, where promissory and proprietary estoppel have merged to become equitable estoppel. In *Waltons Stores (Interstate) Ltd v Maher*, Mason CJ and Wilson J said,

> One may therefore discern in the cases a common thread which links them together, namely, the principle that equity will come to the relief of a plaintiff who has acted to his detriment on the basis of a basic assumption in relation to which the other party to the transaction has "played such a part in the adoption of the assumption that it would be unfair or unjust if he were left free to ignore it." Equity comes to the

---

227 *Thorner*, above note 190 at para 61.
228 *Cowper-Smith*, above note 184.
229 *Ibid* at para 35 [citations omitted].

relief of such a plaintiff on the footing that it would be unconscionable conduct on the part of the other party to ignore the assumption.[230]

That case was different from the cases of proprietary estoppel because the plaintiffs (Mr and Mrs Maher) were not expecting to acquire an interest in the defendant's land but were instead expecting to grant an interest in their land to the defendant (Waltons Stores). The parties were negotiating the grant of a lease to Waltons Stores. The Mahers believed that the formalities would soon be completed and began to demolish their existing building in order to construct a new building suitable for Waltons Stores. Meanwhile, Waltons Stores was looking at other locations, and even though they were aware of the demolition, they did not tell the Mahers that they might not take a lease after all. Waltons Stores then decided not to take the lease.

The parties never had a contract, but Waltons Stores was ordered to pay damages to the Mahers in lieu of specific performance of the contract that the Mahers thought they were going to make. Their right to damages was generated by estoppel: Waltons Stores' silence amounted to a representation that they intended to take a lease, and the Mahers had relied on it to their detriment.

G. SALE OF GOODS

As discussed at the beginning of this chapter, goods can be transferred by delivery or by deed. In this part, we consider how they can be transferred by contract of sale. A sale of goods is very different from a sale of land. A contract to sell land can create an equitable interest (as discussed above) but cannot transfer legal title. The contract is a promise to transfer title, which is then achieved by deed or registration. For goods, the contract of sale is usually the event that causes legal ownership to be transferred from seller to buyer. No separate act of conveyance is required.

Every jurisdiction in Canada (except Quebec) has a *Sale of Goods Act*,[231] which was copied from the English *Sale of Goods Act 1893*.[232] That Act codified the common law of sale and dealt with a variety of different issues, including the standard warranties made by sellers and

---

230 [1988] HCA 7, 164 CLR 387 at 404, quoting Dixon J in *Grundt v Great Boulder Pty Gold Mines Ltd*, [1937] HCA 58, 59 CLR 641 at 675.

231 RSBC 1996, c 410; RSA 2000, c S-2; RSS 1978, c S-1; CCSM, c S10; RSO 1990, c S.1; RSNB 2016, c 110; RSNS 1989, c 408; RSPEI 1988, c S-1; RSNL 1990, c S-6; RSY 2002, c 198; RSNWT 1988, c S-2.

232 The current English version is the *Sale of Goods Act 1979*.

remedies for breach of contract. We are concerned here with the transfer of legal title. The Saskatchewan version is quoted below, but the others are essentially no different.

1) What Is a Sale of Goods?

Goods are defined in the *Sale of Goods Act* to include "all chattels personal other than things in action or money and includes emblements, industrial growing crops and things attached to or forming part of the land which are agreed to be severed before sale or under the contract of sale."[233] In other words, goods are physical objects other than land or money, but things attached to the land can be regarded as goods for the purposes of the *Sale of Goods Act*. As discussed in Chapter 7, a right to take the natural produce of the land (including minerals) can be either a *profit à prendre* (which is an interest in land) or a sale of goods. A right to harvest a sown crop is an emblement.

The *Sale of Goods Act* states that "[a] contract of sale of goods is a contract by which the seller transfers or agrees to transfer the property in goods to the buyer for a money consideration, called the price."[234] A contract of *barter*, in which goods are exchanged for other goods, is not a contract of sale of goods because the consideration is not money. In *Hearns v Rizzolo*,[235] the plaintiff traded his Dodge for the defendant's Jeep. Unknown to both parties, the Jeep was subject to a security interest in favour of a finance company, which repossessed it. The plaintiff paid $10,738 to the finance company to get the Jeep back and then sued the defendant for that amount in small claims court. His claim was dismissed. Since their contract was a barter and not a sale, the implied warranty in the *Sale of Goods Act* that the buyer would get good title did not apply. On appeal to the Supreme Court, Pickup J said, "I see no error in the adjudicator applying *caveat emptor* because there was no evidence of fraud on the part of the respondent, or of an expressed warranty as to freedom from encumbrances in the agreement between the parties."[236]

A supply of goods can occur pursuant to a contract that is not a contract of sale but a contract for services. In *Ter Neuzen v Korn*,[237] a woman contracted HIV from infected semen used in an artificial insemination procedure. She sued her doctor for negligence and for breach of the implied warranty in the *Sale of Goods Act* that goods are fit for the

---

233   RSS 1978, c S-1, s 2.
234   *Ibid*, s 3.
235   2012 NSSC 256.
236   *Ibid* at para 17.
237   [1995] 3 SCR 674, 127 DLR (4th) 577.

purpose for which they are bought. The Supreme Court of Canada held that their contract was for medical services, not a sale of semen; therefore, the warranty did not apply. Sopinka J said,

> In order for the *Sale of Goods Act* to apply, a contract must primarily be for the purpose of selling goods. If the sale of a good is merely incidental to what is primarily a contract for services, then the statute will not imply a warranty. As Legg J. observed in *Gee v. White Spot Ltd.* (1986), 7 B.C.L.R. (2d) 235 (S.C.), in order to come within the *Sale of Goods Act*, a contract need not be one exclusively for the sale of goods. However, the sale of a good must be the primary purpose of the contract. . . .
>
> [T]he contract to perform the AI procedure on the appellant was primarily a contract for medical services and not a sale of semen. To hold otherwise would be to distort the true nature of the whole agreement between the parties. The provision of the semen was obviously an important component to the AI procedure; however the primary reason the appellant went to a gynaecologist was for professional medical services and expertise.[238]

2) Transfer of Property

The *Sale of Goods Act* organizes goods into several categories. *Specific goods* are "goods identified and agreed upon at the time a contract of sale is made," and *future goods* are "goods to be manufactured or acquired by the seller after the making of the contract of sale."[239] The statute also refers to *ascertained goods* and *unascertained goods*, but without defining those terms. Atkin LJ said, "'Ascertained' probably means identified in accordance with the agreement after the time a contract of sale is made, and I shall assume that to be the meaning."[240]

The *Sale of Goods Act* provides rules for determining when ownership is transferred from the seller to the buyer. Normally, that depends on the intentions of the parties as expressed or implied by the terms of their contract. Regardless of their intentions, ownership cannot be transferred to the buyer unless the goods are identified. This is the same as the requirement of certainty of subject matter for the creation of a trust (discussed above). The *Sale of Goods Act* makes that clear: "Where

---

238 *Ibid* at paras 67 and 71.
239 RSS 1978, c S-1, s 2 [*Sale of Goods Act*].
240 *Re Wait*, [1927] 1 Ch 606 at 630 (CA). See also *Re Western Canada Pulpwood Co Ltd*, [1930] 1 DLR 652, 38 Man R 378 (CA); *Humboldt Flour Mills Co Ltd v Boscher* (1974), 50 DLR (3d) 477 (Sask QB).

there is a contract for the sale of unascertained goods no property in the goods is transferred to the buyer unless and until the goods are ascertained."[241]

In *Re Goldcorp Exchange Ltd*,[242] Goldcorp sold gold, silver, and platinum bullion to more than 1,000 customers. Its promotional literature stated, "Basically, you agree to buy and sell as with physical bullion, but receive a certificate of ownership rather than the metal. The metal is stored in a vault on your behalf."[243]

The customers believed that they owned the bullion they had purchased. Goldcorp became hopelessly insolvent, and the Privy Council (on appeal from New Zealand) was asked to decide who owned the bullion in Goldcorp's possession. Unfortunately for the customers, Goldcorp never allocated bullion to specific customers when it was purchased. As Lord Mustill said, "[C]ommon sense dictates that the buyer cannot acquire title until it is known to what goods the title relates."[244]

Ownership can be transferred to the buyer once the goods have been identified. Exactly when that occurs depends on the intentions of the parties as revealed by the terms of their contract:

(1) Where there is a contract for the sale of specific or ascertained goods the property in them is transferred to the buyer at the time the parties to the contract intend it to be transferred.

(2) For the purpose of ascertaining the intention of the parties regard shall be had to the terms of the contract, the conduct of the parties and the circumstances of the case.[245]

The *Sale of Goods Act* provides "rules for ascertaining the intention of the parties as to the time at which the property in the goods is to pass to the buyer," which apply unless a different intention has been expressed or implied by their contract.[246] Many law students and lay people are surprised when they learn the first rule: "Where there is an unconditional contract for the sale of specific goods in a deliverable state the property in the goods passes to the buyer when the contract is made and it is immaterial whether the time of payment or the time of delivery or both be postponed."[247]

---

241 *Sale of Goods Act*, above note 239, s 18.
242 [1994] UKPC 3, [1995] 1 AC 74, [1994] 3 NZLR 385 [cited to AC].
243 *Ibid* at 87.
244 *Ibid* at 90.
245 *Sale of Goods Act*, above note 239, s 19.
246 *Ibid*, s 20.
247 *Ibid*.

People tend to assume that ownership is transferred when the goods are delivered and the price is paid, but unless the seller and the buyer decide otherwise, the buyer becomes the owner of the goods as soon as the contract is made if the goods are identified and in a deliverable state. The seller becomes a bailee pending delivery.

Goods can be sold "on sale or return," in which case the buyer becomes a bailee of the goods until they choose to accept them, at which time they become the owner.[248] When unascertained or future goods are sold by description, the buyer will become the owner when goods matching that description are appropriated to the contract with the consent of the parties.

In *Wardar's (Import & Export) Co Ltd v W Norwood & Sons Ltd*,[249] the seller had 1,500 cartons of frozen ox kidneys in cold storage at Smithfield market in London. The buyer agreed to buy 600 of those cartons and sent a refrigerated truck to pick them up. When the carrier arrived at 8 a.m., the cartons were already stacked on the pavement. It took four hours to load them into the truck, by which time they were "in soft condition." The carrier then turned on the refrigeration and drove to Scotland, where the kidneys were condemned by a medical officer.

The Court of Appeal decided that ownership was transferred to the buyer at 8 a.m. when the carrier arrived. That was when goods were appropriated to the contract with the consent of both parties. They were still frozen and of *merchantable quality* at that time. The damage occurred after they already belonged to the buyer; therefore, the seller was not liable for it.

In *Re Kenron Homes Ltd*,[250] the Kahkewistahaw First Nation in Saskatchewan agreed to buy seven "ready to move" homes. They paid $77,766 to the builder as the homes were being constructed. Unfortunately, the builder became bankrupt, and none of the homes were delivered. The buyers claimed unsuccessfully that they owned the partially constructed homes. Vancise J said,

> In order to ascertain the intention of the parties to the contract as to
> when title passes one must examine the contract as a whole. If it is
> not possible to determine a contrary intention from an examination
> of the contract, the statute governs. It is a question of construction in
> each case and a question of fact in each case. . . .

---

248 See *Atari Corporation (UK) Ltd v Electronics Boutiquestores (UK) Ltd*, [1998] QB 539 (CA).

249 [1968] 2 QB 663 (CA) [*Wardar's*].

250 (1982) 20 Sask R 80 (QB).

In the present case there was no payment by instalment and inspection. There is provision for payment on delivery to the owner but nowhere in the contract does it provide nor can it be inferred that property is to pass prior to placing the goods in a deliverable state. I find that there is no intention that the property would pass to the owner as it is constructed or manufactured.[251]

Since the contract did not express or imply otherwise, the statute governed. The homes were not in a deliverable state and were still owned by the bankrupt builder. The transfer of ownership is a double-edged sword, as *Wardar's*[252] demonstrates. Although it would have given the buyers property rights enforceable against the builder's trustee in bankruptcy, it also would have meant that the homes were at the buyers' risk during construction. Who would have borne the loss if they had been destroyed in a fire?

251 *Ibid* at para 11.
252 *Wardar's*, above note 249.

CHAPTER 9

COMPETING RIGHTS

A. INTRODUCTION

The law of property provides rules to resolve disputes when two or more people claim competing rights to the same thing. Every case discussed in this book concerns a dispute over something. Often the issue before the court is whether someone has a property right at all. Can they have an exclusive right to hire boats to be used on a canal?[1] Can they compel their neighbour to repair their roof?[2] Did they acquire a fee simple estate?[3] Are they the beneficiary of a trust?[4] Sometimes the issue is how far the right extends. Did an airplane flying overhead trespass through a fee simple estate?[5]

In this chapter, we deal with cases in which the dispute is between people who undoubtedly have property rights to the same thing, but their rights are incompatible with one another. Who has the better right to a can of money found under a house: the owner of the house, the boy who found the can, or the authorities who took it away from the boy?[6] The law provides *priority rules* to answer questions like these.

---

1   *Hill v Tupper* (1863), 2 H & C 121, 159 ER 51 (see Chapter 7).
2   *Rhone v Stephens*, [1994] UKHL 3, [1994] 2 AC 310 (see Chapter 7).
3   *Butt v Humber* (1976), 46 APR 92, 17 Nfld & PEIR 92 (Nfld SC) (see Chapter 8).
4   *Paul v Constance*, [1977] 1 WLR 527 (CA) (see Chapter 8).
5   *Bernstein of Leigh v Skyviews & General Ltd*, [1978] QB 479 (see Chapter 3).
6   *Bird v Fort Frances*, [1949] 2 DLR 791 (Ont) (see Chapter 2).

The previous chapter was about the ways in which people can acquire rights. This chapter is about the ways in which people can lose their rights. The resolution of a priority dispute will diminish or destroy the property rights of the losing party. It cannot be helped.

In many cases, both parties are the innocent victims of someone else's wrong. To use an example loved by property law teachers around the world, what should happen if a thief stole my bicycle and sold it to you, who paid full market value and had no way of knowing it was stolen? The loser will have a claim against the thief for damages (mine is for the tort of conversion, and yours is for breach of contract), but that is probably not worth pursuing. Who should win?

There is no natural answer to that question. The common law has chosen to protect my ownership rather than your purchase in good faith, but that is an artificial choice. Other legal systems may make different choices. For example, in *Winkworth v Christie Manson and Woods Ltd*,[7] works of art were stolen from the plaintiff in England, sold to an honest buyer, and then offered for sale in England by auction. If that was the whole story, the plaintiff would win. However, the artworks were sold to the honest buyer in Italy and then returned to England for sale. The sale in Italy was governed by Italian law, under which the honest buyer wins. The plaintiff's ownership did not revive when the artworks were back in England.

We have several different sets of priority rules. The rules that determine the priority of *legal* property rights are different from the rules that protect *equitable* property rights. This is one reason why it matters whether rights are legal or equitable. Most property rights to land are governed by registration systems, which provide different priority rules. The priority of security interests in personal property also depends on registration. Each of these different sets of rules is discussed below.

This chapter then looks at competing claims to goods that get attached to land (as fixtures) or to other goods (as accessories). Property rights to goods can be lost if those goods lose their separate identity and become part of land or other goods belonging to someone else. They can also be lost if goods are used to manufacture other goods. Finally, it sometimes happens that goods of the same type get mixed together, so it is impossible to tell them apart. The law provides rules to resolve the competing claims of those who owned the goods that went into the mixture.

---

7   [1980] Ch 496 (Ch D).

B. COMMON LAW

1) *Nemo Dat*

When dealing with a competition between legal property rights, the best place to start is with the principle called *nemo dat quod non habet* (or *nemo dat* for short), which means that no one can give what they do not have. It explains why the owner of the stolen bicycle wins in the example above. The honest buyer cannot get a better title than the thief who sold it. They acquired the thief's title, which is a right to possession that is enforceable against everyone else in the world, except someone with a better right.[8] The owner has a better right because the theft did not destroy their right to possession or transfer it to the thief. The thief acquired a new right to possession when they stole the bicycle (subject to the owner's better right), and that is all they could sell.

Normally, it does not matter whether the owner was careless and might have avoided the loss. As Morris LJ said in *Central Newbury Car Auctions Ltd v Unity Finance Ltd*, "The improvident householder who has left a window open at night which gives easy access for a thief is not in a worse position in asserting ownership of stolen articles than is the cautious householder who has checked the secure closing of his house."[9]

Another example is provided by *Northern Counties of England Fire Insurance Co v Whipp*.[10] Mr Crabtree was the plaintiff's manager. He mortgaged his land to the plaintiff in exchange for £7,000. The mortgage deed and his title deeds were kept in the plaintiff's safe, to which Crabtree had a key. He then mortgaged the land to Mrs Whipp for £3,500 and gave her the title deeds, which he had stolen from the safe. She thought she was getting a first legal mortgage, but since the land had already been mortgaged to the plaintiff, she could not get a mortgage of anything more than Crabtree had to give, which was his equity of redemption.

The vice-chancellor held that Whipp's equitable mortgage had priority over the plaintiff's older legal mortgage because the plaintiff had been careless with the title deeds by allowing Crabtree to have access to them. That was reversed by the Court of Appeal. Fry LJ said,

> The decisions on negligence at common law have been pressed on us in the present case, but it appears to us enough to observe, that the action at law for negligence imports the existence of a duty on the

---

8   *Costello v Derbyshire Constabulary*, [2001] EWCA Civ 381, [2001] 1 WLR 1437 at para 31.

9   [1957] 1 QB 371 at 394 (CA). See also *Farquharson Brothers & Co v King & Co*, [1902] AC 325 at 335–36 (HL) [*Farquharson Brothers*].

10   (1884) 26 Ch D 482 (CA) [*Northern Counties*].

part of the defendant to the plaintiff, and a loss suffered as a direct consequence of the breach of such duty; and that in the present case it is impossible to find any duty undertaken by the Plaintiff company to the Defendant, Mrs. Whipp. The case was argued as if the legal owner of land owed a duty to all other of Her Majesty's subjects to keep his title deeds secure; as if title deeds were in the eye of the law analogous to fierce dogs or destructive elements, where from the nature of the thing the Courts have implied a general duty of safe custody on the part of the person having their possession or control.[11]

The court said that the plaintiff's mortgage would have been postponed to Whipp's mortgage if the plaintiff had been a party to Crabtree's fraud or had appointed Crabtree as their agent with the authority to mortgage the land, but "the Court will not postpone the prior legal estate to the subsequent equitable estate on the ground of any mere carelessness or want of prudence on the part of the legal owner."[12]

Nemo dat is just the starting point. There are many exceptions to that principle. The person with the older legal property right (whether it is ownership, possession, or something else) will rely on *nemo dat*. The person who acquired a newer, competing property right for value in good faith will hope that one of the exceptions applies in their favour. It is important to remember that none of the exceptions will help someone who acquired their property right as a gift or with knowledge of the older right. There is no good reason to make an exception to *nemo dat* unless the newer right was acquired for value and in good faith. As *Northern Counties* shows, being an honest buyer is not enough on its own. It is necessary, but not sufficient. There is always some other good reason to make an exception to *nemo dat*.

2) Money

The most important exception to *nemo dat* concerns cash money. The ownership of bills and coins does not pass to the thief when they are stolen. However, another person can acquire ownership of the stolen money if it is paid to them as currency and they give value in exchange without knowledge that it was stolen. In *Sinclair v Brougham*, Viscount Haldane LC said,

> If a sovereign or banknote be offered in payment it is, under ordinary circumstances, no part of the duty of the person receiving it to inquire

---

11   *Ibid* at 493.
12   *Ibid* at 494, Fry LJ.

into title. The reason of this is that chattels of such a kind form part of what the law recognises as currency, and treats as passing from hand to hand in point, not merely of possession, but of property.[13]

For example, if a thief stole a $20 bill, they acquired a right to possess it subject to the owner's better right to possession. If the thief then used it to buy coffee and received $15 in change, the coffee shop acquired ownership of the bill free from the owner's right to possession. The shop acquired the thief's right to possession, and their receipt in good faith of money used as currency destroyed the owner's better right. The thief acquired ownership of the coffee and $15 in change because those things belonged to the shop and they chose to transfer their rights to the thief.[14]

This exception to *nemo dat* is necessary if money is to fulfill its function as a medium of exchange. A $20 bill is worth $20 because the person who accepts it honestly as payment need not worry that they might not get good title.

3) Agents

Another exception to *nemo dat* is made when agents exceed their authority. No exception is needed when an agent acts with the authority of their principal. Their authorized actions bind their principal and can cause the principal's legal title to be transferred, mortgaged, and so on. The problem occurs when an agent acts without authority. Who should bear the consequences: the principal who chose the agent, or the buyer who relied on the agent's apparent authority to sell?

Every jurisdiction provides a statutory exception to *nemo dat* for mercantile agents who deal in goods in the ordinary course of their business.[15] The exception applies if they have possession of the goods or documents of title with the consent of the owner. The transaction

---

13   [1914] AC 398 at 418. See also *Miller v Race* (1758), 1 Burrow 452, 97 ER 398; *Ilich v The Queen*, [1987] HCA 1, 162 CLR 110.

14   There is a good argument that thieves hold items purchased with stolen money in trust for the victims of their theft, but that is a different issue concerning trusts arising by operation of law in response to unjust enrichment: *Black v S Freedman & Co*, [1910] HCA 58, 12 CLR 105; *Evans v European Bank Ltd*, [2004] NSWCA 82, 61 NSWLR 75.

15   *Sale of Goods Act*, RSBC 1996, c 410, s 59; *Factors Act*, RSA 2000, c F-1; *Factors Act*, RSS 1978, c F-1; *Factors Act*, CCSM, c F10; *Factors Act*, RSO 1990, c F.1; *Factors and Agents Act*, RSNB 2011, c 153; *Factors Act*, RSNS 1989, c 157; *Factors Act*, RSPEI 1988, c F-1; *Sale of Goods Act*, RSNL 1990, c S-6, s 27; *Factors Act*, RSY 2002, c 82; *Factors Act*, RSNWT 1988, c F-1.

is valid so long as the other party acts in good faith and does not know that the owner did not consent to it.[16]

The exception applies because the owner allowed the agent to have the goods or documents of title and took the risk that they might deal with them improperly. In *Brandon v Leckie*,[17] two motor homes were stolen from the two plaintiffs and sold to a mercantile agent in Calgary, who resold them to the two defendants. The plaintiffs agreed that each defendant was "a bona fide purchaser for value without notice of any defects in title."[18] The defendants argued that they should get good title because they dealt with a mercantile agent in good faith and that it should not matter whether the agent had possession with the consent of the owners or not. That was rejected by the court. Moore J said,

> It simply does not seem logical that the Legislature of this Province, in its wisdom, would enact legislation, the effect of which would be to preclude a true owner, who has done no wrongful act, from attempting to regain and in fact regaining a chattel stolen from him. Never at any time from the moment of the original theft of each motor home has title passed from the original owners. As counsel for the plaintiff argued — *nemo dat quod non habet*. Nobody can give good title to what he does not possess.[19]

4) Estoppel

The *Sale of Goods Act* in every province and territory has a section that codifies the principle of *nemo dat* along with an important exception to it:

> Subject to this Act, if goods are sold by a person who is not the owner of them, and who does not sell them under the authority or with the consent of the owner, the buyer acquires no better title to the goods than the seller had, unless the owner's conduct precludes the owner from denying the seller's authority to sell.[20]

---

16   *St John v Horvat*, [1994] 5 WWR 22, 113 DLR (4th) 670 (BCCA); *MJ Jones Inc v Henry* (2002), 58 OR (3d) 529 (CA).

17   [1972] 6 WWR 113, 29 DLR (3d) 633 (Alta QB) [cited to DLR].

18   *Ibid* at 634.

19   *Ibid* at 637–38.

20   RSBC 1996, c 410, s 26; see also RSA 2000, c S-2, s 23; RSS 1978, c S-1, s 23; CCSM, c S10, s 23; RSO 1990, c S.1, s 22; RSNB 2016, c 110, s 28; RSNS 1989, c 408, s 24; RSPEI 1988, c S-1, s 23; RSNL 1990, c S-6, s 23; RSY 2002, c 198, s 22; RSNWT 1988, c S-2, s 25.

Normally, when goods are sold by someone who is not the owner, *nemo dat* applies unless the seller was acting properly as the owner's agent. The exception that "precludes the owner from denying the seller's authority to sell" is often referred to as the defence of *estoppel*.[21] This occurs when the owner is responsible for the buyer's mistaken belief that the seller did have authority. Merely giving possession of goods to the seller is not enough.[22] Otherwise, every bailment would put the owner's title at risk.

The owner will be estopped from denying the seller's authority if the owner tells the buyer that the seller is the owner or an authorized agent. In *Peoples Bank of Halifax v Estey*,[23] the plaintiff bank agreed to sell logs to a lumber manufacturer in Fredericton named McKendrick. They were delivered to him, but it was a term of their contract that he would not get title until the purchase price was paid. The defendant Estey called the bank's manager to ask if the logs were for sale and was told that they had been sold to McKendrick. Estey then bought some of the logs from McKendrick. The bank sued Estey and was awarded damages for conversion at trial, but that was overturned on appeal. A majority of the Supreme Court of Canada held that the bank was estopped from denying McKendrick's authority to sell.

In most cases, there is no direct communication between the owner and the buyer. The question is whether the owner enabled the seller to pretend to be the owner or their agent. In *Canaplan Leasing Inc v Dominion of Canada General Insurance Co*,[24] the owner of a BMW made an arrangement with a car dealer for the sale of the car to a stockbroker in Hamilton in exchange for an older BMW and $10,000. The deal fell through, so the dealer sold the car in Vancouver for $22,470, which the dealer kept to cover expenses and the owner's past debt to the dealer. The owner reported the car stolen, it was resold, and the police seized it from the buyer. The court held that the owner was estopped from denying the dealer's authority to sell because the owner had provided the dealer "with all keys to the vehicle, warranty books, owner's manual and the automobile registration, endorsing the space on the back as the seller of the vehicle."[25] Lander J said,

---

21 See, for example, *Central Newbury Car Auctions Ltd v Unity Finance Ltd*, above note 9; *Mortimer-Rae v Barthel* (1979), 105 DLR (3d) 289, 11 Alta LR (2d) 66 (QB); *Canaplan Leasing Inc v Dominion of Canada General Insurance Co* (1990), 69 DLR (4th) 531 (BCSC) [*Canaplan*].

22 *Nachtigal v Premier Motors Ltd*, [1929] 2 DLR 190, 24 Alta LR 80 (CA); *McVicar v Herman* (1958), 13 DLR (2d) 419 (Sask CA).

23 (1904) 34 SCR 429 [*Peoples Bank*].

24 *Canaplan*, above note 21.

25 *Ibid* at para 6, Lander J.

From the case law it is apparent that the primary concern in determining whether a person will be estopped from denying an individual's authority to deal with a property, is whether the individual was armed with some indicia which would make it appear that he was either the owner or authorized to sell. Mere possession of the chattel, carelessness with respect to the ownership documents, deception or theft in obtaining the necessary documents to convey title is not sufficient. One must look to the conduct of the person that was handing over the chattel and what they intended when the chattel and documents were handed over. The individual must intend to clothe the agent with either apparent ownership or authority to deal with the chattel before an estoppel argument can be sustained.[26]

Estoppel will not apply unless the owner's conduct amounts to a representation that the seller is the owner or their agent and the buyer relies on that representation. In *Farquharson Brothers & Co v King & Co*,[27] the owners were merchants who imported timber and stored it in a warehouse at the Surrey Commercial Docks (which then existed in east London and had docks named after places from where cargo was imported, including Canada Dock and Quebec Pond). The owners wrote to the secretary of the dock company to authorize their clerk, Mr Capon, to accept deliveries of timber and transfer it to their customers. Capon pretended to be a man named Brown. As Capon, he signed orders for the transfer of timber to Brown, and the dock company transferred it in their books into Brown's name. Pretending to be Brown, he then sold the timber to the buyers, who purchased it in good faith. The Court of Appeal held that the owners were estopped from denying Capon's authority to sell, but that was reversed on appeal to the House of Lords. Lord Halsbury LC said,

> Estoppel arises where you are precluded from denying the truth of anything which you have represented as a fact although it is not a fact; but no such question arises here.... Capon was unknown; the appellants were unknown; nobody dreams of suggesting that the respondents here acted upon the faith of Capon being invested with that authority. They never heard of Capon, they never heard of the appellants, but the clerk who has committed the fraud, ingeniously availing himself of his power of signing orders for delivery, gave a

---

26   *Ibid* at para 29.
27   *Farquharson Brothers*, above note 9.

delivery order to change the name in which the goods were stored in the dock company's books to the name of Brown.[28]

Lord Halsbury LC went on to discuss the exception in the *Sale of Goods Act*:

> My Lords, I think the state of the law would have been perfectly clear without it, but the *Sale of Goods Act* has disposed of any such question, because it says, "Subject to the provisions of this Act, where goods are sold by a person who is not the owner thereof, and who does not sell them under the authority or with the consent of the owner, the buyer acquires no better title to the goods than the seller had, unless the owner of the goods is by his conduct precluded from denying" — what? — "the seller's authority to sell." Now, where comes in here the operation of that saving clause? What authority was there to sell? None. What representation was there of Capon's authority to sell? None. . . . This was a theft, and the thief could give no better title than he himself had, which was none.[29]

5) Buyer or Seller in Possession

The *Sale of Goods Act* provides exceptions to *nemo dat* that apply if (1) the buyer obtains possession of the goods while the seller retains title or (2) the seller retains possession of the goods while the buyer obtains title.[30] A buyer in possession can transfer good title to someone who deals with the buyer in good faith without notice of the seller's title. Conversely, a seller in possession can transfer good title to someone who deals with the seller in good faith without notice of the buyer's title. Both exceptions are now subject to the *Personal Property Security Act* (*PPSA*), discussed below.

If the *Sale of Goods Act* had been in force in New Brunswick in 1904, this exemption would have applied in *Peoples Bank*.[31] As discussed above, the bank retained title to the logs it sold and delivered to McKendrick. He was a buyer in possession, and Estey would have received good title from him even if he had not called the bank to inquire about the logs.

---

28   *Ibid* at 330–31. See also *Nachtigal v Premier Motors Ltd*, [1929] 2 DLR 190, 24 Alta LR 80 (CA).

29   *Farquharson Brothers*, above note 9 at 333.

30   RSBC 1996, c 410, s 30; RSA 2000, c S-2, s 26; RSS 1978, c S-1, s 26; CCSM, c S10, s 28; RSO 1990, c S.1, s 25; RSNB 2016, c 110, s 31; RSNS 1989, c 408, s 28; RSNL 1990, c S-6, s 27; RSY 2002, c 198, s 24; RSNWT 1988, c S-2, s 27. In Prince Edward Island, these exceptions are found in the *Factors Act*, RSPEI 1988, c F-1, ss 9, 10.

31   *Peoples Bank*, above note 23.

The normal reason why parties to a contract of sale choose to separate ownership from possession is to create a security interest (as discussed in Chapter 6). The seller retains title to make sure they get paid. The seller retains possession when they sell the goods to the buyer and lease them back. This is essentially a loan from the buyer who received title (but not possession) to hold as security for the loan.[32] If the parties choose to separate ownership and possession under their contract of sale, the owner takes the risk that the possessor might deal with the goods in breach of their agreement. The owner can protect their security interest by registration (as discussed below). Otherwise, there is no reason why other people should be adversely affected by the particular terms of a private contract of sale dealing with the passing of title.

6) Voidable Title

Every *Sale of Goods Act* has a section that deals with voidable contracts of sale. A voidable contract is not void. It exists and can transfer ownership of goods to the buyer. It is voidable if the seller has the power to rescind the contract for some reason. The usual reason is the buyer's fraud. In other words, the seller was induced to enter into the contract by the buyer's fraudulent misrepresentation. Contracts can also be rescinded because of duress, undue influence, or innocent misrepresentations.

Normally, the contract of sale causes ownership of goods to be transferred from the seller to the buyer (as discussed in the previous chapter). The rescission of that contract will remove the source of the buyer's legal title, which will revert to the seller. A difficulty arises if the buyer has dealt with the goods in the meantime. The *Sale of Goods Act* deals with that problem as follows: "When the seller of goods has a voidable title to them, but the seller's title has not been avoided at the time of the sale, the buyer acquires a good title to the goods, if they are bought in good faith and without notice of the seller's defect of title."[33]

This section refers only to two characters (the seller and the buyer), but it presupposes that the seller has a backstory. The seller's title is voidable because they purchased the goods from a previous seller, who has the right to rescind that transaction. The whole story will involve at least three characters. There are two different issues: (1) did the seller

---

32 See, for example, *Westcoast Leasing Ltd v Westcoast Communications Ltd* (1980), 22 BCLR 285 (SC) [*Westcoast*].

33 RSBC 1996, c 410, s 28; see also RSA 2000, c S-2, s 24; RSS 1978, c S-1, s 24; CCSM, c S10, s 24; RSO 1990, c S.1, s 24; RSNB 2016, c 110, s 30; RSNS 1989, c 408, s 26; RSPEI 1988, c S-1, s 25; RSNL 1990, c S-6, s 25; RSY 2002, c 198, s 23; RSNWT 1988, c S-2, s 26.

with voidable title sell the goods to the buyer before or after the previous seller rescinded the previous sale, and (2) did the buyer have notice of the previous seller's right to rescind? Both issues were raised in *Car & Universal Finance Co Ltd v Caldwell*.[34]

On 12 January 1960, Caldwell was induced by fraud to sell his Jaguar to Norris in exchange for £10 in cash and a cheque for £965. Caldwell went to the bank the next day, where he discovered that the cheque was worthless and was advised to contact the police. He reported the fraud to the police and called the Automobile Association later that day. Norris sold the Jaguar that same day to Motobella Co Ltd, which resold it to G & C Finance Corp Ltd on 15 January. Motobella had notice of Norris's fraud, but G & C Finance did not.

The contract of sale from Caldwell to Norris was voidable. A difficult issue in the case was whether Caldwell was able to rescind it without communicating with Norris. Upjohn LJ said,

> If one party, by absconding, deliberately puts it out of the power of the other to communicate his intention to rescind which he knows the other will almost certainly want to do, I do not think he can any longer insist on his right to be made aware of the election to determine the contract. In these circumstances communication is a useless formality. I think that the law must allow the innocent party to exercise his right of rescission otherwise than by communication or repossession. To hold otherwise would be to allow a fraudulent contracting party by his very fraud to prevent the innocent party from exercising his undoubted right. I would hold that in circumstances such as these the innocent party may evince his intention to disaffirm the contract by overt means falling short of communication or repossession.[35]

Caldwell avoided the contract on 13 January "by overt means" when he contacted the police and the Automobile Association. This is an issue that students may study in the law of contracts. Of interest to students of property law is the effect of Caldwell's rescission on ownership of the Jaguar. It would not matter whether he rescinded the contract before or after the car was sold to Motobella because they had notice that Norris's title was defective. They could not acquire a better title than Norris, whose title was subject to Caldwell's power to rescind.

The order in which Caldwell's rescission and the sale to G & C Finance occurred is crucial because they bought the car in good faith and without notice. When Caldwell rescinded on the 13th, ownership of

---

34 [1965] 1 QB 525 (CA).
35 *Ibid* at 555.

the car reverted to him. When Motobella sold the car to G & C Finance on the 15th, they were no longer the owner. *Nemo dat* applied. All that G & C Finance acquired was Motobella's right to possession, which was subject to Caldwell's better right. If Caldwell had not rescinded by the 15th, the story would have been different. G & C Finance would have acquired good title by virtue of the exception in the *Sale of Goods Act*, and Caldwell's power to rescind the contract would have been lost.

A voidable contract should not be confused with a void contract. A voidable contract has legal effect until it is rescinded. It might never be rescinded if the party with the power to do so decides to affirm the contract or waits too long and it is no longer possible to unwind the transaction. A void contract, on the other hand, has no legal effect.

In *Manning v Algard Estate*,[36] a collection of rare Swedish coins (worth $58,000) was stolen from Mr Algard in Vancouver in 1994. Ms Ovsenek bought them for $5 at a garage sale in 2000. They were given to her daughter, Ms Manning, in 2005. After she inquired about their value, the police seized the coins and returned them to Algard, who died soon afterwards from heart failure. Manning then sued his estate to recover the coins.

Manning relied on the section of the *Sale of Goods Act* (quoted above) regarding a seller with voidable title because her mother bought the coins in good faith without notice. The court was prepared to assume that the seller was an honest finder and not a thief, but that made no difference. Algard's title to the coins was never transferred by sale or gift, voidable or otherwise. He never lost his right to possess them. The finder acquired a new right to possession, which was sold to Ovsenek and then given to Manning, but that right was always subject to Algard's better right to possession. *Nemo dat* applied. The section regarding voidable transactions did not. As Butler J said,

> Voidable title describes the situation where the title of a seller of goods may be voided at the option of the true owner. This may occur on grounds of fraud at common law or in equity, misrepresentation, non-disclosure, duress or undue influence. A finder does not have voidable title. Rather, a finder acquires a right to retain a chattel she has found. The right can be exercised against all but the true owner or those claiming through the true owner.[37]

In *Holat v Wettlaufer*,[38] the plaintiff purchased a Peterbilt commercial truck for $95,200 in Prince George and leased it to Mr Wettlaufer.

---

36   2008 BCSC 1129 [*Manning*].
37   *Ibid* at para 73 [citations omitted].
38   2014 BCSC 425.

He forged a transfer of ownership from the plaintiff to himself and became the registered owner. He then sold it for $65,000 to Mr Robson, who claimed ownership of the truck on the basis that he had acquired it in good faith from a seller with voidable title. There was no doubt that he acted in good faith and without notice of the plaintiff's rights. However, there was no transaction to be avoided. As Funt J said, a "forged document is a pure nullity."[39]

Registration of ownership in Wettlaufer's name did not change the outcome. It did not cause ownership to be transferred to him, nor did it provide a guarantee by the province that he was the owner. As discussed in the previous chapter, ownership of goods is transferred when the owner intends to transfer their ownership and gives effect to that intention by delivery, deed, or contract of sale. That never occurred. All Wettlaufer ever had was possession as a bailee, and that was all he could transfer to Robson.

7) Market Overt

There used to be an exception to *nemo dat* in the English *Sale of Goods Act 1979* for a sale of goods in *market overt*, but that was repealed in 1994.[40] British Columbia is the only place in Canada where this exception might still exist. British Columbia's *Sale of Goods Act* states,

> (1) If goods are sold in market overt, according to the usage of the market, the buyer acquires a good title to the goods, as long as they are bought in good faith and without notice of any defect or want of title on the part of the seller.
>
> (2) This section does not affect the law relating to the sale of horses.[41]

The Ontario *Sale of Goods Act* states, "The law relating to market overt does not apply to a sale of goods that takes place in Ontario."[42] The statutes in other provinces and the territories are silent on the issue. But without an express exception for market overt, it could not survive the general rule in every *Sale of Goods Act* that "if goods are sold by a person who is not the owner of them, and who does not sell them under the authority or with the consent of the owner, the buyer acquires no

---

39   *Ibid* at para 53.

40   *Sale of Goods (Amendment) Act 1994* (UK) repealed s 22 of the *Sale of Goods Act 1979*.

41   RSBC 1996, c 410, s 27.

42   RSO 1990, c S.1, s 23.

better title to the goods than the seller had"[43] (discussed above in the section on estoppel).

The term *market overt* means open market, but this exception has a special legal meaning. To qualify as a sale in market overt, it must take place between sunrise and sundown in a market that is legally constituted by Crown grant or by statute.[44] By custom, a sale in the open part of a shop in the City of London (meaning the "square mile" in the heart of greater London) would be treated as a sale in market overt if that shop ordinarily sold goods of that type.[45] In *Clayton v Le Roy*, Scrutton J described the history of this exception to *nemo dat* and said,

> The original ground of the rule was that the market was overt, and the sale could be seen by people attending the market, including those looking for goods stolen from them. The word "shop" appears to be derived from the old high German "schopf," or "scopf," which meant a building without a front wall, such as a barn or vestibule. The judges in the time of Elizabeth seem to me to have attached considerable importance to the question whether passers-by could see the sale taking place.[46]

In *Reid v Commissioner of Police of the Metropolis*, Scarman LJ said,

> The reason why the law permitted a sale in market overt to confer a good title upon the *bona fide* purchaser was the openness of the trans-action.... When shops were scarce, the market was the place, and market day the occasion, for the public to buy and sell. The market was regulated by the franchise-holder. The place, the day, and the hours of business were established under the authority of the franchise and were well known. Thus any person whose goods had been stolen would know where and when the thief was likely to seek to dispose of them, and would have an opportunity of finding and recovering them before they were sold in the open market.[47]

It is clear that the justifications for this exception to *nemo dat* are long gone, which is why it no longer exists in most jurisdictions. Although

---

43 *Sale of Goods Act*, RSA 2000, c S-2, s 23; RSS 1978, c S-1, s 23; CCSM, c S10, s 23; RSNB 2016, c 110, s 28; RSNS 1989, c 408, s 24; RSPEI 1988, c S-1, s 23; RSNL 1990, c S-6, s 23; RSY 2002, c 198, s 22; RSNWT 1988, c S-2, s 25. Also see *Mackenzie v Blindman Valley Co-operative Association Ltd* [1947] 4 DLR 687, [1947] 2 WWR 443 (Alta QB); *McTavish v Kellett*, (1989) 62 Man R (2d) 146 (QB).

44 *Bishopsgate Motor Finance Corp v Transport Brakes Ltd*, [1949] 1 KB 322 (CA); *Reid v Commissioner of Police of the Metropolis*, [1973] QB 551 (CA) [*Reid*].

45 *Clayton v Le Roy*, [1911] 2 KB 1031 (KB and CA).

46 *Ibid* at 1045 (KB).

47 *Reid*, above note 44 at 562.

it still survives in the BC statute (having been copied from the English version), it is not clear whether there are any markets or shops in British Columbia that would qualify. In *Westcoast Leasing Ltd v Westcoast Communications Ltd*,[48] radio equipment was sold in the service department located above a shop. The buyers argued unsuccessfully that it was a sale in market overt. Murray J said,

> Does the concept of market overt as it applies in the City of London also apply to a shop on Broadway in the city of Vancouver? I think not and I reach that conclusion by saying that there is no evidence before me of any custom in British Columbia which would constitute the shop in question as a market overt. Even if I am wrong in that conclusion I do not think that the upstairs portion of the shop where the equipment was sold forms part of a market overt.[49]

C. EQUITY

When dealing with competing claims to the same thing, the starting point at common law is the principle of *nemo dat quod non habet*, as discussed above. In equity, it is the defence of bona fide purchase for value without notice. The choice between the two depends on the nature of the property rights in competition. If the older of the two rights is legal, the holder of that right will rely on *nemo dat*, whereas the holder of the newer right hopes to find an exception. If the older right is equitable, *nemo dat* is unlikely to be helpful, as explained below. The question is whether the holder of the newer right is entitled to the defence of bona fide purchase for value without notice. The common law and equitable priority rules are similar because the exceptions to *nemo dat* also require a purchase in good faith without notice. However, they operate on different principles.

An example may help. If a trustee sells the trust assets in breach of trust, the beneficiary may seek to recover them from the purchaser. *Nemo dat* will not help them. The trustee had legal title to the trust assets and the power to sell them even when acting in breach of trust. The purchaser acquired what the trustee had to give, which was legal ownership. A court of equity will not take their legal ownership away because it must recognize the legal title conferred on the purchaser by the common law. The question is whether the purchaser will be allowed to use their legal ownership for their own benefit or will be required by

---

48   *Westcoast*, above note 32.
49   *Ibid* at para 23.

the rules of equity to hold it in trust for the beneficiary. That depends on whether the purchaser is entitled to the equitable defence of bona fide purchase.

This same principle applies to all equitable property rights, including equitable mortgages and restrictive covenants. Those rights are enforced by a court of equity, which will not enforce them against a bona fide purchaser. Back when the courts were separate and equity was enforced by the Court of Chancery, this was a question of jurisdiction. In *Pilcher v Rawlins*,[50] a trustee mortgaged the trust property in breach of trust and absconded with the proceeds. The beneficiaries claimed that their equitable interests under the trust had priority over the legal mortgage. That was rejected. James LJ said,

> I propose simply to apply myself to the case of a purchaser for valuable consideration, without notice, obtaining, upon the occasion of his purchase, and by means of his purchase deed, some legal estate, some legal right, some legal advantage; and, according to my view of the established law of this Court, such a purchaser's plea of a purchase for valuable consideration without notice is an absolute, unqualified, unanswerable defence, and an unanswerable plea to the jurisdiction of this Court. Such a purchaser, when he has once put in that plea, may be interrogated and tested to any extent as to the valuable consideration which he has given in order to shew the *bona fides* or *mala fides* of his purchase, and also the presence or the absence of notice; but when once he has gone through that ordeal, and has satisfied the terms of the plea of purchase for valuable consideration without notice, then, according to my judgment, this Court has no jurisdiction whatever to do anything more than to let him depart in possession of that legal estate, that legal right, that legal advantage which he has obtained, whatever it may be.[51]

1) Bona Fide Purchase

The defence of bona fide purchase for value without notice has four elements. *Bona fide* means good faith, which seems to be satisfied if the purchaser did not have notice of the prior equitable interest. Lord Wilberforce explained it as follows in *Midland Bank Trust Co Ltd v Green*:

> My Lords, the character in the law known as the *bona fide* (good faith) purchaser for value without notice was the creation of equity. In order to affect a purchaser for value of a legal estate with some equity or

---

50   (1872) LR 7 Ch App 259 (CA).
51   *Ibid* at 268–69.

equitable interest, equity fastened upon his conscience and the composite expression was used to epitomise the circumstances in which equity would or rather would not do so. I think that it would generally be true to say that the words "in good faith" related to the existence of notice. Equity, in other words, required not only absence of notice, but genuine and honest absence of notice.[52]

Purchase for value may seem redundant, but the word *purchase* once had a special meaning. Land could be either inherited or purchased. As Sir John Baker said, it was "a principle of the common law that the heir took 'by descent' and not 'by purchase,' which meant that he took his land by right of succession and not by virtue of a direct grant to himself."[53] Anyone who received a direct grant of land took it by purchase even if it was a gift. We no longer have inheritance, but we still use the term *purchase* in this context to mean the transfer of legal title. A person who acquires only an *equitable* interest cannot use the defence even if they acquired it in good faith, for value, and without notice.

The receipt of legal title is necessary but not sufficient. The purchaser must also give value for it and not have notice of the prior equitable interest. There is no reason to allow a donee to use the defence. They may be bitterly disappointed that their gift is not as good as they had hoped or is possibly even worthless to them, but they will not be left worse off than if the gift had never been made. If someone did acquire legal title for value, they cannot use the defence if they knew or should have known about the prior equitable interest.

The consideration needed to make a binding contract might not be enough to support the defence of bona fide purchase for value. A promise to pay money is good consideration for a contract, but for the defence of bona fide purchase, the money must be paid before notice is received.[54] Also, the defence requires more than nominal consideration.[55] Value does not have to be full market value. Someone can be a bona fide purchaser for value even if they get an amazing bargain. In *Manning*[56] (discussed above), a woman purchased rare Swedish coins worth $58,000 at a garage sale for $5. It was an arm's-length transaction in which she paid the asking price. It did not matter because the coins had been stolen, and there was no exception to *nemo dat* that worked

---

52 [1981] AC 513 at 528 (HL).

53 John Baker, *An Introduction to English Legal History*, 5th ed (Oxford: Oxford University Press, 2019) at 282.

54 *Thomas v Thomas*, [1939] 4 DLR 202 (NBCA); *Currie v McNair* (1991), 81 DLR (4th) 744, 117 NBR (2d) 43 (CA).

55 *Glenelg Homestead Ltd v Wile* (2005), 248 DLR (4th) 427, 230 NSR (2d) 289 (CA).

56 *Manning*, above note 36.

in her favour. If, instead, the coins had been sold by a trustee acting in breach of trust, she probably would have been entitled to the defence of bona fide purchase. The low sale price might have raised questions about her good faith and lack of notice, but it was a purchase for value.

Most of the cases in this area concern the question of notice.[57] There are three types of notice: *actual*, *constructive*, and *imputed*. A person has *actual notice* of an equitable interest if they were informed of it or its possible existence at some point. Actual notice is different from knowledge. Someone can have actual notice of something without knowing whether it really does exist. A "beware of the dog" sign is actual notice that there may be a dog in the yard, not proof that there is one. Also, a person can know something at one point and forget it. They no longer have knowledge but still have actual notice.[58]

A person has *constructive notice* of something when they are treated as if they received actual notice even though they never did. This artificially restricts the defence of bona fide purchase but still leaves the absence-of-notice requirement unchanged (at least formally). Someone will have constructive notice of an equitable interest if a reasonable person in their shoes would have discovered its possible existence. What a reasonable person does depends on the circumstances. No one bothers to investigate the title to goods on offer at a garage sale, but they would be foolish to buy an airplane, a business, or a home without making some inquiries.

In *Joseph v Lyons*,[59] a jeweller in Worcester executed a bill of sale of his stock-in-trade to the plaintiff to secure a debt. He then pledged some of his jewellery to the defendant, who was a pawnbroker. This was a competition between two security interests: the plaintiff's older equitable charge and the defendant's newer legal pledge (see Chapter 6). The plaintiff argued that his charge had priority because the defendant had constructive notice of the registered bill of sale. That was rejected by the Court of Appeal. Cotton LJ said,

> Then the defendant had the legal title: he had no notice of the equitable title existing in the plaintiff: at least nothing has been proved shewing that he had notice: here the defendant was a pawnbroker, and he was not bound to search the register of bills of sale: he was not bound to inquire as to goods pledged with him in the course of his business. Of course, if he had been informed of the existence of

---

57   See, for example, *Hawker v Hawker* (1969), 3 DLR (3d) 735 (Sask QB).

58   *MCP Pension Trustees Ltd v Aon Pension Trustees Ltd*, [2011] 3 WLR 455 at 461–62 (CA); see also *Re Montagu's Settlement Trusts*, [1987] 1 Ch 264 at 284 (Ch D).

59   (1884) 15 QBD 280 (CA).

the bill of sale, he would have been bound to search the register in order to inform himself of its contents; but I think that the doctrine as to constructive notice has gone too far, and I shall not extend it.[60]

Resolving disputes on the basis of constructive notice does have advantages. What a reasonable person would have discovered is an objective test, whereas a determination of what a party actually discovered is a more difficult inquiry into their state of mind at the relevant time. A finding that someone had constructive notice does not carry a suggestion of impropriety, which might be inferred from a finding of actual notice. However, constructive notice does mean that honest people can pay money in good faith and be surprised by equitable interests that they would have discovered if they had taken more care.

The failure to make inquiries is not negligence or any other breach of duty. Purchasers do not owe duties to themselves. They are free to take risks and trust the vendor's promises. Of course, if they are acting on behalf of someone else (e.g., as a solicitor, an agent, a company officer, or a trustee), they may be in breach of their duty of care to that person. But that is a different story.

Most cases of constructive notice involve real estate transactions. Although the general principles apply to other assets, the details concerning land are not that important today because land registration systems are designed to alleviate the problems associated with constructive notice (as discussed below).

A person has constructive notice of things that a competent solicitor would have discovered by doing the normal searches and making the usual inquiries on behalf of their client. Someone acquiring an interest in land has constructive notice of the rights of any tenant in possession of the land. They do not have constructive notice of the landlord's rights, but if they know that the tenant is paying rent to someone other than the person they are dealing with, they have actual notice that someone else might have an interest in the land.[61] If someone other than the vendor is in occupation, a prudent purchaser would make inquiries. The same goes for someone proposing to take a mortgage or lease.

When an agent acquires notice while engaged in a transaction on behalf of their principal, the agent's notice is *imputed* to their principal. In other words, the principal is treated as having the same notice as their agent even if the agent does not communicate that information to the principal. Typically, these are cases in which a solicitor is working

---

60   *Ibid* at 286.
61   *Hunt v Luck*, [1902] 1 Ch 428 (CA); *MacArthur v Hastings* (1905), 15 Man R 500 (QB); *Thistlethwaite v Sharp* (1912), 7 DLR 801, 1 WWR 774 (Sask DC).

on behalf of a client or an officer or a director is working on behalf of their company. The agent may have actual or constructive notice. Either will be imputed.

There are two major qualifications. First, the notice must come to the agent as part of the transaction in which they are acting on behalf of the principal. For example, a solicitor may work on a large number of different transactions during their career. Notice received in one transaction on behalf of a client will not be imputed to a different client in a different transaction. Second, if the agent is acting fraudulently against their principal's interests, their notice will not be imputed to their principal. As Perdue J said in *MacArthur v Hastings*,

> In ordinary transactions the knowledge of the solicitor in respect of a matter passing through his hands is the imputed knowledge of his client. If the solicitor knows a material fact respecting a title, such as a prior incumbrance, it is assumed that he will communicate this fact to the client, and consequently the client is fixed with notice. Where, however, the circumstances of the case show that the solicitor in the very transaction intended a fraud which would require the suppression of the knowledge of the material fact from the person on whom he was committing the fraud, then notice is not to be imputed to such person.[62]

2) First in Time

The defence of bona fide purchase is available only to people who acquire legal title. The priority rule that applies to two competing equitable interests is *qui prior est tempore potior est jure*, which means that the person who is first in time is preferred in law. An older equitable interest may be postponed to a newer equitable interest if (1) the newer interest was acquired in good faith, for value, and without notice of the older interest and (2) the holder of the older interest bears some responsibility for the problem. This resembles the exception to *nemo dat* based on estoppel because both depend on the holder of the newer right being misled by the holder of the older right. In contrast, the defence of bona fide purchase can destroy the equitable interest of someone who is wholly blameless.

In *Rice v Rice*,[63] the plaintiffs sold their leasehold estate to Michael Rice. The purchase price was not paid in full, but the deed contained

---

62 *MacArthur v Hastings*, above note 61 at 506 (QB). See also *Re Monserat Investments Ltd* (1978), 87 DLR (3d) 593, 20 OR (2d) 181 (CA).

63 (1854) 2 Drew 73, 61 ER 646 [cited to Drew].

the usual acknowledgement by the vendors that they had received payment of the purchase price. Rice then granted an equitable mortgage to the defendant created by giving them possession of the title deeds. This meant that Rice's legal estate was subject to two equitable security interests: the plaintiffs' older vendors' lien and the defendant's newer equitable mortgage. Kindersley VC held that the lien was postponed to the mortgage:

> The vendors, when they sold the estate, chose to leave part of the purchase-money unpaid, and yet executed and delivered to the purchaser a conveyance by which they declared in the most solemn and deliberate manner, both in the body and by a receipt indorsed, that the whole purchase-money had been duly paid. They might still have required that the title-deeds should remain in their custody, with a memorandum by way of equitable mortgage as a security for the unpaid purchase-money, and, if they had done so, they would have been secure against any subsequent equitable incumbrance; but that they did not choose to do, and the deeds were delivered to the purchaser. Thus they voluntarily armed the purchaser with the estate as the absolute legal and equitable owner, free from every shadow of incumbrance or adverse equity.[64]

Kindersley VC also said that "in a contest between persons having only equitable interests, priority of time is the ground of preference last resorted to," which should be used only if "their equities are in all other respects equal."[65] That view was rejected by the House of Lords in *Shropshire Union Railways and Canal Co v The Queen*[66] and by the Privy Council in *Abigail v Lapin*, where Lord Wright said,

> The opinion of the Vice-Chancellor no doubt has not been approved in so far as he says that priority in time is only taken as the test where the equities are otherwise equal: it is now clearly established that *prima facie* priority in time will decide the matter unless, as laid down by Lord Cairns L.C. in *Shropshire Union Rys. and Canal Co. v. The Queen*, that which is relied on to take away the pre-existing equitable title can be shown to be something tangible and distinct having grave and strong effect to accomplish the purpose.[67]

---

64 *Ibid* at 83–84.
65 *Ibid* at 78.
66 (1875) LR 7 HL 496.
67 [1934] AC 491 at 504 (PC).

3) Mere Equities

The term *mere equity* is confusing. The rights classified as mere equities include both rights *in personam* and rights *in rem*. If a mere equity is a personal right, then it is enforceable only against specific persons and will not affect anyone else, even if they have knowledge of it.[68] If it is property, then it can be enforced against others. However, mere equities are less durable than other equitable property rights.

An equitable right to rescind a contract or other transaction is a mere equity.[69] Rights to rescind are often only personal. If exercised, the parties will be released from contractual obligations and give up personal rights. However, the rescission of a transaction can lead to the recovery of assets previously transferred to the other party. If someone has the power to recover assets by rescinding a transaction, they have an equitable interest in those assets. This is consistent with equity's treatment of powers to acquire ownership of assets in other contexts, such as the power of a donee to complete a gift without the donor's help or the power to acquire land through specific performance of a contract of sale (discussed in the previous chapter).

A power to acquire assets through rescission is similar to an option to purchase. The option holder has a choice whether or not to exercise the option. If its exercise will give rise to a specifically enforceable contract of sale, then the option is an equitable property right even before it is exercised. As Martland J said in *Canadian Long Island Petroleums Ltd v Irving Industries Ltd*, "forthwith upon the granting of the option, the optionee upon the occurrence of certain events solely within his control can compel a conveyance of the property to him."[70] A person with the right to recover assets through rescission is in the same position, but instead of compelling someone to sell their land, they are making them give it back. Lord Millett said that "the right to reconveyance is a form of specific performance (or 'specific unperformance')."[71]

The right to rectify a transaction is also a mere equity. If it leads to the recovery of assets, then it is also an equitable interest in those assets. In *Taitapu Gold Estates Ltd v Prouse*,[72] the vendors sold land excluding the mineral rights, which they intended to keep. By mistake, they failed to make an exception for mineral rights in the transfer, so the purchasers acquired legal title to those rights when the transfer was registered.

---

68   *National Provincial Bank Ltd v Ainsworth*, [1965] AC 1175 (HL).

69   *Phillips v Phillips* (1862), 4 De GF & J 208, 45 ER 1164.

70   [1975] 2 SCR 715, 50 DLR (3d) 265 at 277.

71   PJ Millett, "Restitution and Constructive Trusts" (1998) 114 *Law Q Rev* 399 at 416.

72   [1916] NZLR 825 (HC).

The vendors had a right to rectify the transfer to correct the mistake; therefore, the purchasers held the mineral rights in trust for them.

A similar problem occurred in *Blacklocks v JB Developments (Godalming) Ltd.*[73] The vendors sold their farm, intending to keep the portion with their house for themselves. By mistake, the plan they attached to the transfer did not exclude that portion. That portion was held in trust for them by the purchasers, and that trust was enforceable against a subsequent purchaser because the surviving vendor continued to occupy the house.

A mere equity, like all equitable property rights, is subject to the defence of bona fide purchase. However, a mere equity can also be defeated by someone who acquires a newer *equitable* interest for value without notice of the mere equity.[74] The usual first-in-time rule does not apply. In this way, an equitable right to recover assets through rescission or rectification is similar to the common law right to avoid a sale of goods (discussed above). The resale of the goods to a buyer in good faith and without notice will destroy the previous owner's legal right to rescind their sale.

The right to recover assets through rescission at common law or in equity or through rectification in equity is less durable than other legal and equitable property rights. This is probably because it is hard to discover. Someone dealing with the legal owner of assets will probably have no way to find out whether the owner's title is voidable due to a mistake in a previous transaction. If the right to avoid that transaction was protected by the normal rules of *nemo dat* or first in time, it could easily and unfairly take priority over the rights of an honest buyer, who could do nothing to avoid the problem.

D. LAND REGISTRATION

As discussed in chapters 6 and 8, there are two main types of land registration systems in Canada: *deed registration* and *title registration*. Title registration exists in every province and territory except Prince Edward Island and Newfoundland and Labrador, which have deed registration systems. Manitoba, Ontario, New Brunswick, and Nova Scotia have both systems, with a process for changing from deed to title registration.

Both systems make significant changes to the common law and equitable priority rules discussed above. They both provide protection

---

73   [1982] Ch 183 (Ch D).
74   *Latec Investments Ltd v Hotel Terrigal Pty Ltd*, [1965] HCA 17, 113 CLR 265.

to someone who registers their interest in land by giving them priority over older unregistered interests and newer interests. Land title registration goes further than deed registration. The changes to the priority rules in a land title system are so extensive that they almost completely replace the old rules.

1) Deed Registration

Despite the name, a deed registration system is not limited to the registration of deeds but provides for the registration of almost any document that creates or transfers an interest in land.[75] The registration of a document is not normally the event that creates or transfers the interest. The document does the work, and registration protects its priority.

One of the limitations of a deed registration system is that registration of a document does not guarantee that it is valid, nor does it guarantee that the grantor had any rights to give. In other words, the principle of *nemo dat* still applies in part. A purchaser will need to investigate the validity of their vendor's chain of title if they want to be satisfied that they will acquire the expected interest.

The person who registers a document gains several advantages: they are protected from (1) the effects of constructive notice of older interests, (2) loss of priority to newer interests, and (3) some of the problems associated with *nemo dat*. The main work is done by a section in every *Registry Act*, such as this one in Ontario:

> After the grant from the Crown of land, ... every instrument affecting the land or any part thereof shall be adjudged fraudulent and void against any subsequent purchaser or mortgagee for valuable consideration without actual notice, unless the instrument is registered before the registration of the instrument under which the subsequent purchaser or mortgagee claims.[76]

This section does not make an unregistered document void but means that it can be treated as non-existent by anyone who registers a document that creates a competing property interest so long as the

---

75   *Registry Act*, CCSM, c R50, s 1; *Registry Act*, RSO 1990, c R.20, s 1; *Registry Act*, RSNB 1973, c R-6, s 1; *Registry Act*, RSNS 1989, c 392, s 2; *Registry Act*, RSPEI 1988, c R-10, s 1; *Registration of Deeds Act, 2009*, SNL 2009, c R-10.01, s 2.

76   *Registry Act*, RSO 1990, c R.20, s 70; see also *Registry Act*, CCSM, c R50, s 56; *Registry Act*, RSNB 1973, c R-6, s 19; *Registry Act*, RSNS 1989, c 392, s 18; *Registry Act*, RSPEI 1988, c R-10, s 43; *Registration of Deeds Act, 2009*, SNL 2009, c R-10.01, s 37.

registrant acquired their interest for value and without actual notice of the interest created by the unregistered document. This is equivalent to the defence of bona fide purchase, with two major differences. First, the registrant is not affected by constructive notice of unregistered interests. Second, registration can also protect equitable interests.

a) Notice

The statutes in Manitoba and Ontario expressly state that priority over an older, unregistered interest is available only to a registrant "without actual notice" of it.[77] The statutes in New Brunswick and Newfoundland and Labrador do not make priority conditional upon the absence of notice, but the courts insist upon it. Registration will not defeat an unregistered interest if the registrant had actual notice of it. Lord Cairns LC said this about the Irish deed registration statute:

> My Lords, any person reading over that Act of Parliament would perhaps in the first instance conclude, as has often been said, that it was an Act absolutely decisive of priority under all circumstances, and enacting that under every circumstance that could be supposed, the deed first registered was to take precedence of a deed which, although it might be executed before, was not registered till afterwards. But ... notwithstanding the apparent stringency of the words contained in this Act of Parliament, still if a person in Ireland registers a deed, and if at the time he registers the deed either he himself, or an agent, whose knowledge is the knowledge of his principal, has notice of an earlier deed, which, though executed, is not registered, the registration which he actually effects will not give him priority over that earlier deed.... [I]nasmuch as the object of the statute is to take care that, by the fact of deeds being placed upon a register, those who come to register a subsequent deed shall be informed of the earlier title, the end and object of the statute is accomplished if the person coming to register a deed has ... notice of a deed affecting the property executed before his own.[78]

This has been followed in Canada.[79] A registered interest will not have priority over an older, unregistered interest if the registrant had actual notice of it. Constructive notice will not do. As Strong J said in *Ross v Hunter*, "It is well settled that nothing short of actual notice, such notice as makes it a fraud on the part of a purchaser to insist on the

---

77 *Registry Act*, CCSM, c R50, s 56; *Registry Act*, RSO 1990, c R.20, s 70.

78 *Agra Bank Ltd v Barry* (1874), LR 7 HL 135 at 147–48.

79 *Ross v Hunter* (1882), 7 SCR 289 [*Ross*]; *Rose v Peterkin* (1885), 13 SCR 677; *Fortis Trust Corp v Deloitte & Touche Inc* (1997), 159 Nfld & PEIR 91, 492 APR 91 (NLCA).

registry laws, is sufficient to disentitle a party to insist in equity on a legal priority acquired under the statute."[80]

Ross v Hunter was an appeal to the Supreme Court of Canada from Nova Scotia in 1882, when the *Registry Act* contained no express exception for notice. The current version now states,

> Every instrument shall, as against any person claiming for valuable consideration *and without notice* under any subsequent instrument affecting the title to the same land, be ineffective unless the instrument is registered in the manner provided by this Act before the registering of such subsequent instrument.[81]

The express exception in Nova Scotia is not limited to actual notice, but courts still hold that the registrant is not affected by constructive notice. As Jones J said in *O'Toole v Walters*, "[A]ctual notice of the prior instrument is required."[82] This means that the law is the same in Nova Scotia (where there is an express exception for notice), in Manitoba and Ontario (where the exception is limited to actual notice), and in New Brunswick and Newfoundland and Labrador (where there is no express exception). Only Prince Edward Island is different, where the *Registry Act* protects the registrant from notice of any kind:

> No constructive or other notice of any unregistered deed or mortgage shall defeat, impeach, or affect, or be construed to affect, any deed or mortgage relating to all or any part of the same lands, tenements or hereditaments, which has been registered under this Act, but every such unregistered deed or mortgage shall be deemed to be fraudulent and void against subsequent purchasers or incumbrancers for valuable consideration, whose deeds or mortgages are previously registered, whether the purchasers or incumbrancers had notice thereof or not.[83]

This means that a registrant in Prince Edward Island will not be bound by prior unregistered interests even if they have actual notice of them.[84] Nothing will protect a registrant if they are engaged in actual fraud (e.g., knowingly participating in a breach of trust), but actual notice by itself is not fraud.

---

80   *Ross*, above note 79 at 321. See also *New Brunswick Ry Co v Kelly* (1896), 26 SCR 341; *Re McKinley and McCullough* (1919), 51 DLR 659, 46 OLR 535 (CA); *Canadian Imperial Bank of Commerce v Rockway Holdings Ltd* (1996), 29 OR (3d) 350 (SC); *Walshe v Citizens Bank of Canada* (2003), 63 OR (3d) 702 (SC).

81   *Registry Act*, RSNS 1989, c 392, s 18 [emphasis added].

82   (1979) 96 DLR (3d) 202 at 206 (NSSC) [*O'Toole*]. See also *Winter v Keating* (1978), 35 APR 633, 24 NSR (2d) 633 (CA).

83   RSPEI 1988, c R-10, s 43.

84   See *Peddie v Eagles and Lai* (2012), 325 Nfld & PEIR 177, 1009 APR 177 (PEI SC).

b) *Nemo Dat*

Registration can operate as an exception to *nemo dat*, as demonstrated by *O'Toole v Walters*.[85] A father gave a portion of his land to his son by deed in 1961. The father then sold a portion of his land in 1966 to Mr DePierro, who registered his deed in January 1969. Mr O'Toole purchased that land in August and registered his deed in September. The son registered his deed three days later. Unfortunately, the land that O'Toole purchased from DePierro included most of the land that the son had acquired in 1961, including his house.

When the father sold the land to DePierro in 1966, he no longer owned the part he had given to his son in 1961. DePierro could not buy more than the father had to sell (*nemo dat*), so the son still owned his land, even though most of it was included in the plan attached to DePierro's deed. The case does not say whether DePierro had actual notice of the son's interest. If he did, then nothing changed when he registered his deed in 1969. If not, then he acquired legal title to the son's land through registration. In any event, O'Toole had only constructive notice of the son's interest, so he obtained legal title to the son's land when he registered his deed, even if DePierro did not already own it.

Registration operated as an exception to *nemo dat*. It caused the purchaser to acquire land that the vendor did not own and caused the son to lose his legal fee simple estate without his consent. This may seem harsh or unfair, but it is necessary if the deed registration system is to function properly. People can search the registry to see if there are any competing interests in the land they wish to acquire and need not worry about being adversely affected by unregistered interests. Anyone with an interest in land can protect it by registration. If they fail to do so, they risk losing it.

If documents are registered in the same order in which they are executed, then registration will not change the normal priority of the interests created by those documents. Older interests (including equitable interests) will prevail over newer interests (which are acquired with notice of the older registered interests). However, if documents are registered in reverse order, then registration can change the normal priority, as it did in *O'Toole v Walters*. Perhaps the easiest way to understand this effect is to treat the document that is registered first as if it was executed first if the registrant acquired their interest for value and without actual notice of the older unregistered interest. Treat the document that is registered second as if it was executed second with notice of the registered interest. Then apply the normal rules.

---

85 *O'Toole*, above note 82. See also *Jemco Holdings Ltd v Medlee Ltd* (1975), 78 DLR (3d) 604, 14 NSR (2d) 662 (NSCA).

c) Short Leases

In Manitoba and New Brunswick, leases up to three years do not need to be registered if the tenant is in actual occupation.[86] The exemption in Ontario applies to leases up to seven years.[87] It is three years in Nova Scotia, but occupation is not a requirement.[88]

2) Land Title Registration

Land title registration exists in every province and territory except Prince Edward Island and Newfoundland and Labrador. There are wide variations among the different title registration systems in Canada, but they share two common principles. The first is that legal rights are transferred or created by registration of a document and not by the document itself.[89] This is designed to alleviate the problems associated with *nemo dat* because the rights created by registration do not depend on a chain of title. The registrant obtains the legal rights that the registered document purports to convey whether the grantor held them or not. Second, the registrant is not affected by notice of unregistered interests.[90] This obviates the need to search for competing interests and alleviates the problems associated with the defence of bona fide purchase for value without notice. Some systems achieve these objectives better than others.

When someone acquires a registered interest in land for value and without fraud, they obtain what is often called *indefeasibility of title*. This is shorthand for the protection provided by the priority rules of the registration system. As Lord Wilberforce said in *Frazer v Walker*, "[It] is a convenient description of the immunity from attack by adverse claim to the land."[91] The registrant's title is subject to older registered interests (with priority between registered interests based on order of registration) but free from all unregistered interests except those that

---

86   *Registry Act*, CCSM, c R50, s 2; *Registry Act*, RSNB 1973, c R-6, s 19(3).

87   *Registry Act*, RSO 1990, c R.20, s 70(2).

88   *Registry Act*, RSNS 1989, c 392, ss 2(e), 25.

89   *Land Title Act*, RSBC 1996, c 250, ss 20, 22; *Land Titles Act*, RSA 2000, c L-4, ss 53, 54; *Land Titles Act, 2000*, SS 2000, c L-5.1, ss 25, 26; *Real Property Act*, CCSM, c R30, s 66; *Land Titles Act*, RSO 1990, c L.5, ss 78, 86; *Land Titles Act*, SNB 1981, c L-1.1, s 15; *Land Registration Act*, SNS 2001, c 6, ss 45, 49; *Land Titles Act, 2015*, SY 2015, c 10, ss 38, 39; *Land Titles Act*, RSNWT 1988, c 8, ss 64, 65, 70.

90   *Land Title Act*, RSBC 1996, c 250, s 29; *Land Titles Act*, RSA 2000, c L-4, s 203; *Land Titles Act, 2000*, SS 2000, c L-5.1, s 23; *Real Property Act*, CCSM, c R30, s 80; *Land Titles Act*, RSO 1990, c L.5, s 72; *Land Titles Act*, SNB 1981, c L-1.1, s 61; *Land Registration Act*, SNS 2001, c 6, s 4; *Land Titles Act, 2015*, SY 2015, c 10, s 40; *Land Titles Act*, RSNWT 1988, c 8, s 75.

91   [1967] 1 AC 569 at 580, [1967] NZLR 1069.

are listed as exceptions in the statute and those that are protected by a *caveat* or *caution*.

A person with an unregistered interest in land can protect it by lodging a caveat or caution that prevents or restricts further dealing with the land.[92] Any subsequent registrations will be subject to the caveator's claim. Unlike registration, a caveat or caution does not create an interest in land. It merely protects whatever interest the caveator actually has, which might be nothing.

The Saskatchewan system no longer uses caveats but allows for the registration of *interests*, which are legal or equitable interests in land that are less than *ownership* (which is a fee simple estate).[93] Like a caveat, registration of an interest in Saskatchewan does not create it or guarantee that it exists but merely protects it if it does.[94] Nova Scotia is similar. Fee simple estates, life estates, and remainders can be *registered*, whereas other interests in land are *recorded*.[95]

Every system makes an exception for leases of up to three years and at least some easements.[96] A registrant will take subject to those leases and easements even though they are unregistered and the registrant may be unaware of their existence. The exception for short leases continues a tradition that goes back to the *Statute of Frauds 1677*[97] (as discussed in Chapter 8). The costs of registration, both to tenants and the registration system, outweigh the potential costs to people who acquire competing interests in the land.

The exception for easements can also be justified in terms of relative cost. In Alberta, Manitoba, Ontario, and Nova Scotia, an exception is made for all easements.[98] In the other provinces and territories, the exception is limited to "any public highway or right of way or other

---

92 *Land Title Act*, RSBC 1996, c 250, ss 31, 282; *Land Titles Act*, RSA 2000, c L-4, ss 130, 135; *Real Property Act*, CCSM, c R30, ss 148, 152; *Land Titles Act*, RSO 1990, c L.5, ss 128, 129; *Land Titles Act*, SNB 1981, c L-1.1, ss 30, 31; *Land Titles Act, 2015*, SY 2015, c 10, ss 136, 139; *Land Titles Act*, RSNWT 1988, c 8, ss 59.3, 143.

93 *Land Titles Act, 2000*, SS 2000, c L-5.1, s 12(7).

94 *Ibid*, s 54.

95 *Land Registration Act*, SNS 2001, c 6, ss 17, 47, 49, 55.

96 *Land Title Act*, RSBC 1996, c 250, s 23; *Land Titles Act*, RSA 2000, c L-4, s 61; *Land Titles Act, 2000*, SS 2000, c L-5.1, s 18; *Real Property Act*, CCSM, c R30, s 58; *Land Titles Act*, RSO 1990, c L.5, s 44; *Land Titles Act*, SNB 1981, c L-1.1, s 17; *Land Registration Act*, SNS 2001, c 6, s 73; *Land Titles Act, 2015*, SY 2015, c 10, s 59; *Land Titles Act*, RSNWT 1988, c 8, s 69.

97 29 Car 2, c 3.

98 *Land Titles Act*, RSA 2000, c L-4, s 61(1)(f); *Real Property Act*, CCSM, c R30, s 58(1)(c); *Land Titles Act*, RSO 1990, c L.5, s 44(1)(2); *Land Registration Act*, SNS 2001, c 6, s 73(1)(e).

public easement."[99] Highways and utility rights of way may require long corridors of easements over a large number of servient tenements. The loss of an easement over one of those tenements could have massive costs that far outweigh the cost to the owner of that tenement to allow the easement to continue. Even for private easements, the benefit to the dominant tenement may be much greater than the cost imposed on the servient tenement. For example, a right of way may be a minimal intrusion over the servient tenement but provide the only convenient route from the dominant tenement to a public road or beach.

a) Fraud

In every land title registration system, the benefits of indefeasibility are not available to someone who obtains a registered interest by their own fraud. Most statutes expressly state that it is not fraud to obtain registration with actual knowledge that an unregistered exists.[100] The exceptions are British Columbia, Ontario, and Nova Scotia (discussed below).

In *Union Bank of Canada v Phillips*,[101] Frank Phillips made an agreement to purchase land by instalments, which gave him an equitable interest in the land. He assigned that agreement as security for a loan and thus created an equitable mortgage. The lender lodged a caveat to protect their equitable interest in the land. Phillips completed the purchase and became the registered owner of the legal fee simple estate, subject to the lender's caveat. He then granted a registered legal mortgage to the Union Bank of Canada, which served notice on the other lender to prove the interest they claimed to have. The other lender failed to take action, and their caveat lapsed. They then claimed that their older equitable mortgage had priority over the bank's newer legal mortgage because the bank had actual notice of it. This was rejected by the Supreme Court of Canada.

Davies CJ quoted the provisions of Saskatchewan's *Land Titles Act* (then in section 194) that a purchaser for value is not "affected by any notice direct, implied or constructive, of any trust or unregistered interest in the land, any rule of law or equity to the contrary notwithstanding" and that "knowledge on the part of any such person that any trust

---

99   *Land Titles Act, 2000*, SS 2000, c L-5.1, s 18(1)(c); *Land Titles Act, 2015*, SY 2015, c 10, s 59(d); *Land Titles Act*, RSNWT 1988, c 8, s 69(c). See also *Land Title Act*, RSBC 1996, c 250, s 23(1)(e); *Land Titles Act*, SNB 1981, c L-1.1, s 17(4)(f) and (g).

100 *Land Titles Act*, RSA 2000, c L-4, s 203; *Land Titles Act, 2000*, SS 2000, c L-5.1, s 23; *Real Property Act*, CCSM, c R30, s 80; *Land Titles Act*, SNB 1981, c L-1.1, s 61; *Land Titles Act, 2015*, SY 2015, c 10, s 40; *Land Titles Act*, RSNWT 1988, c 8, s 75.

101 (1919) 58 SCR 385, 46 DLR 41 [cited to SCR].

or unregistered interest is in existence shall not of itself be imputed as fraud."[102] He went on to say,

> The authorities relied upon in the argument at bar were to the effect that a purchaser or mortgagee for value of an equitable interest in lands with actual or constructive notice of other equitable unregistered interests prior to that which he acquired took subject to those interests. But it seems to me that the object and purpose of this section, apart from cases of fraud, was to lay down a different rule which should govern in cases coming within its ambit, and, unless we are prepared to ignore the section altogether or fritter away its language and meaning, we must hold that, except in cases of fraud, these equitable rules established by the authorities, however just and equitable they may seem to be under ordinary circumstances, are not applicable to cases coming within section 194 of *The Land Titles Act*.[103]

In *Hackworth v Baker*,[104] Elizabeth Hackworth had an equitable interest in her mother's land because she held an unregistered transfer from her mother. Percy Baker wanted to buy the land and was told that it belonged to Hackworth and was not for sale. He later discovered that the mother was the registered owner, so he bought the land from her and became the registered owner. Hackworth sued on the basis that Baker had acquired title by fraud, but that was rejected by the Saskatchewan Court of Appeal. It was argued (by future prime minister John Diefenbaker KC) that "he who takes and registers an instrument after notice of another person's equity or unregistered interest is protected only if that other person is not 'hurt' by the transaction."[105] Turgeon JA said,

> [T]he mere fact that the holder of an unregistered interest is "hurt" or "deprived of his property" by the act of a person who, with notice, or knowledge, of that interest, acquires and registers an adverse interest, does not affect the position of that person. That person has the statute in his favour. But he must abstain from fraud. . . .
>
> Of course, the effect of the registration of Baker's transfer was to destroy whatever right in the land the plaintiff had . . . and a man must be considered as having intended the effect of his act. But this must happen every time a person is given by statute, and takes, an advantage over another person.[106]

---

102 *Ibid* at 387.
103 *Ibid.*
104 [1936] 1 WWR 321 (Sask CA).
105 *Ibid* at para 46, Turgeon JA.
106 *Ibid* at paras 50 and 64.

In *Loke Yew v Port Swettenham Rubber Co Ltd*,[107] a vendor sold 322 acres of land in Selangor after receiving an undertaking from the purchaser that they would make their own arrangements to purchase the interest of Loke Yew, who was the unregistered owner of fifty-eight of those acres. The purchase price was reduced accordingly. After the purchaser became the registered owner, they sued Loke Yew to evict him from the land. The Privy Council advised that the purchaser was guilty of actual fraud because they obtained the land by giving a false undertaking to the vendor.

The *Land Registration Act* in Nova Scotia defines fraud as follows:

> A person obtains an interest through fraud if that person, at the time of the transaction, (a) had actual knowledge of an interest that was not registered or recorded; (b) had actual knowledge that the transaction was not authorized by the owner of the interest that was not registered or recorded; and (c) knew or ought to have known that the transaction would prejudice the interest that was not registered or recorded.[108]

This means that the fraud exception in Nova Scotia is similar to the exception for persons with actual notice that operates in most deed registration systems.[109]

The *Land Title Act* in British Columbia states,

> Except in the case of fraud in which he or she has participated, a person contracting or dealing with or taking or proposing to take from a registered owner . . . a transfer of land . . . is not, despite a rule of law or equity to the contrary, affected by a notice, express, implied, or constructive, of an unregistered interest affecting the land.[110]

Without the usual statement that knowledge is not fraud, there is some confusion in British Columbia over the difference between actual notice and fraud.[111] Something more than actual notice is required, but it is not clear what that is. In *Hudson's Bay Co v Kearns*,[112] a man purchased land in Vancouver for $300 in 1892, with constructive notice that it was subject to an equitable mortgage. The trial judge held that

---

107 [1913] UKPC 17, [1913] AC 491.

108 SNS 2001, c 6, s 4(4).

109 See *CitiFinancial Canada East Corp v Touchie*, 2010 NSSC 149.

110 RSBC 1996, c 250, s 29(2).

111 See British Columbia Law Institute, *Report on Section 29(2) of the Land Title Act and Notice of Unregistered Interests* (2011), online: www.bcli.org/sites/default/files/report_58_Land_Title_Act_Section_29(2)_Notice_of_Unregistered_Interests_FINAL.pdf.

112 (1896) 4 BCR 536 (SC).

his title was subject to the mortgage, but this was reversed on appeal. Davie CJ said,

> In conclusion, therefore, I am of opinion that the effect of section 35 of the *Land Registry Act* must be taken as absolutely protecting a purchaser for value against attack on the ground of notice of any character or nature whatsoever; but its otherwise absolute effect must be held to be subject to this qualification, that a man who in consequence of any knowledge constituting actual notice of a prior unregistered title or interest does any act for the direct purpose of bringing himself within the words of the section, as distinguished from any act in the ordinary course of business or in the natural course of any pending dealing or transaction, and thereby prejudicing the holder of the unregistered title, must be held to be guilty of actual fraud and to be estopped from invoking the protection of the enactment, under the inflexible rule that an Act of Parliament shall not be used as an instrument of, or in defence of, actual fraud.[113]

In *Vancouver City Savings Credit Union v Serving for Success Consulting Ltd*, Bracken J surveyed the cases since *Hudson's Bay Co v Kearns* and noted that there are two different approaches taken by BC courts:

> The law in British Columbia appears to have developed so as to create two arguably divergent lines of authority. The first line of authority . . . states that a purchaser of real property who takes title to a property with knowledge of a prior unregistered adverse interest, and who then attempts to rely on s. 29 of the *Land Title Act*, may be found to have committed equitable fraud. The second line of authority . . . requires something more than knowledge; usually conduct that constitutes some form of dishonesty. Both lines of authority seem to rely, at least in part, on *Kearns*.[114]

Bracken J decided that the second approach was correct: "In my view, before a finding of equitable fraud can be made there must be evidence of actual notice coupled with some act of dishonesty or deceit on the part of the person seeking the protection of s. 29 of the *Land Title Act*."[115]

In Ontario, a registrant is subject to older unregistered interests if they have actual notice of them even in the absence of fraud. This was the conclusion of the majority of the Supreme Court of Canada in *United Trust Co v Dominion Stores Ltd*.[116] Dominion Stores had an unregistered

---

113 *Ibid* at para 42.
114 2011 BCSC 124 at paras 62–64.
115 *Ibid* at para 70.
116 [1977] 2 SCR 915, 71 DLR (3d) 72 [cited to SCR].

lease of commercial space at 418 Spadina Avenue in Toronto. The land-lord sold their reversion to United Trust, who became the registered owner with actual notice of the lease. There was no allegation of fraud.

The Court noted that the *Land Titles Act* in Ontario "is modelled not on the Torrens system, which got its start in South Australia in 1857, but on the English *Land Transfer Act, 1875*."[117] Therefore, it differs significantly from the registration systems in the western provinces and the territories, which are based on the Torrens system. Referring to the statutes in western Canada, Spence J said, "In every case, those enact-ments contained an express provision making actual notice ineffect-ive to encumber the registered title.... In Ontario, no such provision appeared."[118] He went on to say,

> [I]n Ontario, only a few years after the enactment of *The Land Titles Act*, the courts have expressed a disinclination to imply such an extinction of the doctrine of actual notice. There is no doubt that such doctrine as to all contractual relations and particularly the law of real property has been firmly based in our law since the beginning of equity. It was the view of those courts, and it is my view, that such a cardinal principle of property law cannot be considered to have been abrogated unless the legislative enactment is in the clearest and most unequivocal of terms.[119]

Laskin CJ dissented on the basis that an exception for notice would defeat the very purpose of title registration:

> We face here another instance of a temptation to construe a statute in the light of the common law, to qualify a statute by an equitable doctrine alien to the purpose (a clear purpose in the circumstances underlying its enactment) which the statute sought to achieve. Because notice of unregistered interests was not expressly excluded as a qualifying consideration, the integrity of the land titles register is shaken by the judgment in appeal, although the scheme and lan-guage of *The Land Titles Act* are, in my opinion, adequate enough to show the irrelevancy of such notice. A system of registration of title is treated, in respect of the effect of notice of unregistered interests, as if it were a system of registration of documents, such as exists under *The Registry Act....*
>
> To import actual notice in a title registration system without its express preservation is to change the basic character of the system.

---

117   *Ibid* at 919, Laskin CJ.
118   *Ibid* at 951.
119   *Ibid* at 952.

It is impossible, in my view, to adhere to the principle of the primacy of the register and at the same time to make it yield to a doctrine of notice.[120]

b) Forgery

A significant problem created by title registration is the risk of forgery. Although forged documents can be used to deceive people, they have no legal effect in a deed registration system in which *nemo dat* continues to operate. However, in a title registration system, a forged document will have the legal effect that it purports to have if it is accepted for registration. This can cause innocent people to lose their estates through no fault of their own. A hardship is imposed on a few people so that land can be conveyed cheaply and efficiently by everyone else without the need to confirm the validity of the title being conveyed. The few who suffer are compensated by an assurance fund created as part of the system.

The effect of registration of a forged document has been debated since the nineteenth century. There are two theories: *deferred indefeasibility* and *immediate indefeasibility*. The difference is easiest to explain by example. Imagine that I am the registered owner of a fee simple estate and someone forges a transfer of that estate to you, an honest purchaser for value. You grant a mortgage to the bank to borrow the purchase price, which you pay to the forger, who is never seen again. You are the registered owner of the fee simple estate subject to a registered mortgage to the bank. What should happen?

Under *deferred indefeasibility*, your title is defeasible because your loss was caused by the forger's deception and not by the registration system. However, the bank loaned money to you in reliance on the registration system, which guaranteed that you were the owner of the fee simple estate. Having relied on the register that stated that you were the owner, the bank's mortgage is indefeasible. This means that I get my estate back subject to the bank's mortgage, but the assurance fund will compensate me for the loss caused by the registration system, and I will use that money to discharge the mortgage. Unfortunately, your only claim is against the forger, who has disappeared or is in prison and not worth suing.

Under *immediate indefeasibility*, your title is indefeasible because you obtained it for value without fraud (on your part) and the system guarantees it. I will be compensated by the assurance fund because my loss was caused by the registration system. Immediate indefeasibility

---

120 *Ibid* at 919 and 936.

has been accepted in New Zealand and Australia,[121] but the situation in Canada is not clear.

Immediate indefeasibility was accepted by the Saskatchewan Court of Appeal in *Hermanson v Martin*.[122] Valerie and Edward Schmidt were joint owners of 540 Osler Street in Regina. They divorced, and she moved to Calgary and married Allen Hermanson. Edward sold the land to Ralph Martin in 1975 for $13,500. Edward signed the transfer along with an unidentified woman posing as Valerie. He died two years later, when Valerie discovered the forgery. Her claim against Ralph Martin failed because he had purchased the land without fraud on his part.

Ontario has gone the other way with what might be called *double deferred indefeasibility*. In *Lawrence v Maple Trust Co*,[123] a forged transfer of Susan Lawrence's home in Toronto was registered in the name of Thomas Wright, who was a party to the crime. He then granted a mortgage to Maple Trust Co, who advanced the proceeds honestly and in good faith. There is no doubt that the transfer to Wright should be set aside, but the Ontario Court of Appeal held that the mortgage to Maple Trust was invalid even though they relied on the register in good faith. Gillese JA said,

> Wright never took valid title to the Property because he obtained it by fraud. He was, therefore, not a registered owner. . . . [O]nly a registered owner may give valid charges on land. Maple Trust is the intermediate owner of an interest in the Property. It had an opportunity to avoid the fraud. It did not take from a registered owner. Therefore, despite registering its charge, Maple Trust loses in a contest with the true registered owner, Ms. Lawrence. Accordingly, the charge against the Property in favour of Maple Trust should be set aside.[124]

The problem is that Wright was the registered owner when Maple Trust took their mortgage. His title was based on forgery and reversible, but how was Maple Trust supposed to know that? A search of the register would not reveal the truth, which could only be discovered by hiring a private detective. Presumably, if Wright had sold the land to an honest buyer who became the registered owner and then mortgaged it, the buyer would not get good title, but the mortgagee would. There is no discernible difference between an honest lender who relies on the registered title of a fraudster and one who relies on the registered title

---

121 *Frazer v Walker*, above note 91; *Pyramid Building Society v Scorpion Hotels Pty Ltd*, [1988] 1 VR 188 (CA).

122 [1987] 1 WWR 439, 33 DLR (4th) 12 (Sask CA).

123 (2007) 278 DLR (4th) 698, 84 OR (3d) 94 (CA).

124 *Ibid* at para 68.

of the victim of a fraudster. In both cases, the lender has relied on a registered title that will be set aside. The distinction made by the Court of Appeal means that people cannot rely on the register and must search the chain of title or purchase title insurance.

The law in British Columbia is equally problematic, but it was imposed by the legislature and not the courts. An amendment to the *Land Title Act* states that a "person who purports to acquire land or an estate or interest in land by registration of a void instrument does not acquire any estate or interest in the land on registration of the instrument."[125] This resurrects all the problems associate with *nemo dat*, which title registration was designed to avoid. The statute then provides an exception to the exception for people who acquire a fee simple estate "in good faith and for valuable consideration."[126] This is a return to the old equitable defence of bona fide purchase, but limited to people who acquire the fee simple.

The difficulties created by this were revealed in *Gill v Bucholtz*.[127] Gurjeet Gill become the registered owner of land by registration of a forged transfer. She was a party to the forgery. She then granted a registered mortgage to Mr and Mrs Bucholtz, who paid $40,000 to her. The BC Court of Appeal held that Ms Gill's title was void; therefore, the mortgage was also void, even though Mr and Mrs Bucholtz had relied on the register in good faith. The statutory exception to *nemo dat* applies only in favour of someone who acquires a fee simple estate.

In British Columbia, a person who acquires a fee simple estate by registration of a forged transfer will acquire immediate indefeasibility if they acted in good faith and gave value for it. Other interests in land do not receive the benefit of any indefeasibility unless they are granted by someone with an indefeasible fee simple estate. For example, if Mr and Mrs Bucholtz had assigned their mortgage, the assignee would receive nothing. If Ms Gill had granted a long lease that was mortgaged and then assigned, no one would get anything even though they all obtained registered interests for value in good faith in reliance on the register. *Nemo dat* will apply to all of these lesser interests, however long the chain of title, because they are based on a void fee simple estate (and title cannot be acquired by adverse possession in British Columbia).

125 *Land Title Act*, RSBC 1996, c 250, s 25.1(1).
126 *Ibid*, s 25.1(2).
127 2009 BCCA 137.

E. PERSONAL PROPERTY SECURITY

As discussed in Chapter 6, security interests in personal property are governed by the *PPSA* (*Personal Property Security Act*) in every Canadian province and territory (except Quebec).[128] The Saskatchewan version of the *PPSA* is cited and quoted in this section. The versions elsewhere in Canada are substantially the same.

The *PPSA* applies to many different kinds of personal property, including bank accounts, bonds, commercial consignments, company shares, crops, and futures contracts. An asset that is subject to a security interest is called *collateral*.[129] To keep things simple, this section focuses on security interests in goods.

The *PPSA* applies "to every transaction that in substance creates a security interest, without regard to its form and without regard to the person who has title."[130] Since the form of the transaction is irrelevant, it does not matter whether a security interest is legal or equitable. The *PPSA* also applies to "a lease for a term of more than one year . . . that does not secure payment or performance of an obligation."[131] As discussed in Chapter 6, it is not easy to tell whether or not a lease creates a security interest, so the inclusion of all leases over one year avoids that problem. Also, a person in possession of goods appears to be the owner, whether they are a bailee under a lease or pursuant to a secured transaction. Registration giving notice of the interest of a lessor or secured creditor helps avoid the problem that people will deal with the possessor of goods in the mistaken belief that they are the owner.

The *PPSA* provides a set of priority rules that are used if one or more of the competing rights is a security interest governed by the *PPSA*. The first question is whether the security interest is *enforceable* against third parties. There are two ways to create an enforceable security interest: (1) the creditor has possession or control of the collateral or (2) the debtor has signed a security agreement.[132] If the security interest is not enforceable against third parties, there is no priority dispute. The third party wins.

The second question is whether the security interest is *perfected*. There are two ways to perfect a security interest: (1) the creditor has

---

128 RSBC 1996, c 359; RSA 2000, c P-7; SS 1993, c P-6.2; CCSM, c P35; RSO 1990, c P.10; SNB 1993, c P-7.1; SNS 1995-96, c 13; RSPEI 1988, c P-3.1; SNL 1998, c P-7.1; RSY 2002, c 169; SNWT 1994, c 8.
129 *PPSA*, SS 1993, c P-6.2, s 2(1)(g) [*PPSA*, SS 1993].
130 *Ibid*, s 3(1)(a).
131 *Ibid*, s 3(2).
132 *Ibid*, s 10(1).

possession or control of the collateral or (2) the creditor has registered a financing statement.[133] Control of the collateral relates to certain forms of intangible personal property, such as company shares and futures contracts. It is a subject best undertaken in an advanced study of personal property security. If we focus on goods, then we have two options. If the creditor has possession of the goods (like a pawnbroker), their security interest is both enforceable and perfected. If the creditor does not have possession, they will need a security agreement signed by the debtor to make their security interest enforceable against third parties and will need to register a financing statement to perfect that interest.

1) Priority Between Security Interests

The basic priority rules for competing security interests in goods are relatively simple: (1) a perfected security interest takes priority over an unperfected security interest, (2) the priority between perfected security interests depends on the order in which they were perfected, and (3) the priority between unperfected security interests depends on the order of attachment (which occurs when the creditor has given value and the debtor acquires rights to the collateral).[134] There are numerous wrinkles and two important exceptions. The first exception is for liens arising by operation of law:

> Where a person in the ordinary course of business furnishes materials or services with respect to goods that are subject to a security interest, a lien that the person has with respect to those materials or services has priority over a perfected security interest unless the lien is given by an Act that provides that the lien does not have the priority.[135]

The second exception is for *purchase money security interests*, which are given super priority if they are perfected.[136] A purchase money security interest includes "a security interest taken in collateral . . . to the extent that it secures all or part of its purchase price" and an "interest of a lessor of goods pursuant to a lease for a term of more than one year."[137] This includes a seller or lessor of goods as well as a creditor who finances their purchase. A purchase money security interest will have priority over other security interests even if those other interests were perfected earlier. If there are two purchase money security interests in

---

133 *Ibid*, ss 19, 24, & 25.
134 *Ibid*, s 35.
135 *Ibid*, s 32.
136 *Ibid*, ss 34.
137 *Ibid*, s 2(1)(jj).

the same goods, the interest of a seller or lessor will have priority over a creditor who financed the purchase.

Without super priority for purchase money security interests, creditors may be reluctant to sell goods on credit or provide purchase financing because their security interests would rank behind previously perfected security interests in the debtor's after-acquired property. The super priority is limited to the newly acquired asset (or its proceeds if it is sold), so it does not detract from security interests already in existence.

2) Priority over Other Interests

The *PPSA* provides an exception for people who buy or lease goods from someone who sells or leases them in the ordinary course of their business:

> A buyer or lessee of goods sold or leased in the ordinary course of business of the seller or lessor takes free of any perfected or unperfected security interest that is given by the seller or lessor ... whether or not the buyer or lessee knows of it, unless the buyer or lessee also knows that the sale or lease constitutes a breach of the security agreement pursuant to which the security interest was created.[138]

There are numerous cases dealing with the question of what constitutes a sale in the ordinary course of the seller's business. For example, in *Camco Inc v Olson (Frances) Realty (1979) Ltd*,[139] Muxlow Development Corp was involved in a new condominium project in Regina with 171 units. It purchased four appliances (fridge, stove, washer, and dryer) for each unit from Camco subject to its perfected security interests in those appliances. Muxlow sold the units with each sale, including the appliances. Muxlow became insolvent, and Camco wanted to seize the appliances. The Saskatchewan Court of Appeal held that the appliances had been sold in the ordinary course of Muxlow's business even though it was a property developer and not in the business of selling appliances.

For the exception to operate, the security interest must be granted by the seller or lessor. In *Royal Bank of Canada v Wheaton Pontiac Buick Cadillac GMC Ltd*,[140] the bank had a perfected security interest in the inventory of Key West Motor Products Ltd, which was a car dealer in Saskatoon. Key West became insolvent, and some if its cars were later sold at auction. One of those cars was accepted as a trade-in by Wheaton

---

138   *Ibid*, s 30(2).
139   [1986] 6 WWR 258, 50 Sask R 161 (CA).
140   (1990) 88 Sask R 151 (QB).

and sold to a buyer. Although the sale by Wheaton was in the ordinary course of its business as a car dealer, the bank's security interest was not granted by Wheaton. The previous sale of the car at auction was not in the ordinary course of Key West's business since it was no longer in business when the car was sold. Therefore, Wheaton paid $7,000 to the bank to discharge its security interest.

The *PPSA* provides a different exception for people who buy or lease *consumer goods* worth up to $1,000 ($1,500 in Saskatchewan).[141] These are "goods that are used or acquired for use primarily for personal, family or household purposes."[142] This exception is not limited to security interests granted by the seller or lessor.

If a debtor becomes bankrupt, a security interest in their personal property "is not effective against" their trustee in bankruptcy unless it is perfected at the time of the bankruptcy.[143] In *Re Giffen*,[144] Telecom Leasing Canada leased a car to BC Tel, which leased it to an employee, Carol Anne Giffen. The lease was longer than one year, but neither Telecom nor BC Tel registered a financing statement under the *PPSA*. Giffen became bankrupt one year later. Telecom seized the car and sold it at auction for $10,154 with the consent of Giffen's trustee in bankruptcy. The Supreme Court of Canada decided that her trustee in bankruptcy was entitled to the money.

Telecom argued that the trustee in bankruptcy had acquired the *property of the bankrupt* and no more; therefore, the trustee's only interest in the car was Giffen's right to possession under the lease (which was terminated). However, Telecom could not enforce its interest in the car against the trustee since it was deemed to be a security interest under the *PPSA* and was unperfected when Giffen became bankrupt. Therefore, Giffen's trustee had good title to the car even though she did not.

This exception to the *nemo dat* principle is consistent with relativity of title (discussed in Chapter 2). Giffen had a right to possess the car that was enforceable against everyone else in society except someone with a better right. Telecom had a better right to possession (upon termination of the lease), but Giffen's right to possession had already been transferred to the trustee in bankruptcy. Therefore, Telecom could not enforce its right to possession against the trustee, which meant that the trustee had the best right to possession (i.e., ownership).

---

141 *PPSA*, SS 1993, above note 129, s 30(3).
142 *Ibid*, s 2(1)(i).
143 *Ibid*, s 20.
144 [1998] 1 SCR 91, 155 DLR (4th) 332 [*Re Giffen*].

F. FIXTURES

When goods are attached to land, they may become *fixtures*, in which case they are no longer goods. They become part of the estate in the land. As discussed in Chapter 3, an estate is a right to possess a space on the earth. It includes any physical things within that space that the law regards as part of the estate. This includes the soil, trees, and so on, and normally any buildings. However, it is not always clear whether goods brought into that space remain as goods or become part of the estate.

Normally, it is not important whether things are goods or fixtures. For example, if you own a house, you are free to replace the windows. The old windows become goods when they are removed, and the new windows cease to be goods when they are installed. You can cut down or plant trees, install a new furnace, paint the house, and so on. This has no legal significance because you own the things in question whether they are goods or fixtures.

There are several different reasons why it can matter whether things are goods or fixtures. Tax is one reason.[145] If a tax is based on the value of the land, then it matters whether expensive items are part of that land or exist separately as goods. In *Zellstoff Celgar Ltd v British Columbia*,[146] a company purchased a pulp mill and was required to pay a property transfer tax of $4,554,510 because the machinery and equipment were fixtures. The tax would have been $286,298 if those items were goods and excluded from the value of the land.

The distinction between goods and fixtures also matters when land is sold. Unless the parties agree otherwise, the contract of sale will include the land and fixtures and exclude everything else. This is why the parties specify what is included. When a home is sold, the contract should state whether appliances, curtains, and so on, are included to resolve any doubt about things that may be fixtures. The contract may include some goods (e.g., washer and dryer) and exclude some fixtures (e.g., an antique chandelier).

Most of the cases in this area concern competing claims to things (which is why it is discussed in this chapter). One person claims ownership of the things as goods, whereas another claims ownership of them as part of the estate in land. This can happen if goods are taken without the owner's permission and attached to land belonging to someone else. The rival claimants may be secured creditors, with one having a

---

145 See *Melluish v BMI (No 3) Ltd*, [1996] AC 454 (HL).
146 2014 BCCA 279.

security interest in the goods and another a mortgage over the land. In days gone by, when personal property could be given away by will but real property was inherited, an issue regarding fixtures could arise on the death of the owner. That can still happen if a testator leaves their land to one beneficiary and personal property to another. Fixtures also feature in disputes between landlords and tenants. A fixture may be a *tenant's fixture*, which the tenant is entitled to remove during or at the end of lease.

1) Goods or Fixtures?

Whether things are goods or fixtures depends on the *degree of annexation* and the *object of annexation*. In other words, *how* are they attached to the land and *why* are they attached? The starting assumption is that things are goods if they are not attached at all and fixtures if they are attached even slightly. The greater the attachment, the more likely they are fixtures. That is only a starting point. Unattached things can be fixtures, and attached things can be goods. This depends on the object of annexation. Why were the items placed on the land: as an improvement to the land or for the better enjoyment of the items themselves?

In *Holland v Hodgson*, Blackburn J gave this example of unattached things being goods or fixtures depending on the apparent purpose for their placement on the land:

> When the article in question is no further attached to the land than by its own weight it is generally to be considered a mere chattel. But even in such a case, if the intention is apparent to make the articles part of the land, they do become part of the land. Thus blocks of stone placed one on the top of another without any mortar or cement for the purpose of forming a dry stone wall would become part of the land, though the same stones, if deposited in a builder's yard and for convenience sake stacked on the top of each other in the form of a wall, would remain chattels.[147]

The object of annexation does not depend on the subjective intentions of the people who placed the items on the land but on the apparent reason for their placement. What would an objective observer think when viewing the land? Goods can become fixtures even if their owner stated that they did not want them to be fixtures.[148]

---

147 (1872) LR 7 CP 328 at 334–35 (Exch) [*Holland*].
148 *Hobson v Gorringe*, [1897] 1 Ch 182 at 193 (CA); *Melluish v BMI (No 3) Ltd*, above note 145 at 473.

Perhaps the clearest statement of these rules is found in *Stack v T Eaton Co.*[149] Land was sold, and the Ontario Divisional Court was asked to decide whether shelves and light fittings were transferred to the purchaser as fixtures or still belonged to the vendor as goods. They were attached by screws and easily removeable without damage to the building. The court held that they were fixtures. Meredith CJ said,

I take it to be settled law:

1. That articles not otherwise attached to the land than by their own weight are not to be considered as part of the land, unless the circumstances are such as shew that they were intended to be part of the land.

2. That articles affixed to the land even slightly are to be considered part of the land unless the circumstances are such as to shew that they were intended to continue chattels.

3. That the circumstances necessary to be shewn to alter the *prima facie* character of the articles are circumstances which shew the degree of annexation and object of such annexation which are patent to all to see.

4. That the intention of the person affixing the article to the soil is material only so far as it can be presumed from the degree and object of the annexation.

5. That even tenants' fixtures, put in for the purposes of trade, form part of the freehold, with the right, however, to the tenant, as between him and his landlord, to bring them back to the state of chattels again by severing them from the soil, and that they pass by a conveyance of the land as part of it, subject to this right of the tenant.[150]

In *Leigh v Taylor*,[151] Madame de Falbe was the tenant for life of the Luton Hoo estate (which has appeared in many films and is now a hotel). She attached valuable tapestries to the walls of the manor house by tacking them to strips of wood that were nailed to the walls. After her death, the House of Lords decided that the tapestries were not fixtures but formed part of her personal estate (although the same result could be achieved by treating them as tenant's fixtures). The attachment

---

149 (1902) 4 OLR 335 (Div Ct).
150 *Ibid* at 338, quoted in *Lasalle Recreations Ltd v Canadian Camdex Investments Ltd* (1969), 4 DLR (3d) 549 at 554 (BCCA); *Bank of Nova Scotia v Mitz* (1979), 106 DLR (3d) 534, 27 OR (2d) 250 at para 13 (CA); *Zellstoff Celgar Ltd v British Columbia*, above note 146 at para 9.
151 [1902] AC 157 (HL).

was necessary in order to display the tapestries properly. Lord Halsbury CJ said,

> It never was intended to remain a part of the house; the contrary is evident from the very nature of the attachment, the extent and degree of which was as slight as the nature of the thing attached would admit of. Therefore, I come to the conclusion that this thing, put up for ornamentation and for the enjoyment of the person while occupying the house, is not under such circumstances as these part of the house.[152]

In *Holland v Hodgson*,[153] looms in a mill were attached to the floor of the mill with nails, which was necessary to keep them stable when operating. The court held that they were fixtures intended as lasting improvements to land being used as a factory.

In *Berlin Interior Hardware Co Ltd v Colonial Investment*,[154] theatre chairs were sold under a conditional sales agreement by which the seller retained title until the purchase price was paid. They were screwed to the floor of the Empire Theatre in Saskatoon. The Saskatchewan Court of Appeal held that they were fixtures. Elwood J said,

> It seems to me that, bearing in mind the nature of the building for which these chairs were bought, the intention of affixing them to the building was to make them become part of the freehold. As the learned trial Judge remarked: "A theatre is not much good without chairs," and it would seem to me that chairs to a theatre are as essential as seats or pews in a church.[155]

In *Lasalle Recreations Ltd v Canadian Camdex Investments Ltd*,[156] wall-to-wall carpets were sold under a conditional sales agreement and installed in a hotel. The BC Court of Appeal held that they were fixtures. McFarlane JA said, "Weighing all these circumstances, I am of the opinion that the object of the annexation was the better and more effectual use of the building as a hotel and not the better use of the goods as goods."[157]

Buildings are normally regarded as fixtures. However, courts have held that buildings can be goods if they can be moved relatively easily. Mobile homes have been regarded as goods in some cases and fixtures in other. Many of these cases were surveyed in *Plaza Equities Ltd v Bank*

---

152 *Ibid* at 161.
153 *Holland*, above note 147.
154 (1918) 38 DLR 643, 11 Sask LR 46 (CA).
155 *Ibid* at para 5.
156 *Lasalle Recreations*, above note 150.
157 *Ibid* at 556.

of Nova Scotia,[158] where the Alberta Court of Queen's Bench held that a large mobile home was a fixture. It had been transported in two halves, which were placed on a concrete foundation and joined together to look like a bungalow.

2) Tenant's Fixtures

A tenant's fixture is a fixture. The question of whether something is a tenant's fixture or a landlord's fixture is different from the question of whether or not it is a fixture. Things firmly affixed to the land for the improvement of the land can be tenant's fixtures. If something is a tenant's fixture, then the tenant has a right to remove it during the lease or possibly shortly afterwards. That right will be lost if the lease ends and the tenant does not continue in possession.[159]

Tenant's fixtures have been divided into three categories: *trade fixtures* (installed by commercial tenants), *ornamental and domestic fixtures* (installed by residential tenants), and *agricultural fixtures* (installed by farming tenants). At common law, agricultural fixtures could not be removed by the tenant at the end of the lease, but that was changed by statute in England, starting with the *Landlord and Tenant Act 1851*.[160] In *Carscallen v Leeson*,[161] a farming tenant installed a windmill and wire fences and removed them at the end of the lease. The Alberta Court of Appeal held that the *Landlord and Tenant Act 1851* could not help her because she had not complied with its conditions but decided that she was not liable because those things never became fixtures.

The rules regarding tenant's fixtures are subject to the terms of the lease. In *Cherry v Bredin*,[162] a farming tenant leased land from the Canadian National Railway (CNR). According to a term of the lease, he could remove any fence he installed within 60 days after the end of the lease. He removed the fence more than two years after the lease ended and was ordered to pay $2 in damages. The Saskatchewan Court of Appeal said that his right to remove the fence was granted as a term of the lease and did not exist at common law because it was an agricultural

---

158 [1978] 3 WWR 385, 84 DLR (3d) 609 (Alta QB).
159 *National Trust Co v Palace Theatre Ltd*, [1928] 2 DLR 739, [1928] 1 WWR 805 (Alta CA); *New Zealand Government Property Corp v HM & S Ltd*, [1982] QB 1145 (CA) [*New Zealand Government Property Corp*]; *Re Gortler and Mister Donut Shops Ltd* (1983), 150 DLR (3d) 185, 43 OR (2d) 59 (HCJ).
160 14 & 15 Vict, c 25.
161 [1927] 4 DLR 797, [1927] 3 WWR 425 (Alta CA).
162 [1927] 3 DLR 326, [1927] 2 WWR 314 (Sask CA).

fixture. There was no mention of the *Landlord and Tenant Act 1851*. Turgeon JA said,

> And the defendant's right to sever and remove this fence, a purely agricultural fixture, was created by his express agreement with the C.N.R. In the absence of such an agreement he would have lost all right to the fence, and could not have removed it at the expiration of his term: *Elwes v. Maw* (1802) 3 East 38 (102 E.R. 510).[163]

In *New Zealand Government Property Corp v HM & S Ltd*,[164] Her Majesty's Theatre on Haymarket in London was leased in 1898, and the lease was renewed in 1970 with rent for part of the new term set at "open market rental for the demised premises." The Court of Appeal held that the value of the tenant's fixtures should be excluded from the value of the premises when deciding what the rent should be. The court distinguished tenant's fixtures from landlord's fixtures. The seats and lights installed by the tenant were tenant's fixtures. Improvements made by the tenant to the structure of the building, including replacement doors and windows, were landlord's fixtures, which the tenant could not remove at the end of the lease.

In *859587 Ontario Ltd v Starmark Property Management Ltd*,[165] HK Auto Centre was a tenant of commercial space in Markham, Ontario. They purchased an automotive spray booth under a conditional sales agreement but fell behind on their payments for the booth and their rent. The landlord exercised their right to distrain for rent, which is a right to seize the tenant's goods in the rented premises, and seized the spray booth (without removing it). The Ontario Court of Appeal held that the spray booth was a tenant's fixture, which was nailed to the floor and attached to electrical, water, and air pipes. Since it was a fixture, it was part of the land and not goods that could be seized by the landlord. Doherty JA said,

> A trade fixture is as much a part of the freehold as any immovable fixture as long as the trade fixture has not been severed from the freehold by the tenant at the time of the distraint. As distraint runs against the tenant's property found on the land and not against the land itself, it follows that trade fixtures which are part of the land at the time of the purported distraint cannot be subject to distraint.[166]

---

163 *Ibid* at para 5.
164 *New Zealand Government Property Corp*, above note 159.
165 (1998) 164 DLR (4th) 167, 40 OR (3d) 481 (CA).
166 *Ibid* at para 9.

In *Scott v Filipovic*,[167] land in British Columbia was leased for the purpose of growing blueberries. The tenant agreed that the blueberry plants would be removed at the end of the lease and that the lease was not assignable. The tenant sold the lease to the plaintiffs, who spent the winter in Arizona. When they returned, the landlord would not let them continue the lease. They sued and were awarded $90,000 in damages for conversion of the blueberries planted by the former tenant. This was reversed by the BC Court of Appeal. The blueberry plants were fixtures, not goods; therefore, there was no valid claim for conversion (which is wrongful interference with the possession of goods). The plants were tenant's fixtures, which the tenant was entitled to remove, but the plaintiffs were not tenants because the lease was not assignable. Therefore, they had no claim against the landlord. The lease had been abandoned by the former tenant, and the right to remove tenant's fixtures had been lost.

3) Personal Property Security

Many of the cases on fixtures are competitions involving secured creditors. Goods are sold on credit with the creditor retaining legal title to the goods, which are attached to land that is mortgaged. The debtor becomes bankrupt, and there is a competition between the security interest in the goods and the security interest in the land. If the goods become fixtures, then any interest in them as goods ceases to exist. However, the contract between the creditor and the debtor gives the creditor the right to enter the land and repossess the fixtures (and turn them into goods again). That right is sufficient to give the creditor an equitable interest in the land (not the goods), which can be enforced against others subject to the defence of bona fide purchase.[168]

Today, the priority between a creditor with a security interest in goods that become fixtures and anyone with an interest in the land is governed by the *PPSA*.[169] If the security interest attached to the goods *before* they became fixtures, then it has priority over any interest in the land that existed when the goods became fixtures. If a newer interest in the land is acquired for value and without fraud (or without knowledge

---

167 2015 BCCA 409.

168 *Re Samuel Allen & Sons Ltd*, [1907] 1 Ch 575 at 581–82 (Ch D); *Re Morrison, Jones & Taylor Ltd*, [1914] 1 Ch 50 (CA); *Kay's Leasing Corp Pty Ltd v CSR Provident Fund Nominees Pty Ltd*, [1962] VR 429.

169 RSBC 1996, c 359, s 36; RSA 2000, c P-7, s 36; SS 1993, c P-6.2, s 36; CCSM, c P35, s 36; RSO 1990, c P.10, s 34; SNB 1993, c P-7.1, s 36; SNS 1995-96, c 13, s 37; RSPEI 1988, c P-3.1, s 36; SNL 1998, c P-7.1, s 37; RSY 2002, c 169, s 35; SNWT 1994, c 8, s 36.

of the security interest in Ontario), then it will have priority over the security interest unless the secured creditor has registered a notice of their interest in the appropriate land registry.

If the security interest attached to the goods *after* they become fixtures, then it will not have priority over existing interests in the land unless the holders of those interests consented to the security interest. Notice of the security interest will need to be registered in the land registry in order to have priority over newer interests in the land.

G. SPECIFICATION, ACCESSION, AND MIXTURES

Property rights to goods can be lost if those goods are (1) used to make other goods, (2) attached to other goods in such a way that it is impractical to separate them, or (3) mixed with other goods, and it is impossible tell them apart. These three situations raise three different legal issues: *specification*, *accession*, and *mixtures*. Specification is the creation of a new thing, and accession is the loss of goods that become attached to other goods. Mixtures are self-explanatory.

These three situations can overlap and sometimes be confused with one other. A great Canadian example is *Jones v De Marchant*,[170] in which a husband stole eighteen beaver skins from his wife, added four beaver skins of his own, and paid $50 to have them made into a fur coat with a lining. He then gave the coat to his mistress. The Manitoba Court of Appeal ordered the mistress to deliver the coat to the wife. Richards JA discussed mixtures and accession:

> The fact that it is impossible now, in examining the coat, to say which parts of it constitute the 18 skins, does not shew their identity to be lost. They are traced to the coat and shewn to be part of it, which sufficiently identifies them.
>
> It is said that, as she cannot say which, are hers, she cannot separate them. She is not called upon to do so. The case is governed by the law of accession, and the loss has to be borne by the wrongdoer or the defendant who claims through him.[171]

However, the case is really one of specification. The legal existence of the beaver skins was lost when they were made into a new thing, the

---

170 (1916) 26 Man R 455 (CA) [*Jones*].
171 *Ibid* at 459.

coat. A better outcome (from a property lawyer's perspective) would be to order the husband to pay damages for conversion, as discussed below.

1) Specification

Specification is the legal term for the creation of new goods. (It is also used in the law of patents, which requires inventors to provide a *specification of the invention*,[172] but that is unrelated to the topic at hand.) It comes from *specificatio* in Roman law, which is the making of a *nova species* (i.e., a new thing).

Specification occurs naturally when plants grow, animals give birth, hens lay eggs, and so on. Human assistance may be required to help produce the new goods, for example, by picking fruit, milking cows, or shearing sheep. New goods are also manufactured, like cars and cakes.

When new goods come into existence, the law allocates new property rights to them. These are default rules that can be altered by agreement. The default rules for goods created naturally are based on the civilian concept of ownership, which entitles the owner to "the *usus* (right to use of the thing), *fructus* (right to its fruits) and *abusus* (right to alienate or destroy the thing)."[173] The owner of a thing is entitled to its fruits, so the owner of a tree owns the fruit, nuts, or syrup it produces, just as milk and eggs belong to the owners of the cows and hens and a baby animal belongs to the owner of its mother.

By default, manufactured goods belong to the manufacturer, but people often agree to change that rule. An artisan who handcrafts a musical instrument or a baker who makes loaves of bread may be working on behalf of an employer who will own the fruits of their labour. In *Jones*,[174] discussed above, the coat was made for the husband with beaver skins he supplied, and (normally) he would have become its owner when it was made, not the furrier who made it.

A problem can arise when goods are made from raw materials without the consent of the owner of those materials, as in *Jones*. The solution in that case was to allocate ownership of the new coat to the wife who owned most of the beaver skins from which it was made. Although that may be a just result in that case, it is a rule that has the potential to impose substantial hardship on manufacturers and their customers.

As discussed at the beginning of this chapter, the *nemo dat* principle means that honest people can buy goods and be liable for the tort

---

172 *Patent Act*, RSC 1985, c P-4, s 27.
173 Daniel Clarry, "Fiduciary Ownership and Trusts in a Comparative Perspective" (2014) 63 ILCQ 901 at 907.
174 *Jones*, above note 170.

of conversion if their seller did not have good title to those goods. It is a hardship the law imposes on innocent buyers to protect property rights. However, it would be taken too far if it was used to protect the owner of raw materials that have been used without their consent to manufacture new goods. The manufacturer may have no idea that their supplier did not have good title to the raw materials they purchased. If you buy a new car, for example, you can be confident that the manufacturer owned the car that was shipped to the dealer. What if it was made from steel that the supplier did not own? What about a guitar or piano made from wood that the supplier did not own? Should the finished product belong to the owner of the raw materials, in which case the honest customer is guilty of the tort of conversion and liable for the full value of the item purchased?

The manufacturer who consumes raw materials without the owner's consent will be liable for the tort of conversion even if they acted honestly. That will fully compensate the owner, who can use the award of damages to purchase new materials. The manufactured product may be far more valuable than the materials from which it is made. To allocate ownership of the product to the owner of the materials could produce a massive windfall for them at the expense of honest manufacturers and their customers.

There is a temptation, as in *Jones*, to ignore the fact that a new thing has been made and resolve the dispute based on the continuing ownership of the raw materials. However, if specification has occurred, the raw materials no longer exist at law. New goods have come into existence, and the property rights to those goods are new rights.

It is not always easy to tell whether specification has occurred. As Bryson J said in the Australian case of *Associated Alloys Pty Ltd v Metropolitan Engineering and Fabrication Pty Ltd*,

> The question whether goods which have been used in some manufacturing process still exist in the goods produced by that process, or have gone out of existence on being incorporated in the derived product is, in my opinion, a question of fact and degree not susceptible of much exposition. When wheat is ground into flour it is reasonably open to debate whether the wheat continues to exist; when flour is baked into bread there could be little doubt that the flour does not. Many examples might be encountered or imagined, and each must be addressed separately.[175]

---

175 [1996] NSWSC 119, 20 ACSR 205 at 209, aff'd [2000] HCA 25, 202 CLR 588.

In that case, pressure vessels had been made from steel plates that belonged to Associated Alloys, and an issue was whether their steel continued to exist. That depended on whether it was practical to reconvert the pressure vessels into steel plates. Bryson J said,

> [W]hether goods are reducible to the original materials is not simply a matter of physics. Other perspectives have to be considered, including the economic perspective. The scraps of leather produced by cutting up a manufactured shoe could not in reality be regarded as the original leather from which the shoe was manufactured. The steel which would be produced by cutting up a pressure vessel and flattening out the cylindrical parts would not be the steel which Associated Alloys delivered under the sale; it would be scrap steel. In my finding, disregarding the offcuts, the steel plate supplied under these invoices no longer exists and Associated Alloys has no property in the derived products.[176]

It would not have been practical to turn the fur coat in *Jones* back into beaver skins. Therefore, those skins no longer existed at law, and the dispute should not have been resolved on the basis that the wife continued to own them. Instead, the essential question was whether the new coat should belong to her. Although that may have been the most satisfying outcome in this case, the allocation of ownership of manufactured goods to an unwitting supplier of raw materials is a priority rule that can produce unfair windfalls and losses, as discussed above. Instead, the husband should have been liable to the wife for conversion of the skins. The mistress was not liable for conversion because the skins no longer existed when she received the coat as a gift. However, the wife could have an equitable lien on the coat for the value of the skins (see Chapter 6), which would have been enforceable against the mistress because she was not a bona fide purchaser for value.

2) Accession

Accession occurs when goods become attached to other goods, and it is impractical to separate them again. This is similar to fixtures, in which goods get attached to land, but the rules are completely different. That is because of the fundamental distinction between possession of land and possession of goods. An estate in land is a right to possess a space on the earth, and the law of fixtures is used to determine what physical things inside that space form part of the estate. Things can be fixtures

---

176 *Ibid* at 209–10.

and part of an estate even though they are not attached and are easily removable from that space.

Possession of goods is not possession of a space but possession of a physical object. When goods become attached to other goods, neither party should lose their right to possession unless it is impractical to separate them again. If they cannot be separated, the owner of the *principal chattel* is entitled to the whole, but possibly with a duty to pay the owner of the *accessory* for the value of their goods that have ceased to exist at law.

In *Firestone Tire & Rubber Co of Canada v Industrial Acceptance Corp*,[177] a truck was sold under a conditional sales agreement. The buyer then bought new tires for it under a conditional sales agreement. When the buyer defaulted on their payments, the seller of the truck seized it and claimed ownership of the tires as accessories. The Supreme Court of Canada held that the tires had not lost their separate identity because they were "removable without physical injury to the body of the truck or to any of its constituent parts."[178] This was followed in *Ilford-Riverton Airways Ltd v Aero Trades (Western) Ltd*,[179] where a rented engine was installed in an airplane. Although the process of removing an engine is more complex than removing tires, it can be done without injury to the engine or the airplane.

In the Australian case of *McKeown v Cavalier Yachts Pty Ltd*,[180] Cavalier Yachts had agreed to build a custom yacht for McKeown. He provided the hull worth $1,777 and paid $20,000. They did not build the yacht. Instead, they sold their entire business to Spartech Marine Industries, which built the yacht in the hull according to McKeown's instructions. Spartech did not receive the $20,000 paid by McKeown. Their work was valued at $24,409. Spartech demanded payment, and McKeown sued on the basis that the hull belonged to him; therefore, the yacht built using his hull was an accessory that belonged to him. The court agreed with McKeown but ordered him to pay $4,409 to Spartech, which was the value of their work less the $20,000 he had paid to Cavalier Yachts.

The case is odd for several reasons. The court did not address the question of specification. Was the yacht a new thing, or was it just an improved version of the hull? If the yacht was new, then the hull ceased to exist (at law), and Spartech would be liable for converting it. The court treated it as a case of accession.

177 [1971] SCR 357 [*Firestone*].
178 *Ibid* at 358, Laskin J.
179 [1977] 5 WWR 193, 76 DLR (3d) 742 (Man CA) [*Ilford-Riverton*]. See also *First City Capital Ltd v Price Waterhouse Ltd* (1984), 57 BCLR 354 (SC).
180 (1988) 13 NSWLR 303.

Spartech argued that the yacht was the principal chattel because it was much more expensive than the hull, but that was rejected. The yacht was built into the hull piece by piece, and at the end of each day's work the new bits became part of the hull. It is odd that the legal outcome should depend on the manufacturing process. If a large, pre-fabricated portion had been attached to the hull, would the result have been different?

Finally, to say that McKeown should pay $4,409 because he was unjustly enriched by that amount seems odd. He was enriched by $24,409 worth of work. The fact that he paid $20,000 to someone other than the person who did the work seems irrelevant.

3) Mixtures

Mixtures occur when goods belonging to different people get mixed or mingled together and it is impossible to tell them apart. Roman law distinguished *confusio* from *commixtio*. A mixture of fluids (e.g., oil or wine) was a *confusio*, whereas a mixture of solids (e.g., bales of hay or grains of wheat) was a *commixtio*. The contributors to a *confusio* would become tenants in common of the whole mixture, but the contributors to a *commixtio* would continue to be sole owners of their goods in the mixture. The distinction was based on the idea that any portion of a fluid mixture may contain fluids from more than one source, whereas every grain of a solid mixture must belong solely to one contributor or another.

We no longer bother to draw that distinction because the problem is the same in both cases. There is no way to know which parts of the mixture belong to whom. If the mixture is divided up again, each con-tributor will take away goods that used to belong to another contributor whether the goods are fluids or solids. The only sensible solution is for the contributors to become tenants in common regardless of the nature of the goods that are mixed, and this seems to be the current law. Ten-ancies in common have been created by accidental mixtures of bales of cotton,[181] cattle,[182] and scaffolding.[183]

A mixture is not a problem if the contributors consented to it. They can agree on how it will be owned and divided up. An unintended mixture is not really a problem so long as none of the goods are lost or damaged. The contributors can each take back a portion of the goods equal to their contributions. The problem arises when a mixture was

---

181   *Spence v Union Marine Insurance Co Ltd* (1868), LR 3 CP 427 [*Spence*].
182   *Big Top Hereford Pty Ltd v Thomas*, [2006] NSWSC 1159.
183   *Hill v Reglon Pty Ltd*, [2007] NSWCA 295.

unintended and some of the goods have been lost or damaged. The law provides rules to resolve the competing claims to the surviving and undamaged goods. If one of the contributors wrongly caused the mixture, they must wait until the claims of the other contributors are satisfied before they can take what is left. Innocent contributors will share the mixture in proportion to their contributions up to the total amount of their contributions.

It used to be the law that a person would lose their ownership of goods if they wrongly mixed them with goods belonging to someone else. In *Spence v Union Marine Insurance Co Ltd*,[184] bales of cotton were being shipped with each bale marked to identify its owner. The ship sank and most of the bales were recovered, but the identifying marks had been washed away. It was an accidental mixture, so the rule regarding wrongdoers did not apply, but Bovill CJ stated it as an *obiter dictum* in 1868:

> In our own law there are not many authorities to be found upon this subject; but, as far as they go, they are in favour of the view, that, when goods of different owners become by accident so mixed together as to be undistinguishable, the owners of the goods so mixed become tenants in common of the whole, in the proportions which they have severally contributed to it. The passage cited from the judgment of Blackburn J. in the case of the tallow which was melted and flowed into the sewers, is to that effect: *Buckley v. Gross* (1863) 3 B. & S. 574. And a similar view was adopted by Lord Abinger in the case of the mixture of oil by leakage on board ship in *Jones v. Moore* (1841) 4 Y. & C. Ex. 351. It has been long settled in our law, that, where goods are mixed so as to become undistinguishable, by the wrongful act or default of one owner, he cannot recover, and will not be entitled to his proportion, or any part of the property, from the other owner: but no authority has been cited to show that any such principle has ever been applied, nor indeed could it be applied, to the case of an accidental mixing of the goods of two owners.[185]

That *obiter dictum* was not applied by the Supreme Court of Canada in 1882. In *McDonald v Lane*,[186] the defendant had wrongly mixed 513 of his logs with 930 logs belonging to the plaintiffs, who claimed to be entitled to all 1,443 logs. The Court held that the plaintiffs were entitled to the number of logs they contributed to the mixture and were free to choose the logs they liked best but could not keep more than that.

---

184 *Spence*, above note 181.
185 *Ibid* at 437–38.
186 (1882) 7 SCR 462.

In *Indian Oil Corp Ltd v Greenstone Shipping Co SA*,[187] Russian crude oil was transported on a ship to the Indian Oil Corporation in Madras. The amount delivered to Indian Oil was 1,287 barrels less than the amount loaded in Russia. An arbitrator awarded damages of $46,014 for the shortfall. The missing oil had been wrongfully mixed with crude oil that was already on board the ship before the Russian crude oil was loaded. Indian Oil appealed the arbitrator's award on the basis that they were entitled to all the oil on the ship (valued at $388,000) because it had been wrongfully mixed with their own. The English court dismissed their appeal. Staughton J reviewed the authorities and concluded,

> Seeing that none of the authorities is binding on me, although many are certainly persuasive, I consider that I am free to apply the rule which justice requires. This is that, where B wrongfully mixes the goods of A with goods of his own, which are substantially of the same nature and quality, and they cannot in practice be separated, the mixture is held in common and A is entitled to receive out of it a quantity equal to that of his goods which went into the mixture, any doubt as to that quantity being resolved in favour of A. He is also entitled to claim damages from B in respect of any loss he may have suffered, in respect of quality or otherwise, by reason of the admixture.[188]

One of the authorities that helped Staughton J reach this conclusion was *Armory v Delamirie*,[189] discussed in Chapter 2. That was the case in which a chimney sweeper's boy found a piece of jewellery and took it to a goldsmith for appraisal. The goldsmith removed the gemstone and returned the jewellery to the boy with an empty socket. In Chapter 2, we were concerned with the relativity of title and the boy's better right to possession. Here, we are interested in the measure of damages awarded:

> As to the value of the jewel several of the trade were examined to prove what a jewel of the finest water that would fit the socket would be worth; and the Chief Justice directed the jury, that unless the defendant did produce the jewel, and shew it not to be of the finest water, they should presume the strongest case against him, and make the value of the best jewels the measure of their damages: which they accordingly did.[190]

The goldsmith's wrongful act had made it impossible to know how much the boy had lost, so the facts were presumed against the goldsmith

---

187 [1988] QB 345 [*Indian Oil Corp*].
188 *Ibid* at 370–71.
189 (1722) 1 Strange 505, 93 ER 664.
190 *Ibid*.

within the limits of the available evidence. The size of the socket was known, but the quality of the gemstone was not, so the presumption was limited to the best gemstone that could fit in the socket. In the same way, if someone wrongfully mixes their goods with goods belonging to others, presumptions will be made against the wrongdoer, but subject to the available evidence. Staughton J said,

> [I]f the wrongdoer has destroyed or impaired the evidence by which the innocent party could show how much he has lost, the wrongdoer must suffer from the resulting uncertainty. Thus the jury in *Armory v. Delamirie*, 1 Str. 505 were directed by Pratt C.J. to award the plaintiff the value of the finest jewel which the socket would hold, not the finest jewel that had ever been known. . . . [W]here it is totally unknown how much of the innocent party's goods went into the mixture, the whole should belong to him. But I do not see that they require or justify the same result where it is known how much was contributed by the innocent party, or even what the maximum quantity is that he can have contributed, being something less than the whole.[191]

4) Personal Property Security

Many of the cases of specification, accession, or mixtures involve secured creditors. The *PPSA* applies if they do.

a) Accessions

Accessions are defined in the *PPSA* as "goods that are installed in or affixed to other goods."[192] This changes the common law rule that goods do not become accessions unless it is impractical to remove them. In fact, this inverts the common law rule because goods will only be accessions under the *PPSA* if they are removable. If not, they will be subject to the rule that deals with specification and mixtures, discussed below.[193]

The *PPSA* treats accessions much like it treats fixtures (discussed above). If a security interest attached to an accessory *before* it was installed or affixed to other goods (the whole), then it has priority over any claim to the accessory by someone with an existing interest in the whole.[194] If the security interest is perfected, then it will continue to have priority over newer competing interests. If it is not perfected, then

---

191 *Indian Oil Corp*, above note 187 at 369.
192 *PPSA*, SS 1993, above note 129, s 2(1)(a).
193 Ronald CC Cuming, Catherine Walsh & Roderick Wood, *Personal Property Security Law*, 2d ed (Toronto: Irwin Law, 2012) at 602 and 606 [Cuming, Walsh & Wood].
194 *PPSA*, SS 1993, above note 129, s 38.

it will lose priority to newer interests in the whole that are acquired for value without knowledge of it.

If the security interest in the accessory is acquired *after* it is installed or affixed to other goods, then it will be subject to existing interests in the other goods unless the holders of those interests consented to the security interest in the accessory. If unperfected, the security interest in the accessory will be subject to newer interests in the whole acquired for value and without knowledge of it.

The result under the *PPSA* would have been the same as the result under the common law in *Firestone*,[195] discussed above. The secured creditor's interest attached to the tires before they were installed on the truck. Although the tires would be accessions under the *PPSA*, the creditor's unperfected security interest would have priority over the interests in the whole truck that existed when the tires were installed.

The outcome would have been different in *Ilford-Riverton*.[196] Under the *PPSA*, the lease of the aircraft engine for more than a year was a security interest, and the engine became an accession when it was installed in the airplane. The security interest in the engine would have priority over existing interests in the whole airplane, but the owner of the airplane became bankrupt. Therefore, the owner of the engine would not be able to enforce their right to possess the engine against the trustee in bankruptcy, as in *Giffen*,[197] discussed above.

b) Specification and Mixtures

The *PPSA* has one section to deal with specifications and mixtures: "A perfected security interest in goods that subsequently become part of a product or mass continues in the product or mass if the goods are so manufactured, processed, assembled or commingled that their identity is lost in the product or mass."[198]

As mentioned above, this also applies to goods that would be regarded as accessions at common law because they cannot practically be removed again. The reference to goods losing their identity by being assembled should cover that situation.

This section of the *PPSA* states that a perfected security interest continues in the product, but that does not mean that the raw materials

---

195 *Firestone*, above note 177.
196 *Ilford-Riverton*, above note 179. See also *First City Capital Ltd v Price Waterhouse Ltd*, above note 179.
197 *Re Giffen*, above note 144.
198 *PPSA*, SS 1993, above note 129, s 39.

continue to exist if specification occurs. The security interest continues to exist, but in newly created goods. However, the priority rules will be based on the date when the interest in the raw materials was perfected.

In *Unisource Canada Inc v Hongkong Bank of Canada*,[199] Unisource Canada supplied paper to Johanns Graphics (located in Waterloo, Ontario), which used it to make pamphlets and brochures. It was argued "that the paper content in this case did not become part of commingled goods, that the paper never lost its identity as such"; therefore, this section of the *PPSA* did not apply.[200] Reilly J rejected that argument:

> I conclude first that the paper supplied by Unisource to Johanns did indeed become "part of a product" (commingled goods). In my view, the goods were "so processed ... that their identity was lost in the product." I come to this conclusion as a matter of common sense. Unisource supplied blank paper to Johanns. Putting aside any "change" in identity as a result of cutting, Johanns then "processed" the paper by printing on it, adding graphics, *et cetera*, and then binding it into an advertising brochure, a pamphlet, or whatever. It had lost its identity as blank paper stock. If one holds up a magazine and asks a friend, "What is this?," the answer will be, "It's a magazine," or, upon closer inspection, "It's a copy of *MacLeans*." The answer will not be, "It's a number of blank pieces of paper on which words and pictures have been printed and then the pages were stapled together." Such an answer would be completely ridiculous, because the original identity (blank paper) has been lost forever (subject to recycling).[201]

For this section to apply, the creditor must have a perfected security interest in goods that become part of the product. It will not be sufficient if goods are consumed in the process but never become part of the product, such as food for livestock or fuel for a furnace.[202]

Each creditor's security interest in the product will be limited to the value of the goods that become part of the product or mixture. If multiple creditors have perfected security interests in different goods that become part of the manufactured product or mixture, they will share it in proportion to the value of the obligations secured by their interests.[203]

199   (1998) 43 BLR (2d) 226, 14 PPSAC (2d) 112 (Ont SC).
200   *Ibid* at para 168, Reilly J.
201   *Ibid* at para 171.
202   Cuming, Walsh & Wood, above note 193 at 606.
203   *Ibid* at 608–9.

TABLE OF CASES

0742848 BC Ltd v 426008 BC Ltd, 2019 BCSC 1869 120–21
1244034 Alberta Ltd v Walton Int Group Inc, 2007 ABCA 372 221
1465152 Ontario Ltd v Amexon Development Inc, 2015 ONCA 86 69
1832732 Ontario Corp v Regina Properties Ltd, 2018 ONSC 7643 141
2123201 Ontario Inc v Israel Estate, 2016 ONCA 409 224
859587 Ontario Ltd v Starmark Property Management Ltd (1998),
    164 DLR (4th) 167, 40 OR (3d) 481 (CA) 281
880682 Alberta Ltd v Molson Breweries Properties Ltd, [2003]
    2 WWR 642, 4 RPR (4th) 271 (Alta QB) 164, 165

Abigail v Lapin, [1934] AC 491 at 504 (PC) 255
Adderley v Dixon (1824), 1 Sim & St 607, 57 ER 239 218–19
Adeyinka Oyekan v Musendiku Adele (1957), 1 WLR 876 (PC) 59
Agra Bank Ltd v Barry (1874), LR 7 HL 135 259
Air Canada v M & L Travel Ltd, [1993] 3 SCR 787, 108 DLR (4th) 592 183
Air Jamaica Ltd v Charlton, [1999] UKPC 20, [1999] 1 WLR 1399 57
Alati v Kruger, [1955] HCA 64, 94 CLR 216 69
Albion Securities Co Ltd v Nathanson, 2003 BCSC 232 104
Alfred F Beckett Ltd v Lyons, [1967] Ch 449 (CA) 135
Aluminium Industrie Vaassen BV v Romalpa Aluminium Ltd,
    [1976] 1 WLR 676 (CA) 110
Anderson v Rolandi Brothers Logging Co (1955),
    17 WWR (NS) 119 (BCSC) 135
Aquadel Golf Course Ltd v Lindell Beach Holiday Resort Ltd,
    2009 BCCA 5 160
Arbutus Bay Estates Ltd v Canada, 2017 BCCA 374 142

Armitage v Nurse, [1997] EWCA Civ 1279, [1998] Ch 241 77
Armory v Delamirie (1722), 1 Strange 505, 93 ER 664 .... 28, 290–91
Associated Alloys Pty Ltd v Metropolitan Engineering and
    Fabrication Pty Ltd, [1996] NSWSC 119, 20 ACSR 205,
    aff'd [2000] HCA 25, 202 CLR 588 .... 285, 286
Asten v Asten, [1894] 3 Ch 260 185
Aston Cantlow and Wilmcote with Billesley Parochial Church Council v
    Wallbank, [2003] UKHL 37, [2004] AC 546 130
Atari Corporation (UK) Ltd v Electronics Boutiquestores (UK) Ltd,
    [1998] QB 539 (CA) 233
Atlantic Concrete Ltd v Levatte Construction Co Ltd (1975),
    62 DLR (3d) 663, 12 NSR (2d) 179 (CA) 135, 137
Atlantic Developments Inc v Fowler, 2013 NLCA 58 150
Attorney General for Alberta v Huggard Assets Ltd, [1951] SCR 427,
    [1951] 2 DLR 305 33
Attorney General for Alberta v Huggard Assets Ltd, [1953] UKPC 11 33
Attorney General v Guardian (No 2), [1990] 1 AC 109 8–9
Attorney-General of Southern Nigeria v John Holt & Co
    (Liverpool) Ltd, [1915] AC 599 (PC) 141
Aussie Traveller Pty Ltd v Marklea Pty Ltd, [1997] QCA 2, [1998] 1 Qd R 1 47
AYSA v Canada (Revenue Agency), 2007 SCC 42 74

Backhouse v Judd, [1925] SASR 16 .... 9, 10
Baird v British Columbia (1992), 77 CCC (3d) 365 (BCCA) 25, 26
Bank of Canada v Wheaton Pontiac Buick Cadillac GMC Ltd (1990),
    88 Sask R 151 (QB) 274–75
Bank of Montreal v Dynex Petroleum Ltd, 2002 SCC 7,
    [2002] 1 SCR 146, 208 DLR (4th) 155 .... 129, 133–34
Bank of Nova Scotia v Boisselle (1985), 63 AR 283 (QB) 121
Bank of Nova Scotia v Mitz (1979), 106 DLR (3d) 534,
    27 OR (2d) 250 (CA) 278
Barber v Glen, [1987] 6 WWR 689, 59 Sask R 49 (CA) 96, 180
Barton v Raine (1980), 114 DLR (3d) 702, 29 OR (2d) 685 (CA) 153
Batchelor v Marlow, [2001] EWCA Civ 1051, [2003] 1 WLR 764 145
Batty v Toronto, 2011 ONSC 6862 17
BC Teachers' Credit Union v Betterly (1975), 61 DLR (3d) 755 (BCSC) 78, 114
Beaver v The Queen, [1957] SCR 531, 118 CCC 129 23
Beemer v Brownridge, [1934] 1 WWR 545 (Sask CA) 189
Behnke v Bede Shipping Co Ltd, [1927] 1 KB 649 218
Bergler v Odenthal, 2020 BCCA 175 210
Berkheiser v Berkheiser, [1957] SCR 387, 7 DLR (2d) 721 .... 135, 137
Berlin Interior Hardware Co Ltd v Colonial Investment (1918),
    38 DLR 643, 11 Sask LR 46 (CA) 279
Bernstein of Leigh v Skyviews & General Ltd, [1978] QB 479 .... 36, 38, 235
Berrisford v Mexfield Housing Co-operative Ltd, [2011] UKSC 52,
    [2012] 1 AC 955 44

Bettison v Langton, [2002] UKHL 24, [2002] 1 AC 27, aff'g
    [2000] Ch 54 (CA).. 136
Beyer v Clarke, 2010 BCSC 1190.. 142
Big Top Hereford Pty Ltd v Thomas, [2006] NSWSC 1159 288
Birch v Treasury Solicitor, [1951] Ch 298 (CA) 200
Bird v Fort Frances, [1949] 2 DLR 791 (Ont).. 26, 235
Birmingham v Renfrew (1937), 57 CLR 666... 212
Bishopsgate Motor Finance Corp v Transport Brakes Ltd, [1949]
    1 KB 322 (CA).. 248
Black v Blair Athol Farms Ltd, [1996] 5 WWR 516,
    110 Man R (2d) 84 (CA) 45
Black v S Freedman & Co, [1910] HCA 58, 12 CLR 105.................................. 239
Blackburn v McCallum, (1903) 33 SCR 65 161
Blacklocks v JB Developments (Godalming) Ltd, [1982] Ch 183 (Ch D) 257
Blackwell v Blackwell, [1929] UKHL 1, [1929] AC 318 .... 209, 210, 211
Blankstein v Walsh, [1989] 1 WWR 277, 55 Man R (2d) 125 (QB),
    aff'd [1989] 4 WWR 604, 58 Man R (2d) 269 (CA).................................... 142
BMP Global Distribution Inc v Bank of Nova Scotia, 2009 SCC 15.................. 114
Boardman v Phipps, [1966] UKHL 2, [1967] 2 AC 46 76
Bocardo SA v Star Energy UK Onshore Ltd, [2010] UKSC 35,
    [2011] 1 AC 380.. 37, 38
Bolton v Forest Pest Management Institute, [1985] 6 WWR 562,
    21 DLR (4th) 242 (BCCA)... 135
Booth v Knibb Developments Ltd, 2002 ABCA 180 216
Borwick Development Solutions Ltd v Clear Water Fisheries Ltd,
    [2020] EWCA Civ 578... 27
Boyce v Boyce (1849), 16 Sim 476, 60 ER 959.. 185
Bradford Investments (1963) Ltd v Fama (2005), 257 DLR (4th) 347,
    77 OR (3d) 127 .... 20, 35
Brandon v Leckie, [1972] 6 WWR 113, 29 DLR (3d) 633 (Alta QB) 240
Bridges v Hawkesworth (1851), 21 LJQB 75... 23
British Columbia (Director of Civil Forfeiture) v Onn, [2009]
    12 WWR 626, 312 DLR (4th) 739 48–49
British Columbia (Public Trustee) v Mee, [1972] 2 WWR 424,
    23 DLR (3d) 491 (BCCA) 94
Brown v Rotenberg, [1946] OR 363 (CA)... 200
Butt v Humber (1976), 46 APR 92, 17 Nfld & PEIR 92 (Nfld SC)............... 175, 235

Cadbury Schweppes Inc v FBI Foods Ltd, [1999] 1 SCR 142,
    167 DLR (4th) 577 8
Cain v Moon, [1896] 2 QB 283.. 198
Caldwell v Elia (2000), 129 OAC 379, 30 RPR (3d) 295 153
Camco Inc v Olson (Frances) Realty (1979) Ltd, [1986] 6 WWR 258,
    50 Sask R 161 274
Cameron v Silverglen Farms Ltd (1982), 132 DLR (3d) 505,
    51 NSR (2d) 64 (SC) 135, 137

Canada (Director of Soldier Settlement) v Snider Estate, [1991]
2 SCR 481, 81 DLR (4th) 161 117
Canada Cement Co v Fitzgerald (1915), 9 OWN 79 (Ont CA)........................ 142
Canada Safeway Ltd v Thompson (City), [1996] 10 WWR 252,
112 Man R (2d) 94 (QB), aff'd [1997] 7 WWR 565,
118 Man R (2d) 34 (CA) 157, 162, 163
Canadian Imperial Bank of Commerce v Conrad, 2019 NSSC 37 121–22
Canadian Imperial Bank of Commerce v Haley (1979),
100 DLR (3d) 470, 25 NBR (2d) 304 (SC AD)......................................121
Canadian Imperial Bank of Commerce v Rockway Holdings Ltd (1996),
29 OR (3d) 350 (SC) 260
Canadian Long Island Petroleums Ltd v Irving Industries Ltd,
[1975] 2 SCR 715, 50 DLR (3d) 265 .... 224, 256
Canaplan Leasing Inc v Dominion of Canada General Insurance Co
(1990), 69 DLR (4th) 531 (BCSC)...241
Car & Universal Finance Co Ltd v Caldwell, [1965] 1 QB 525 (CA) 245
Caratun v Caratun (1992), 96 DLR (4th) 404, 10 OR (3d) 385 (CA) 5, 71
Cargill v Gotts, [1981] 1 WLR 441 (CA) 142
Carscallen v Leeson, [1927] 4 DLR 797, [1927] 3 WWR 425 (Alta CA)........... 280
Carson v Wilson, [1961] OR 113, 26 DLR (2d) 307 (CA) 176, 177
Carter v Sigmund (1996), 75 BCAC 93.. 142
Case of Mines (1567), 75 ER 472, 1 Plowden 310 38
Central Newbury Car Auctions Ltd v Unity Finance Ltd, [1957]
1 QB 371 (CA)... 237
Chase Manhattan Bank NA v Israel-British Bank (London) Ltd,
[1981] Ch 105 114
Chase v Chase (1962), 36 DLR (2d) 351 (NBCA) 176, 177
Chaulk v Fairview Construction Ltd (1977), 14 Nfld & PEIR 13 (Nfld CA) 222
Cherry v Bredin, [1927] 3 DLR 326, [1927] 2 WWR 314 (Sask CA)......... 280, 281
Cholmondeley v Clinton (1820), 37 ER 527, 2 Jac & W 1 29–30
Church v Hill, [1923] SCR 642, [1923] 3 DLR 1045 109
CIBC Mortgage Corp v Vasquez, 2002 SCC 60...111
CitiFinancial Canada East Corp v Touchie, 2010 NSSC 149......................... 266
Claflin v Claflin, 20 NE 454 (Mass 1889) 80
Clapman v Edwards, [1938] 2 All ER 507.. 145
Clark, Drummie & Co v Ryan (1999), 170 DLR (4th) 266 (NBCA)..................88
Clayton v Le Roy, [1911] 2 KB 1031 (KB and CA).. 248
Clement v Jones, [1909] HCA 11, 8 CLR 133..20
Clos Farming Estates v Easton, [2002] NSWCA 389...................................... 142
Clough Mill Ltd v Martin, [1985] 1 WLR 111 (CA)...................................... 110
Co-op Centre Credit Union Ltd v Greba, [1984] 5 WWR 481, 1
0 DLR (4th) 449 (Alta CA).. 117, 119, 120
Cochlin v Massey Harris Co Ltd (1915), 8 Alta LR 392 (CA)......................... 135
Cochrane v Moore (1890), 25 QBD 57 at 76... 173
Committee for the Commonwealth of Canada v Canada, [1991]
1 SCR 139, 77 DLR (4th) 385 ....17, 18

Coogan v News Group Newspapers Ltd, [2012] EWCA Civ 48, 2 WLR 848........8
Cook v Johnston, [1970] 2 OR 1 (HCJ) 99
Corporate Affairs Commission v ASC Timber Pty Ltd (1989),
   18 NSWLR 577 ....137, 138
Costello v Derbyshire Constabulary, [2001] EWCA Civ 381, [2001]
   1 WLR 1437 ....24–25, 237
Cottage Holiday Associates Ltd v Customs and Excise Commissioners,
   [1983] QB 735..............45
Coutinho & Ferrostaal GmbH v Tracomex (Canada) Ltd, 2015 BCSC 787......110
Cowan v Scargill, [1985] Ch 270..............76
Cowper-Smith v Morgan, 2017 SCC 61..............216, 227, 228
Crabb v Arun District Council, [1975] EWCA Civ 7, [1976] Ch 179 ....155, 225
Crump v Kernahan (1995), 32 Alta LR (3d) 192 (QB)..............165
Cuckmere Brick Co Ltd v Mutual Finance Ltd, [1971] Ch 949 (CA)..............121
Cummings v Claremont Petroleum NL, [1996] HCA 19, 185 CLR 124 5
Cummings v Cummings (2004), 235 DLR (4th) 474, 69 OR (3d) 398 (CA) 197
Currie v Currie Estate (1995), 425 APR 144, 166 NBR (2d) 144 (CA) 197
Currie v McNair (1991), 81 DLR (4th) 744, 117 NBR (2d) 43 (CA)..............251
Cusack v Day, [1925] 3 DLR 1028, [1925] 2 WWR 715 (BCCA)..............200

Dalton v Henry Angus & Co (1881), 6 App Cas 740..............139
Danicki v Danicki, [1995] OJ No 3995, 59 ACWS (3d) 1097..............201, 202
Day v Harris, [2013] EWCA Civ 191, [2014] Ch 211..............169
Dear v Reeves, [2001] EWCA Civ 277, [2002] Ch 1 222
Dedrick v Ashdown (1888), 15 SCR 227..............110
Delgamuukw v British Columbia, [1993] 5 WWR 97, 104 DLR (4th) 470..........35
Delgamuukw v British Columbia, [1997] 3 SCR 1010,
   153 DLR (4th) 193 ....60, 61, 62
Delgoffe v Fader, [1939] Ch 922 (Ch D)..............200
Depew v Wilkes (2002), 216 DLR (4th) 487, 60 OR (3d) 499 (CA) 142
Devlin v Wilson, [1936] 1 WWR 705 (Sask QB)..............120
Dibattista v Menecola (1990), 74 DLR (4th) 569, 75 OR (2d) 443 (CA)..............99
Dickson v Chamberland (1926), 22 Alta LR 270 (CA) 206
Didow v Alberta Power Ltd, [1988] 5 WWR 606,
   60 Alta LR (2d) 212 (CA) 37
DKLR Holding Co (No 2) Pty Ltd v Commissioner of Stamp Duties,
   [1982] HCA 14, 149 CLR 431 80
Doodeward v Spence, [1908] HCA 45, 6 CLR 406..............11, 12
Dougan v Ley [1946] HCA 3, 71 CLR 142..............218
Downsview Nominees Ltd v First City Corp Ltd, [1993] AC 295 at 312 (PC)..116
Dowty Boulton Paul Ltd v Wolverhampton Corp (No 2), [1976] Ch 13 (CA)...142
Duchess of Argyll v Duke of Argyll, [1967] 1 Ch 302 8
Duffield v Elwes (1827), 1 Bli NS 497, 4 ER 959 (HL) 201
Dukart v District of Surrey, [1978] 2 SCR 1039, 86 DLR (3d) 609..............142
Duke of Sutherland v Heathcote, [1892] 1 Ch 475 136–37
Dunbar v Plant, [1997] EWCA Civ 2167, [1998] Ch 412..............97

Durham Condominium Corp No 123 v Amberwood Investments Ltd,
(2002) 211 DLR (4th) 1, 58 OR (3d) 481 (CA) 159–60
Durrani v Augier (2000), 190 DLR (4th) 183, 50 OR (3d) 353 (SC) 118
Dyce v Lady James Hay (1852), 1 Macq 305 142
Dyck v Shingle Estate, 1984 ABCA 185, 54 AR 382 201
Dyer v Dyer (1788), 2 Cox 92, 30 ER 42 87

Earl Putnam Organization Ltd v Macdonald (1978), 91 DLR (3d) 714,
21 OR (2d) 815 (CA) 139
Eastern Trust Co v McTague (1963), 39 DLR (2d) 743 (PEI SC AD) 54
Easton v Isted, [1903] 1 Ch 405 (CA) 139
Eaves v Hickson (1861), 30 Beav 136, 54 ER 840 75
Edmonds v Armstrong Funeral Home Ltd, [1931] 1 DLR 676 (Alta CA).... 12, 193
Edmonton Regional Airports Authority v Canada Life Assurance Co,
[2004] 4 WWR 192, 24 Alta LR (4th) 251 (QB) 161
Edwards v State Trustees Ltd, [2016] VSCA 28 97
Erie Sand and Gravel Ltd v Tri-B Acres Inc, 2009 ONCA 709 216
Evans v European Bank Ltd, [2004] NSWCA 82, 61 NSWLR 75 239

F Moyer Boot & Shoe Co v Moellendorf, [1930] 3 WWR 311,
25 Alta LR 76 (CA) 135
Fales v Canada Permanent Trust Co, [1977] 2 SCR 302, 70 DLR (3d) 257 75
Farquharson Brothers & Co v King & Co, [1902] AC 325 (HL) 237, 242, 243
Fields of Athenry Resort Corporation v Grey, 2018 NLSC 230 107
Firestone Tire & Rubber Co of Canada v Industrial Acceptance Corp,
[1971] SCR 357 .... 287, 292
First City Capital Ltd v Price Waterhouse Ltd (1984),
57 BCLR 354 (SC) 287, 292
Firstpost Homes Ltd v Johnson, [1995] 1 WLR 1567 (CA) 216
Firth v BD Management Ltd (1990), 73 DLR (4th) 375 (BCCA) 48
Fisher v Mansfield, [1997] 2 NZLR 230 212
Fisher v Wigg (1700), 1 Salk 391, 91 ER 339 85–86
Flack v National Crime Authority (1998), 156 ALR 501 .... 22, 24
Flannigan v Wotherspoon, [1953] 1 DLR 768, 7 WWR (NS) 660
(BCSC) 95, 108
Foley v Hill (1848), 2 HLC 28, 9 ER 1002 7
Fortis Trust Corp v Deloitte & Touche Inc (1997), 159 Nfld & PEIR 91,
492 APR 91 (NLCA) 259
Foskett v McKeown, [2000] UKHL 29, [2001] 1 AC 102 .... 78, 114
Foundling Hospital Governors and Guardians v Crane, [1911]
2 KB 367 (CA) 176
Four-Maids Ltd v Dudley Marshall (Properties) Ltd, [1957] Ch 317 119
Franklin v St John's (City), 2012 NLCA 48 153
Fraser v Thames Television Ltd, [1984] QB 44 8
Frazer v Walker, [1967] 1 AC 569, [1967] NZLR 1069 .... 262, 270
Frederick Gerring Jr (Ship) v The Queen (1897), 27 SCR 271 21

Fredkin v Glines (1908), 9 WLR 393, 18 Man R 249 (CA)................135, 137, 138
Frith v Alliance Investment Co (1914), 49 SCR 384, 20 DLR 356.................... 215
Frost Ltd v Ralph, (1980) 115 DLR (3d) 612.. 122

Galbraith v Madawaska Club Ltd, [1961] SCR 639, 29 DLR (2d) 153.............. 163
Gibson Holdings v Principal Investments, [1964] SCR 424,
    44 DLR (2d) 673 .... 45, 163
Gilchrist Watt & Sanderson Pty Ltd v York Products Pty Ltd,
    [1970] 1 WLR 1262 (PC).. 27
Gill v Bucholtz, 2009 BCCA 137 271
Glenelg Homestead Ltd v Wile (2005), 248 DLR (4th) 427,
    230 NSR (2d) 289 (CA) 251
Grant v Lowres, 2018 BCCA 311 142
Grant v MacDonald, [1992] 5 WWR 577, 68 BCLR (2d) 332 (CA) 142
Grey v Grey (1677), 2 Swans 594, 36 ER 742 88
Greymac Trust Co v Ontario (Ontario Securities Commission). See Re Ontario
    Securities Commission and Greymac Credit Corp
Grundt v Great Boulder Pty Gold Mines Ltd, [1937] HCA 58, 59 CLR 641...... 229
Gypsum Carrier Inc v The Queen, [1978] 1 FC 147, 78 DLR (3d) 175.............. 150

Hackworth v Baker, [1936] 1 WWR 321 (Sask CA)... 265
Hale v Westfair Foods Ltd, [1995] 3 WWR 293, 127 Sask R 223 (QB) 16
Hall v Hebert, [1993] 2 SCR 159, 101 DLR (4th) 129 25
Hall v McLaughlin Estate (2006), 25 ETR (3d) 198 (Ont SC)......................... 212
Harbour Authority v Simpson Aqua, 2016 PECA 20 147
Harrison v Carswell, [1976] 2 SCR 200 19
Hatch v Mackedie, 1998 CanLII 1080 (BCSC) 173
Hawker v Hawker (1969), 3 DLR (3d) 735 (Sask QB)................................... 252
Hearns v Rizzolo, 2012 NSSC 256...230
Heath v Tang, [1993] 1 WLR 1421 (CA) 5
Hedley v Roberts, [1977] VR 282 142
Henderson v Henderson, 2016 SKQB 282 9
Henderson v Volk, (1982) 132 DLR (3d) 690, 35 OR (2d) 379 (CA) 154–55
Henry v Hammond, [1913] 2 KB 515 182–83
Henry v Henry (1999), 126 OAC 372...181
Hermanson v Martin, [1987] 1 WWR 439, 33 DLR (4th) 12 (Sask CA) 270
Hill v Nova Scotia (Attorney General), [1997] 1 SCR 69,
    142 DLR (4th) 230 ....155, 216
Hill v Reglon Pty Ltd, [2007] NSWCA 295..288
Hill v Tupper (1863), 2 H & C 121, 159 ER 51 ....131–32, 235
Hilliard v Lostchuk, [1993] OJ No 2204, 42 ACWS (3d) 1097...................... 206
Hobson v Gorringe, [1897] 1 Ch 182 at 193 (CA) 277
Hoj Industries Ltd v Dundas Shepard Square Ltd (1978),
    95 DLR (3d) 354, 23 OR (2d) 295.. 179
Holat v Wettlaufer, 2014 BCSC 425...246–47
Holden v Tanase, 2002 ABQB 1025...222

Holland v Hodgson (1872), LR 7 CP 328 (Exch) 277, 279
Hollett v Hollett (1993), 334 APR 271, 106 Nfld & PEIR 271 (Nfld SC) 175
Holroyd v Marshall (1862), 10 HLC 191, 11 ER 999 ....111–12, 220
Hongkong Bank of Canada v Wheeler Holdings Ltd, [1993] 1 SCR 167,
    100 DLR (4th) 40 32
Hoyl Group Ltd v Cromer Town Council, [2015] EWCA Civ 782, [2015]
    HLR 43 155
Humboldt Flour Mills Co Ltd v Boscher (1974), 50 DLR (3d) 477 (Sask QB)....231
Hunt v Luck, [1902] 1 Ch 428 (CA) 253
Hunter v Hunter, [1930] 4 DLR 255, 65 OLR 586 (SC) 193
Hunter v Moss, [1993] EWCA Civ 11, [1994] 1 WLR 452 184
Husky Oil Operations Ltd v Shelf Holdings Ltd, [1989] 3 WWR 692,
    56 DLR (4th) 193 (Alta CA) 142
Hutchings v Campbell, Wilson and Horne Ltd, [1924] 1 WWR 1070,
    [1924] 2 DLR 299 (Alta CA) 147

i Trade Finance Inc v Bank of Montreal, 2011 SCC 26 114
ICBC v Lo, 2006 BCCA 584 .... 76, 180
Ilford-Riverton Airways Ltd v Aero Trades (Western) Ltd, [1977]
    5 WWR 193, 76 DLR (3d) 742 (Man CA) 287, 292
Ilich v The Queen, [1987] HCA 1, 162 CLR 110 239
Imperial Oil Ltd v Young (1996), 142 Nfld & PEIR 280,
    445 APR 280 (Nfld SC) 150
In Hudson's Bay Co v Kearns (1896), 4 BCR 536 (SC) 266, 267
In re Hagger, [1930] 2 Ch 190 212
Income Tax Commissioners v Pemsel, [1891] UKHL 1, [1891] AC 531 74
Indian Oil Corp Ltd v Greenstone Shipping Co SA, [1988] QB 345 290
Inwards v Baker, [1965] 2 QB 29 (CA) 226

J & W Investments Ltd v Black (1963), 38 DLR (2d) 251 (BCCA) 116
JA Pye (Oxford) Ltd v Graham, [2002] UKHL 30, [2003] 1 AC 419 .... 20, 22
Jackson Estate v Young, 2020 NSSC 5 195
Janicki v Hospital of St Raphael, 744 A (2d) 963 (Superior Ct
    Connecticut 1999) 12
Jankowski v Perpetual Trustee Co Ltd, [1996] 2 WWR 457,
    131 DLR (4th) 717 (Man CA) 208, 209–10
JAR Leaseholds Ltd v Tormet Ltd, [1965] 1 OR 347, 48 DLR (2d) 97 (CA) 113
JCM v ANA, 2012 BCSC 584 12
JE Gibson Holdings v Principal Investments, [1964] SCR 424,
    44 DLR (2d) 673 .... 45–46, 163
Jemco Holdings Ltd v Medlee Ltd (1975), 78 DLR (3d) 604,
    14 NSR (2d) 662 (CA) 261
Jerome v Kelly, [2004] UKHL 25, [2004] 1 WLR 1409 220–21
John Burrows Ltd v Subsurface Surveys Ltd, [1968] SCR 607,
    68 DLR (2d) 354 225
Johnson v Farney (1913), 14 DLR 134 (Ont CA) 181, 182

Johnston v Roode, 2019 NSCA 98..20
Joly v Pelletier, [1999] OJ No 1728 (Ont HC).. 10
Jones v Davidson Partners Ltd (1981), 121 DLR (3d) 127,
    31 OR (2d) 494 (SC).. 104
Jones v De Marchant (1916), 26 Man R 455 (CA).....................283, 284, 285, 286
Jones v Pritchard, [1908] 1 Ch 630.. 148
Joseph v Lyons (1884), 15 QBD 280 (CA).. 252–53

Kay's Leasing Corp Pty Ltd v CSR Provident Fund Nominees Pty Ltd,
    [1962] VR 429.. 282
Kellogg Brown & Root Inc v Aerotech Herman Nelson Inc,
    2004 MBCA 63 69
Kendrick v Dominion Bank (1920), 58 DLR 309, 48 OLR 539 (CA)............... 200
Kenworthy v Ward (1853), 11 Hare 196, 68 ER 1245 85
Keppell v Bailey (1834), 2 My & K 517, 39 ER 1042 130–31
Kerri (Guardian of) v Decker, 2002 NFCA 11.. 110
Kim v Choi, 2020 BCCA 98...25
Kirk v Ford, [1920] 3 WWR 91, 53 DLR 644 (Sask CA)................135, 137, 138
Klippstein v Kapasiwin (Summer Village), 2020 ABCA 32 142
Knight v Knight (1840), 3 Beav 148 at 172, 49 ER 58.................................. 181
Komari Inc v Feddema (1988), 55 DLR (4th) 595, 67 OR (2d) 135 (SC)........... 135
Kowbel v Marusiak (1957), 7 DLR (2d) 424, 21 WWR (NS) 35 (Alta CA) 113

Lace v Chandler, [1944] KB 368 (CA)...45
Lake v Gibson (1729), 1 Eq Cas Abr 290, 21 ER 1052 87
Langer v McTavish Bros Ltd, [1932] 4 DLR 90 (BCCA).................. 172, 173, 174
Lasalle Recreations Ltd v Canadian Camdex Investments Ltd (1969),
    4 DLR (3d) 549 (BCCA) 278, 279
Latec Investments Ltd v Hotel Terrigal Pty Ltd, [1965] HCA 17,
    113 CLR 265 257
Lawen Estate v Nova Scotia (Attorney General), 2019 NSSC 162 197
Lawrence v Maple Trust Co (2007), 278 DLR (4th) 698,
    84 OR (3d) 94 (CA)... 270
Le Corporation Episcopale Catholique Romane of St Albert v
    RJ Sheppard & Co (1913), 9 DLR 619, 3 WWR 814 (Alta QB) 178
Leacock v Leacock, 2009 ABQB 525.. 113
Legg v Burton, [2017] 4 WLR 186 (Ch D)..181, 213
Lehmann v BRM Enterprises Ltd (1978), 88 DLR (3d) 87, 7 BCLR 8 (SC)....... 113
Leigh v Taylor, [1902] AC 157 (HL) 278, 279
Lensen v Lensen, [1984] 6 WWR 673, 14 DLR (4th) 611 (Sask CA),
    rev'd [1987] 2 SCR 672, 44 DLR (4th) 1... 216
Leoppky v Meston, 2008 ABQB 45 215
Levet v Gas Light and Coke Co, [1919] 1 Ch 24 139
Lewis v Alliance of Canadian Cinema Television and Radio Artists,
    [1996] 6 WWR 588, 18 BCLR (3d) 382 (CA) 181, 186
Liverpool City Council v Irwin, [1976] UKHL 1, [1977] AC 239.......................47

Lockwood v Brentwood Park Investments Ltd (1970), 10 DLR (3d) 143,
1 NSR (2d) 669 (CA) 143
Lohia v Lohia, [2001] EWCA Civ 1691 88
Loke Yew v Port Swettenham Rubber Co Ltd, [1913] UKPC 17,
[1913] AC 491 266
London and South Western Railway Co v Gomm (1881), 20 Ch D 562
(CA) 223–24
Lumsden v Miller, [1980] 4 WWR 143, 110 DLR (3d) 226 (Alta QB) 199
Lutz Estate v Lutz, 2020 SKCA 14 197
Lutz v Kawa (1980), 112 DLR (3d) 271 30
Lysaght v Edwards (1876), 2 Ch D 499 (CA) 220

MA Hanna Co v Provincial Bank of Canada, [1935] SCR 144,
[1935] 1 DLR 545 183
Mabo v Queensland (No 2), [1992] HCA 23, 175 CLR 1 ....34, 58, 59, 61, 62
Mabo v Queensland, [1988] HCA 69, 166 CLR 186 63
MacArthur v Hastings (1905), 15 Man R 500 (QB) 253, 254
MacDonald v MacDonald, 2003 NSSC 8 189
MacIntyre v Spierenburg (1979), 41 NSR (2d) 584, 76 APR 584 (SC) 215
Mackenzie v Blindman Valley Co-operative Association Ltd, [1947]
4 DLR 687, [1947] 2 WWR 443 (Alta QB) 248
MacLeod v Montgomery Estate, [1980] 2 WWR 303,
108 DLR (3d) 424 (Alta CA) 191
Maddison v Alderson (1883), 8 App Cas 467 (HL) 215, 216, 217
Madsen Estate v Saylor, 2007 SCC 18 179
Majeau Carrying Co Pty Ltd v Coastal Rutile Ltd, [1973] HCA 22, 129
CLR 48 104
Malayan Credit Ltd v Jack Chia-Mph Ltd, [1986] 1 AC 549 (PC) 89
Manning v Algard Estate, 2008 BCSC 1129 ....246, 251
Maracle v Travellers Indemnity Co of Canada, [1991] 2 SCR 50,
80 DLR (4th) 652 225
March Brothers & Wells v Banton (1911), 45 SCR 338 109
Marsh v Alabama, 326 US 501 (1946) 18
Mascall v Mascall, [1984] EWCA Civ 10, 50 P & CR 119 191
Mason v Mason, 2018 NBCA 20 192–93
Mason v Partridge, 2005 NSCA 144 153
McAuley v Genaille, 2017 MBCA 69 198
McCartney v Londonderry & Lough Swilly Railway Co Ltd,
[1904] AC 301 143
McDonald v Bode Estate, 2018 BCCA 140 134
McDonald v Eckert, 2004 BCSC 323 94
McDonald v Lane (1882), 7 SCR 462 289
McDonald v McDonald (1903), 33 SCR 145 200
McEwen v Ewers and Ferguson, [1946] 3 DLR 494 at 495 (Ont HCJ) 86, 87
McHugh v Union Bank of Canada, [1913] AC 299, 10 DLR 562 (PC) 121
McKeown v Cavalier Yachts Pty Ltd (1988), 13 NSWLR 303 ....287, 288

McManus v McManus, 2019 BCSC 123 88
McNeil v Corbett (1907), 39 SCR 608...216
MCP Pension Trustees Ltd v Aon Pension Trustees Ltd,
    [2011] 3 WLR 455 (CA)...252
McPhail v Doulton, [1970] UKHL 1, [1971] AC 424 ....72, 186
McTavish v Kellett (1989), 62 Man R (2d) 146 (QB)...................248
McVicar v Herman (1958), 13 DLR (2d) 419 (Sask CA) 241
Mehta Estate v Mehta Estate, [1993] 6 WWR 457,
    104 DLR (4th) 24 (Man CA)...88
MEL Industries Ltd v Pioneer Machinery Co Ltd (1981),
    121 DLR (3d) 103, 15 Alta LR (2d) 140 (CA)........................110
Melluish v BMI (No 3) Ltd, [1996] AC 454 (HL) 276, 277
Metro-Matic Services Ltd v Hulmann, [1973] 4 OR (2d) 462,
    48 DLR (3d) 326, (CA), rev'g [1970] 2 OR 707,
    12 DLR (3d) 21 (HCJ)..44
Midland Bank Trust Co Ltd v Green, [1981] AC 513 (HL)........250–51
Mihaylov v 1165996 Ontario Inc, 2017 ONCA 116 ....142, 150
Miller v Emcer Products Ltd, [1956] Ch 304 (CA)...................142
Miller v Race (1758), 1 Burrow 452, 97 ER 398........................239
Miller v Tipling (1918), 43 OLR 88, 43 DLR 469 (CA) 147
Milroy v Lord (1862), 4 De G F & J 264, 45 ER 1185 (CA) 190
Miner v CPR (1910), 18 WLR 476, 3 Alta LR 408 (CA) 193
MJ Jones Inc v Henry (2002), 58 OR (3d) 529 (CA) 240
Moncrieff v Jamieson, [2007] UKHL 42, [2007] 1 WLR 2620..........142, 145
Moody v Steggles (1879), 12 Ch D 261..............................144–45
Moore v Regents of the University of California, 793 P (2d) 479 (1990)...........12
Mordo v Nitting, 2006 BCSC 1761 191
Morguard Mortgage Investments Ltd v Faro Development Corp Ltd,
    [1975] 1 WWR 737, 50 DLR (3d) 426 (Alta CA)................118–19
Mork v Bombauer (1977), 4 BCLR 127 (SC) 113
Morris v Redland Bricks Ltd, [1970] AC 652.........................140
Morris v Whiting (1913), 15 DLR 254 at (Man KB)..................189
Mortimer-Rae v Barthel (1979), 105 DLR (3d) 289,
    11 Alta LR (2d) 66 (QB)..241
Mountford v Scott, [1975] Ch 258....................................224
Mulvaney v Jackson, [2002] EWCA Civ 1078, [2003] 4 All ER 83 ....141, 142
Myers v Johnston, [1923] 4 DLR 1152, 52 OLR 658 (CA) 142

Nachtigal v Premier Motors Ltd, [1929] 2 DLR 190,
    24 Alta LR 80 (CA) 241, 243
National Provincial Bank Ltd v Ainsworth, [1965] AC 1175 (HL)............256
National Trust Co v Palace Theatre Ltd, [1928] 2 DLR 739,
    [1928] 1 WWR 805 (Alta CA)...280
Neazor v Hoyle (1962), 32 DLR (2d) 131 (Alta SC AD)................88
Nelson (City) v Mowatt, 2017 SCC 8...................................29
Nelson v 1153696 Alberta Ltd, 2011 ABCA 203.....................138, 151

Nevsun Resources Ltd v Araya, 2020 SCC 5..11
New Brunswick Ry Co v Kelly (1896), 26 SCR 341 260
New Zealand Government Property Corp v HM & S Ltd, [1982]
    QB 1145 (CA).. 280, 281
Nicholls Estate v Nicholls Estate, [1972] 5 WWR 99 (Alta CA) 171, 173, 174
Noble v Alley, [1951] SCR 64, [1951] 1 DLR 321........................ 157, 161
Nordin v Faridi, [1996] 5 WWR 242, 17 BCLR (3d) 366 (CA) 142
Northern Counties of England Fire Insurance Co v Whipp (1884),
    26 Ch D 482 (CA)... 237–38
Novak v Gatien (1975), 25 RFL 397 (Man QB) 96
Nylar Foods Ltd v Roman Catholic Episcopal Corp of Prince Rupert,
    (1988) 48 DLR (4th) 175 (BCCA)... 162

O'Toole v Walters (1979), 96 DLR (3d) (NSSC) 260, 261
Ocean Harvesters Ltd v Quinlan Brothers Ltd, [1975] 1 SCR 684,
    44 DLR (3d) 687 44
Ong v Ping, [2017] EWCA Civ 2069... 188
Ontario Hydro-Electric Power Commission v Brown, [1960] OR 91,
    21 DLR (2d) 551 (CA)... 182
Opetchesaht Indian Band v Canada, [1997] 2 SCR 119, 147 DLR (4th) 1...........61
Oppenheim v Tobacco Securities Trust Co, [1950] UKHL 2, [1951] AC 297...... 74
Orchard Trading Estate Management Ltd v Johnson Security Ltd,
    [2002] EWCA Civ 406... 134, 148

Pallot v Douglas, 2017 BCCA 254 ....71, 98
Palmer v Bowman, [2000] 1 WLR 842 (CA)............................... 143
Parker v British Airways Board, [1982] 1 QB 1004 (CA).....................23, 24, 27
Parker v Parker (1989), 100 NBR (2d) 361, 252 APR 361 (QB) 150
Parkland Mortgage Corp v Therevan Development Corp, [1982]
    1 WWR 587, 130 DLR (3d) 682 (Alta QB) 180
Patton v OH Ranch Ltd (1996), 138 DLR (4th) 381,
    43 Alta LR (3d) 445 (CA) 136
Paul v Constance, [1977] 1 WLR 527 (CA)........................... 182, 190, 235
Pearse v Green (1819), 1 J & W 135, 37 ER 327................................. 75
Pecore v Pecore, 2007 SCC 17 ....88, 90
Peddie v Eagles and Lai (2012), 325 Nfld & PEIR 177,
    1009 APR 177 (PEI SC)...260
Pegg v Pegg (1992), 1 Alta LR (3d) 249, 21 RPR (2d) (QB)........................ 129
Peoples Bank of Halifax v Estey (1904), 34 SCR 429.....................241, 243
Pepper v Brooker, 2017 ONCA 532 30
Performance Industries Ltd v Sylvan Lake Golf & Tennis Club Ltd,
    2002 SCC 19 70
Phillips v Halliday, [1891] AC 228 142
Phillips v Phillips (1862), 4 De GF & J 208, 45 ER 1164.........................256
Phipps v Pears, [1964] EWCA Civ 3, [1965] 1 QB 76 140–41
Pickering Square Inc v Trillium College Inc, 2014 ONSC 2629........ 134

Pierce v Proprietors of Swan Point Cemetery, 14 Am Rep 667 (1872) 12
Pilcher v Rawlins (1872), LR 7 Ch App 259 (CA) 250
Pitt v Holt, [2013] UKSC 26, [2013] 2 AC 108 76
Plaza Equities Ltd v Bank of Nova Scotia, [1978] 3 WWR 385,
    84 DLR (3d) 609 (Alta QB) 279–80
Popov v Hayashi, 2002 WL 31833731 (Cal Super 2002) 21
Prince George (City) v Columbus Hotel Co (1991) Ltd, 2010 BCSC 149 49
Pritchard v Briggs, [1980] Ch 338 (CA) 224
Project Research Group Ltd v Acumen Investments Ltd (1986),
    33 DLR (4th) 118, 57 OR (2d) 332 (SC) 117
Prudential Assurance Co Ltd v London Residuary Body, [1991]
    UKHL 10, [1992] 2 AC 386 44–45
PruneYard Shopping Center v Robins, 447 US 74 (1980) 18
Punch v Savoy's Jewellers Ltd (1986), 26 DLR (4th) 546,
    54 OR (2d) 383 (CA) 27
Pyramid Building Society v Scorpion Hotels Pty Ltd, [1988]
    1 VR 188 (CA) 270

R (Von Goetz) v Tower Hamlets LBC, [1998] EWCA Civ 1507,
    [1999] QB 1019 221
R & R Cunningham Enterprises Ltd v Vollmers, [1973] 4 WWR 339
    (Alta QB) 105
R v Adams, [1996] 3 SCR 101, 138 DLR (4th) 657 61
R v Air Canada, [1978] 2 WWR 694, 86 DLR (3d) 631 (Man CA),
    aff'd [1980] 2 SCR 303, 111 DLR (3d) 513 37
R v Alexson, [1989] 6 WWR 275, 68 Alta LR (2d) 255 (Prov Ct) 136
R v Bentham, [2005] UKHL 18, [2005] WLR 1057 13
R v Esquimalt, [1972] 5 WWR 362 at 365 129
R v Ford, 2010 BCCA 105 96
R v Kelly, [1998] EWCA Crim 1578, [1999] QB 621 12
R v Lowden (1981), 15 Alta LR (2d) 250, 27 AR 91 at 101 (CA) 183
R v Ngan, [2007] NZSC 105 27
R v Powley, [2003] 2 SCR 207, 230 DLR (4th) 1 .... 61, 62–63
R v Tang, [2008] HCA 39, 237 CLR 1 11
R v Tener, [1985] 1 SCR 533, 17 DLR (4th) 1 135
Rammage v Roussel Estate, 2016 ONSC 1857 211–12
Rangeley v Midland Railway Co (1868), LR 3 Ch App 306 147
Rawlinson v Mort (1905), 21 TLR 774, 93 LT 555 171
Raymond v Anderson, 2011 SKCA 58 .... 69, 219–20
Re Allen, [1953] Ch 810 54–55
Re Amland Estate (1975), 10 NBR (2d) 285 (QB) 191
Re Astor's Settlement Trusts, [1952] Ch 534 72
Re Babour, [1967] Qd R 10 85
Re Barnes (1918), 42 OLR 352 206
Re Bayoff Estate, 2000 SKQB 23 .... 199, 200
Re Beardmore Trusts, [1952] 1 DLR 41, [1951] OWN 728 183

Re Beaumont, [1902] 1 Ch 889 (Ch D) 203
Re Bowes Co Ltd and Rankin, [1924] 4 DLR 406, 55 OLR 601 164–65
Re Boyes (1884), 26 Ch D 531 .... 207, 210–11
Re Cole, [1964] Ch 175 (CA) 170–71, 172, 174
Re Community Youth Services Inc, 2011 NBQB 19 161
Re Demaiter and Link, [1973] 3 OR 140 (SC) 83
Re Dillon (1890), 44 Ch D 76 (CA) 200
Re Dreger (1976), 12 OR (2d) 371, 69 DLR (3d) 47 (SC) 96
Re Drummond Wren, [1945] 4 DLR 674 (Ont HC) 157, 161
Re Ellenborough Park, [1955] EWCA Civ 4,
    [1956] Ch 131 ....142, 143, 144, 145, 146, 149
Re Freud, [2014] EWHC 2577 (Ch) 208
Re Gape, [1952] Ch 743 (CA) 54
Re Giffen, [1998] 1 SCR 91, 155 DLR (4th) 332 ....126, 275, 292
Re Goldcorp Exchange Ltd, [1994] UKPC 3, [1995] 1 AC 74,
    [1994] 3 NZLR 385 232
Re Gonin, [1979] Ch 16 at 35 (Ch D) 205
Re Goodchild, [1996] 1 All ER 670 212
Re Gore, [1972] 1 OR 550, 23 DLR (3d) 534 (SC) 96
Re Gortler and Mister Donut Shops Ltd (1983), 150 DLR (3d) 185,
    43 OR (2d) 59 (HCJ) 280
Re Green, [1951] Ch 148 212
Re Hallett's Estate (1879), 13 Ch D 696 (CA) 114
Re Harvey (1932), 41 OWN 420 206
Re Hogg Estate (1987), 83 AR 165 (QB) 206
Re James, [1935] Ch 449 (Ch D) 205
Re Jessop Estate (1987), 55 Sask R 18 (CA) 181
Re Keen, [1937] Ch 236 (CA) 207, 208, 210
Re Kenron Homes Ltd (1982), 20 Sask R 80 (QB) 233–34
Re Korvine's Trust, [1921] 1 Ch 343 203–4
Re Londonderry's Settlement, [1965] Ch 918 (CA) 76
Re McColgan, [1969] 2 OR 152, 4 DLR (3d) 572 54
Re McKinley and McCullough (1919), 51 DLR 659, 46 OLR 535 (CA) 260
Re McLeod Estate, 2012 ABQB 384 173
Re Mihalopulos (1956), 5 DLR (2d) 628, 19 WWR 118 (Alta SC) 208
Re Monserat Investments Ltd (1978), 87 DLR (3d) 593,
    20 OR (2d) 181 (CA) 254
Re Montagu's Settlement Trusts, [1987] 1 Ch 264 at 284 (Ch D) 252
Re Morrison, Jones & Taylor Ltd, [1914] 1 Ch 50 (CA) 282
Re North Gower Township Public School Board and Todd, [1968]
    1 OR 63, 65 DLR (2d) 421 (CA) 53, 54
Re Nottage, [1895] 2 Ch 649 74
Re Ontario Securities Commission and Greymac Credit Corp (1986),
    30 DLR (4th) 1, 55 OR (2d) 673 (CA), aff'd, [1988] 2 SCR 172 114
Re Rose, [1949] Ch 78 (Ch D) 190
Re Rose, [1952] EWCA Civ 4, [1952] Ch 499 .... 190, 191

Re Sammon (1979), 94 DLR (3d) 594, 22 OR (2d) 721 (CA) 176
Re Samuel Allen & Sons Ltd, [1907] 1 Ch 575 (Ch D) 282
Re Southern Livestock Producers Ltd, [1964] 1 WLR 24................................ 105
Re Stewart, [1908] 2 Ch 251 (Ch D)...204–5
Re Stoneham, [1918] 1 Ch 149 (Ch D) 169, 170
Re Tachibana (1968), 66 DLR (2d) 567, 63 WWR (NS) 99 (Man CA) 193
Re Taylor Estate, [1982] 6 WWR 109, 19 Sask R 361 (SK SU)........................ 42
Re Tilbury West Public School Board and Hastie, [1966] 2 OR 20,
    55 DLR (2d) 407 53–54
Re Vandervell Trustees Ltd (No 2), [1974] EWCA Civ 7, [1974] Ch 269 21
Re Wait, [1927] 1 Ch 606 (CA)..231
Re Western Canada Pulpwood Co Ltd, [1930] 1 DLR 652,
    38 Man R 378 (CA)...231
Re Weston, [1902] 1 Ch 680 (Ch D)..200
Re Whatmough and National Trust Co Ltd (1979), 96 DLR (3d) 382,
    23 OR (2d) 452 (SC) 121
Re White, [1928] 1 DLR 846, 8 CBR 544 (Ont SC).................................... 96
Regency Villas Title Ltd v Diamond Resorts (Europe) Ltd, [2017]
    EWCA Civ 238, [2017] Ch 516, varied [2018] UKSC 57,
    [2019] AC 553 .... 141, 142
Reid v Commissioner of Police of the Metropolis, [1973] QB 551 (CA)............ 248
Reid v Whiteford (1883), 1 Man R 19 (QB) 41
Renehan v Malone (1897), 1 NB Eq 506 181
Rennick v Rennick (1962), 33 DLR (2d) 649 (Sask CA)................................206
Rhone v Stephens, [1994] UKHL 3, [1994] 2 AC 310 ....101, 158–59, 235
Rice v Rice (1854), 2 Drew 73, 61 ER 646...254–55
Richards v Delbridge (1874), LR 18 Eq 11.. 190
Riffel Estate (1987), 64 Sask R 190 (QB) 210
Riley v Penttila, [1974] VR 547...20
Riverlate Properties Ltd v Paul, [1975] Ch 133 (CA)..................................... 70
RMH Teleservices v BCGEU, 2003 BCSC 278 19
Robillard v Staaf, 2008 BCSC 1266...135, 137, 138
Roche v Douglas, [2000] WASC 146, 22 WAR 331................................... 12–13
Rochefoucauld v Boustead, [1897] 1 Ch 196 at 206 (CA)...............188, 210, 216
Rogers v Hosegood, [1900] 2 Ch 388.. 163
Rose v Peterkin (1885), 13 SCR 677 259
Ross v Hunter (1882), 7 SCR 289 ....139, 259–60
Royal Bank of Canada v Oliver, [1992] 1 WWR 320,
    85 DLR (4th) 122 (Sask CA) 96
Rufenack v Hope Mission, [2003] 3 WWR 161, 10 Alta LR (4th) 172 (QB)...... 210
Russo v Field, [1973] SCR 466, 34 DLR (3d) 704 ....157, 162

SA v Metro Vancouver Housing Corp, 2019 SCC 4 ....72, 78
Sadaka v Saleh, 2011 SKQB 416...215
Saleh v Reichert (1993), 104 DLR (4th) 384 (Ont)... 193
Sanderson v Halstead, [1968] 1 OR 749, 67 DLR (2d) 567 (HCJ) 191

Sandford v Porter (1889), 16 OAR 565 (CA) 75
Saskatchewan Minerals v Keyes, [1966] 1 WLR 363 (CA) 129–30
Saulnier v Anderson (1987), 43 DLR (4th) 19, 83 NBR (2d) 1 (QB) 199, 200
Saulnier v Royal Bank of Canada, 2008 SCC 58 .... 5, 71
Saunders v Vautier (1841), Cr & Ph 240, 41 ER 482 80
Schobelt v Barber, [1967] 1 OR 349, 60 DLR (2d) 519 .... 96, 180
Scott v Filipovic, 2015 BCCA 409 282
Semelhago v Paramadevan, [1996] 2 SCR 415,
    136 DLR (4th) 1 .... 219, 220, 221, 222, 224
Sen v Headley, [1991] EWCA Civ 13, [1991] Ch 425 202
Shamac Country Inns Ltd v 412765 Alberta Ltd (1994),
    18 Alta LR (3d) 396 (QB) 178
Sharpe v The Bishop of Worcester, [2015] EWCA Civ 399 130
Shaw v Foster (1872), LR 5 HL 321 220
Shepherd Homes Ltd v Sandham (No 2), [1971] 1 WLR 1062 (Ch D) 160
Shkuratoff v Shkuratoff, 2007 BCSC 1061 191
Shropshire Union Railways and Canal Co v The Queen (1875),
    LR 7 HL 496 255
Siewert v Seward, [1975] 3 WWR 584, 54 DLR (3d) 161 (Alta CA) 135
Sifton v Sifton, [1938] AC 656 (PC) 54
Silaschi v 1054473 Ontario Ltd (2000), 48 OR (3d) 313,
    186 DLR (4th) 339 (CA) 113
Silver v Fulton, 2011 NSSC 127 57
Sinclair v Brougham, [1914] AC 398 238–39
Slagboom v Kirby, 1993 CanLII 449 199
Smith and Snipes Hall Farm Ltd v River Douglas Catchment Board,
    [1949] 2 KB 500 (CA) 157, 158
Smith v Marrable (1843), 11 M & W 5, 152 ER 693 49
Snitzler v Snitzler, 2015 ONSC 2539 .... 200, 202–3
Snyder v Chisholm, 2015 NSCA 39 136
Sorensen (Estate) v Sorensen (1977), 90 DLR (3d) 26, 3 AR 8 (CA) 201
Soulos v Korkontzilas, [1997] 2 SCR 217, 146 DLR (4th) 214 180
South West Marine Estates Ltd v Bank of BC (1985),
    65 BCLR 328 (CA) 121
Southern Centre of Theosophy Inc v South Australia, [1981] UKPC 41,
    [1982] AC 706 36
Southwark London Borough Council v Mills, [1999] UKHL 40,
    [2001] 1 AC 1 .... 47, 49
Spence v Union Marine Insurance Co Ltd (1868), LR 3 CP 427 .... 288, 289
St John v Horvat, [1994] 5 WWR 22, 113 DLR (4th) 670 (BCCA) 240
Stacey v Anglican Churches of Canada (1999), 182 Nfld & PEIR 1,
    554 APR 1 (NL CA) 16
Stack v T Eaton Co (1902), 4 OLR 335 (Div Ct) 278
Stall v Yarosz (1964), 43 DLR (2d) 255, 47 WWR (NS) 113 (Man CA) 153
Stanbarr Services Ltd v Metropolis Properties Inc, 2018 ONCA 244 118
Stearman v Powers, 2014 BCCA 206, 373 DLR (4th) 539 47

Stephens v Gulf Oil Canada Ltd, (1975) 65 DLR (3d) 193,
11 OR (2d) 129 (CA)..161
Stiles v Tod Mountain Development Ltd (1992), 88 DLR (4th) 735,
64 BCLR (2d) 366 (SC) 226
Street v Mountford, [1985] AC 809 (HL) 43
Strong v Bird (1874), LR 18 Eq 315..204, 206
Strother v 3464920 Canada Inc, 2007 SCC 24 76
Sturgeon Hotel Ltd v St Albert (City) (2010), 504 AR 202 (QB) 145
Surrey Metro Savings Credit Union v West, [1996] BCWLD 2468 (BCSC)...... 120
Swift 1st Ltd v Chief Land Registrar, [2015] EWCA Civ 330, [2015] Ch 602.....80
Switzer's Investments Ltd v Burn (1964), 47 DLR (2d) 280 (Alta QB).............. 215

T Choithram International SA v Pagarani, [2000] UKPC 46,
[2001] 1 WLR 1 .... 186–87, 190
Taitapu Gold Estates Ltd v Prouse, [1916] NZLR 825 (HC) 256
Tapling v Jones (1865), 11 HL Cas 290, 20 CBNS 166 139
Tappenden v Artus, [1964] 2 QB 185 (CA) 105–6
Tataryn v Tataryn Estate, [1994] 2 SCR 807, 116 DLR (4th) 193 ....196, 197, 198
Taylors Fashions Ltd v Liverpool Victoria Trustees Co Ltd, [1982] QB 133..... 225
Temma Realty Co Ltd v Ress Enterprises Ltd, [1968] 2 OR 293,
69 DLR (2d) 195 (CA) 139
Ter Neuzen v Korn, [1995] 3 SCR 674, 127 DLR (4th) 577......................230, 231
Third Eye Capital Corp v Dianor Resources Inc, 2018 ONCA 253.................. 134
Thistlethwaite v Sharp (1912), 7 DLR 801, 1 WWR 774 (Sask DC) 253
Thomas v Brown (1876), 1 QBD 714 215
Thomas v Canada (Attorney General), 2006 ABQB 730............................. 26
Thomas v The Times Book Co Ltd, [1966] 1 WLR 911 (Ch D) 169, 170
Thomas v Thomas, [1939] 4 DLR 202 (NBCA) 251
Thompson v Guaranty Trust Co, [1974] SCR 1023, 39 DLR (3d) 408........216, 217
Thompson v Mechan, [1958] OR 357, 13 DLR (2d) 103 (CA) 198, 199
Thomson v Neil (1974), 7 OR (2d) 438.. 142
Thorner v Major, [2007] EWHC 2422 (Ch), [2008] WTLR 155 225
Thorner v Major, [2008] EWCA Civ 732 226
Thorner v Major, [2009] UKHL 18, [2009] 1 WLR 776............ 218, 225, 226, 228
Tod v Barton, [2002] EWHC 265 (Ch), 4 ITELR 715............................. 80
Toomer v Witsell, 334 US 385 at 402 (1948) 19
Torkington v Magee, [1902] 2 KB 427 4
Toronto Standard Condominium Corp No 1487 v Market Lofts Inc,
2015 ONSC 1067...134
Toronto-Dominion Bank v Wise, 2016 ONCA 629 151
Tsilhqot'in Nation v British Columbia, 2007 BCSC 1700 .... 60, 61, 62, 64
Tsilhqot'in Nation v British Columbia 2014 SCC 44.................. 58, 59, 60, 64, 65
Tulk v Moxhay (1848), 2 Ph 774, 41 ER 1143..................................... 156, 158, 160
Turner v Turner, [1984] Ch 100 76

Union Bank of Canada v Phillips (1919), 58 SCR 385, 46 DLR 41 264–65

Unisource Canada Inc v Hongkong Bank of Canada (1998),
    43 BLR (2d) 226, 14 PPSAC (2d) 112 (Ont SC)..293
United States v Arora, 860 F Supp 1091 (US DC Maryland 1994)....................12
United Trust Co v Dominion Stores Ltd, [1977] 2 SCR 915, 71 DLR (3d)
    72 267–69
University of Manitoba v Sanderson Estate, [1998] 7 WWR 83,
    155 DLR (4th) 40 (BCCA) 212, 213, 214

Vancouver City Savings Credit Union v Serving for Success
    Consulting Ltd, 2011 BCSC 124...267
Vandervell v Inland Revenue Commissioners, [1966] UKHL 3,
    [1967] 2 AC 291 180
Vannini v Public Utilities Commission of Sault Ste Marie,
    [1973] 2 OR 11, 32 DLR (3d) 661 (HCJ)..142
VJF v SKW, 2016 BCCA 186..88

Wagner v Van Cleeff (1991), 5 OR (3d) 477 (Div Ct) 76
Waldman v Melville (City), [1990] 2 WWR 54, 65 DLR (4th) 154
    (Sask QB) 193
Walker v Dubord (1992), 92 DLR (4th) 257, 67 BCLR (2d) 302 (CA) 92, 93
Wallbridge Estate, 2010 ONSC 3409...193
Walsh v Lonsdale (1882), 21 Ch D 9 (CA) 221
Walshe v Citizens Bank of Canada (2003), 63 OR (3d) 702 (SC).....................260
Waltons Stores (Interstate) Ltd v Maher, [1988] HCA 7, 164 CLR 387.......228–29
Wardar's (Import & Export) Co Ltd v W Norwood & Sons Ltd,
    [1968] 2 QB 663 (CA)...233, 234
Warren v Keen, [1954] 1 QB 15 (CA)..48
Washington University v Catalona, 490 F (3d) 667 (USCA 8th 2007)..............12
Watson v Jackson (1914), 19 DLR 733 (Ont CA)..143
Watt v Watt Estate, [1988] 1 WWR 534, 49 Man R (2d) 317 (CA).......87, 187, 190
Wauchope v Maida, [1972] 1 OR 27, 22 DLR (3d) 142 (CA)............................215
Waverley Borough Council v Fletcher, [1995] 4 All ER 756 (CA)................23, 24
Wells v Mitchell, [1939] 3 DLR 126, [1939] OR 378 (CA) 142
West Flamborough v Pretuski, [1931] 1 DLR 520, 66 OLR 210 (CA)...............143
Westcoast Leasing Ltd v Westcoast Communications Ltd (1980),
    22 BCLR 285 (SC)...111, 244, 249
Westsea Construction Ltd v Land Title Office, [1995] 4 WWR 725,
    3 BCLR (3d) 56..53, 55
Wheeldon v Burrows (1872), 12 Ch D 31 (CA) 150, 152, 153
White v Gicas, 2014 ONCA 490 181
White v Lauder Developments Ltd (1975), 60 DLR (3d) 419,
    9 OR (2d) 363 (CA) 161
Whitelaw v Wilson, [1934] 3 DLR 554, [1934] OR 415 (SC) 97
Whittlesea City Council v Abbatangelo, [2009] VSCA 188, 259 ALR 56 20
Wilkes v Allington, [1931] 2 Ch 104 (Ch D)..199, 201
Williams v Hensman (1861), 1 J & H 546, 70 ER 862....................................92

Willman v Ducks Unlimited (Canada), [2005] 2 WWR 1,
   245 DLR (4th) 319 (Man CA) 147
Winkworth v Christie Manson and Woods Ltd, [1980] Ch 496 (Ch D) 236
Winter v Keating (1978), 35 APR 633, 24 NSR (2d) 633 (CA) 260
Wylie v McCarron, 2020 NBCA 28 153

Yanner v Eaton, [1999] HCA 53, 201 CLR 351 .... 19, 62
Yaxley v Gotts, [1999] EWCA Civ 3006, [2000] Ch 162 227
Yearworth v North Bristol NHS Trust, [2009] EWCA Civ 37, [2010] QB 1 12
Yorkshire Railway Wagon Co v Maclure (1882), 21 Ch D 309 (CA) 111
Young v Hichens (1844), 6 QB 606... 20–21
Your Response Ltd v Datateam Business Media Ltd, [2014]
   EWCA Civ 281, [2015] QB 41 107

Zbarsky v Lukashuk, [1992] 1 WWR 690, 61 BCLR (2d) 349 (CA) 140
Zellstoff Celgar Ltd v British Columbia, 2014 BCCA 279 .... 276, 278

TABLE OF LEGISLATION

Alberta Land Stewardship Act, SA 2009, c A-26.8 147
An Act to Repeal the Statute of Frauds, CCSM, c F158 .... 178, 215
An Act to Repeal the Statute of Frauds, SNB 2014, c 47 .... 178, 215
Animal Keepers Act, SA 2005, c A-40.5 .... 105, 106

Bankruptcy and Insolvency Act, RSC 1985, c B-3 .... 4, 5, 102
Builders Lien Act, RSY 2002, c 18 106
Builders Lien Act, SBC 1997, c 45 106
Builders' Lien Act, CCSM, c B91 106
Builders' Lien Act, RSA 2000, c B-7 106
Builders' Lien Act, RSNS 1989, c 277 106
Builders' Lien Act, SS 1984-85-86, c B-7.1 106

Canadian Charter of Rights and Freedoms, Part I of the
    Constitution Act, 1982, being Schedule B to the
    Canada Act 1982 (UK), 1982, c 11 .... 18, 19, 63–65
Commercial Liens Act, SS 2001, c C-15.1 .... 105, 106
Community Easements Act, SNS 2012, c 2 147
Companies Act 2006 (UK) 110
Condominium Act, 1998, SO 1998, c 19 100
Condominium Act, 2009, SNL 2009, c C-29.1 100
Condominium Act, CCSM, c C170 100
Condominium Act, RSBC 1996, c 64 100
Condominium Act, RSNS 1989, c 85 100
Condominium Act, RSNWT 1988, c C-15 100
Condominium Act, RSPEI 1988, c C-16 100

Condominium Act, RSY 2002, c 36 100
Condominium Property Act, 1993, SS 1993, c C-26.1 100
Condominium Property Act, RSA 2000, c C-22 100
Condominium Property Act, SNB 2009, c C-16.05 100
Conservation Easements Act, RSNB 2011, c 130 147
Conservation Easements Act, SNS 2001, c 28 147
Conservation Easements Act, SS 1996, c C-27.01 147
Conservation Land Act, RSO 1990, c C.28 147
Constitution Act, 1867, (UK), 30 & 31 Vict, c 3, reprinted in
    RSC 1985, App II, No 5 .... 63, 64, 65
Constitution Act, 1982, being Schedule B to the Canada Act 1982 (UK),
    1982, c 11 .... 8, 18, 65
Construction Act, RSO 1990, c C.30 106
Controlled Drugs and Substances Act, SC 1996, c 19 96
Conveyancing Act, RSNL 1990, c C-34 98
Conveyancing Act, RSNS 1989, c 97 .... 40, 175
Conveyancing and Law of Property Act, RSO 1990,
    c C.34 .... 40, 41, 86, 93, 157, 175
Copyright Act, RSC 1985, c C-42 8
Court of Queen's Bench Act, CCSM, c C280 .... 66, 67
Courts of Justice Act, RSO 1990, c C.43 .... 66, 67
Crown Lands Act, CCSM, c C340 38

Dependants of a Deceased Person Relief Act, RSPEI 1988, c D-7 196
Dependants Relief Act, CCSM, c D37 .... 195, 198
Dependants Relief Act, RSNWT 1988, c D-4 196
Dependants Relief Act, RSY 2002, c 56 196
Dependants' Relief Act, 1996, SS 1996, c D-25.01 195
Devolution of Estates Act, RSNB 1973, c D-9 .... 41, 194

Easements Act, RSNB 2011, c 143 154
Environment Act, RSY 2002, c 76 147
Estate Administration Act, RSY 2002, c 77 .... 41, 194, 195
Estate Administration Act, SA 2014, c E-12.5 4
Expropriation Act, CCSM, c E190 16
Expropriation Act, RSA 2000, c E-13 16
Expropriation Act, RSBC 1996, c 125 16
Expropriation Act, RSNB 1973, c E-14 16
Expropriation Act, RSNL 1990, c E-19 16
Expropriation Act, RSNS 1989, c 156 16
Expropriation Act, RSNWT 1988, c E-11 16
Expropriation Act, RSPEI 1988, c E-13 16
Expropriation Act, RSS 1978, c E-15 16
Expropriation Act, RSY 2002, c 81 16
Expropriations Act, RSO 1990, c E.26 16

Factors Act, CCSM, c F10 239
Factors Act, RSA 2000 239
Factors Act, RSNS 1989, c 157 239
Factors Act, RSNWT 1988, c F-1 239
Factors Act, RSO 1990, c F.1 239
Factors Act, RSPEI 1988, c F-1 .... 239, 243
Factors Act, RSS 1978 239
Factors Act, RSY 2002, c 82 239
Factors and Agents Act, RSNB 2011, c 153 239
Family Law Act, RSNL 1990, c F-2 .... 88, 100
Family Law Act, RSO 1990, c F.3 .... 88, 100
Family Law Act, RSPEI 1988, c F-2.1 .... 88, 100
Family Law Act, SBC 2011, c 25 100
Family Law Act, SNWT 1997, c 18 .... 88, 100
Family Property Act, CCSM, c F25 100
Family Property Act, RSA 2000, c F-4.7 .... 88, 100
Family Property Act, SS 1997, c F-6.3 .... 88, 100
Family Property and Support Act, RSY 2002, c 83 .... 88, 100
Family Relief Act, RSNL 1990, c F-3 196
Fish and Wildlife Act, SNB 1980, c F-14.1 19
Forest Act, RSBC 1996, c 157 64
Forestry Workers Lien for Wages Act, RSO 1990, c F.28 107

Garage Keepers Act, CCSM, c G10 106
Garage Keepers Lien Act, RSNWT 1988, c G-1 106
Garage Keepers Lien Act, RSY 2002, c 99 106
Garage Keepers' Lien Act, RSPEI 1988, c G-1 106

Historic Resources Act, RSNL 1990, c H-4 147
Home Owner Grant Act, RSBC 1996, c 194 15
Hotel Keepers Act, CCSM, c H150 106
Hotel Keepers Act, RSBC 1996, c 206 106
Hotel Keepers Act, RSNWT 1988, c H-5 106
Human Rights Act, RSPEI 1988, c H-12 157
Hydro and Electric Energy Act, RSA 2000, c H-16 37

Income Tax Act, RSC 1985, c 1 (5th Supp) 73, 77
Industrial Design Act, RSC 1985, c I-9 7
Intestate Succession Act, 2019, SS 2019, c I-13.2 .... 41, 194, 195
Intestate Succession Act, CCSM, c I85 .... 41, 194, 195
Intestate Succession Act, RSNL 1990, c I-21 .... 41, 194
Intestate Succession Act, RSNS 1989, c 236 .... 41, 194, 195
Intestate Succession Act, RSNWT 1988, c I-10 .... 41, 194

Judicature Act, RSA 2000, c J-2 .... 66, 67
Judicature Act, RSNB 1973, c J-2 .... 66, 67

Judicature Act, RSNL 1990, c J-4 .... 66, 67
Judicature Act, RSNS 1989, c 240.. 66, 67
Judicature Act, RSNWT 1988, c J-1 .... 66, 67
Judicature Act, RSPEI 1988, c J-2.1 .... 66, 67
Judicature Act, RSY 2002, c 128... 67
Judicature Act, SNWT (Nu) 1998, c 34... 66, 67

Land Act, RSBC 1996, c 245...38, 147
Land Registration Act, SNS 2001, c 6..............30, 117, 118, 120, 147, 149, 154, 177,
    178, 262, 263, 266
Land Title Act 1994 (Queensland)...94
Land Title Act 2000 (Northern Territory) 94
Land Title Act, RSBC 1996, c 250 ....40, 117, 118, 120, 147, 153, 157, 177, 178,
    262, 263, 264, 266, 271
Land Titles Act 1980 (Tas) 94
Land Titles Act, 2000, SS 2000, c L-5.1.....................30, 40, 41, 117, 118, 149, 153,
    177, 178, 262, 263, 264
Land Titles Act, 2015, SY 2015, c 10 .... 30, 40, 117, 118, 147, 149, 153, 157,
    177, 178, 262, 263, 264
Land Titles Act, RSA 2000, c L-4 .... 117, 118, 149, 177, 178, 262, 263, 264
Land Titles Act, RSNWT 1988, c 8 ....40, 117, 118, 147, 149, 177, 178, 262,
    263, 264
Land Titles Act, RSO 1990, c L.5 .... 30, 117, 118, 154, 177, 178, 262, 263
Land Titles Act, SNB 1981, c L-1.1 ....30, 117, 118, 120, 154, 177, 178,
    262, 263, 264
Landlord and Tenant Act 1851, 14 and 15 Vict, c 25 .... 280, 281
Lands Act, SNL 1991, c 36...30
Law and Equity Act, RSBC 1996, c 253 ....66, 67, 178, 215, 217
Law of Property (Miscellaneous Provisions) Act 1989, s 2, sch 2..................... 216
Law of Property Act 1925 (UK), 15 & 16 Geo V, c 20 ....94, 174
Law of Property Act, CCSM, c L90 ....40, 41, 86, 93, 98, 154, 157
Law of Property Act, RSA 2000, c L-7..........................40, 41, 86, 93, 98, 153, 224
Law Reform Act, RSNB 2011, c 184 16
Liens on Goods and Chattels Act, RSNB 2014, c 117................................ 105, 106
Limitation Act, SBC 2012, c 13 .... 29, 30
Limitation of Actions Act, CCSM c L150.. 29
Limitation of Actions Act, RSNWT 1988, c L-8 .... 29, 30, 153
Limitation of Actions Act, RSY 2002, c 139.. 29, 153
Limitation of Actions Act, SNB 2009, c L-8.5.. 29
Limitation of Actions Act, SNS 2014, c 35... 29
Limitations Act, 2002, SO 2002, c 24 29
Limitations Act, RSA 2000, c L-12 .... 29, 30
Limitations Act, SNL 1995, c L-16.1.. 29
Livestock Lien Act, RSBC 1996, c 272 .... 105, 106

Marital Property Act, RSNB 2012, c 107...88, 100

Married Women's Property Act 1882, 45 & 46 Vict, c 75 82
Matrimonial Property Act, RSNS 1989, c 275 .... 88, 100
Mechanics Lien Act, RSNWT 1988, c M-7 106
Mechanics' Lien Act, RSNB 1973, c M-6 106
Mechanics' Lien Act, RSNL 1990, c M-3 106
Mechanics' Lien Act, RSPEI 1988, c M-4 106
Mineral Resources Act, RSPEI 1988, c M-7 39
Mineral Resources Act, SNS 1990, c 18 39
Miners Lien Act, RSNWT 1988, c M-12 107
Miners Lien Act, RSY 2002, c 151 107
Mines and Minerals Act, RSA 2000, c M-17 38
Modern Slavery Act 2015 (UK) 11
Museum Act, RSPEI 1988, c M-14 147

Occupiers Liability Act, RSBC 1996, c 337 16
Occupiers' Liability Act, CCSM, c O8 16
Occupiers' Liability Act, RSA 2000, c O-4 16
Occupiers' Liability Act, RSO 1990, c O.2 16
Occupiers' Liability Act, RSPEI 1988, c O-2 16
Occupiers' Liability Act, SNS 1996, c 27 16
Ontario Heritage Act, RSO 1990, c O.18 147
Ontario Trails Act, 2016, SO 2016, c 8 147
Ownership of Minerals Act, RSNB 2011, c 200 38–39

Partition Act, RSNS 1989, c 333 98
Partition Act, RSO 1990, c P.4 .... 98, 99
Partition of Property Act, RSBC 1996, c 347 98
Patent Act, RSC 1985, c P-4 .... 8, 284
Perpetuities Act, RSA 2000, c P-5 .... 54, 58
Perpetuities Act, RSNWT 1988, c P-3 .... 54, 58
Perpetuities Act, RSO 1990, c P.9 .... 54, 58
Perpetuities Act, RSY 2002, c 168 .... 54, 58
Perpetuities Act, SNS 2011, c 42 54
Perpetuities and Accumulations Act, CCSM, c P33 57
Perpetuity Act, RSBC 1996, c 358 .... 54, 58
Personal Property Security Act, CCSM, c P35 .... 122, 272, 282
Personal Property Security Act, RSA 2000, c P-7 .... 122, 272, 282
Personal Property Security Act, RSBC 1996, c 359 .... 122, 272, 282
Personal Property Security Act, RSO 1990, c P.10 .... 122, 123, 272, 282
Personal Property Security Act, RSPEI 1988, c P-3.1 .... 122, 272, 282
Personal Property Security Act, RSY 2002, c 169 .... 122, 272, 282
Personal Property Security Act, SNB 1993, c P-7.1 .... 122, 272, 282
Personal Property Security Act, SNS 1995-96, c 13 .... 122, 272, 282
Personal Property Security Act, SNWT 1994, c 8 .... 122, 272, 282
Personal Property Security Act, SS 1993, c P-6.2 .... 122, 123, 272, 282
Petroleum and Natural Gas Act, RSNL 1990, c P-10 39

Plant Breeders' Rights Act, SC 1990, c 20 7
Possessory Liens Act, RSA 2000, c P-19 .... 105, 106
Prescription Act 1832, 2 and 3 Will 4, c 71 154
Prevention of Cruelty to Animals Act 1908 (No 995) 10–11
Probate Act, RSPEI 1988, c P-21 .... 4, 41, 193, 194, 213
Probate Act, SNS 2000, c 31 4
Property Act, RSNB 1973, c P-19 .... 40, 41, 85, 86, 93, 147, 175
Property Law Act, RSBC 1996, c 377 .... 41, 86, 93, 149, 178, 224
Provincial Lands Act, 2016, SS 2016, c P-31.1 38
Provision for Dependants Act, RSNB 2012, c 111 196
Public Lands Act, RSA 2000, c P-40 38
Public Lands Act, RSO 1990, c P.43 38
Public Utilities Easements Act, RSS 1978, c P-45 147

Queen's Bench Act, 1998, SS c Q-1.01 .... 66, 67
Quia Emptores 1290, 18 Edw 1, c 1 .... 32, 161

Real Property Act 1845, 8 and 9 Vic, c 119 174
Real Property Act, CCSM, c R30 .... 30, 40, 117, 118, 147, 177, 178, 262, 263, 264
Real Property Act, RSNS 1989, c 385 .... 41, 86
Real Property Act, RSPEI 1988, c R-3 .... 93, 98, 175
Real Property Limitations Act, RSNS 1989, c 258 154
Real Property Limitations Act, RSO 1990, c L.15 154
Registration of Deeds Act, 2009, SNL 2009, c R-10.01 .... 117, 177, 258
Registry Act, CCSM, c R50 .... 117, 177, 258, 259, 262
Registry Act, RSNB 1973, c R-6 .... 117, 177, 258, 262
Registry Act, RSNS 1989, c 392 .... 117, 177, 258, 260, 262
Registry Act, RSO 1990, c R.20 .... 117, 177, 258, 259, 262
Registry Act, RSPEI 1988, c R-10 .... 117, 177, 258, 260
Rental of Residential Property Act, RSPEI 1988, c R-13.1 .... 49, 51
Repair and Storage Liens Act, RSO 1990, c R.25 ....105, 106
Repairers Lien Act, RSBC 1996, c 404 106
Residential Landlord and Tenant Act, SY 2012, c 20 .... 49, 51
Residential Tenancies Act, 2006, SO 2006, c 17 .... 49, 51
Residential Tenancies Act, 2006, SS 2006, c R-22.0001 .... 49, 51
Residential Tenancies Act, 2018, SNL 2018, c R-14.2 .... 49, 51
Residential Tenancies Act, CCSM, c R119 .... 49, 51
Residential Tenancies Act, RSNS 1989, c 401 .... 49, 51
Residential Tenancies Act, RSNWT 1988, c R-5 .... 49, 51
Residential Tenancies Act, SA 2004, c R-17.1 .... 49, 51
Residential Tenancies Act, SNB 1975, c R-10.2 .... 49, 51
Residential Tenancy Act, SBC 2002, c 78 .... 49, 51
Rules of Court, NB Reg 82-73 98

Sale of Goods (Amendment) Act 1994 (UK) 247
Sale of Goods Act 1979 (UK) 229, 247

Sale of Goods Act, CCSM, c S10 .... 6, 229, 240, 243, 244, 248
Sale of Goods Act, RSA 2000, c S-2 .... 6, 229, 240, 243, 244, 248
Sale of Goods Act, RSBC 1996, c 410 .... 6, 229, 239, 240, 243, 247
Sale of Goods Act, RSNB 2016, c 110 .... 6, 229, 240, 243, 244, 248
Sale of Goods Act, RSNL 1990, c S-6 .... 6, 229, 239, 240, 243, 244, 248
Sale of Goods Act, RSNS 1989, c 408 .... 6, 229, 240, 243, 244, 248
Sale of Goods Act, RSNWT 1988, c S-2 .... 6, 229, 240, 243, 244, 248
Sale of Goods Act, RSO 1990, c S.1 .... 6, 229, 240, 243, 244, 247
Sale of Goods Act, RSPEI 1988, c S-1 .... 6, 229, 240, 244, 248
Sale of Goods Act, RSS 1978, c S-1 .... 6, 229, 230, 231, 240, 243, 244, 248
Sale of Goods Act, RSY 2002, c 198 .... 6, 229, 240, 243, 244, 248
Slavery Convention, 15 September 1926 and amended 7 December 1953,
    212 UNTS 2861, arts 1 & 2 (entered into force 7 July 1955) 11
Stable Keepers Act, CCSM, c S200 .... 105, 106
Statute of Frauds 1677, 29 Car 2, c 3 .... 174, 175, 176, 178, 179, 188, 210,
    214–15, 263
Statute of Frauds, RSNS 1989, c 442 .... 178, 179, 188, 215
Statute of Frauds, RSO 1990, c S.19 .... 178, 188, 215
Statute of Limitations, RSPEI 1988, c S-7 .... 29, 30
Statute of Wills 1540, 32 Hen 8, c 1 .... 40, 192
Storage Warehouse Keepers Act, RSNS 1989, c 447 106
Storer's Lien Act, RSNB 2011, c 225 .... 105, 106
Strata Property Act, SBC 1998, c 43 100
Succession Law Reform Act, RSO 1990, c S.26 .... 41, 91, 193, 194, 195, 213
Survivorship Act, 1993, SS 1993, c S-67.1 .... 91, 100
Survivorship Act, CCSM, c S250 91
Survivorship Act, RSNB 2012, c 116 91
Survivorship Act, RSNL 1990, c S-33 91
Survivorship Act, RSNS 1989, c 454 91
Survivorship Act, RSNWT 1988, c S-16 91
Survivorship Act, RSY 2002, c 213 91

Tenants in Common Act, RSNWT 1988, c T-1 86
Tenants in Common Act, RSY 2002, c 216 86
Tenures Abolition Act 1660, 12 Car 2, c 24 33–34
Testators' Family Maintenance Act, RSNS 1989, c 465 196
The Limitations Act, SS 2004, c L-16.1 29
Threshers' Lien Act, RSS 1978, c T-13 107
Threshers' Liens Act, CCSM, c T60 107
Trademarks Act, RSC 1985, c T-13 7
Trust (Jersey) Law 1984, art 12 72
Trustee Act, 2009, SS 2009, c T-23.01 .... 57, 77, 85
Trustee Act, CCSM, c T160 .... 77, 80, 85
Trustee Act, RSA 2000, c T-8 .... 77, 80, 85
Trustee Act, RSBC 1996, c 464 .... 77, 85
Trustee Act, RSNL 1990, c T-10 .... 77, 85

Trustee Act, RSNS 1989, c 479 .... 77, 85
Trustee Act, RSNWT 1988, c T-8 .... 77, 85
Trustee Act, RSO 1990, c T.23 .... 77, 85
Trustee Act, RSPEI 1988, c T-8 85
Trustee Act, RSY 2002, c 223 .... 77, 85
Trustees Act, SNB 2015, c 21 .... 77, 85
Tugboat Worker Lien Act, RSBC 1996, c 466 107

Warehouse Keepers Lien Act, RSNWT 1988, c W-2 .... 105, 106
Warehouse Keepers Lien Act, RSY 2002, c 226 .... 105, 106
Warehouse Lien Act, RSBC 1996, c 480 .... 105, 106
Warehousemen's Lien Act, RSA 2000, c W-2 .... 105, 106
Warehousemen's Lien Act, RSNS 1989, c 499 .... 105, 106
Warehousemen's Lien Act, RSPEI 1988, c W-1 .... 105, 106
Warehousemen's Liens Act, CCSM, c W20 .... 105, 106
Warehouser's Lien Act, RSNL 1990, c W-2 .... 105, 106
Water Act, RSA 2000, c W-3 19
Wildlife Act, 1998, SS 1998, c W-13.12 19
Wildlife Act, CCSM, c W130 19
Wildlife Act, RSA 2000, c W-10 19
Wildlife Act, RSBC 1996, c 488 19
Wildlife Act, RSNS 1989, c 504 19
Wildlife Act, RSY 2002, c 229 19
Wildlife Conservation Act, RSPEI 1988, c W-4.1 .... 19, 147
Wills Act, 1996, SS 1996, c W-14.1 .... 193, 194
Wills Act, CCSM, c W150 .... 193, 194, 213
Wills Act, RSNB 1973, c W-9 .... 193, 194, 213
Wills Act, RSNL 1990, c W-10 .... 193, 194, 213
Wills Act, RSNS 1989, c 505 .... 193, 194, 213
Wills Act, RSNWT 1988, c W-5 .... 193, 194, 214
Wills Act, RSY 2002, c 230 .... 193, 194, 213–14
Wills and Succession Act, SA 2010, c W-12.2 .... 4, 41, 91, 193, 194, 195, 196
Wills Variation Act, RSBC 1979, c 435 196
Wills, Estates and Succession Act, SBC 2009, c 13 ..... 4, 41, 91, 193, 194, 195, 196
Woodmen's Lien Act, RSNS 1989, c 507 107
Woodmen's Lien Act, RSS 1978, c W-16 107
Woodmen's Liens Act, CCSM, c W190 107
Woods Workers' Lien Act, RSNB 1973, c W-12.5 107
Woodworker Lien Act, RSBC 1996, c 491 107

INDEX

Abate, testamentary gift, 194
Aboriginal title, 58–65
    Canadian law, 58–59
        constitutional protection, 63–65
        content of title, 59–62
        possessory title, differences, 60–61
        alienation or encumbrance, 60
        communal property, 60
        future generations, 60
        non-transferable, 60–61
        proof of title, 62–63
        radical title of Crown, 34–35
        site-specific rights, 61–62
Accession, 286–88
    defined, 283, 286, 291
    fixtures, distinguished, 286–87
    overlap with specification and mixture, 283–84
    personal property security, 291–92
Actual notice, 252
    constructive notice, differences, 253
    deed registration systems, 259–60
    title registration systems, 264, 266–68
Adeem, testamentary gift, 194
Administrator, 192. See also Executor
Administratrix, 192. See also Administrator
Adverse possession, 29–30

prescriptive easements, distinguished, 155
Advowson, 130
Affidavit of execution of will, 193
Affirmative easements. See Positive easements
After-acquired property, 127
Agency, 239–40
    imputed notice, 253–54
Agreement for sale, 108–9, 221
Agricultural fixtures, 280
Air space, 36–37
Allodial title, 35
Allodium, 35
Animals, property rights, 6, 9–11. See also Living things
    possessory rights, 27–28
Ascertained goods, 231–32
Assignable rights, 3–6
    administration of estates, 3–4
    bankruptcy, 4–5
    licences, 5
Assignment of leases, 50–51. See also Sublet
Attachment
    fixtures, 277–80
    security interests, 126, 273

Bailment, 27, 28

Bankruptcy, 102
    assignment of rights, 4–5, 96
    builders, 233–34
    joint tenancies, severance, 96
    profits à prendre and, 138
    property of the bankrupt, 4–5, 275
    secured creditors and, 102–3
    unperfected security interests, 126,
        275
Beneficial ownership
    land contracts, 220–21
    trustees, 79–81
Beneficiaries, 71–73
    beneficiary principle, 72
    rights, 78–79
    rule against perpetuities, 55–58
Bequest, 194
Bill of sale, 110
Bona fide purchase, 79, 249, 250–54
    agent, from, 240
    deed registration system, 257
    fixtures, 282
    title registration system, 177–78, 262,
        271
Builders' lien, 106–7
Buyer in possession, 243–44

Caution, 263
Caveat, 263
Certainty of intention, 181–83
Certainty of objects, 185–86
Certainty of subject matter, 183–85
Certainty of term, 44–46
    fixed-term leases, 44–46
    periodic tenancies, 46
Certificate of title, 118
Chain of title, 30, 177, 258, 262, 271
Chancel repairs, 130
Charge
    equitable charge. *See* Equitable
        charge
    registered charge, 117. *See also* Land
        title mortgage
Charitable donations, 167
Charitable-purpose trusts, 73–74
Charter of *feoffment*, 174
Charter rights
    Aboriginal rights, 63–65
    freedom of expression, 18–19
Chattel mortgage, 110, 123

Chose in action, 4–5
Civil enforcement, 68
Codicil, 193, 209, 211
Collateral, 124
Commixtio, 288
Common law lien, 104–7
    general liens, 104
    nature of, 105–6
    non-possessory liens distinguished,
        106–7
    particular liens, 104–5
    pledges, differences, 104
Common law mortgage, 110, 114–15
    deed registration system, 117
    enforcement, 119–22
    land title mortgage, switch to, 117–18
    right to possession, 114, 115, 119
Common ownership. *See* Tenancy in
    common
Competing rights, 235–93
    priority rules. *See* Priority rules
Conditional gift, 198–200
Conditional sales, 110
Conditions precedent, 53
Conditions subsequent, 53. *See also*
    Defeasible estates
Condominiums, 100–1, 135
Confidential information, property
    rights, 8–9
Confusio, 288
Conservation easements, 147–48
Constitution of trust, 186–87
Constructive notice, 252–53
    deed registration systems, 260
Constructive trusts, 96, 179–80
    incomplete gifts, 191
    land contracts, 220–21
    mutual wills, 212–13
Consumer goods, 275
Contingent remainder, 52
    rule against perpetuities, 55–58
Contracts, property rights
    gifts, distinguished, 167–68
    land contracts. *See* Land contracts
Conversion, 28, 236, 282, 284–86
Conveyance, 175
Co-ownership, 82–101
    common ownership. *See* Tenancy in
        common
    condominiums, 100–1

generally, 82–83
joint ownership. *See* Joint Tenancy
partition, 98–100
severance, 91–98
unity of possession, 83–84
Co-parcenary, 83
Corporal hereditaments, 129
Covenants
    freehold covenants. *See* Restrictive
        covenants
    leasehold covenants. *See* Leasehold
        covenants
Criteria certainty, 186
Crops, 6, 135, 230, 272
    PPSA, 125
Crown ownership, 17–19
    freedom of expression and, 18–19
    natural resources, 19
    radical title, 34–35
Currency, 7, 238–39
Curtain principle, 118

Dead pledge, 114
Debt, 2–3, 4–5, 102
    secured. *See* Security interests
Deed, 168, 175–77
Deed registration system, 117, 177,
        258–62. *See also* Common law
        mortgages
    priority rules, 258–62
        nemo dat, 261
        notice, 259–60
        short leases, 262
Defeasible estates, 53–55
    determinable estates distinguished,
        53–54
Deferred indefeasibility, 269
    double deferred indefeasibility,
        270–71
Degree of annexation, 277
Delivery of goods, 168–74
    donatio mortis causa, 200
Determinable estates, 53–55
    defeasible estates distinguished,
        53–54
Detrimental reliance, 225
    land contracts, 216–18
Devise, 194
Discretionary trust, 77–78
Documents, property rights, 7

Domestic animals, property rights, 9.
    See also Animals
    possessory rights, 28
Domestic fixtures, 280
Dominant tenements
    easements, 147–49. *See also*
        Easements
    accommodate the dominant tene-
        ment, 143–45
    restrictive covenants, 163. *See also*
        Restrictive covenants
    benefit to dominant tenement,
        163–65
Donatio mortis causa, 198–204
    conditional gift, 198–200
    delivery, 200
    inter vivos or testamentary, 203–4
    land, 201–3

Easement of necessity, 150–51
Easements, 138–55. *See also* Incorporeal
        hereditaments
    creation, 149–55
        implied easements, 150–53
            necessity, easements of,
                150–51
            other implied easements, 153
            Wheeldon v Burrows, rule in,
                152–53
        prescriptive easements, 153–55
            adverse possession, distin-
                guished, 155
            lost modern grant, 154
            statutory, 154–55
        proprietary estoppel, 155
        statutory easements, 147–49
            conservation easements,
                147–48
    defined, 128
    land title registration, 263–64
    limits on rights, 132
    positive and negative easements,
        139–43
        negative easements. *See* Negative
            easements
        positive easements. *See* Positive
            easements
    profit à prendre, differences, 138
    quasi-easements, 152–53
    requirements for valid easement, 143

accommodate the dominant tenement, 143–45
dominant and servient tenements,
147–49
subject matter of a grant, 145–47
Emblement, 135
Encumbrances, 111–14
equitable charge, 111–12
equitable lien, 106–7, 112–14
mortgages. *See* Mortgages
Entailed estate, 41–42
Equitable charge, 111–12
floating versus fixed charges, 112
Equitable estoppel
promissory estoppel, 225
proprietary estoppel, 225–29. *See
also* Proprietary estoppel
Equitable lease, 221
Equitable liens, 106–7, 112–14
purchaser's lien, 113
unpaid vendor's lien, 113
Equity, 66–70
overview, 66–68
property rights, 168
competing rights, 249–57
remedies, 68–70
injunctions, 69
rectification, 69–70
rescission, 69
specific performance, 69. *See also*
Specific performance
Equity of redemption, 115–16, 118–19
Estate of deceased person. *See* Estates
administration
Estate tail, 41–42
Estates administration, 3–4, 31. *See also*
Wills and estates
intestate succession, 192, 194–95
joint property, 89–90
overview, 192–93
personal representative, 192. *See also*
Executor
Estates in land, 31, 35–51. *See also* Title
to land
fixtures. *See* Fixtures
freehold estates, 39–42
fee simple estate, 31–41
fee tail, 41–42
leaseholds distinguished, 42
life estate, 42

future interests, 51–58
defeasible estates, 53–55
determinable estates, 53–55
remainders, 52
contingent remainders, 52, 55
rule against perpetuities,
55–58
reversions, 52–53
leasehold estates, 42–51
certainty of term, 44–46
fixed-term leases, 44–46
periodic tenancies, 46
freeholds distinguished, 42
leasehold covenants, 46–49
maintenance of common areas,
47, 49
no derogation by landlord,
47–48
no waste by tenant, 48–49
quiet enjoyment, 47
tenant-like use, 48
licences distinguished, 43
possession, 43–44
privity of estate, 50–51
assignment, 50–51
residential tenancies, 49
overview, 35–38
air space, 36–37
underground, 37–38
tenure, 31–35
feudal services, 33–34
radical title, 34–35
subinfeudation, 32
Estoppel
common law, 225
competing rights, 240–43
promissory estoppel, 225
proprietary estoppel, 225–29. *See
also* Proprietary estoppel
Exclusive possession, 22
Executor, 192. *See also* Wills and estates
duties, 192–93
incomplete gifts to, 204–6
Executrix, 192. *See also* Executor
Express trust, 170

Factual possession, 20
Fee simple estate, 31, 39–41. *See also*
Estates in land
Fee tail estate, 41–42

Feoffment, 174–75
Feudalism, 32
  feudal services, 33–34
  subinfeudation, 32
Fiduciaries
  constructive trust, 180
  trustees, 75–77
Finders, 23, 167, 246
  wrongdoers, 24–26
First in time, 254–55
Fixed charge, 112
Fixed-term leases, 44–46
Fixtures, 276–83
  accession, distinguished, 286–87
  goods or fixtures, 277–80
    degree of annexation, 277
    object of annexation, 277
    personal property security, 282–83
  tenant's fixtures, 280–82
    agricultural fixtures, 280
    ornamental and domestic fixtures,
      280
    trade fixtures, 280
Floating charge, 112
Forced heirship, 195
Foreclosure, 115, 120–22
Forgery, 269–71
Formalities
  land contracts, 214–18
  trusts, 187–89
  wills, 193–94
Four unities, 83–85
Franchise, 130
Fraud, 264–69
Freedom of expression, 18–19
Freedom of testation, 195
Freehold covenants. *See* Restrictive
  covenants
Freehold estates, 39–42. *See also* Estates
  in land
  fee simple estate, 31–41
  fee tail, 41–42
  leaseholds distinguished, 42
  life estate, 42
Fructus industrials, 135
Fructus naturales, 135
Fully secret trust, 206–9
Future goods, 138, 231, 233
Future interests, 51–58
  defeasible estates, 53–55

determinable estates, 53–55
  remainders, 52
    contingent remainders, 52, 55
    rule against perpetuities, 55–58
  reversions, 52–53

Gage, 114
General liens, 104
Gifts, 168–79
  contract rights, distinguished,
    167–68
  delivery of goods, 168–74, 200
  *donatio mortis causa. See Donatio
    mortis causa*
  incomplete gifts, 190–91
    executors, to, 204–6
  testamentary gifts. *See* Wills and
    estates
  transfer of land, 174–79
  trusts. *See* Trusts
Goods
  definition, 6
  delivery of goods, 168–74
    donatio mortis causa, 200
  gifts. *See* Gifts
  living things as, 6, 9
  property rights, 6
  security interests. *See* Security
    interests
  title. *See* Title to goods

Half-secret trust, 206–9
Hereditaments
  corporal hereditaments, 129
  incorporeal hereditaments,
    128–30. *See also* Incorporeal
    hereditaments
Hire-purchase agreement, 109–10
Holograph wills, 193–94
Human beings, status as persons, 10–11
Human tissue, property rights, 11–13
Hypothec, 111, 133

Illegality, 24–26
Immediate indefeasibility, 269–70
Implied easements, 150–53
  necessity, easements of, 150–51
  other implied easements, 153
  Wheeldon v Burrows, rule in, 152–53
Imputed notice, 253–54

In personam rights, 2–3. *See also* Personal rights
assignable rights, 3–6
In rem rights, 2–3. *See also* Property rights
assignable rights, 3–6
Incomplete gifts, 190–91
executors, to, 204–6
Incorporeal hereditaments, 128–30
advowson, 130
easements. *See* Easements
franchise, 130
limits on property rights, 130–34
profits à prendre. See Profits à prendre
rentcharges. *See* Rentcharges
Indefeasibility of title, 262–63
deferred indefeasibility, 269
double deferred indefeasibility, 270–71
immediate indefeasibility, 269–70
Injunctions, 69
Intangible property, 7, 107, 126, 129, 168, 273
Intellectual property rights, 7–8
Inter vivos, 167, 203–4
gifts. *See* Gifts
Intestacy. *See* Intestate succession
Intestate succession, 192, 194–95

Joint tenancy, 83–91
common ownership differences, 83, 85
four unities, 83–85
interest, 84
possession, 83–84
time, 84–85
title, 84–85
murder and, 96, 180
partition, 98–100
presumption in favour of, 86–87
resulting trust, 87–89
business partners, 88
joint mortgagees, 89
unequal contributions, 87–88, 90
right of survivorship, 83, 89–91
severance, 91–98
course of dealing, 95–96
effect of severance, 97–98
mutual agreement, 95–96
operation of law, 96–97

unilateral act, 92–95
Judicial remedy, 68
Jus accrescendi, 83

Land
donatio mortis causa, 201–3
property rights, 6. *See also* Estates in land; Land interests
transfer of. *See* Transfer of land
Land contracts, 214–24
defined, 214
formalities, 214–18
oral contracts, 215–18
options to purchase, 223–24
part performance, 216–18
detrimental reliance, 216–18
proprietary estoppel, 227
rights of first refusal, 223–24
specific performance, 218–23
Land interests. *See also* Estates in land
equity of redemption, 115–16
incorporeal hereditaments. *See* Incorporeal hereditaments
possessory rights. *See* Possession
security interests. *See* Mortgages
title to land. *See* Title to land
transfer. *See* Transfer of land
Land registration systems, 117, 257–71
deed registration. *See* Deed registration system
overview, 257–58
title registration. *See* Title registration system
Land title mortgage, 117–19
common law mortgage, benefits over, 117–18
enforcement, 119–22
registration system. *See* Title registration system
right to possession, 119–20
Land title registration. *See* Title registration system
Lapse of testamentary gift, 194
Lateral support, right to, 139–40. *See also* Negative easements
Law of property. *See* Property law
Lease contracts, 221
Lease of personal property, 124
Lease of real property. *See* Leasehold estates

Leasehold covenants, 46–49, 155–56.
    See also Leasehold estates
    maintenance of common areas, 47, 49
    no derogation by landlord, 47–48
    no waste by tenant, 48–49
    quiet enjoyment, 47
    tenant-like use, 48
Leasehold estates, 42–51. *See also*
    Estates in land
    certainty of term, 44–46
        fixed-term leases, 44–46
        periodic tenancies, 46
    condominium alternative, 101
    freeholds distinguished, 42
    leasehold covenants. *See* Leasehold
        covenants
    licences distinguished, 43
    possession, 43–44
    privity of estate, 50–51
        assignment, 50–51
    registration, 178, 262, 263
    rent, 134
    rentcharges, 134–35
    residential tenancies. *See* Residential
        tenancies
Legacy, 194
Licences
    assignable right, 5
    leases distinguished, 43, 131–32
    property rights distinguished, 3, 130
Liens
    common law liens. *See* Common law
        liens
    equitable liens. *See* Equitable liens
    statutory liens. *See* Statutory liens
Life estate, 42, 51
Life in being, 56–57
Light and air, right to, 139. *See also*
    Negative easements
List certainty, 185
Livery of seisin, 174–75
Livestock. *See* Domestic animals
Living pledge, 114
Living things
    goods, status as, 6, 9
    persons, distinguished, 10–11
    property rights, 9–11
Lost modern grant, 154

Market overt, 247–49

Market rent, 179
Market value, 17, 28, 35, 69, 81, 109, 219
    equity of redemption, 116
Mechanics' lien, 106–7
Mercantile agents, 239–40
Mere equity, 256–57
Mirror principle, 118
Mixtures, 288–91
    defined, 283, 288
    overlap with specification and acces-
        sion, 283–84
    personal property security, 293
Money, property rights, 7
    competing rights, 238–39
Mortgages, 114–22
    chattel mortgages, 110
    common law mortgages, 110, 114–15,
        117
    enforcement, 119–22
    equity of redemption, 115–16
    foreclosure, 115
    land title mortgage, 117–19
Murder, 96, 180
Mutual wills, 211–14

Native title, 34–35, 62
Natural resources
    Crown ownership, 19
    profits, 135
        overriding royalty, 133–34
Negative covenants, 157–60. *See also*
    Restrictive covenants
Negative easements, 139–43. *See also*
    Easements
    restrictive covenants, distinguished,
        157
    right to lateral support, 139–40
    right to light and air, 139
Negative equity, 116
Nemo dat quod non habet, 177, 237–38
    exceptions
        agency, 239–40
        buyer or seller in possession,
            243–44
        deed registration, 261
        estoppel, 240–43
        market overt, 247–49
        money, 238–39
        voidable title, 244–47
    sale of goods, 240–49

Notice, 252–53
actual notice, 252. *See also* Actual notice
constructive notice, 252–53. *See also* Constructive notice
deed registration systems, 259–60
imputed notice, 253–54
Nova species, 284
Numerus clausus, 132–33

Object of annexation, 277–79
Object of trust, 185–86
Operation of law, 96–97, 166
Option to purchase, 223–24
Option to renew lease, 46
Ornamental fixtures, 280
Overriding royalty, 133–34
Ownership, 14–19
beneficial ownership. *See* Beneficial ownership
co-ownership. *See* Co-ownership
Crown ownership. *See* Crown ownership
Professor Honoré, 15–17
standard incidents of ownership, 15–17

Part performance, 216–18
detrimental reliance, 216–18
Particular liens, 104–5
Partition, 98–100
Pawn, 103–4
PPSA application, 123–24
Perfection, 126–27, 272–73
Periodic tenancies, 46
Perpetuity. *See* Rule against perpetuities
Personal property security, 122–27, 272–75. *See also* Security interests
accessions, 291–92
after-acquired property, 127
chattel mortgages, 110, 123
enforceability, 123, 126
fixtures, 282–83
form, 123
intangible property, 126
leases, 124
mixtures, 292–93
PPSA regime. *See* PPSA regime
purchase money security interest, 273–74

specifications, 292–93
Personal representative, 192. *See also* Executor
Personal rights, 2–3
assignable rights, 3–6
licences, 3, 5
Persons, things distinguished, 10–11
Pets. *See* Domestic animals
Plants, property rights, 6, 9–11. *See also* Living things
Pledge, 103–4
common law lien, differences, 104
dead pledge, 114
living pledge, 114
PPSA application, 123
Positive covenants, 157–60
Positive easements, 139–43, 157. *See also* Easements
right of way, 139
varieties, 142–43
Possession, 20–30
adverse possession, 29–30
control, 20–22
factual possession, 20
co-ownership, 83–84
exclusive possession, 22
importance, 14
intention to possess, 22–23
landowners, 23–24
necessary elements, 20
ownership, differences, 16–17, 20, 26
standard incidents, 16–17
relativity of title, 28–29
rights to possession, 26–28
bailment, 27
distinguished from possession, 26
land estates. *See* Estates in land
loss of rights, 27
animals, 27–28
security interests, 103–7
common law lien, 104–7
common law mortgage, 114, 115, 119
land title mortgage, 119–20
pawn or pledge, 103–4
things in public places, 23–24
unity of possession, 83–84
wrongdoing and, 24–26
Possessory title, 28–29
Aboriginal title, differences, 60–61

adverse possession, 29–30
Possibility of reverter, 54, 55
PPSA regime, 122–27. *See also* Personal
   property security
  advantages, 122
  application, 122, 123–24
   deemed security interests, 124
   exclusions, 123–24
  collateral, 125
  attachment, 126
  priority rules, 272–75
   accessions, 291–92
   between security interests,
    273–74
   fixtures, 282–83
   over other interests, 274–75
   specifications and mixtures,
    292–93
  proceeds, 125–26
  registration, 124–25
  security interests, 123–24, 126
   after-acquired property, 127
   enforceability, 123, 126
   perfection, 126–27
Preemptive right, 223
Prescription, 140–41, 153–55
Prescriptive easements, 153–55
  adverse possession, distinguished,
   155
  lost modern grant, 154
  statutory, 154–55
Presumption of advancement, 88
Presumption of resulting trust, 87–89
  business partners, 88
  joint mortgagees, 89
  unequal contributions, 87–88, 90
Priority rules
  common law, 237–49
   agents, 239–40
   buyer or seller in possession,
    243–44
   estoppel, 240–43
   market overt, 247–49
   money, 238–39
   nemo dat, 237–38
   voidable title, 244–47
  equity, 249–57
   bona fide purchase, 250–54
   first in time, 254–55
   mere equities, 256–57

   overview, 249–50
  generally, 235–36
  land registration, 257–71
   deed registration, 258–62
   land title registration, 262–71
  personal property security, 272–75
   accessions, 291–92
   between security interests,
    273–74
   fixtures, 282–83
   over other interests, 274–75
   specifications and mixtures,
    292–93
Privity of estate, 50–51, 156
Proceeds, 125–26
Profits à prendre, 5, 135–38. *See also*
   Incorporeal hereditaments
  defined, 128
  duration of the profit, 137
  easement, differences, 138
  exclusive profits, 136–37
  non-exclusive profits, 136–37
  overriding royalty, 133–34
  profits appurtenant, 136
  profits in gross, 136
  sale of goods distinguished, 137–38
Profits appurtenant, 136
Profits in gross, 136
Property law
  equity. *See* Equity
  introduction, 1–2
  land interests. *See* Land interests
  meaning of property, 2
  ownership. *See* Ownership
  possession. *See* Possession
  rights. *See* Property rights
  security interests. *See* Security
   interests
  trusts. *See* Trusts
Property of the bankrupt, 4–5, 275. *See*
  also Bankruptcy
Property rights, 2–6
  assignable rights, 3–6
  competing rights, 235–93
   priority rules. *See* Priority rules
  creation or transfer, 167
   gift or contract, 167–68
   intention or operation of law, 166
   inter vivos or testamentary, 167
   law or equity, 168

easements. *See* Easements
in rem rights, 2–3
licences, distinguished, 3
mere equities, 256–57
ownership. *See* Ownership
possession. *See* Possession
profit à prendre. See Profits à prendre
rentcharges. *See* Rentcharges
restrictive covenants. *See* Restrictive
    covenants
sources of rights. *See* Sources of
    rights
things subject to, 6–13
    confidential information, 8–9
    documents, 7
    goods, 6
    human tissue, 11–13
    intellectual property, 7–8
    land, 6
    living things, 9–11
    money, 7
Property, what is, 1–13
meaning of property, 2
rights. *See* Property rights
Proprietary estoppel, 225–29
easements, 55
land contracts, 216–18
Purchase money security interest, 273–74
Purchaser's lien, 113

Quasi-easement, 152–53
Quasi-property, 12
Qui prior est tempore potior est jure,
    254–55
Quiet enjoyment of leased premises, 47

Radical title, 34–35
Real estate, 31. *See also* Estates in land
Real right, 132–33
Reciprocal wills, 211
Rectification, 69–70
mere equity, 256–57
Re-entry, 54–55
Registration
    land. *See* Land registration systems
    personal property security, 124–25
Relativity of title, 28–29
Remainders, 52
    contingent remainders, 52
    rule against perpetuities, 55–58

Remedy, 68
breach of contract, 218
    specific performance, 218–23
equitable remedies, 68–70
    injunctions, 69
    rectification, 69–70
    rescission, 69
    specific performance, 69
Rent, 134. *See also* Leasehold estates
Rent services, 134
Rentcharges, 134–35. *See also* Incorpor-
    eal hereditaments
defined, 128
Rescission, 69
mere equity, 256
Residential tenancies, 46, 49
sublet, 51
Residuary estate, 194
Residue of estate, 194
Restitutio in integrum, 69
Restraint on alienation, 161
Restrictive covenants, 155–65
benefit to dominant tenement,
    163–65
defined, 128
negative easements, distinguished,
    157
positive covenants, 157–60
use of servient tenement, 161–63
Resulting trust, 87–89, 179–80
business partners, 88
joint mortgagees, 89
unequal contributions, 87–88, 90
Reversion
future interests, 52–53
landlords, 50
Right *in personam. See In personam*
    rights
Right *in rem. See In rem* rights
Right of first refusal, 223–24
Right of pre-emption, 223
Right of re-entry, 54–55
Right of survivorship, 83, 89–91
Right of way, 16, 128, 138, 139, 148, 151,
    263–64. *See also* Positive easements
Right to assign. *See* Assignable rights
Right to lateral support, 139–40. *See*
    also Negative easements
Right to light and air, 139. *See also* Nega-
    tive easements

Right to possess, 26–28. *See also* Possession

Rights in equity. *See* Equity

Romalpa clause, 110

Royalties
feudal services, 33–34
oil and gas, 34, 133–34

Rule against perpetuities, 52, 55–58
legislative intervention, 57–58

Sale and lease back, 110–11

Sale of goods, 229–34
competing rights, 240–49
bona fide purchaser, 250–54
buyer or seller in possession, 243–44
estoppel, 240–43
market overt, 247–49
nemo dat, 240
voidable title, 244–47
defined, 230–31
profit à prendre, distinguished, 137–38
transfer of property, 231–34

Sale of land by creditor, 120–22

Secret trusts, 206–11

Secured creditor, 102–3, 108–9, 272, 282–83. *See also* Security interests

Security interests, 102–27
encumbrances, 111–14
equitable charge, 111–12
equitable lien, 106–7, 112–14
mortgages. *See* Mortgages
generally, 102–3
personal property. *See* Personal property security
possession, 103–7
common law lien, 104–7
pawn or pledge, 103–4
real property. *See* Mortgages
title, 108–11
creditor selling to debtor, 108–10
debtor transfers title, 110–11
common law mortgages, 110, 114–15

Self-help remedy, 68

Seller in possession, 243–44

Servient tenements
easements, 138, 147–49
profit à prendre, 136

restrictive covenants, 161–63

Settlor, 70, 180–81

Severance of joint tenancy, 91–98
course of dealing, 95–96
effect of severance, 97–98
mutual agreement, 95–96
operation of law, 96–97
unilateral act, 92–95

Short leases, 178–79, 262, 263

Site-specific right, 61–62

Socage tenure, 33–34

Sources of rights, 166–234
contractual
goods. *See* Sale of goods
land. *See* Land contracts
distinctions, 166–68
creation or transfer, 167
gift or contract, 167–68
intention or operation of law, 166
inter vivos or testamentary, 167
law or equity, 168
estoppel. *See* Proprietary estoppel
gifts. *See* Gifts
trusts. *See* Trusts
wills. *See* Wills and estates

Specific goods, 231
unconditional contract, 232

Specific performance, 69
land contracts, 218–23

Specification, 284–86
defined, 283, 284
conversion, 284–86
overlap with accession and mixture, 283–84
personal property security, 292–93

Statute of Frauds, 174
leases up to three years, 178–79
transfer of land, 175–76
land contracts, 214–15
trusts, 188–89

Statutory easements, 147–49

Statutory liens, 106–7
PPSA exclusion, 123

Strata title, 100–1

Subinfeudation, 32

Subject of trust, 183–85

Sublet, 26, 50–51, 167

Survivorship, 83, 89–91

Tenancies. *See* Leasehold estates

Tenancy at will, 44
Tenancy by entireties, 83
Tenancy in common, 83–91
  joint ownership
    conversion to, 91–98
    differences, 83, 85
    partition, 98–100
    presumption of, 86–87
    resulting trust, 87–89
      business partners, 88
      joint mortgagees, 89
      unequal contributions, 87–88, 90
    undivided shares, 84
    unity of possession, 83–84
    words of severance, 86, 91
Tenancy, joint. *See* Joint tenancy
Tenant
  leases. *See* Leasehold estates
  life tenants, 42
  residential tenancies. *See* Residential
    tenancies
Tenant's fixtures, 280–82
Tenure, 31–35
  feudal services, 33–34
  radical title, 34–35
  subinfeudation, 32
Testamentary, 167, 203–4. *See also* Wills
  and estates
Testator, 192. *See also* Wills and estates
Testatrix, 192. *See also* Testator
Theft, 24–24
  agent, by, 240
  money, 238–39
  nemo dat, 237–38
Thing in action, 4–5
Three certainties of a trust, 181–86
  intention, 181–83
  objects, 185–86
  subject matter, 183–85
Title insurance, 271
Title registration system, 117–19,
    177–78, 262–71. *See also* Land title
    mortgages
  certificate of title, 118
  curtain principle, 118
  indefeasibility of title, 262–63
    deferred indefeasibility, 269
      double deferred indefeasibility,
        270–71
    immediate indefeasibility, 269–70

mirror principle, 118
  priority rules, 262–71
    caveats and cautions, 263
    easements, 263–64
    forgery, 269–71
    fraud, 264–69
    short leases, 178–79, 263
Title to goods
  possessory title. *See* Possessory title
  relativity of title, 28–29
  retention of title clause, 110
  security interests, 108–11
    bill of sale, 110
    chattel mortgages, 110
    conditional sales, 110
    hire-purchase agreements, 109–10
Title to land, 31–65. *See also* Land
  interests
  Aboriginal title. *See* Aboriginal title
  certificate of title, 118
  estates. *See* Estates in land
  possessory title. *See* Possessory title
  radical title, 34–35
  relativity of title, 28–29
  security interests, 108–11
    agreement for sale, 108–9
    mortgages. *See* Mortgages
Torrens mortgage, 117
Torrens system, 117
Tracing, 125–26
Trade fixtures, 280
Transfer of goods
  contract of sale. *See* Sale of goods
  deed, 168
  delivery. *See* Delivery of goods
Transfer of land, 174–79
  contracts. *See* Land contracts
  deed, 168
  donatio mortis causa, 201–3
  registration. *See* Land registration
    systems
Transfer of rights, 167
Trespassing, 24
Trustees
  bankruptcy trustees. *See* Bankruptcy
  beneficial ownership, 79–81
  duties, 75–77
Trusts, 70–81, 179–91
  beneficial ownership, 79–81
  beneficiaries, 71–73

rights, 78–79
charitable purposes, 73–74
constitution, 186–87
constructive trusts. *See* Constructive
    trusts
duties of trustees, 75–77
equitable rights, 68
express trusts, 170
formalities, 187–89
incomplete gifts, 190–91
modern discretionary trusts, 77–78
resulting trusts. *See* Resulting trusts
rule against perpetuities, 55–58
secret trusts, 206–11
settlor, 70, 180–81
subject of the trust, 70–71
three certainties, 181–86
    intention, 181–83
    objects, 185–86
    subject matter, 183–85

Unascertained goods, 231–32, 233
Underground space, 37–38
Unity of interest, 84
Unity of possession, 83–84
    partition, 98–100
Unity of time, 84–85
Unity of title, 84–85
Unpaid vendor's lien, 113
Unsecured creditor, 103, 138

Value
    bona fide purchase for. *See Bona fide*
        purchase
    debt, of, 102
    documents, 7
    equity of redemption, 116
    intellectual property, 7

market value. *See* Market value
restrictive covenants, 163–64
security interest, attachment, 126, 273
Vendor's lien, 113
Vif-gage, 114
Voidable title, 244–47

Waste by tenant, 48–49
Wheeldon v Burrows, rule in, 152–53
Wild animals, 27–28. *See also* Animals
Wills and estates, 192–214. *See also*
    Estates administration
    adequate provision for families,
        195–98
    donatio mortis causa, 198–204
        conditional gift, 198–200
        delivery, 200
        inter vivos or testamentary, 203–4
        land, 201–3
    generally, 192–93
    incomplete gifts to executors, 204–6
    intestate succession, 194–95
    personal representative, 192. *See also*
        Executor
    residue of estate, 194
    secret trusts, 206–11
    testamentary gifts, 194
        bequest, 194
        devise, 194
        legacy, 194
    wills, 193–94
        affidavit of execution, 193
        codicil, 193
        holograph wills, 193–94
        mutual wills, 211–14
        reciprocal wills, 211
Words of severance, 86, 91
Wrongdoing, 24–26

ABOUT THE AUTHOR

Robert Chambers is a professor at Thompson Rivers University. He practised as a barrister and solicitor in Alberta before obtaining his DPhil from the University of Oxford. He has been teaching and writing about property law for over twenty-five years in Canada, England, and Australia. He was Professor of Private Law at King's College London, Professor of Property Law at University College London, a professor at the University of Alberta, and a senior lecturer at the University of Melbourne. He is also the author of *Resulting Trusts* (Oxford, 1997) and *An Introduction to Property Law in Australia*, 4th ed (Sydney, 2019).

ABOUT THE AUTHOR